Multiple
Methods
of
Teaching
Mathematics
in
the
Elementary
School

Multiple
Methods
of
Teaching
Mathematics
in
the
Elementary
School

SECOND EDITION

Charles H. D'Augustine
OHIO UNIVERSITY

Harper & Row, Publishers
NEW YORK, EVANSTON, SAN FRANCISCO, LONDON

To Dr. Robert L. Morton

Sponsoring Editor: Lane Akers
Project Editor: Sandra G. Turner
Designer: Frances Torbert Tilley
Production Supervisor: Valerie Klima

Multiple Methods of Teaching Mathematics in the
Elementary School, Second Edition

Library of Congress Cataloging in Publication Data

D'Augustine, Charles H.
  Multiple methods of teaching mathematics in the
elementary school.
    1. Mathematics—Study and teaching (Elementary)
I. Title.
QA135.5.D28   1973   372.7'3'044   73-9993
ISBN 0-06-041546-0

Contents

7 Teaching Subtraction on the Set of Whole Numbers 110

8 Teaching Multiplication on the Set of Whole Numbers 133

Preface

This text is designed to be used in courses that stress performance objectives in elementary school mathematics.

Primary emphasis is given to acquainting the pre-service and in-service teacher with a variety of methods of developing mathematical concepts with elementary school age children. The following table highlights the methods, techniques and vehicles for instruction emphasized in this text.

Using models	With whom? What are the limitations? How are they used? Under what circumstances are they used?
Analysis	With whom? What are the advantages and disadvantages? What role do prerequisites play in using this method?
Using Structure of a Topic	How can the structure of a topic sometimes give insight into the method of developing the topic with children? What role does structure play in insuring comprehensive topic development? What role does structure play in utilizing transfer of learning methods?
Using Analogies	With whom? What are the limitations? How are analogies developed?
Involvement	With whom? How are oral, physical, and written involvement techniques employed? What are the advantages and disadvantages?
Using discovery	With whom? How are discovery activities constructed? What are the advantages and disadvantages of the discovery method?
Using examples	How are examples used in instruction? What role do examples play in remediation?
Using definitions	Under what circumstances are definitions used? What are the advantages and disadvantages of using definitions?

Using games and simulations	What role do games and simulations play in the development of problem solving?
Using modified experiments	Under what circumstances are modified experiments used? With whom? What are the advantages and disadvantages?
Using rules	What are the advantages and disadvantages of using rules? Under what circumstances are rules used?

The methods in this text are developed around the mathematical concepts taught at the elementary school level. Specific content objectives are:

Problem Solving	The nature of problem solving. The teacher's responsibilities. Vehicles for developing problem solving. Two methods of developing "story problems."
Number and Numeration	Two methods of teaching number. The characteristics and techniques of teaching numeration.
Operations	Multiples methods of teaching the facts meaningfully. Memorization techniques. Evaluation techniques. Teaching sequences. Multiple methods of teaching algorithms.
Geometry	The geometric concepts are developed concurrently with the methods of teaching the concepts. Major emphasis given to developing applications of geometry.
Measurement	Not only are specific measurement topics presented, but the basic structure of teaching measurement in general is also explored.

The first three chapters of this book are designed to be completed as an independent study activity and have included in them self-scoring tests.

With the exception of Chapter 19, which may be introduced at any point the instructor deems wise, all chapters on number, numeration, operation, geometry, and measurement are designed to be covered in the sequence they are included in the text. However, this does not mean that some chapters cannot be omitted entirely, depending on how a specific course is designed.

C.H.D'A.

Acknowledgments

I am indebted to those teachers and children in the following school systems, where the methods described in this book were tested under actual classroom conditions:

Arizona
  Scottsdale
Florida
  Casselberry
  Fort Lauderdale
  Orlando
  Oviedo
  Tallahassee
  West Palm Beach
  Winter Park
Idaho
  Nampa
Illinois
  Rock Island
Indiana
  Richmond
  Terre Haute

Kansas
  Pratt
Massachusetts
  Framingham
Minnesota
  Minneapolis Suburbs
Missouri
  Pattonville
New Jersey
  East Orange
New York
  Endicott
  Bronx
Ohio
  Athens
  Cincinatti
  Lancaster

Logan
  Marietta
Texas
  Abilene
  Brownsville
  Dallas
  El Paso
  Fort Worth
  Tyler
  Ysletta
Utah
  Salt Lake City
Washington
  Port Washington
  Seattle
Wisconsin
  Oshkosh

I am also indebted to teachers in the following states for providing comments on methods:

Connecticut
Rhode Island
Iowa

Oregon
West Virginia

Pennsylvania
Maryland

1

The making of a mathematics teacher

BEHAVIORAL OBJECTIVES

Student can . . .

List six considerations given in planning a mathematics lesson.

Cite an example and/or a definition for each of six planning steps.

Identify nine questions that might be considered when selecting methods and modes of instruction.

Identify nine factors that play a role in the successful execution of a lesson.

Mention seven considerations one makes in designing practice materials for children.

List four types of enrichment activities.

Identify seven circumstances that would warrant the need for remediation.

Specify four devices that can be used for appraising readiness for a topic.

Name five devices for appraising mastery of a concept.

1.1 INTRODUCTION

In this chapter we will examine the broad objectives you will have to attain to teach mathematics efficiently and creatively. We will also see how this book is designed to help you meet those objectives.

This text emphasizes the basic skills necessary to prepare, execute, evaluate, and follow up on mathematics lessons for elementary school children. Background is given to acquaint you with historical and philosophical insights of teaching mathematics. And we will consider peripheral skills such as reporting student progress, classroom management, and developing positive attitudes for mathematics by students.

This chapter presents an overview of how the book is designed to teach skills related to the following:

1. Planning an introductory lesson in mathematics
2. Executing a lesson in mathematics
3. Practice, maintenance, and extension of a concept
4. Enrichment and remediation

1

5. Appraising readiness for—and mastery of—mathematical concepts
6. Classroom management
7. Evaluating the mathematics curriculum and materials

1.2 PLANNING A LESSON IN MATHEMATICS

It is a rare individual who can spontaneously develop a mathematical concept efficiently, clearly, and without gaps in learning sequences. Usually good teaching is preceded by each of the following steps:

1. Examination of the nature of the concepts to be taught
2. Identification of the specific behavioral objectives you wish to elicit from your students
3. Identification of the prerequisite skills you wish to review before introducing the new concept
4. Selection of the methods and media you wish to employ to develop the concepts
5. Consideration of the types of practice activities you will provide to promote mastery
6. Consideration of how you will evaluate the effectiveness of your teaching

In Chapter 2 we will discuss the nature of some of the broad topics of mathematics, including the nature of number, numeration, operation, problem solving, measurement, and geometry. In Chapters 4 through 16 the nature of each specific concept being taught is integrated with methods of presentation.

After you know the nature of what you are going to teach, you will need to select the behaviors the students must exhibit. These behaviors will give you an insight into the students' depth of understanding. For example, suppose you wish to know whether a child *understands* the concepts of triangle. You might use one or more of the following behavioral objectives as evidence that the students understand the concept of triangle:

1. When told to draw a triangle, the child uses a pencil, straightedge, and piece of paper to draw a picture of a triangle.

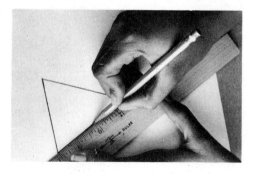

2. When given a set of figures, some of which are triangles, the child correctly points out figures that are triangles.

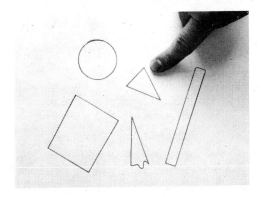

3. Given a definition of a triangle, the child correctly identifies figures that fit the definition.

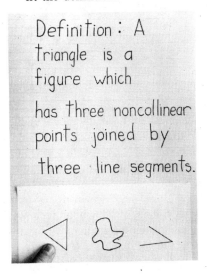

Definition: A triangle is a figure which has three noncollinear points joined by three line segments.

4. Given the word "triangle," the child constructs a precise definition for a triangle.

A teacher selects behavioral objectives to meet certain short-range—usually weekly or biweekly—goals. These short-range goals in turn are part of a set of long-range goals.

Choosing just the right behavioral objective is a delicate task, because the behaviors you expect not only determine the depth of understanding you desire, but they also determine the methods you will use to introduce the concept.

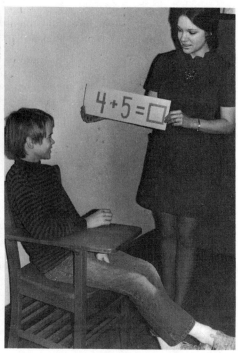

For example, your objective in giving the sentence *Four plus five equals what number?* may be that the child will put a set of 4 objects with a set of 5 objects and determine that the resulting set has 9 objects. Then your introductory activities will be directed toward getting the child to associate the concept of addition with the putting together of sets of a known number and then determining the number of the resulting set. However, if your objective is that the child will automatically respond " nine " when given the sentence *Four plus five equals what number?* then your activities will emphasize automatic recall and memorization techniques. *distinct objectives only for primaries*

After identifying your behavioral objectives you should make a careful note of the prerequisite skills you wish to review before beginning with the new concept. For example, if your behavioral objective is *When given a one-digit divisor and a three-digit dividend the child will find the quotient by repeated subtraction,* then you will consider reviewing the following skills and concepts:

1. Multiplication facts
2. Multiplying ones and tens
3. Multiplying ones and hundreds

4. Greater than and less than
5. Subtraction skills
6. Addition skills
7. Estimating products

Prerequisite skills will be emphasized throughout this text through the technique of teaching you learning sequences and also through a method called analysis.

After you have identified the concepts, your behavioral objectives, and your prerequisite skills you reach a critical point in achieving your objectives. You must now give careful consideration to the teaching techniques or methods you will employ to reach your objectives.

Chapter 3 presents a variety of teaching methods that form a core of methods upon which you can build as you develop toward a master teacher. These methods will be expanded throughout the text.

In planning the teaching of a lesson, you may wish to consider the following questions:

1. Are some of the concepts of such a nature that a child could readily discover them by:
   a. Experiments
   b. Structured practice
   c. Manipulations with objects and devices
2. Are some of the concepts of such a nature that one or more of the following would simplify the presentation:
   a. Models
   b. Analogies
   c. Examples
3. Is the major emphasis discrimination and if so, does the subject warrant a development through definitions?
4. Are the concepts best organized around:
   a. Principles
   b. Properties
   c. Patterns
   d. A unit
   e. A fusion with another curriculum area
5. Are commercial materials available which develop the concepts efficiently, precisely, and interestingly?
6. Are the concepts essentially oriented toward "how to do something," *skill* thus suggesting the incorporation of rules into the methods?
7. Is a primary concern a "depth of understanding," suggesting that an analysis approach may be the most productive? *concept*

8. Is automatic recall of concepts desired, thus suggesting emphasis on speed recall techniques?
9. Are physical skills involved, thus necessitating the inclusion of physical activities among the instructional activities?

1.3 EXECUTING A LESSON IN MATHEMATICS

Every chapter in this text is directed toward teaching you how to conduct lessons in mathematics. To successfully execute a lesson in mathematics you will have to be able to:

1. Manage your classroom efficiently and with minimum disruptions
2. Elicit active participation from your students
3. Recognize and solve students' learning difficulties (inability to read at grade level, physical handicaps, emotional problems, low skill levels, and so on)
4. Communicate mathematical concepts precisely, in the proper inductive sequence, and at a level consistent with children's ability
5. Adapt the pace and direction of instruction to the group you are teaching
6. Provide an atmosphere where mistakes are accepted as a part of learning and where students feel free to ask questions when they do not understand a concept

7. Motivate students to want to learn mathematics
8. Develop in students positive attitudes toward mathematics
9. Select and use methods appropriate for given behavioral objectives and concepts

No two teachers ever execute a lesson in exactly the same way. Each individual's personality, experiences, and training influence not only how he chooses to present concepts, but how he reacts to individuals and the class as the instruction proceeds.

Although each teacher executes a lesson uniquely, there are elements of commonality from teacher to teacher. In each chapter you will gain an insight into some of the more common methods of executing lessons.

In Chapter 3 we discuss some of the broad universal methods of introducing mathematical concepts. These methods will be reviewed continuously throughout the text and related to the teaching of specific concepts. Chapter 3 will concentrate on the following methods:

1. **Involvement:** A teaching technique which can involve physical, written, and oral activities on the part of *every* member of the class as concepts are developed.

2. **Discovery:** A teaching technique which requires that the child study structured or unstructured situations and thus uncover some concept or generalization that is new to him.

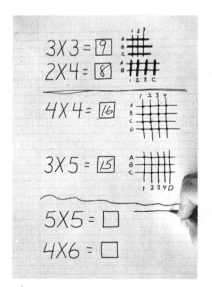

3. Analogy: A teaching technique in which a story is made up to illustrate the "how" of a concept. (This method often sacrifices mathematical precision in order to simplify the concept.)

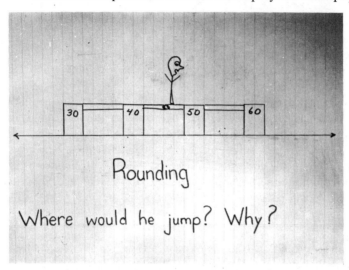

4. Analysis: A teaching technique which breaks a concept down into a step-by-step explanation. (This technique usually emphasizes the "why" of a concept and provides a depth of understanding not normally associated with the other methods of teaching.)

27×35

renaming

$(20 + 7) \times 35$

distributive property of multiplication over addition

$(20 \times 35) + (7 \times 35)$

renaming

$[20 \times (30 + 5)] + [7 \times (30 + 5)]$

distributive property of multiplication over addition

$[(20 \times 30) + (20 \times 5)] + [(7 \times 30) + (7 \times 5)]$

multiplication skills

$600 + 100 + 210 + 35$

renaming

$600 + 100 + 200 + 10 + 30 + 5$

addition skills

$900 + 40 + 5$

renaming

945

5. **Modified experimental method:** A method in which a question is presented, children speculate on the answer, data or information are obtained, and the speculations are either verified or modified.

6. **Direct presentations:** Methods that use lectures or visual or audio displays to rapidly disseminate information.

7. Discussion and inquiry: Methods that promote the interaction of students and permit students to provide input into the learning process.

8. Highly limited teacher-controlled presentations: These methods use commercial films, filmstrips, programed materials, and audio materials as well as noncommercial activities such as guest speakers, school-level field trips, and similar activities.

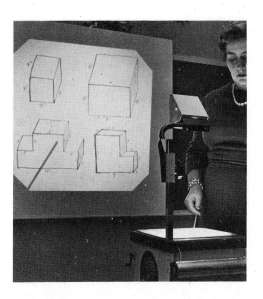

9. Visual and/or audio presentations: Methods that involve teacher-made or teacher-modified commercial devices. The method is controlled to a limited extent by the nature of the devices being employed. Audio and visual devices in this category permit teacher input and control.

10. Games and simulations: A game is a procedure that employs both skill and chance and usually has a winner or winners. A simulation is a modified reconstruction of a situation or event or series of events which happen in society. Both methods of teaching promote high-interest learning levels.

Sometimes the "*what* is being presented" so dominates the "*how*" that there is a tendency to let the "what" accomplish the teaching of the concepts. This dominance is especially evident when rules, definitions, properties, and principles are being employed.

1. **Organization around principles and properties:** The basic structure of the principles and properties often become the method as well as the instrument around which concepts are developed. Under some circumstances the principles and properties serve as vehicles for independent explorations.

2. **Rules and definitions:** Although rules and definitions are not in themselves methods, teachers frequently let them serve as vehicles for the child attaining a concept. This is especially true in using definitions when the objective is to have a child discriminate between concepts.

Although these are not all the methods you will use to teach mathematics, they constitute the major methods at your disposal. You will be fully introduced to these methods in Chapter 3, and they will then reoccur throughout the text.

1.4   PRACTICE, MAINTENANCE, AND EXTENSION

A student's mastery of mathematics is dependent not only on how well he understands a concept during its introduction but also on the type and amount of practice that follow the introduction. In order to maintain the desired mastery level for a child, planned periodic maintenance activities must be included in a long-range plan of practice activities.

When people think of practicing mathematical skills, many think of written practice. As suggestions for practice and maintenance are developed throughout the text the major emphasis is given to developing materials that:

1. Are clear and precise
2. Are varied in nature
3. Include maintenance activities
4. Include extension activities
5. Vary in level of difficulty
6. Are either self-scoring or easily scored
7. Contain enrichment activities

Practice activities are not limited to written materials but can take many interesting and highly motivating guises. For example, there are many games that provide highly stimulating practice with computational skills as well as other concept areas.

Certain concepts can be practiced through simulations set up by the teacher. For example, a simulated grocery store at the first level or a simulated bank at the fourth level will provide students with valuable practice in the area of money measurement.

Oral activities also provide a useful vehicle for practice and maintenance. In some instances, when oral skills are listed among the behavioral objectives (e.g., the child can count orally from 1 to 10), oral practice activities are the mandated type of practice activity.

In Chapter 19 you will learn techniques for constructing written practice materials as well as investigating many other vehicles for developing practice and maintenance activities.

In order to take every child as far as he is capable of going with a concept it will be necessary for you to be continually previewing the next level of abstraction for mathematical concepts. This previewing of concepts, without complete development, for the purpose of taking a child as far as he can go on his own, is referred to as extending a concept. Techniques of extension will be developed throughout the text.

1.5 ENRICHMENT AND REMEDIATION

The meaning of enrichment and remediation is often limited by the novice teacher. The novice teacher frequently interprets enrichment activities as being intended only for the better students and remedial activities as being intended only for the less able students. However, under some circumstances, every child needs enrichment and remediation activities. *i.e. there is no such thing as "normal" & these terms are antiquated + misleading*

In Chapter 19 we will examine enrichment activities that:

1. Provide depth to the child's problem-solving repertoire
2. Promote an understanding of the nature and scope of mathematics
3. Develop a child's creative skills
4. Promote an understanding of avocational applications of mathematical skills

Each of these types of enrichment is to some extent a desirable activity for every child in a school.

Remediation of some type will be necessary when a child

1. Returns to school after an absence
2. Does not focus his attention on a concept as it is being developed
3. Has faulty work habits
4. Was not presented the concepts effectively in a previous learning situation
5. Has developed inefficient mathematical skills
6. Is below level in reading or language skills and will need special attention when these aspects are present in a mathematical learning situation

7. Has not mastered skills and experiences prerequisite to the understanding of a given concept

When a child has participated in a detailed introduction to a concept, but the topic still needs to be introduced in greater detail than a normal review or maintenance activity, then this type of topic introduction is referred to as a remediation activity. In Chapter 19 we discuss some of the basic remediation techniques for individuals as well as groups.

1.6 APPRAISING READINESS FOR— AND MASTERY OF—MATHEMATICAL CONCEPTS

Appraising a student's readiness for a concept, that is, predicting the probability a student will learn a given concept, is a very complex problem, outside the scope of this text. In this book appraising readiness focuses on determining mastery of prerequisite skills for a concept and the preintroductory level of understanding a student has of the concept about to be introduced.

If you do not determine "readiness," then your students may lack the skills needed to learn the concept you are introducing. At the other extreme, if children already have a high skill level with the concept being introduced, then you may waste your students' time dwelling on aspects they have already mastered.

Chapter 19 will be devoted to investigating both of these aspects of readiness. In appraising readiness you will be concerned with the construction and utilization of checklists, pretests, diagnostic tests, inventory tests, achievement tests, and anecdotal records.

Appraisal of your students' mastery of mathematical concepts will not only evaluate your students but will also evaluate your effectiveness as a teacher. It will also focus your attention on concepts that need additional development. In some instances these appraisals will identify students who need remediation. In Chapter 19 we will consider some of the introductory techniques for constructing and using the following methods of appraisal:

1. Diagnostic tests
2. Achievement tests
3. Teacher-made tests
4. Oral and show-me evaluations
5. Practice materials for evaluations

1.7 CLASSROOM MANAGEMENT

Being an efficient and skillful manager is an important part of being a skillful teacher. If you are inept at managing a classroom, your teaching efficiency will be affected almost directly proportional to the degree of your ineptness.

In Chapter 19 we will highlight some of the factors that lead to efficient management, including:

1. Classroom control techniques
2. Record keeping
3. Parent-teacher communication
4. Professional relations and ethics
5. Grouping techniques
6. Classroom learning situations
7. Special human relations problems

1.8 EVALUATING THE MATHEMATICS CURRICULUM AND MATERIALS

It is not within the scope of this text to provide you with the skills and techniques necessary for you to evaluate a school's mathematics curriculum. However, at some point in the life of every teacher she will be involved in the selection of mathematics materials for teaching elementary school mathematics. To make rational decisions, each teacher should be aware of (1) school curricular objectives, (2) scope and sequence charts, (3) evaluative criteria for selecting materials, and (4) trends and research in elementary school mathematics. One of the basic objectives of Chapter 19 is to familiarize you with these areas and acquaint you with resources that will give you a more detailed view of these areas.

Although this book cannot train you to be an expert in evaluating mathematics curricula, you will be introduced to some basic introductory ideas that will serve as a basis for future study in this area.

Self-Scoring Test

The following test will sample your understanding of the material presented in this chapter. If you score 8 or less you may wish to reread this chapter and outline the major concepts presented.

1. What two aspects of teaching are determined by the types of behavioral objectives you select? (1 point) *method, evaluation*
2. For each of the following, identify one method or mode of presentation that you would choose if you wished to:
   a. Get the child to discover a concept on his own. *Discovery*
   b. Reduce the level of abstraction in a presentation. *analogy*
   c. Get a child competent in the "how" aspect of a learning situation. (3 points)
3. In executing a lesson, to what extent do any two teachers present the concept in the same manner? (1 point)
4. In a modified experimental method what role do the children play after a question is presented? (1 point) *speculate, experiment, verify/modify*
5. Identify two limited-control presentations where other people, to some extent, determine the presentation of a concept. (1 point) *film, speaker*

oral, show me

6. Identify two practice methods in addition to a paper and pencil method. (1 point)

7. Who needs enrichment in a school program? (1 point) *everyone*

8. Identify two types of test for appraising mastery of mathematics. (1 point)

achievement.. test, diagnostic.

Answers for Self-Test

1. The depth of the child's understanding and the methods of presentation you select to introduce a concept.   2. a. Experiments, structured practice, or manipulations with objects or devices. b. Models, analogies, or examples. c. Rules. 3. Each teacher has his or her unique style based on training and experience. 4. They provide speculations on the answer to the question before data are gathered. 5. Two of the following: field trips, guest speakers, commercial materials such as films, filmstrips, video tapes, audio tapes, records, and programed materials.   6. Games and simulations.   7. Every child under some circumstances needs enrichment. 8. Two of the following: diagnostic, achievement, readiness, and teacher-made tests.

BIBLIOGRAPHY

Historical Insight

Betz, William. "Five Decades of Mathematical Reform—Evaluation and Change," *The Mathematics Teacher* (October 1967), pp. 600–610.

Clark, John R. "Perspective in Programs of Instruction in Elementary Mathematics," *The Arithmetic Teacher* (December 1965), pp. 604–612.

Trends

The Cambridge Conference on School Mathematics, Educational Services, Inc., Boston: Houghton Mifflin, 1963.

Major, John R. "Science and Mathematics: 1970s—A Decade of Change," *The Arithmetic Teacher* (April 1970), pp. 293–297.

2
The nature of mathematical concepts

BEHAVIORAL OBJECTIVES

Student can . . .

List five ways that your teaching of a mathematical concept might be influenced by knowing the mathematical nature of that concept.

Identify two elements relating to the concept of a whole number that play a role in a child's understanding the concept of a number.

Distinguish between a number concept and its symbolic representation.

State two examples of both binary and singulary operations.

Describe the role that models play in the development of operations.

Define problem solving.

Cite two examples of real problem-solving situations appropriate for an elementary school child.

State two examples of what is meant by "measurement being concerned with making comparisons."

Describe the role of properties in classifying figures.

2.1 INTRODUCTION

To paraphrase an old adage: Before one can *teach* a concept, one must *know* the concept. In this chapter we will explore the nature of some of the basic concepts of mathematics. This chapter is not designed to make you a mathematician, but by exploring the nature of basic primitive mathematical concepts, you will be sensitized to the need of refreshing your memory on the nature of what you are about to teach before you begin teaching a new concept. In this chapter we will investigate the nature of number, numeration, operation, problem solving, measurement, and geometry. In each of these investigations, the primary emphasis will be on the nature of a concept's role in determining methods, structure, language, and sequences for presenting concepts.

2.2 THE NATURE OF NUMBER

A young child asks, "What does the number 4 mean?" Which of the following do you think will give him a permanent understanding of the concept of the number 4?

1. Point to a numeral 4 and tell him this is 4.
2. Hold up 4 fingers and tell him this is a set of 4.
3. Show him several sets of 4 and tell him that each of the sets has 4 things.
4. Tell him that 4 is 1 more than 3.
5. Tell him that 4 is 1 less than 5.

None of these examples would result in the child's permanent understanding of the concept of 4, since none reflects the true nature of fourness. Before we explore the nature of fourness, let us explore the nature of something you clearly understand by having experienced the nature of the concept many times.

If you wished to teach a child the concept of sweetness, you would have him taste objects with the property of sweetness pointing out each time that the sensation he is experiencing in his mouth is caused by the object being sweet. He would then transfer these experiences to other situations in which he experiences the same sensation. He would then associate the word "sweet" with the sensations he experiences.

What we mean when we say a certain set has 4 members is that it and all the sets in the world that can be matched one-to-one with a person's hands and feet have the property of fourness. We could have chosen any commonly recognized set of 4 (the set of sides of a square, the set of legs on a cow, etc.).

Understanding the nature of fourness thus provides a teacher with insight into the mode of presenting the concepts to children. From the nature of the concept we see there are two ingredients that must be present:

1. A set of 4 must be identified as such for the child.
2. The child is then given the task of finding other sets of 4 by matching one-to-one the members of his set with members of other sets of 4.

In summary, the concept of fourness is that property of all sets which can be put into one-to-one correspondence with the set of letters *a*, *b*, *c*, and *d*. (Remember any set of 4 could have served as the reference set.)

This discussion of the concept of 4 focused on only one aspect of the nature of 4. The concept of 4 taught and learned independently of the other number concepts would serve a limited purpose, and it is not intended to suggest a viable method of teaching whole numbers one at a time.

2.3 THE NATURE OF NUMERATION

In early recorded history, we find evidence that people tried to record symbolically the concept of the number of a set. The cave man pictured 3 deer on the cave wall to denote the number of deer killed in a hunt. There is evidence in ancient burial sites that an inventory of the number of pieces of pottery that were buried with a body was recorded as corresponding notches on a stick left in the hand of the deceased.

Although there exists only one number 4, its symbolic representation (called numeration) has many guises. The following table depicts just a few of the many names for the concept of 4.

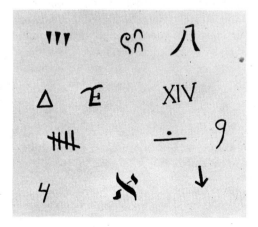

Names for the Number Four

four	2^2	$\sqrt{16}$
IV	$8 \div 2$	$\frac{8}{2}$
IIII	$2 + 2$	$\sqrt[3]{64}$
Vier	$3 + 1$	100_{two}
Quatro	$(2 \times 3) - 2$	....
$7 - 3$	$4! - 20$	$(13 \times 0) + 4$

The nature of numeration is such that one must constantly be aware that a numeration system is nothing more than names for numbers.

If the teacher is not aware of the distinction between the number concept and names for that concept, he can lead the student to serious misconceptions.

For example: How many twos in 22?

If your impulse was to say 2, then you view 22 as a name.

If I write the word "Mary" on the board and make the statement, "I am going to erase Mary," no one would think I was about to erase Mary "the girl." They would think I was about to remove Mary's name from the board.

If there is a possibility of misconceptions developing, you should make the distinction between number and numeral when talking to children.* You will then refer to names of numbers as numerals. It is generally accepted procedure that when you do not specify the word "number" or "numeral" you are referring to the number concept. For example, 3 and 2 is 5 clearly refers to the number 3, the number 2, and the number 5. If we had been referring to names we might have said, the numeral 3 and the numeral 2 are used to make the numeral 32.

Sometimes, as with the concept of numeration, an understanding of the nature of the concept will help you avoid ambiguity in the development of the concepts. An understanding of the nature of the concept will provide you with the background to effect this clarity of thought, and thus promote precise, nonambiguous developments.

2.4 THE NATURE OF OPERATIONS

Most of an elementary school child's mathematical experiences will be with *binary operations*. By binary operations we mean we take two numbers ("bi" meaning two) and arrive at a third. For example, if the binary

---

* Care should be exercised not to overemphasize this distinction with children. This distinction probably should be made *only* when it is clear that without a distinction misconceptions will arise.

operation is addition and we start with the two numbers 2 and 3, then we obtain 5. If the binary operation is multiplication and we start with 2 and 3, then we obtain 6.

The nature of both of these operations is that they represent an abstraction and generalized concept derived from real-life situations. For example, in the accompanying illustration we see three situations that suggest $2 \times 3 = 6$. The nature of operations is such that for a development

of an operation to be meaningful during the initial introduction of an operation, a teacher needs to point out to the child real-life situations or models that suggest these operations.

There are some *singulary operations* with which a child will have to become knowledgeable. A singulary operation involves one number. For example, if the operation is squaring, and the number is 3, we obtain the number 9. The term "squaring" probably was derived from the real-life situation where the area of a square was determined by multiplying the length of a side by itself. Finding the square root of a number is another singulary operation. For example, the square root of 9 is 3.

Understanding the nature of the models that suggest operations will provide you with the means to develop understandable operations for children. Select your models from real life carefully, making sure that you have picked sufficient representations so that when the child encounters a real-life application, he will choose the appropriate operation to solve his problem.

In Chapter 4 the concept of using models to suggest operations will be fully explored.

2.5 THE NATURE OF PROBLEM SOLVING

Problem solving is the process of reorganizing concepts and skills into a new pattern of application that opens a path to a goal. This is in contrast to the application of a habitual pattern to reach a previously attained goal. For example, suppose your goal on the first day of school was to find a new classroom. There are several alternative ways of reaching this goal, including the following:

1. You could look up the classroom number and location in the schedule of classes and then, using this information, find your way to class.
2. You could find someone who is taking this class and follow him to class.

3. You could attempt to reach your goal by visiting each classroom in the school and asking the people in each classroom what course is being taught in that room.
4. If you have an idea in which building courses of this type are taught, you could come to this building and asked someone in the hall where the class is being taught.

Perhaps each of these techniques had helped you solve similar problems in the past. Or perhaps you selected one of them as the method that had been the most efficient in the past. However, getting to class on the second day is a habitual application of your recent problem-solving experience and hence ceases to be identified as a problem-solving situation.

The nature of real problem solving has great implications for your development of problem-solving skills and concepts. When you have children work "story problems" in a text, you are not accomplishing the task of teaching problem solving. These "story problems" are only a prelude to the task of developing problem-solving skills.

Chapter 3 will be devoted to exploring the teacher's responsibilities and goals with respect to problem solving, as well as suggesting a variety of ways that the goals he sets can be achieved.

2.6 THE NATURE OF MEASUREMENT

The basis of all measurement is *comparison*. Before a child has any hope of mastering concepts relating to measurement, he must understand the nature of that measurement. The child should be sensitized by his teacher to investigate the nature of the comparison as soon as he encounters any new type of measurement.

Let us consider the following example:

What do we mean when we say a person is 20 years old?

Before you try to answer this question, consider the following:

Two children are placed in a line on the playground. They are sent simultaneously on a race across the playground. One child crosses the finish line and wins the race and the second child completes the race.

QUESTION: "Who took the least amount of time?"
"How do you know?"
QUESTION: "Under what circumstances would you say that both children took the same amount of time?"

Time is the comparison of two events. For example, when we say that an event took a day to happen (a 24-hour day) we mean that while the event was happening the Earth was making one complete revolution.

Now that you understand the basic nature of the comparison of time, what has occurred 20 times while the 20-year-old has been existing on the Earth?

Sometimes, as with measurement, the basic nature of a concept determines the initial starting point.

2.7   THE NATURE OF GEOMETRY

In this section we will explore geometric properties and how they influence your teaching classification concepts in geometry. This section is designed to highlight the role that the nature of a concept plays in providing a coherent structure to your teaching.

Often the act of giving consideration to the basic nature of a concept will enable you to build a complete learning structure for a set of concepts. For example, let us examine how this sequencing of concepts based on the elemental nature of a concept leads to a coherent structure.

Directions

Place two dots on a piece of paper. Place your pencil lead on one of these dots. Scribble around on your paper without lifting your pencil, draw over to the other dot. Study what you see located at the site of the two original dots. These two dots picture what are called *endpoints* of the figure.

Directions

Now draw one dot on a piece of paper. Place your pencil on this dot and scribble around on your paper without raising your pencil. Still without raising your pencil, draw back to the original dot.

Notice that this second figure has no endpoints.

Study both of the figures that you made. Can you find places where you crossed over previously made paths? These "crossing over" *intersections* are called *crosspoints*.

Let us now see how the understanding of the basic nature of the properties of a figure having or not having endpoints and having or not having crosspoints can be used to classify figures. In Chapter 17 on teaching geometry, you will find that properties are only one of the categories of basic elemental concepts used to classify figures.

Figures with endpoints	Figures with crosspoints	Figures with no crosspoints and no endpoints

Simple closed curves

The basic structure of many branches of mathematics, such as geometry, determines the way to sequence concepts in developing a concept area. However, in an area such as geometry, greater understanding of the nature of the concepts you are teaching will help you find more alternate and equally valid sequences for presenting concepts.

Self-Scoring Test

The following test will sample your understanding of the material presented in this chapter. If you score 8 or less you may wish to reread this chapter and outline the major concepts presented.

1. You are trying to teach a child the concept of threeness so you give the child 3 buttons and tell the child he has a set of 3. What directions must be given at this point to complete the concept of threeness? (1 point) *show + ask for other sets of 3*
2. Write five names for the number 9. (1 point) 3^2, IX
3. Illustrate two different models that suggest $2 \times 4 = 8$. (1 point)
4. What type of measurement is based on comparing the happening of events? (1 point)
5. Identify a geometric property that the numeral 5 possesses. (1 point)
6. Identify five ways in which knowing the nature of mathematical concepts will influence your teaching. (5 points)

Answers for Self-Test

1. Find other sets of 3 by matching the members of your set to other things one-to-one.   2. There are an infinite number of possibilities. Some of these are 3×3, $6 + 3$, 3^2, $27 \div 3$, nine, IX, and 11_{eight}.   3. Two of the following types:

Sets

Arrays

Cross product or street intersections

4. Time.   5. Endpoints.   6. Any five of the following: a. Provides insight into the best probable mode of presentation. b. Gives guidance in choosing vocabulary which will insure a precise presentation. c. Gives guidance in reducing the level of abstraction. d. Helps you keep in perspective the fact that much of mathematics is the result of man's abstracting aspects of nature. e. The nature of a topic often has an inherent structure which dictates sequencing. f. The better you understand a topic, the more chance you have to reduce the level of abstractness.

BIBLIOGRAPHY

Esty, Edward. "Functions," *The Arithmetic Teacher* (December 1967), pp. 657–664.
Freitag, Herta T. and Arthur R. Freitag. *The Number Story* (Washington, D.C.: National Council of Teachers of Mathematics), 1960.
Smart, James R. and John L. Marks. "Mathematics of Measurement," *The Arithmetic Teacher* (April 1966), pp. 283–287.
Stiel, Edsel F. "Relations and Functions," *The Mathematics Teacher* (November 1965), pp. 623–628.
Williford, Harold. "What Does Research Say About Geometry in the Elementary School," *The Arithmetic Teacher* (February 1972), pp. 92–104.

3

Major methods of teaching mathematics concepts

BEHAVIORAL OBJECTIVES

Student can . . .

Identify three types of involvement by giving an example of each.

State those phases of instruction that use involvement.

List four characteristics of teaching by involvement.

Cite five characteristics of teaching by analogies.

Identify those phases of instruction that use analogies.

Give an analogy for some mathematical concept.

Identify six characteristics of teaching by analysis.

Analyze a mathematical concept.

State the phase of instruction that uses analysis.

Identify four characteristics of teaching by rules.

Cite a rule that is used to develop a mathematical concept.

List three characteristics of teaching by definition.

State a definition that can be used to teach a mathematical concept.

List the three steps of a modified experiment.

Identify four characteristics of teaching by modified experiments.

Name one concept that can be taught by a modified experiment.

Identify two characteristics of teaching by examples.

List four characteristics of teaching by using models.

Cite three characteristics of teaching by games and simulations.

State four characteristics of teaching by discovery.

3.1 INTRODUCTION

This chapter presents an overview of eleven major teacher-controlled methods of presenting mathematical concepts to children. These methods form the structure around which you will present concepts to children. Although you may not master these methods in this chapter, you should be able to describe the nature and characteristics of each method. In addition, you will be expected to know the phase of introducing a concept (introductory, mastery, maintenance) during which each method is pedagogically best employed.

In addition to the eleven methods presented in this chapter, other chapters consider variations of these methods as well as discussing further basic techniques of teaching.

Rarely is one method used in isolation from other methods. Each method presented in this chapter contains elements of other methods.

3.2 TEACHING BY INVOLVEMENT # 1

Teaching by involvement is one of the most useful methods in teaching mathematics. Involvement is the process of engaging every child simultaneously in the learning process. It usually takes one of the three following forms in the classroom:

1. Oral involvement, for example, choral counting activities.
2. Physical involvement, for example, clapping hands to denote the number of animals displayed on a felt board.
3. Written or symbolic involvement, for example, every child writing an answer to a stated problem and displaying it simultaneously when the teacher says "Show me."

Involvement can take two or more forms at once, perhaps clapping and oral counting activities.

Some of the characteristics of teaching by involvement are:

1. High interest—when students are involved you can maintain concept development for an extended period of time.
2. Excellent class control techniques when used with discretion and skill, since students who are actively engaged in the learning process have little time for other endeavors. The group dynamics at work with this

method places great pressure on a child for conformity, and thus must be used with care and discretion.

3. The oral and physical types of involvement necessitate a higher noise level than may be permissible in some teaching situations. (Children tend to get "keyed up" using this method.)

4. Written and physical involvement are excellent diagnostic devices that help you assess how well each child is learning the concept. Oral involvement is not suitable for this purpose.

When you are employing oral involvement techniques, intermittent quiet written involvement will help in maintaining an acceptable noise level.

Involvement can be used during introductory, mastery, or maintenance phases of instruction. For example, let us assume we have taught children to count rotely (counting by saying the words in order, without the presence of objects) by tens and ones. We now want to teach them to count rationally (counting where objects are used in the counting process). The teacher might proceed as follows. (Display on the board 2 sets of ten and 3 ones not grouped.)

Sample Dialogue

  • • •

Teacher: Listen as I count, because following my counting you will have to count just as I have counted.

Teacher (Touching each of the tens in sequence, she begins counting): 10, 20, (now touching each of the ones in sequence, she continues the counting) 21, 22, 23. Now everyone count with me as I touch the sets.

Children and Teacher: 10, 20, 21, 22, 23.

As each child counts you are employing the techniques of oral involvement.

Sometimes when your goal is for each child to master a previously introduced concept, involvement will prove a very useful device.

Assume everyone in your class has missed the fact that $7 \times 9 = 63$. (This type of activity would not be employed until after the child had mastered the meaning of multiplication.) You might then proceed as follows:

Sample Dialogue

7
9
63
7
9
63
7
9
63
7
9
63
7
9
63

Teacher: Everyone take a plain sheet of paper. Begin at the top of the paper and write a 7, under the 7 write a 9, then under the 9 write 63, now under the 63 write a 7 again. Continue in this manner writing 7, then 9, then 63 until you reach the bottom of the page. As you write this be saying silently to yourself, 7 times 9 equals 63.

This procedure is a written involvement method that might be used during a mastery phase.

Maintenance can become a tedious, distasteful activity for children unless the teacher uses a great amount of ingenuity. Physical involvement is one of the methods he has in his repertoire to enliven maintenance activities.

Concept: Review of the concept of less than and greater than for numbers 999 or less.

465   Teacher: (Writes the numeral 465 on the board.) Here we have the numeral 465. I am going to write another numeral on the board. If the number named is less than 465, touch the floor. If the number named is greater than 465, raise your hand.

430   Teacher: (Writes 430 on the board.) On your mark! Get set! Go!
Children: The children touch the floor to indicate 430 is less than 465.

In summary, involvement is a high-interest teaching technique that offers the possibility of evaluation. It also provides a device for controlling classroom behavior as concepts are developed.

3.3   TEACHING BY ANALOGIES

Teaching by analogies is the process of making up a story to illustrate a concept. Some of the characteristics of involvement are:

1. High interest. (The story aspect of this method maintains the child's interest.)
2. Some precision of language is lost by utilizing analogies.
3. A concept may have to be retaught to develop a mathematically precise understanding and to avoid misconceptions promoted by the analogy.
4. Analogies are more often used for the "how" than the "why" skill.
5. Well-devised analogies reduce the level of abstraction of a presentation and frequently succeed in conveying a concept when more abstract methods fail.

You will need to exercise a great amount of caution in creating and utilizing analogies.

Analogies are most frequently used during the introductory and mastery phases of instruction and rarely during the maintenance phase.

Let us now examine some sample analogies:

Concept: Assume you have introduced a distributive property $[a \times (b + c) = (a \times b) + (a \times c)]$ by some method other than an analogy. You wish to reinforce this introduction and concentrate on the "how."

Let us examine how an analogy might be used in conjunction with a model to illustrate the distributive property identified in the previous paragraph.

Teacher: A farmer has an orange grove which has a fence that separates the grove into two parts.

The farmer looks on one side of the fence and observes a 3-by-3 array. He knows he can find the number of trees by multiplying 3 and 3.

Teacher: How many trees are in this part of the grove?

Children: 9.

He looks on the other side of the fence and observes a 3-by-2 array. He multiplies 3 and 2 and then knows there are 6 trees in this part of the grove.

Teacher: If he knows there are 9 trees in one part of the grove and 6 trees in another part, how does he find the total number of trees?

Children: Add 9 and 6.

$$(3 \times 2) + (3 \times 3)$$
$$6 \quad + \quad 9$$
$$15$$

The teacher displays the symbolism which parallels the analogy so far.

Teacher: Let us examine another way the farmer could have determined the number of trees.

He could have walked down a row, climbed over a fence, and observed that a row was composed of 3 trees and 2 more trees.

Teacher: How could he have found the total number of trees in a row?

Children: Add 3 and 2.

Teacher: Then he observes he has 3 rows of 5 trees. How can he find the total number of trees?

Children: Multiply the 3 and 5.

$$3 \times (3 + 2)$$
$$3 \times \quad 5$$
$$15$$

The teacher displays the symbolism which parallels the analogy and then gets the children to see that

$$3 \times (3 + 2) = (3 \times 3) + (3 \times 2)$$

Sometimes the analogy can make a mathematician grit his teeth. In a desperate effort to correct a misconception, a teacher may resort to the expedient technique of an analogy like the following. A child has been repeatedly introduced to "why" denominators are not added when working with fractional numbers, but he continues to add denominators.

$\frac{3}{4} + \frac{6}{4} = \square$ Teacher: The 4 is the family name like Jones and the 3 and 6 tell us how many Joneses there are. There are 3 Joneses and 6 more Joneses, how many Joneses in all?
Students: 9.
Teacher: Correct, we write $\frac{9}{4}$ because there are 9 Joneses.

$\frac{1}{5} + \frac{2}{5} = \square$ Teacher: If the 5 tells us the family name is fifths, how many fifths do we have?

In summary, analogies are generally used in the introductory and mastery stages of instruction. A degree of mathematical precision is often sacrificed by using this method to reduce the level of abstraction of the concepts being introduced. Analogies most often are used to emphasize the "how" of a concept and are rarely used to explain the "why." The teacher must use extreme caution in selecting analogies that will not result in gross misconceptions.

3.4 TEACHING BY ANALYSIS

Teaching by analysis is the method of breaking a concept down into a step-by-step explanation. Some of the characteristics of teaching by analysis are:

1. It is a low-interest method.
2. Analysis is one of the best methods to convey thorough understanding of the "why" of a concept.
3. It generally requires extensive prerequisite skill mastery on the part of the students for reasonable chance of successful employment.
4. Some students may get lost in the step-by-step minutiae and fail to get the overall concept.
5. This is the most abstract method of presenting concepts to children, but it sometimes represents the most efficient and logical choice for developing a concept.
6. Analysis is generally used in introducing concepts.

Let us examine two instances in which analysis may be the preferred method of presenting concepts.

Concept: Ones times tens equals tens.

Prerequisite skills:
A   Knowledge of tens factor names
B   Knowledge of associative property of multiplication: $a \times (b \times c) = (a \times b) \times c$
C   Multiplication facts mastery

Sample Dialogue

Analysis	Dialogue
4×30	What is our tens factor name for 30? (Answer: 3×10)
$4 \times (3 \times 10)$	Does it make any difference in the product which two of three factors we chose to multiply first? (Answer: No) Then let's multiply the 4 and 3 first.
$(4 \times 3) \times 10$	What is the product of 4 and 3? (Answer: 12)
12×10	Notice that 4 times 3 tens gives us 12 tens. What is another name for 12 tens? (Answer: 120)

120

This analysis is performed so that the child will see why multiplying ones and tens results in a tens for a product.

The child is not being taught by this method "how" to multiply ones times tens, although it would be a simple matter to establish the routine from this point in either the vertical form

30
×4
___
120

or the horizontal form

$4 \times 30 = 120$

Let us use analysis to examine "why" we "invert" the divisor when we are trying to find the quotient of two fractional numbers.

Prerequisite skills:

A   Reciprocal property for multiplication of fractional numbers: $\dfrac{a}{b} \times \dfrac{b}{a} = 1$

B   Division by 1 property: $\dfrac{a}{b} \div 1 = \dfrac{a}{b}$

C   Compensation property for division: $a \div b = (a \times c) \div (b \times c)$

D   Multiplication by 1 property: $\dfrac{a}{b} = \dfrac{a}{b} \times \dfrac{c}{c} = \dfrac{a \times c}{b \times c}$

Sample Dialogue

Analysis	Dialogue
$\frac{3}{4} \div \frac{2}{3}$	We have learned to divide by 1, but we have not as yet learned to divide by $\frac{2}{3}$. Does anyone know of a way of changing the divisor to 1 by multiplying the $\frac{2}{3}$ by something? Yes, $\frac{3}{2}$. Good, but when we multiply the divisor by a number, what must we do to the dividend in order to keep the quotient the same? (Answer: Multiply the dividend by the same number)
$(\frac{3}{4} \times \frac{3}{2}) \div (\frac{2}{3} \times \frac{3}{2})$	What do we get when we multiply $\frac{2}{3} \times \frac{3}{2}$? (Answer: 1)
$(\frac{3}{4} \times \frac{3}{2}) \div 1$	$(\frac{3}{4} \times \frac{3}{2})$ names some number and we are dividing this number by 1. What will our quotient be? (Answer: The same number that $(\frac{3}{4} \times \frac{3}{2})$ names)
$\frac{3}{4} \times \frac{3}{2}$	How is this expression different from the original expression? (Answer: Instead of dividing by $\frac{2}{3}$, we are multiplying by $\frac{3}{2}$). What do we get when we multiply $\frac{3}{4} \times \frac{3}{2}$? (Answer: $\frac{9}{6}$)
$\frac{9}{6}$	

In summary, analysis used as a method of teaching is a low-interest method, usually requiring extensive prerequisite skills, but probably offering the best hope for the child's achieving a thorough understanding of the "why" of a concept. Analysis is normally used in the introductory phase of concept development.

3.5 TEACHING BY RULES

Teaching by rules is the practice of giving a statement which, if followed, will result in the child accomplishing a task. The rule might be as simple as instructing the child to add the ones first and then the tens in two-digit column addition exercises. Or it might be a complex rule such as: When dividing two fractional numbers to find the quotient, multiply the dividend by the reciprocal of the divisor.

It is generally not considered good teaching technique to introduce a concept with a rule. Rules are saved as a summarizing procedure after the "why" and "how" have been developed by other methods. A rule is used to bring to focus the ideas you have been developing.

Some of the characteristics of teaching by rules are:

1. It is a low-interest method.
2. It is a quick, expedient method sometimes used as a last resort when a child has trouble following a computational scheme.
3. The concept developed by the rule must be maintained by periodic practice or the skill represented is lost through disuse, and there is little hope that the child can reconstruct the concept unless the "why" has been developed by another method.
4. Rules are best used as a summarizing device for concepts.

Let us review some basic arithmetic rules that are developed after the rationale for the rule has been established.

1. In adding fractional numbers with like denominators, we add the numerators and retain the denominator of the addends in our sum.
2. In arranging numerals before adding, place the ones under the ones, the tens under the tens, the hundreds under the hundreds, and so on.
3. If the decimal is moved two places to the right in the divisor, then it is moved two places to the right in the dividend.

Rules are useful in summarizing the development of a concept, but it is not considered good teaching technique to begin the introduction of a concept with a rule. Rules are a low-interest method that must be maintained by practice with the concepts to be effective. Rules per se do not help the child to go back and reconstruct the "why" of a concept if he forgets the rule.

3.6 TEACHING BY DEFINITION

Teaching by definition is the process of presenting a statement to a child which the child then uses to discriminate between those ideas that fit the statement and those that do not. Let us consider one example.

A simple closed figure is a figure with no endpoints and no crosspoints. Find the two figures illustrated that fit this definition.

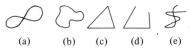

(a)   (b)   (c)   (d)   (e)

If you picked (b) and (c) you are correct.

Some of the characteristics of teaching by using definitions are:

1. It is a low-interest method when used by itself.
2. It is usually the best choice of a method when you wish to have a child make a discrimination.
3. This method requires a high language competency on the part of the child.
4. Teaching by definitions is usually used in the introductory and mastery phases.

Let us examine three definitions of varying degrees of complexity.

1. A *prime number* is a counting number divisible by two and only two distinct counting numbers. For example, 7 is a prime number because it is divisible by 1 and 7 only, but 8 is not a prime because it is divisible by 1, 2, 4, and 8.
2. A *triangle* is a polygon formed by the joining of just three line segments with three noncollinear points.
3. If, on a number line, a number n located to the right of a number m is greater than the number m, then all numbers to the right of m are greater than m. On the accompanying line segment, since 5 is greater than 4, all numbers to the right of 4 are greater than 4.

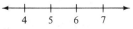

4   5   6   7

In summary, although teaching by definition is not a high-interest method when used by itself, it is usually the best choice of a method when discrimination is a behavior expected of the child.

3.7 TEACHING BY MODIFIED EXPERIMENTS

Teaching by modified experiments is not as sophisticated as the standard science type of experiment. Teaching by modified experiment involves three steps: (1) a question is posed; (2) the students all speculate on the answer; and (3) data are gathered and the question is resolved.

Some of the characteristics of teaching by modified experiments are:

1. It is high-interest method, because every child who has speculated on the answer has a vested interest in the outcome of the data gathering.
2. This method may be more time consuming than another method.
3. Extensive resources may be needed to gather the data.
4. Not every concept lends itself to the modified experimental method.

Let us examine a concept that may be taught by the modified experimental method.

Concept: 4 quarts is equal in measure to 1 gallon.

Procedure: The teacher places two containers, one that will hold a quart of liquid and one that will hold a gallon of liquid, on a table. She asks her class how many of the smaller containers full of liquid it will take to fill the larger container. She gets a variety of answers and keeps soliciting answers until every child has made a guess. Then she tells them the large container will hold a gallon and the small container will hold a quart. She instructs one child to fill the small container and pour the water from the small container to the large container and repeat this process until the large container is full. The class discovers that those children who speculated four are correct.

In summary, the modified experimental method is a high-interest method that can be used when data may be gathered by experimental procedures or observations.

3.8 TEACHING BY TRANSLATION

Teaching by translation is the process of developing a new concept by paralleling old concepts which are structurally similar to new concepts. This is similar to the procedure of looking up the English meaning of words written in a foreign language in order to translate the meaning of a statement written in a foreign language.

Some characteristics of teaching by translation are:

1. It is a medium-interest method because students can identify with those aspects of the translation they are already familiar with.
2. It requires very careful sequencing and knowledge of the finer points of both the new concept and the concept used in the translation.

Let us examine a situation in which translation might be used.

Concept: Multiplication involving decimals where translation from the identical fraction situation is used. Students have already learned to name fractional numbers as tenths and hundredths in decimal form.

Children first solve $\frac{3}{10} + \frac{4}{10} = \square$
Then they use this
information to solve $.3 + .4 = \square$

In summary, teaching by translation is a good method to use provided there is a parallel set of concepts that have already been taught.

3.9 TEACHING BY EXAMPLES

The method of teaching by examples is one of the most versatile of all teaching methods. It is used in all phases of instruction. Some of the characteristics of teaching by examples are:

1. It is a medium-interest method, since a comparatively short amount of time is needed for the presentation of a concept when compared with most other methods.
2. Examples usually are used in conjunction with other methods, except in spot remediation situations.
3. It is used mostly in "how" situations.
4. Generally more than one example should be shown when using this method, especially if several variations of the concept exist.
5. It is an excellent method for one-to-one remediation situations, where the teacher is going around the room checking on the progress that children are making with practice exercises. When slight conceptual errors are present, the teacher can use examples as the method of correcting the misconceptions.

Let us now examine some situations in which it may be desirable to use examples.

Concept: The concept of a quadrilateral.

Definition: A quadrilateral is a four-sided polygon. Figures (a), (b), and (c) are *examples* of quadrilaterals and (d), (e), and (f) are not.

(a) (b) (c) (d) (e) (f)

Sometimes when you are observing a child working practice material you will notice a mistake that can be corrected quickly with a few examples, as in the following case:

Student's incorrect response	Your examples
$3^2 = 6$	$3^2 = 3 \times 3 = 9$
	$3^3 = 3 \times 3 \times 3 = 27$

In summary, teaching by examples is a versatile method often used to clarify a concept introduced by another method. It is also useful as a device for giving spot remediation for minor concept misconceptions.

3.10 TEACHING BY USING MODELS

Models used in the teaching process are pictures or objects that represent some aspect of a concept being developed. This method is widely used to reduce the level of a concept's abstraction.

Some of the characteristics of this method are:

1. It is a high-interest method.
2. Models reduce the complexity of concepts.
3. It is used extensively when introducing number, operation, problem-solving, geometry, and measurement concepts.
4. Care must be exercised in the choice of a model, so that an attribute of the model not related to the concept being developed does not lead the child to developing misconceptions about the concept. For example, repeated use of three red disks in teaching a very young child the concept of threeness may result in the child mistaking the concept of threeness with red things.

Models are used during every phase of instruction. However, they are probably used more often at a beginning introductory stage when you need to reduce the level of abstraction.

Let us examine some of the basic models for elementary school mathematics.

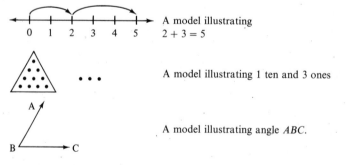

A model illustrating
$2 + 3 = 5$

A model illustrating 1 ten and 3 ones

A model illustrating angle ABC.

In summary, use of models is a high-interest method that generally simplifies the presentation of a concept.

3.11 TEACHING BY USING GAMES AND SIMULATIONS

A game is any device or activity that has a winner or winners and involves elements of both skill and chance. A simulation is any device or activity that employs selected aspects of a real-life situation. Both games and simulations are high-interest types of instructional methods.

Games and simulations often require prerequisite skills on the part of the participant, and they are therefore usually used in the later phases of instruction. However, there are some games and simulations that can be used in the introductory stage of instruction, because they develop the skills as the activity proceeds.

Some of the characteristics of games and simulations are:

1. They promote high interest.
2. They may be more time consuming than other methods, but they may result in greater depth of understanding of a concept or better mastery of a skill.
3. They are high noise level activities.

Two example of games follow:

a game similar to Bingo, where the teacher calls out facts such as "3 + 7 equals what?" If the child has the answer, he places a square on the numeral. The first child who gets a row across or down wins.

a child tosses two bean bags on a set of numerals on the floor. He must give the product of the two numbers to get a point. The first child to get ten correct answers wins.

Many types of simulations can be used in teaching, including the following:

a simulated grocery store can be set up, with one child acting as the grocer and the other children making purchases.

a simulated bank can be created in the room. One child can act as the teller with the other children making deposits and withdrawing money.

In summary, games and simulations are high-interest methods of developing concepts. These methods generally require extra time to develop concepts, but often the cost in time is compensated by children getting a depth of understanding. This is not a recommended technique where noise level must be absolutely minimal.

3.12 TEACHING BY DISCOVERY

Teaching by discovery is the process of providing structured clues to the child in such a way that he uncovers the meaning of the concept without being directly told its meaning. It is usually used in the introductory phase of instruction.

Some characteristics of teaching by discovery are:

1. It is a high-interest method due to the mystery nature of the development.
2. Some students may have to be told the concept after an extended period of time has elapsed "searching" for the discovery.
3. It requires great expertise on the part of the teacher for successful execution.
4. Frequently the child retains a concept longer than when taught by another method.

Let us examine a typical discovery* activity.

Concept: The teacher is attempting to get children to discover the relationship $(n-1) \times (n+1) = n^2 - 1$.

The students have solved the following pairs of equations:

Sample Dialogue

a. $2 \times 2 = 4$	She calls the class's attention to the fact that one factor in
b. $1 \times 3 = 3$	the b equation is 1 less and one factor is 1 more than the
a. $3 \times 3 = 9$	factor in the a equation. She asks the students to compare
b. $2 \times 4 = 8$	the products in the a and b equations. She asks if anyone has
a. $4 \times 4 = 16$	discovered a pattern. When a child raises his hand, the
b. $3 \times 5 = 15$	teacher says all right, if 20×20 is 400, what will 19×21 be
	equal to? If the child can answer this question, she can be
	reasonably sure he has discovered the pattern. (Notice she
	has not asked the child to verbalize what he has discovered.
	Can you guess why?)

In summary, teaching by discovery is a high-interest method often resulting in extended retention of a concept. Its advantages must be weighed against the factor that all children may not discover the concept by this method. The discovery may take an inordinate amount of time.

Self-Scoring Test

The following test will sample your understanding of the material presented in this chapter. If you score 8 or less you may wish to reread this chapter and outline the major concepts presented.
True or False.

1. Behavioral objectives are selected to attain short-range goals.
2. Rules are used in teaching the child to discriminate.
3. No two teachers ever execute a lesson in exactly the same way.
4. Analogies are used to illustrate the "how" of a concept.
5. Analysis emphasizes the "how" of a concept.
6. Direct presentations are methods that are used to rapidly disseminate information.

* Of the many types of discovery, only one is illustrated here.

7. A game is a reconstruction of a situation or event or series of events which happen in society.
8. Simulations and games can be used as practice activities.
9. Enrichment is for the better student and remediation is for the less able student.
10. In this book you will be taught how to predict the predictability a student will learn a given concept.

Answers for Self-Test
1. True   2. False   3. True   4. True   5. False   6. True   7. False
8. True   9. False   10. False

BIBLIOGRAPHY

Historical Insight
Betz, William. "Five Decades of Mathematical Reform—Evaluation and Change," *The Mathematics Teacher* (October 1967), pp. 600–610.
Clark, John R. "Perspective in Programs of Instruction in Elementary Mathematics," *The Arithmetic Teacher* (December 1965), pp. 604–612.

The Cambridge Conference on School Mathematics. *Educational Services, Inc.* (Boston: Houghton Mifflin), 1963.
Major, John R. "Science and Mathematics: 1970s—A Decade of Change," *The Arithmetic Teacher* (April 1970), pp. 293–297.

Methods
Golden, Sarah R. "Fostering Enthusiasm Through Child-Created Games," *The Arithmetic Teacher* (February 1970), pp. 111–115.

4

Introduction to problem solving

BEHAVIORAL OBJECTIVES
Student can . . .

Identify two factors that play a role in problem solving.

List nine vehicles for problem solving.

Describe the function "story problems" play in learning to solve problems.

State three distinct types of problem solving.

Identify six principles that foster flexibility in problem solving.

Describe four steps for oral activities using a models approach with "story problems."

Outline two advantages of the models approach over the translation approach.

Identify one reason for using a translation approach for "story problems."

List six rules for translating and solving "story problems."

Describe two methods of getting children to create their own "story problems."

4.1 INTRODUCTION

This chapter is designed to introduce the nature of problem solving and two methods of developing the child's problem-solving repertoire. It precedes the development of specific concepts, because problem solving is the primary goal for which most concepts and skills are developed.

Methods of teaching problem solving will be supplemented in every subsequent chapter on concept development. As you read each chapter, keep in mind that although it is important that a child add, subtract, multiply, and divide, it is equally important that he apply these skills in problem-solving situations.

4.2 WHAT IS PROBLEM SOLVING?

At this point, you may wish to review the nature of problem solving discussed in Section 2.5. We have seen that the act of problem solving, in simplest terms, involves an individual striving to reach and reaching a goal over a previously untraveled path. For example, if you want to drive a car to the town of Two Egg, Florida, and you have never been to this town before, then the process of your researching where it is, choosing the best route for getting there, driving the route you have chosen, and getting to Two Egg are all part of the problem-solving process. After you arrive at Two Egg you may reevaluate your decision, because unforeseen circumstances—perhaps a detour or a very rough stretch of road—hampered you in driving the route you chose. You may decide another choice would have been better. This reevaluation is also part of the problem-solving process.

Remember the path that you chose to reach your goal is part of the problem-solving process only if you have never traveled the path before. If you traveled the path before, then you are following a habitual response pattern. However, by modifying the habitual response only slightly, you again are involved in a problem-solving situation. For example, riding a bicycle for the first time over a route you have always driven an automobile would contain the potential ingredients for a problem-solving situation.

4.3 THE TEACHER'S RESPONSIBILITIES

As the teacher you have a prime responsibility for nurturing two factors that play a role in problem solving. These are the concepts and skills that a child brings to a problem-solving situation and his repertoire of previously solved problems.

For example, we can pose the following problem to a sixth-grade class.

You are an engineer and it is your responsibility to find the distance across a gorge so that you can draw up plans for a bridge to cross this gorge (see accompanying figure). How would you go about finding the distance across the gorge?

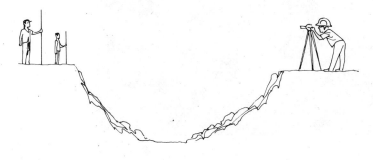

A student might bring to this problem some or all of the following:

1. An understanding of linear measure.
2. A knowledge of measuring instruments.
3. A knowledge of concepts relating to right triangles.
4. A knowledge of proportion and rules of proportion with respect to various geometric figures.
5. Experience in solving problems involving linear measurements where both direct and indirect methods have led to satisfactory solutions.

The child's normal path to the goal of determining the distance across the gorge—that is, by direct measurement—is blocked. He will not be able to use a habitual response pattern and thus is faced with a real problem situation. His solution might consist of getting a string to the other side of the gorge by an arrow, or a helicopter, or by some other means, and then retrieving the string and associating the length of the string with the distance across the gorge. Or it might consist of a more sophisticated approach such as triangulation or using proportional sides of a triangle.

The degree of flexibility and sophistication that the child can exhibit will be directly proportional to the number of concepts you have helped him develop and the extensiveness of his repertoire of solved problems of a similar nature.

4.4　DEVELOPING THE CHILD'S REPERTOIRE

Before investigating some of the areas from which problems can be selected, let us examine some of the vehicles through which a child's repertoire can

be developed. To gain an awareness of how problems arise in a child's environment, you must be able to pose problems from a variety of events and things. The following list is presented to help develop your sensitivity to vehicles for problem solving.

Vehicle	Example
Role playing	Two children are playing store. One child has to make change for the other child.
Current events	A 300-bed hospital was just constructed in Maintown. What is the ratio of potential patients to beds? How would you go about determining if this ratio is an adequate ratio for Maintown?
Advertisements	Brand X tire sells for $19.20 and has an 18-month guarantee. Brand Y sells for $29.20 and has a 24-month guarantee. Find the factors that should influence your decision on which tire to purchase.
Science	Derive a hardness test for a set of rocks.
Graphs	Given a graph depicting traffic densities in each of the school's hallways during the noon hour, devise a traffic pattern that will minimize congestion.
Data	Find an equation to fit the following data:

$\bigcirc$	3	1	8	4	5
$\triangle$	14	6	34	18	22

Maps	Determine a round-trip route between City A and City B such that the traveler will never be on the same road twice and such that he would travel the fewest number of miles by taking this round-trip route.
Constructions	Using a compass and straightedge, construct a hexagon.
Patterns	What would be the next number in the following sequence: 63, 31, 15, 7?

Although the "story problems" found in elementary school texts occasionally are genuine problems for the children, their chief function is to develop the skills and concepts prerequisite to problem solving. These story problems permit application of computational skills and help the child learn the skill of translating problem situations into mathematical equations, but they rarely permit the possibility of many alternative paths to the goal.

The set of story problems found in elementary texts is neither extensive enough nor varied enough to give the child an adequate repertoire of solved problems. It will be your responsibility to supplement these problems with those of your own creation. Therefore, you should begin making your own repertoire as extensive and as varied as possible to prepare yourself to challenge your students with both creative and real problem situations.

4.5 TYPES OF PROBLEM SITUATIONS

When a child learns to translate a problem situation into an open sentence and then finds one or more numbers that make this sentence true, he has mastered only one aspect of problem solving. Not all mathematical problems have as one of their goals a numerical answer, and even when a numerical answer is obtained, it is often an intermediate point in the problem-solving process and an interpretation or value judgement must still be made with regard to it. Sometimes the problem is simply one of developing a system for organizing the data into a usable format. Or the problem may involve breaking down a mathematical model into machine language in such a manner that an efficient translation is effected. Or the problem may involve creating a unit of measurement or developing a measuring instrument that will give better precision than is possible with the measuring instruments currently available.

The great variety of problem situations makes it necessary for you to acquaint yourself with the broad area of applied mathematics. You should be familiar with the problems that arise in the sciences and social sciences and in business, economics, government, and daily social activities. Exercises at the end of this chapter are designed to acquaint you with a variety of sources for story problems.

4.6 GUIDELINES FOR DEVELOPING PROBLEM-SOLVING SKILLS

If everyone faced the same problems in life or if we could readily categorize all of the problems people face or if there existed only a limited number of possible problems, then we could teach children to solve problems by mastering set response patterns that could be applied rationally to problems. However, not only is the number of problems the child may face almost unlimited, but in our rapidly expanding technological society the problems of tomorrow have not yet been identified. Thus we must pursue a program that will foster flexibility in the child's ability to solve problems.

To promote flexibility in problem solving, the following principles are suggested:

1. Not only should the child be given the skills necessary to solve problems, but he should also be taught how to identify and delimit problems.
2. Not only should the child be taught how to translate a problem into a mathematical sentence, but he should also be taught how to translate the problem into a simpler model of the problem.
3. Not only should the child be taught how to find alternative paths to his goal, but he should also be taught how to decide which of these is the most efficient path.
4. Not only should the child be taught how to derive a numerical answer, but he should also be taught how to interpret and use the information practically.
5. Not only should a child be taught to check his results, but he should also be taught to modify his solution as new data become available to him. In other words, he should be made aware of the fact that the answer for today may not be the answer for tomorrow.
6. Not only should a child be taught to solve problems, but he should also be taught to create problems.

4.7   MODELS APPROACH TO TEACHING STORY PROBLEMS

In elementary mathematics series there are between 25 and 40 basic models for whole number and fractional number story problems. This wide variation is due to a refinement of subcases in some series more than any fundamental disagreement between series.

The models approach is the technique of having a child read or listen to a story problem and then having him match the situation to some previously learned model. The matching of models offers several advantages over the translation approach, which will be discussed in the next section.

Some advantages of the models approach are:

1. It offers a greater opportunity for success for the child having a low reading comprehension skill level than the translation approach. Often the child can fit a suitable model to the situation after a quick skim of the story problem, even if he does not comprehend every word. This is in contrast to the careful, step-by-step analysis required by the translation approach.
2. It is probably best to at least supplement the translation approach with the models approach, because the models approach is better suited to oral and audio-tape presentations of story problems.
3. The technique of reducing a problem to a simplified model is a basic problem-solving skill and thus should be included at least as a supplemental method, if for no other reason than it should be among every child's repertoire of problem-solving skills.

When the teacher is orally developing the models approach with children, the following four steps are generally followed:

1. A story problem is presented orally to the class, either by the teacher or by a child.
2. A verbal fitting ensues in which three or four models are discussed (sometimes using models suggesting contrasting operations and other times using different models suggesting a single operation). All of the discussion takes place without reference to specific numbers. As a matter of fact, it would be extremely coincidental if the problem the teacher is discussing matches the quantitative aspect of a model that might have been introduced months ago.
3. The children display their choices through a "show-me" type of activity.
4. A discussion ensues on "why" different models were chosen. Models chosen without some logical basis for selection are dropped. (The teacher must use his discretion and permit a wide latitude of interpretation of models, assuming only that the designated operation is suitable for problem solving.)

Let us examine a sample dialogue that illustrates one approach a teacher might use in presenting story problems by the models approach.

Assumption: It will be assumed that the following four basic models have been introduced one at a time over an extended period of time.

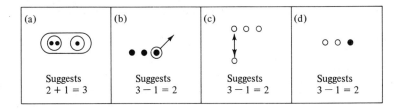

(a)	(b)	(c)	(d)
Suggests 2 + 1 = 3	Suggests 3 − 1 = 2	Suggests 3 − 1 = 2	Suggests 3 − 1 = 2

The teacher places the following story on the board and has a child read it.

Mary unpacked 8 cups.
She found 2 of the cups were broken.
How many were not broken?

The teacher's dialogue might be similar to the following (pointing at each succeeding model in the accompanying illustration):

(a) Are 2 sets of cups being put together, and do we want to know the total number of cups we have?
(b) Are part of the cups being removed, and do we want to know how many cups are left?
(c) Is one set being compared with another set, and do we want to know how many more or less one set has than another set?
(d) Do we know something about the whole set and about part of the set, and do we want to find out something about the rest of the set?

Write on a piece of paper the letter naming the model you feel fits the situation. When I say go, show me your answer. On your mark! Get set. Go! (Most children will probably pick D. However, some children may have answered B because they thought of the broken cups as being removed from the set. Other children might have answered C, because they thought of the 2 broken cups being matched with the unbroken set of 8).

Each of these interpretations would be logically correct for the child with a suitable interpretation. Note the wide latitude permitted for correct answers when using this method.

In the chapters on teaching basic addition, subtraction, multiplication, and division facts as well as chapters on operations with fractional numbers, you will find a basic set of models you can use when applying this method.

4.8 THE TRANSLATION APPROACH TO STORY PROBLEMS

The translation approach does not permit the child the same degree of freedom in interpretation that the models approach permits. However, it is the rigidity of the translation approach that may be its greatest virtue. Some children thrive on the highly structured and rigorous requirements of the translation approach.

The translation approach involves the child reading word-by-word and phrase-by-phrase the content of the story problem and then translating these words and phrases into expressions that are chained together to form an equation. Some of the characteristics of the translation approach are:

1. It requires the child to comprehend the story problem.
2. Skills mastered by this approach are fundamental to algebraic problem-solving skills, which the child will encounter later in his study of mathematics.
3. The order that numerals and operation signs appear in the equations is determined by convention.

Let us examine a sample translation:

Story Problem	Thought	Translation
Mary has some cookies.	☐ stands for the number of cookies Mary has.	☐
Bill gives Mary three more cookies.	Gives is like putting together or forming the union, thus + is linked with the 3.	☐ + 3
Mary now has nine cookies.	What she started with and what Bill gave her equals a total amount of 9.	☐ + 3 = 9
How many cookies did Mary start with?		$\boxed{6}$ + 3 = 9 6 cookies

In some elementary mathematics series the students are given a set of rules to follow in using the translation approach. Although these rules vary from series to series, they contain the following elements:

1. Find out what question you are supposed to answer.
2. Find the essential information.
3. Decide on the appropriate operation.
4. Write the equation.
5. Solve the equation.
6. Put the solution into an English sentence which answers the question.

Notice that the rules in no way instruct the child in "how" to translate the problem into an equation.

There are many recommended techniques for teaching the child proficiency in the skill of translating story problems into an equation. One of the earliest attempts was the technique of having a child identify the key words in the question. For example, (left, in all, total, etc.). This technique was rejected by researchers because it had two flaws:

1. The key words under some circumstances might generate the incorrect equation.
2. The concept of key words did not parallel a real-life problem-solving situation where the child had to create his own key words.

A more successful approach to helping the child master a story problem translation involves the use of action phrases. In this instance, the child is taught to associate the action taking place in the story with a particular operation. This type of activity is closely allied with real problem-solving situations. In the chapters on teaching basic addition, subtraction, multiplication, and division facts, as well as in chapters on operations with fractional numbers, we will use some of the basic action phrases of the translation approach to problem solving.

4.9 GETTING CHILDREN TO CREATE STORY PROBLEMS

It is essential that children be given many opportunities to create story problems, because most of the problems they encounter in real-life situations will be of their own making (e.g., selecting items for purchase in a store) or modifications or interpretations of data where no question accompanies the data (e.g., interpreting graphs, map data, or scores), or they will start with a question and gather data to answer the question.

The models approach lends itself to having the children create their own story problems. Some teachers at selected intervals ask the children to make up stories which seem to fit a particular model or models. These story problems are then discussed and solved by the class.

Other teachers, by modifying this technique, have developed a technique for designing story problems at different vocabulary levels and different levels of abstraction, thus better meeting the needs of their students. To do this, they have each child create a story problem to fit a model on a 3-by-5-inch card, and then the child places his answer to this story problem on another 3-by-5 card. The children place their names on both of these cards. The teacher goes through the cards and sorts them into three or more levels of reading difficulty. (Children will write their problems at a level of competence equivalent to their competence with language arts and reading skills; thus the child who has difficulty reading will write comparatively easy problems in terms of readability, whereas the child who has a high level of reading and language arts competence may create very complex story problems.)

The cards are placed in three shoeboxes. Children are assigned problems from these boxes based on their level of reading competence. Every child should be given the opportunity to try the more advanced problems.

When a child completes a problem, he checks his answer against the originator's answer. When there are discrepancies between the two answers, the child who has just completed the "problem" goes to the originator of the "problem" to discuss the answer. One of the advantages of this activity is that one of the two children will be instructing the other child in the problem-solving process during these discussions of who is correct and why.

Teachers who use this technique believe it helps to meet each child's needs in solving story problems.

When the translation approach is the basic method being utilized by the teacher, he can give each child a different equation and have each child create a story based upon this equation. For example, the teacher could pass out to a child the equation $3 + 5 = \square$. The child would then use this equation as the basis for a story involving a set of 5 being put with a set of 3.

4.10 SUMMARY

Problem solving is the process of striving to reach a goal by a previously untraveled path. Problem solving takes many guises. Some or all of the following take place in solving problems.

1. A problem is recognized.
2. The basic structure of the problem is reduced to a simplified model.
3. Data are gathered or avenues for solution are selected.
4. A value judgment is rendered in selecting the "best" avenue for a solution.
5. The problem is solved and the choice of solution is evaluated.
6. Alternate solutions are tested.

The teacher has three responsibilities in helping each child become a problem solver. These responsibilities are:

1. Development of the child's basic skills.
2. Development of the child's repertoire of simulated problems.
3. Introduction of the child to a wide variety of real problem-solving situations in which the child is required to seek solutions at his level of maturity and with the skills he has mastered at that point in time.

The teacher has several methods from which to choose in developing the child's repertoire of solved "problems." Two of the most common are the models approach, which minimizes difficulties with reading skills, and a translation approach, which forms a foundation for later work with algebraic problem solving.

EXERCISES

1. Find a story problem in a basic elementary mathematics series which fits the following model. (Remember the quantitative aspects between the model and the story problem do not have to match.)

$\odot$ $\odot$ $\odot$ $\odot$

Suggests $3 \times 4 = 12$

2. Copy the following table and complete the translation.

Bill had three books.	3
He lost some of the books.	$3 - \square$
He now has one book.	?
How many books did he lose?	?

3. Create a "story problem" to fit each of the following:
   a. $\circ\ \circ\ \textcircled{\circ\ \circ} \longrightarrow$
   b. $7 + 7 = \square$

BIBLIOGRAPHY

Blanc, S. S. "Mathematics in Elementary Science," *The Arithmetic Teacher* (December 1967), pp. 636–640, 670.

Buswell, G. T. "Solving Problems in Arithmetic," *Education* (January 1959), pp. 287–290.

Conen, L. S. "Open-Sentences—The Most Useful Tool in Problem Solving," *The Arithmetic Teacher* (April 1967), pp. 263–266.

D'Augustine, C. "Reflections on the Courtship of Mathematics and Science," *The Arithmetic Teacher* (December 1967), pp. 645–649.

Earp, N. W. "Problem Solving—Arithmetic's Persistent Dilemma," *School Science and Mathematics* (February 1967), pp. 182–188.

Ginter, J. L., and K. B. Henderson. "Strategies for Teaching Concepts by Using Definitions," *The Mathematics Teacher* (May 1966), pp. 455–457.

Johnson, D. C. "Unusual Problem Solving," *The Arithmetic Teacher* (April 1967), pp. 268–271.

Manhein, J. "Word Problems or Problems with Words." *The Mathematics Teacher* (April 1961), pp. 234–238.

Mathison, S. "Solving Story Problems and Liking It," *The Arithmetic Teacher* (November 1969), pp. 577–579.

National Council of Teachers of Mathematics. *30th Yearbook* (Washington, D.C.), 1969, pp. 477–537.

Van Engen, H. "Teach Fundamental Operations Through Problem Solving," *Grade Teacher* (April 1962), pp. 58–59.

5

Teaching whole numbers

5.1 INTRODUCTION

In this chapter we discuss two basic methods of teaching numbers and methods of teaching names for numbers. This chapter emphasizes the following teaching techniques from Chapter 3:

1. Model usage
2. Analogies
3. Analysis
4. Involvement
5. Translation
6. Discovery

5.2 TECHNIQUES OF PRESENTING SETS

Before we undertake the presentation techniques of teaching specific number properties, and because this presentation will involve, to a large extent, the concept of sets, we shall first investigate techniques of identifying sets. There are essentially four basic ways of presenting sets at the lower elementary school level. In the following table you will see some of the common ways of presenting sets.

Type	Illustrations
1. Using loops, rings, circles, or other outlining around objects.	
2. Using braces where the members of the set are separated by commas.	$\{\triangle \ \square \ \bigcirc\}$
Note: The three dots in the second set tell us this set has an uncountable number of members (infinite set).	$\{$ 1, 2, 3, $\bullet\bullet\bullet\}$
3. Using a roster or listing of the members.	Mary Doe John Smith Sue Mee
4. Objects placed proximate to each other.	$\triangle\square$ $\bigcirc$

5.3 THE NATURE OF SPECIFIC WHOLE NUMBERS

Most children come to the first grade with the skill of being able to identify the number property of a set when that property is the number 1. How did they learn this concept? It was learned by looking repeatedly at sets of 1 (and) hearing someone say, "This is 1, and that is 1, and there is 1," and so on. After a while, the child intuitively grasped the concept of oneness, even though he could not verbalize why a certain set had the property of oneness. He mentally matched a set he knew had the number property of 1 with his new set in order to determine if the new set was also a set of 1.

The whole numbers are defined in much the same way that the child views the number 1. For example, we can tell everyone formally what the number 1 is by the following definition:

Definition: All sets will be said to have the number property of 1 if they can be matched one-to-one with the set $\{Z\}$. (Any set with the number property 1 could have been chosen as our master set against which all other sets will be matched.)

We define the number 2 in a similar manner:

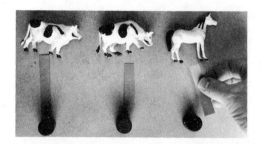

Definition: All sets will be said to have the number property of 2 if they can be matched one-to-one with the set $\{a, b\}$. (Again, any set with the number of 2 could have been chosen as our master set against which all other sets will be matched.)

In general, our method of defining a specific whole number for a child will consist of our selecting a set with this number property and then telling the child that it has this number property. Then we shall tell the child that all sets matching this set one-to-one also have this number property. The child should be given many opportunities to discover sets with the number property of the teacher's master set by searching his environment for sets that can be put into one-to-one correspondence with the master set.

EXERCISES (1)

1. Describe a set whose elements have all of the following properties: shininess, smoothness.
2. Draw a picture of a set of plants, and list three properties common to each element of this set.

3. Present one set by each of the following techniques: braces, listing, looping, proximity.
4. Define the number 4.
5. Define the number zero, using { } as the master set.
6. What is incorrect about the following sentence? "The teacher wrote the number three on the board."

5.4 THE NATURE OF CARDINAL NUMBER AS DISTINGUISHED FROM ORDINAL NUMBER

If you were asked the number property of the set in Figure 5.1 you would say that it is the number 2.

Figure 5.1

You would be giving the cardinal number of this set. Cardinal numbers answer such questions as how many or how much. For example, if you say, "The boy had 3 apples," you are talking about *how many* apples are in the set. Or if you make the statement, "I bought 3 pounds of meat," you are talking about *how much* meat was bought. Such statements as "I saw 3 birds," "I got 6 right on the test," "I weigh 120 pounds," all contain words that identify the cardinal number of a set.

It is also possible to refer to an ordinal number with respect to a set. Numbers that identify *which* object in a set you are talking about are called ordinal numbers. If you say, "This is a set of 3 boys," you are speaking of the cardinal number of a set, but if you say, "This is the third boy," you are referring to an ordinal aspect of the set.

When you identify the *which one* within a set, you are focusing on some specific *ordered* arrangement of the set and, more specifically, on an element within the ordering. A number used to identify which one within an ordered set is called an *ordinal* number. When you identify the number property of the whole set, however, you are giving an answer to the question how many or how much, and you are thus talking about a *cardinal* number.

There are certain things that you, as a teacher, need to do before you can teach the idea of an ordinal number. First, you must establish where a person is supposed to *start* counting the elements of the set. You must also give directions concerning which object is the next one, and the next one, and so on.

For example, assume that you have a series of pictures scattered on the board and you ask the question, "Which is the second one?" Your students cannot answer this question until they have been told how they are to determine which is the first one, and then how they are to find the next, and the next. Notice in Figure 5.2 that it is possible to find the second element or the fourth element because a picture of a path has been superimposed upon the pictures.

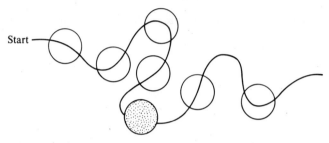

Start

Figure 5.2

If you follow the path, not only will it tell you where to start, but it will also tell you how to find each succeeding element. If you were to start at the other end of the path, the third picture would be the one that is shaded. Sometimes a situation is already prestructured. For example, children lined up at a drinking fountain can tell automatically who is the first and how to find the next one simply by counting down the line one person at a time. But if a set is scrambled, then you, as the teacher, have the task of devising some scheme whereby the children can determine the starting point, and then how to find the next, and the next, and so on.

The child will learn that he determines the name of the ordinal number identifying an element within an ordered set by counting the elements in the set and then modifying the last number name stated in counting. For example, the child might count, "1, 2, 3, 4, 5, 6." He would then say that the last object he counted was the *sixth*.

Generally, a person can identify whether a number is being used in an ordinal sense or in a cardinal sense from the word or the symbol that is being used to name the number. For example, the *th* in the word *fourth* or *th* in the symbol *4th* establishes that 4 is being used in an ordinal sense. However, there are instances when the *th* is omitted, and then we must interpret a number's usage from context. For example, in "I live at 302 North McKinley," the 302 identifies *which* house I live in. Although it is true that there may not be a 301 North McKinley, the number 302 still conveys the idea of which house. If a person were looking for 308 North McKinley and came from the 200 block to 302 North McKinley, he would know that he must continue in that direction to find 308 North McKinley.

Suppose a student is assigned the number 4602. What does this number mean? The number 4602 identifies him in terms of when he came into the school system. We can be sure that 4601 students were assigned numbers before him. This number does not tell us that there are only 4602 students enrolled in school, however. The number 4602 determines *which one* of the students he is in terms of the total set of students.

Sometimes we use names for numbers when we have no desire to talk either about the number of a set or about a particular ordered element of the set. In these cases, we simply use the numeral to label elements of a set. For example, when a football player has the numeral 14 on the back of his shirt, does the 14 mean that he is the fourteenth player? Does the 14 mean that there are 14 players? Obviously, the 14 is not related to order and thus is not an ordinal number. The 14 is only a label. Other examples of this type of symbolic usage are 7-Up, Boeing 747, or Club 21.

What kind of a number is the 3 when one talks of a 3-cent stamp? Does the 3 tell a person how much money the stamp is worth? Does it tell which stamp it is? Does it tell you that it is the third stamp in a sequence of stamps, beginning with a 1-cent stamp and going to a 2-cent stamp, a 3-cent stamp, and so on (assuming that there are no $\frac{1}{2}$-cent stamps issued)? Obviously, the answers to the last three questions are yes, and we see that some numbers can be both cardinal and ordinal.

Another example of this dual usage is found in the sentence: "He is 21 years old today." Does the statement tell us how old he is? Does it also tell "which" year of his life he has completed?

5.5 TEACHING THE CONCEPT OF LESS THAN—GREATER THAN AND EQUAL IN NUMBER

Now that you have reviewed the nature of number, you are ready to investigate how the number concept is presented to the child.

One of the first things to teach a child in the elementary school is to distinguish when one set has more objects, fewer objects, or the same number of objects as another set. Even before you teach him specific cardinal numbers, you must teach him to make these distinctions. You must be able to say and to demonstrate, "This set has more (or fewer or the same number of) objects than another set." You do this by teaching a child to pair the elements of two sets. This pairing can take the form of physically attempting to put each item of one set with each item of a second set, or, when working with pictures of objects, by pairing via connecting marks (see Figure 5.3).

When the child finds elements in one set that he cannot pair in the second set because every item in the second set has been matched, he learns to say that the first set has more objects than the second set. If the sets match one-to-one, he learns to say that the sets are equal in number.

Figure 5.3

When children enter the first grade, they sometimes think that length or size is related to the cardinality of a set. But since length has absolutely nothing to do with the cardinality of a set, experiences should be provided that will correct this misconception. Give the children exercises where one set of objects arranged linearly, whose number is less than another, is actually the longer of the two sets. You might use a set of large boxcars and a set of small boxcars from a toy train. If the child says that the longer set has more objects than the shorter set, he is thinking of "more" in terms of length rather than in terms of number. Ask him to prove that the longer set has more objects than the shorter set by trying to match the elements of the two sets one-to-one. In this way, you will lead the child to see the "moreness" in terms of the set's number property rather than in terms of its length.

After the child has paired the sets, ask him which set has more. It is important for him to understand that if two sets match one-to-one, they have the same number property; if they do not match one-to-one, they do not have the same number property, and the set with unpaired members has more objects than the other set. When a child discriminates in this manner, we say he understands the concept of "one-to-one correspondence."

Another way you can develop this concept is to proceed as follows. After the first few days of school, put away all the chairs that will not have children sitting in them when everyone is in attendance. In other words, have one chair under each desk for every child that you have on your roll. Have the children check attendance for you simply by looking around the room and seeing if any of the chairs are empty. The children determine whether the number of chairs is the same as the number of children in attendance by establishing one-to-one correspondence.

A second activity promoting the concept of one-to-one correspondence is that of having a child pass out a set of things to the class. (Always precount the set to insure that the number of objects will correspond to the number of children in the room.)

A third activity involves having everyone bring a bottlecap or small pebble to school. Place an empty box by the door. As the children go out to the playground, have each child put his bottlecap or pebble in the box. When they come back in from the playground, have each child reach in and pick up one bottlecap or pebble and take it back to his seat. When the children are seated, pass the box among the children to see if everyone came back in from the playground. If there are any objects left in the box, the children know that someone did not come back to the classroom or that a child forgot to pick up a bottlecap or pebble when he came back into the classroom. You cannot discount this possibility.

A fourth activity in which the children can participate is that of lining up in pairs. Each child will be matched with one other child. Ask two questions: "Does everyone have a partner? Are there the same number of people in each line?" (If there is an odd number of children, the teacher may participate.)

5.6 TEACHING NUMBER USING THE MASTER SET APPROACH

The master set approach to teaching number is a very good method under some circumstances and less desirable under others. This method was refined by the author under classroom and clinical situations. The technique was found to be especially useful with the following types of students:

1. Immature. This is due to the protracted length of development and the three-cycle nature of the method.
2. English second language. This is due to the fact that a great amount of emphasis is given in the first and second cycles to listening to the names of numbers stated orally.
3. Minimum preschool number experiences. This is due to the fact that this method does not presuppose the child has received extensive exposure to counting activities or quantitative experiences, as the counting approach to number does assume.

This technique was not found to be satisfactory, especially at the second-cycle stage, when children had had extensive experience with counting activities, either through kindergarten training or through the parents teaching and encouraging the child to count objects.

In the master set approach the child is taught the concepts of numbers 1 through 9 in three cycles. The first cycle, which gives the method its name, has the teacher identify a set and its number property. The children then use this master set to find other sets with the same number property. In the second cycle, the child learns to sight-recognize common dot patterns and subsets of these dot patterns and uses these skills in readiness activities for addition and subtraction.

In the third cycle, the child is formally required to say number words. (This does not mean he will not be using number words before the third cycle.)

Cycle I: Using a master set approach to teach 1 through 9. (The following activities will be developed through a sample dialogue. Each teacher develops his or her own dialogue spontaneously and the following dialogues are not intended to be prescribed modes of discourse but are merely used to illustrate basic techniques.)

> The teacher shows the class a set of 3. She says, "Here is a set of 3, watch me find another set of 3."
> She proceeds to match each element of her master set with another set of 3 in the classroom. She does this several times and then passes out sets of 3 to each member of the class. Each member of the class finds other sets of 3 by matching his master set of 3 with other sets of 3.
> The teacher says, "Find a set of 3 fingers by matching the members of your set with some of your fingers. When I say go I would like you to hold up 3 fingers. On your mark! Get set! Go!"
> The teacher has two options at this point. She can check everyone's response and compliment those who have the correct response by saying, "Very good, yes that's 3," and so on.
> If the child misses the response she can say, "That's almost correct" (correct his fingers, then), "Very good."

As a second option, the teacher can have the children check each other's responses by matching their fingers with a partner's fingers.

The following activities can be used to supplement this approach:

Three patrol: Three children are brought to the front of the room. Each child is asked to raise 1 finger. The rest of the class closes their eyes and each member of the three patrol goes out and touches one child on the head. As soon as a child touches someone on the head, he has a seat and the touched child comes to the front to become a new member of the three patrol.

Three partners: In lining up for recess start the line with 3 partners instead of by pairs.

Three stacks: Pass out sets of 3 objects to each child (blocks, cards, chips, etc.). Pass out a total of 21 objects (any multiple of 3 will do) to each child. Instruct the children to make stacks of 3 with their objects.

As each master set is identified (for 1 through 9) display a picture of the set in the room. For example, if your master set was a set of three kittens, then a picture of 3 kittens could be displayed on the bulletin board.

Cycle II: Mastering dot patterns for 2 through 9.

In developing dot patterns you will wish to use several different dot patterns for each number concept. For example, some common dot patterns for 3 are ∴, ⋰, ..., and ⋮.

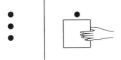

A dot pattern of 3 is placed on the board. The teacher then asks the students to study the dot pattern. She points out that the dot pattern matches the master set of 3 displayed on the bulletin board. Then she has the students close their eyes. While the students' eyes are closed, the teacher covers up part of the pattern. Then she has the students open their eyes. She says, "When I say 'go' I want you to show me with your fingers how many dots I am covering" (assume she covered 2 dots).

She says, "On your mark! Get set! Go!"

She checks everyones' fingers to see that they have noted that two dots are covered. She rewards the children with the correct response by saying, "Very good" (or just "Good"). She lets the children hear the correct word by stating the word "two" over and over again.

She then proceeds to establish the number of dots that are not covered in a similar manner.

For dot patterns of 6, 7, 8, and 9 she uses combinations of previously learned patterns. For example, 8 might be learned as a 4-4 or 5-3 combination.

The following activities can be used to supplement this approach.

Pattern matching: Equip each child with duplicated cards, each of which contains a dot pattern. Place a dot pattern on the board, for example, a pattern of 5. Then say, "When I say 'go' show me a pattern of 5 just like the one I have on the board." Repeat this for other patterns.

Completing the pattern: Place a dot pattern on a sheet of construction paper. Fold the paper over so that part of the pattern is hidden. Show the children the part of the pattern you can see. Now show them the part of the pattern that is hidden. Have them draw the complete pattern, then ask them to show it.

Cycle III: Teaching the child to count. There are two types of counting that must be taught every child. The first is rote counting (counting without the presence of objects) where the child says the counting words in a prescribed sequence (1, 2, 3, 4, etc.). The second type of counting is called rational counting (e.g., counting objects) where the child determines the number of a set by counting.

In helping a child to make the counting words a part of his oral vocabulary, there are many poems and songs the teacher can teach the children. Are you familiar with the following phrases from poems and songs which you may have learned as a child:

1. One, two buckle my shoe
   Three, four knock . . .
2. One little, two little, three little Indians,
   Four little . . .
3. This old man, he played one,
   He played nick knack on my thumb . . .

Counting is a necessary skill for the child even when the master set approach is stressed, because the child will need it to find the number property of sets with many elements. When introducing rational counting, you should encourage the students to try to tell you the number property of the set to be counted by having them use the pattern-recognition technique. You then follow this with the technique of reestablishing the number of the set through counting. Consider the following example.

Ask the class, "How many is this?" ⠪ They would say 5 (or 3 and 2).
Then say, "Let's see how we can find out that we have 5 by counting: 1, 2, 3, 4, 5." (Place your finger on a new dot as you say a new word.)
"Which of these words told us how many there were? The last word we said was 5, and that word also names the number of items in this set. Let's see if this method will work again. How many dots have we here?" ⠿⠿ The children would say 8 (or 4 and 4).
"Let's see if we can find out the number of dots by counting: 1, 2, 3, 4, 5, 6, 7, 8." Ask which of these words told how many dots there were.

There are two skills involved in the act of counting. It requires one skill to count a set of five, and quite a different skill to count 5 from a set containing more than 5. These are two very distinct ideas. It is important that you teach both of these skills. In the first skill, the child knows that when he associates a number word with the last object, this word tells him how many objects are in the set.

It is a far more difficult task to give a child a set of more than 5 objects and to have him count 5 of these. He has to listen for the word 5 as he is performing the act of counting. In the first skill, he stops automatically when his hand reaches the last one. But in the second skill, he has to be aware constantly of the fact that when he hears the word 5 this is his cue to stop. To help a child acquire both of these skills, it is essential that he be given experiences that require him not only to count a set, but also to create a set of a specified number by counting.

In summary, the master set approach is a useful method for children who are immature, or for whom English is a second language, or who have had little or no experience with counting and quantitative concepts prior to the formal introduction of number. It is a much more extensive and protracted development of the concepts of 1 through 9 than is the counting approach, which will be discussed in the next section. The master set approach involves three complete cycles of investigating number and is therefore a useful technique for children who may be frequently absent from school. In addition to developing the number concepts of 1 through 9, the patterning cycle of this approach develops readiness for addition and subtraction.

5.7 TEACHING NUMBER BY THE COUNTING APPROACH

Although teachers who use only the counting approach teach the same basic information as those who exclusively teach the master set approach, there are subtle differences in sequencing and emphasis.

Patterns and master sets are deemphasized and counting is given the primary emphasis in the counting approach. Instead of emphasizing one-to-one matching between the members of two sets, the primary emphasis is on one-to-one matching between the counting words and members of a set.

The counting approach is probably the best technique when a child has had extensive number experiences either in a kindergarten program or via enrichment activities before entering school.

Sometimes the counting approach is called the $n + 1$ approach because of the manner in which the number concepts are introduced. For example, after a teacher has introduced 3 she would put 1 more member in the set to develop the concept of 4. This is in contrast to the master set approach, where the sets start with the desired number of items.

Let us review some of the skills which are involved in learning to count.

They are:

1. The child must make the number words a part of his oral vocabulary. (It has been suggested that poems and songs can be used to accomplish this.)
2. The child must be able to manage a set for counting. (This involves either placing the set in a line or removing members of the set as they are counted, or marking the members of the set as they are counted.)
3. During the beginning phases of learning to count the child must understand that for each member of the set he associates one and only one counting word.
4. The child needs to know that the last counting word he says tells him the total number of members in the set he has counted.

Let us now examine a sample dialogue where the teacher will use the technique of oral involvement or a model.

Assumption: The concepts of 1, 2, 3, and 4 have already been developed.

Teacher: Yesterday we learned that 4 is 3 and 1 more. Here we have a set of 4 on the board. I am putting 1 more member with the set. Listen as I count the members of the set to find out the total number of members. She counts: 1, 2, 3, 4, 5. Now as I touch each of the members of the set I want everyone to count with me.
Class: 1, 2, 3, 4, 5.
Teacher: What does the last word we said tell us?
Child: How many members there are in the set.
Teacher: And how many members are in our set.
Child: 5.

In the counting approach the teaching is limited in development of the concept that if the members of two sets can be matched one-to-one, then they have the same number property.

Similarly, when the counting approach is used the children will probably only be taught to sight-recognize one set of dot patterns for members 2 through 9. This one set of dot patterns is taught primarily to save time later, in the development of place value, since the children will not have to count the members of a set to determine the number. For example, see if you can tell how many tens or how many ones are represented by the following, without counting:

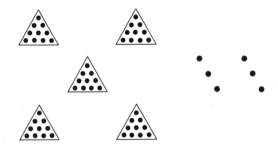

Notice how the patterning of the tens helped you tell that there were five tens without counting. It is this very same skill that will permit you to present concepts related to place value efficiently in terms of time.

In the next section, you will learn how to teach zero. Zero, not being a counting number, cannot be taught by a counting process. Moreover, there are no elements to match one-to-one; therefore it is not possible to use a master set approach to convey the concept. It is for these reasons that zero is presented as a separate concept in the next section.

5.8 TEACHING THE CONCEPT ZERO

The number concept of zero is extremely important and requires a presentation technique different from the techniques used to teach the numbers 1 through 9. For example, the number of 3-legged pink elephants in your room right now is zero. The number of purple-haired fish in the world is zero. Typical statements to first-graders might be "John got zero problems wrong; there are zero people absent today; Mary had zero papers left after she gave everyone a paper." Statements like these, which call the child's attention to sets with the number property of zero, are necessary for teaching this concept.

5.9 TEACHING INEQUALITIES

The concept of inequalities using symbolism is a comparatively recent addition to the elementary mathematics curriculum. Inequalities are essential concepts for a child to have a thorough understanding of number. They will play a role in the child's future study of estimation, long division, statistics, and many other aspects of mathematics.

Let us examine the type of activity that can be used to promote problem solving. You can ask the class to find which of the following sets has more members by matching one-to-one:

X	0		1	a
X	0		2	b
X	0		3	
	0		4	

After you have developed the concept of greater than and less than, you will wish to introduce the symbolism.

The following are activities that can be used to phase in the less than and greater than symbols.

Activity	Oral Directions
$3 < \bigcirc \ \square$	In the loop draw 1 more (or 2 more, etc.) dot than the number named by the numeral on the left. Then write in the placeholder the numeral that tells how many dots you draw. We read this: 3 is less than 4.
$7 \bigcirc > \square$	In the loop draw 1 less (or 2 less, etc.) dot than the number named by the numeral on the left. Then write in the placeholder the numeral that tells how many dots you draw. We read this: 7 is greater than 6.
(• • •) (⦂ ⦂ ⦂) ___ $<$ ___ (⦂ ⦂) (•) ___ $>$ ___	Write the numerals which tell you how many are in each set. Then read the inequality to yourself. (You could have the inequalities read out loud by individual students after all of the students have completed the activity.)
(• •) (⦂ ⦂ •) 2 ⬡ 5 (⦂ ⦂ •) (•) 5 ⬡ 1	Write a true inequality by writing either a less than or greater than symbol in each placeholder.
___ $<$ 7 ___ $>$ 9	Write a numeral which will make the inequalities true.
3 ⬡ 10 34 ⬡ 8	Make the inequalities true by writing either a less than or greater than symbol in each placeholder.

Let us examine an analogy which will serve as a mnemonic device for helping children remember which way the symbols point.

Once there was a crocodile who liked to eat numerals naming numbers! If he had a choice, he would always eat the numeral naming the greater number. For example, given the choice between the numerals 4 and 7, he would choose seven because 7 is greater than 4.

Notice when the crocodile opens his mouth, his mouth makes either a less than or greater than symbol depending upon which way the crocodile is facing.

The teacher places two pictures of crocodiles on the board.

She puts two numerals on the board separated with enough room to draw in a crocodile.

3   8

She draws in the crocodile.

Using the crocodile's mouth as our less than symbol, we read this, "3 is less than 8." The same analogy can be used for the greater than symbol.

As a supplemental class activity, you can pass out a numeral to each child and have them line up from least to greatest or greatest to least as determined by the numbers named by the numerals they have. Another activity is to appoint a Captain of Less Than. When children line up they must whisper in his ear a number greater than the number named by the numeral he is holding.

Before you proceed very far in the development of place value, you will want to be sure students are proficient in the ability to rational count to 100. These skills are taught in the following sequence.

1. Rote and rational counting to 20.
2. Counting by tens to 100. (Note in this section why you do not teach a child to count to 100 by ones before you teach a child to count to 100 by tens.)

The technique of teaching a child to count to 20 is similar to the technique you used to teach him to count to 10, with the exception that there are only a limited number of poems that can aid you in this endeavor.

To develop the skill rotely* you may wish to use the technique of "building up a choral response." The following dialogue will illustrate this.

Teacher: Listen to what I say, then when I stop you repeat what was said: 10, 11, 12.
Class: 10, 11, 12.
Teacher: 10, 11, 12, 13.

This procedure is repeated until the children reach 20.

Following this activity the children should be given activities that involve rational counting of sets up to and including 20 objects.

After a child can count to 20 the remaining counting skills are comparatively easy to teach. The next skill taught is that of counting by tens to 100. Teachers frequently make the mistake of teaching this skill after teaching the child to count by ones to 100. After you examine the next two skills, see if you can identify why counting by tens is taught before counting by ones to 100.

The technique of teaching a child to count rotely to 100 by tens is similar to the technique for teaching children to count from 10 to 20 by ones. The following dialogue will illustrate how you can proceed to develop the skill of counting by tens.

Teacher: Listen to what I say, then when I stop you repeat what was said: 10, 20, 30.
Class: 10, 20, 30.
Teacher: 10, 20, 30, 40.

This procedure is repeated with the children until you reach 100.

* The rote and rational approach can be combined by developing 11 as a set of 10 and 1 more, 12 as a set of 11 and 1 more, and so on.

Following this activity, the children should be given activities that involve rational counting with bundles of 10 sticks, where the bundles are counted by tens.

At this point, the children have the prerequisite skills to be taught to count by ones to 100. A sample dialogue to illustrate how you can accomplish this follows:

Teacher: Listen to what I say and when you see how to count, join me in the counting: 20, 21, 22, 23, 24.
At about this point the class will join in. After you reach 29 say stop.
Teacher (continues): 10, 20—then comes what? When the class responds 30, continue counting from this point 31, 32, 33 . . . . After you and the class have reached 39, say stop. Then
Teacher (repeats): 10, 20, 30, then what comes next? Continue in this manner until you reach 100.

Give the children many rational counting activities where they have to count sets of 100 or less by ones.

The next and last counting skill that should be taught either before or concurrently with the development of two-digit numerals is the skill of counting by tens and ones. The following sample dialogue illustrates how this skill might be taught.

Sample Dialogue

Teacher: Listen as I count this set by tens and ones (as she counts, she touches the sets from left to right): 10, 20, 21, 22, 23.

Now I want you to count with me as I touch the sets: 10, 20, 21, 22, 23. (She emphasizes the 21, because the tendency at this point is for the children to say 30.) What did the last word we said tell us?

Child: How many dots there are in all.

Teacher: Correct, we have 23 dots.

Give the children many opportunities to count sets by tens and ones.

Let us review the counting skills that are prerequisite to the mastery of two-digit addition:

1. Counting by ones to 20
2. Counting by tens to 100
3. Counting by ones to 100
4. Counting sets by tens and ones

There are two behaviors that you may wish to stress when beginning the actual study of two-digit addition:

1. The child can identify the total number of objects present by counting by tens and ones.
2. And the child can identify the number of sets of 10 and the number of sets of 1.

Let us examine a sample dialogue that illustrates this behavior.

Sample Dialogue

10's | 1's

Teacher (holding her hand under the pattern of 4 dots): When I say go, show me with your fingers how many dots are here. On your mark! Get set! Go! (Children hold up 4 fingers, which the teacher checks and tells every child very good.)

Teacher: I will record that there are 4 ones under the word ones.

10's	1's
	4

Teacher (holding her hand under the pattern of 3 tens): Here we have 2 tens and 1 more ten. When I say go, show me with your fingers how many sets of ten are pictured. On your mark! Get set! Go! (The children hold up 3 fingers indicating there are 3 sets of ten.)

Teacher: I will record that there are three of the sets of tens by writing a 3 under the word tens.

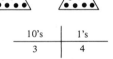

10's	1's
3	4

Teacher: Now let us count by tens and ones and see when we have 3 tens and 4 ones, just how many things we are talking about. (Teacher places her hand by each set as it is counted.)

Teacher and class: 10, 20, 30, 31, 32, 33, 34.

Teacher: When we count, the last words we name tell us what?

Child: How many things there were in all.

Teacher: We see that when we have 3 tens and 4 ones, we have a total of 34 things.

This process is repeated many times with many examples, including situations in which there are zero ones.

Can you guess why the teacher chose to say, "Here we have 2 tens and 1 more ten," rather than just asking how many tens there were? Do you think some of the children would have a tendency at this point in the learning sequence to think the teacher would want them to show her 30 fingers if she had asked how many tens there are?

Can you see now why at least one set of dot patterns is taught when you teach number concepts? Can you see how having to count each set without the aid of patterns would detract from the concept you are trying to develop in terms of cluttering up the thought process as well as losing efficiency in terms of time.

There are a variety of activities which the child will need to participate in to complete this phase of learning two digits. The following exercises are samples of these activities.

1. Draw a dot picture suggested by

tens	ones
4	2

2. Group 35 dots into sets of 10 with loops and then record how many sets of 10 you have and how many ones are left.

tens	ones

Have the children record numerals without the frame in the standard numeral format. (Retaining the frame with immature children may be necessary for an extended period of time, until they have, by repeated exposure, formed the perception of the tens being on the left and the ones on the right. This can be accomplished by sufficient exposure even when the children cannot verbalize which numeral is on the left and which is on the right.)

The following sample dialogue will help in phasing in the standard numeral.

Sample Dialogue

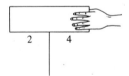

2	4

(Teacher starts the lesson by covering the "tens" and "ones" with a piece of paper.)

Teacher: Who can tell me which of these numerals names the tens without seeing the words written?

Child: The 2.

Teacher: Which numeral names the ones?

Child: The 4.

The teacher uncovers the "tens" and "ones" and verifies the correctness of the responses.

After several activities similar to this she says: If you can remember which numeral names the tens and which numeral names the ones you can stop using the frames with the words.

59

(The teacher places a numeral on the board without the frame or the words.)

Teacher: On a piece of paper write down which numeral is in the tens place. When I say go, hold up your numeral so that I can check your answer. On your mark! Get set! Go! The children display their answers and the teacher notes which children are having difficulty.

This process is repeated several times, with the teacher sometimes asking the class to identify the ones. (This process will identify some children who will have to continue with frames for a longer period.)

Several activities should be included to follow up the introduction The following exercises are samples of these activities.

1. Write a numeral that identifies the number of dots and the way they are grouped.

2. Draw a dot picture suggested by the 5 in 52 and the 2 in 52.

3. Group the dots into sets of 10 with loops and then write the numeral that tells how many dots there are.

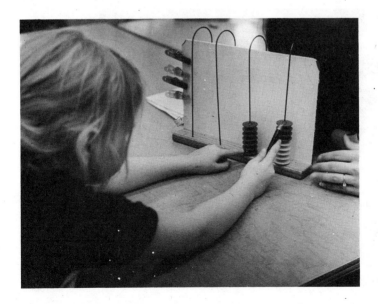

5.10 TEACHING THREE-DIGIT NUMERALS

Three-digit numerals are taught essentially the same way that two-digit numerals are taught. The new skills that the child will need to master are:

1. Counting by hundreds to 1000
2. Counting by ones to 1000
3. Counting by hundreds, tens, and ones

Teaching a child to count by 100 to 1000 is a simple task since he has already mastered counting by ones to 10 and there is direct transfer of this skill to counting by 100.

Sample Dialogue

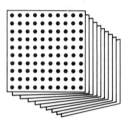

Teacher: As soon as you see how I am counting, I want you to join in the counting: 100, 200, 300, ... (When the teacher gets to 1000, she lets the children say "10-hundred," then she says) Yes, 10-hundred is correct, but we normally say 1000 for 10-hundred.

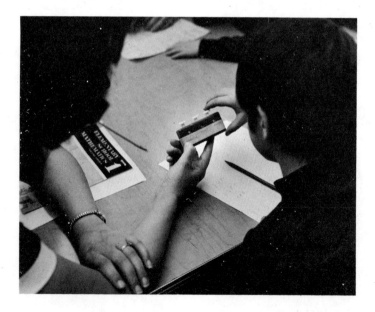

Children should be given an opportunity to count sets of hundreds (e.g., duplicated sheets, each of which contains 100 squares).

In teaching the children to count to 100 by ones, it is not necessary to count all the way to 1000 starting at 1. It is only necessary to concentrate taking the child from just less than each of the hundreds to just greater than each of the hundreds. For example, ... 398, 399, Stop! 100, 200, 300— then comes what? (Continue counting at 401 after the class responds 400.)

You can develop counting by hundreds, tens, and ones concurrently with the recording of three-digit numerals. Let us examine a sample dialogue that illustrates how this can be done.

Sample Dialogue

Teacher: How many ones do we have? How many tens? How many hundreds? (After the number of each type is determined and recorded, the teacher proceeds as follows.)

Teacher: Listen to how I count to determine how many things we have, when we have 2 hundreds, 1 ten, and 3 ones. (First touching the hundreds, then the tens, and then the ones, she counts: 100, 200, 210, 211, 212, 213.) How many dots do we have all together? (The teacher then has the class count various sets by hundreds, tens, and ones.

To complete the learning sequence it is important to include three types of zero cases:

1. Zero in the ones place (e.g., 470, 820, 590).
2. Zero in the tens place (e.g., 508, 701, 905).
3. Zeros in both the tens and ones place.

5.11 TEACHING BILLIONS, MILLIONS, AND THOUSANDS

The author is of the opinion, derived from extensive field testing, that after three-digit numerals have been mastered it is best to develop the concept of a numeral's periods using numerals with three or more periods and working back down to two-period numerals. Let us now examine with a sample dialogue how the concept of periods can be taught after children have mastered three-digit numerals.

Sample Dialogue

347	Teacher: How do we read this numeral? Response: Three-hundred forty-seven.
347, 347, 347, 347	Teacher: We are going to learn to read this numeral. As I put my hand under the numeral each time, I want you to read the numeral and I will say the period's name.
<u>347</u>, 347, 347, 347	Class: Three-hundred forty-seven. Teacher: Billion.
347, <u>347</u>, 347, 347	Class: Three-hundred forty-seven. Teacher: Million.
347, 347, <u>347</u>, 347	Class: Three-hundred forty-seven. Teacher: Thousand.
347, 347, 347, <u>347</u>	Class: Three-hundred forty-seven. Teacher: Correct. We don't say the name of the period when we read. Let me now put together what we said in reading this numeral. Three-hundred forty-seven billion, three-hundred forty-seven million three hundred forty-seven thousand, three hundred forty-seven.

The teacher repeats this process using numerals similar to the following:

1. 487, 265, 347, 214
2. 610, 530, 480, 650
3. 307, 504, 609, 706
4. 400, 300, 800, 600
5.   14, 384, 675, 789
6.   7, 476, 333, 671

Notice which zero cases have been included. There are three types of zero cases that require special teaching:

1. A zero in just the hundreds place
2. A zero in the hundreds and tens place
3. A zero in the hundreds, tens, and ones place

Let us examine a sample dialogue for teaching the periods with a zero in the hundreds place.

Sample Dialogue

17 017	Teacher: Both of these numerals we read "seventeen." When I place my hand under the period you say "seventeen," and I will repeat the period's name.
17, 017, 017	Class: Seventeen Teacher: Million.
17, 017, 017	Class: Seventeen Teacher: Thousand.
17, 017, 017	Class: Seventeen Teacher: Correct.

EXERCISES (2)

1. Describe three-cycle activities for teaching the concept of 4 by the master set approach.

2. Describe three activities for teaching inequality symbolism.

3. Why do you teach a child to count by 10's to 100 before you teach a child to count to 100 by 1's?

4. Describe how you would develop the concept of the numeral 42 using the following set and counting by 10's and 1's.

5. Explain how you would introduce the following numeral to a child:

240, 240, 240, 240

6. The concepts of number and numeration are taught using various sets, grouping devices, and visual aids. Research the "how" and "why" of some devices such as the following which are used to teach number and numeration:

a. Abacus

b. Hundred chart

c. Toy money

d. Place-value chart

BIBLIOGRAPHY

Ellison, A. "That Backward Yllis Math," *The Arithmetic Teacher* (May 1963), pp. 259–261.

Heddens, J. *Today's Mathematics* (Palo Alto, Calif.: Science Research Associates), 1971, pp. 55–65.

National Council of Teachers of Mathematics, *29th Yearbook* (Washington, D.C.), 1964, pp. 1–49.

Reys, Robert E. "Considerations for Teachers Using Manipulative Materials," *The Arithmetic Teacher* (December 1971), pp. 351–358.

Smith, D. E. *Number Stories of Long Ago* (Washington, D.C.: The National Council of Teachers of Mathematics), 1965, pp. 1–12.

Ziesche, S. "Understanding Place Value," *The Arithmetic Teacher* (December 1970), pp. 683–684.

6

Teaching addition on the set of whole numbers

BEHAVIORAL OBJECTIVES
Student can . . .
Give a working definition of addition.
List five ways of reading an addition equation.
Identify two readiness activities for addition.
Construct a dialogue for introducing an addition fact using models.
Construct a dialogue to teach a structural property of addition by

1. A model
2. An analogy
3. A discovery activity

Identify two nonstructural patterns that can be used to teach addition facts.
List three methods of evaluating which facts a child has committed to memory.
Describe a written technique the child can use to promote memorization of facts.
Describe an oral activity that can be used to promote memorization of basic facts.
Sequence a set of exercises in the order they are presented to children.
By using a visual aid or analysis, construct a dialogue to teach any type of addition situation in the learning sequence.
Construct a dialogue to teach column addition.
Translate an addition story problem step-by-step.

6.1 INTRODUCTION

A child's experiences with addition lay the foundation for a large proportion of his later work in arithmetic. That is, his early successes and failures with addition problems play a significant role in his future attitude toward mathematics. The concepts mastered when he is working with addition on the set of whole numbers are an integral part of such later learning as the multiplication algorithm, when addition is utilized in going from a series of partial products to the product; the exploration of multiplication facts, when the distributive property is used; and when addition is used to test the correctness of a difference obtained in subtraction.

6.2   DEFINITION, TERMINOLOGY, AND SYMBOLISM

Before presenting the methods of teaching addition, we shall take a look at the terminology, symbolism, and definitions that will be an integral part of our methods.

Let us now formulate a working definition for *sum* that we can use when trying to convey the idea of addition to children. (A definition is called a working definition when it depicts the procedure a teacher might use in conveying an idea. Working definitions are not to be construed as those the child would be taught, although it is hoped that he would extract the essence of the idea from the teacher's presentation.) This working definition might be stated as follows:

Suppose we wanted to find the sum of two whole numbers $\square$ and $\triangle$; we would take the following steps:

Obtain a set, the number of which is $\square$.
Obtain a set, the number of which is $\triangle$ and that has no elements in common with the first set.
Join or combine or unite the two sets.
Determine the number property of the new set that was obtained by uniting or combining or joining of the two original sets.
The number property of the new set is designated in the sum of $\square$ and $\triangle$.

There are two notations you will want to teach your students (see Figure 6.1). In the horizontal form, we are assuming a left-to-right reading. In the vertical form, we are assuming a top-to-bottom reading.

$$\begin{array}{r} 6 \\ +5 \\ \hline 11 \end{array}$$ Vertical form $6 + 5 = 11$ Horizontal form

Figure 6.1

There are many ways that the mathematical sentences illustrated in Figure 6.1 can be read. A few of the ways of reading them are as follows:

The sum of 6 and 5 is 11.
The sum of 6 and 5 equals 11.
6 and 5 is 11.

6 and 5 equals 11.
5 added to 6 equals 11.
5 added to 6 is 11.
The sum of 6 and 5 is equal to 11.

When a person is referring to objects, he uses a plural verb. For example, 3 cats and 4 cats are 7 cats. When a person refers to numbers, the singular verb form is used. For example, 3 and 4 is 7. In Figure 6.2, the terminology applied to the various numerals in the addition sentences is identified. These are the terms we shall use to refer to the various elements of the addition sentence.

Addend   Addend   Sum   4 Addend
                              +5 Addend
                             ___
4   +   5   =   9   9 Sum

Figure 6.2

6.3 READINESS EXPERIENCES FOR ADDITION

When you have the child recognize that a pattern of 4 and 4 is a pattern of 8, you are building readiness for the concept that 4 plus 4 is 8. When you have the child recognize that a pattern of 5 and a pattern of 3 is a pattern of 8, you are building readiness for the concept that 5 plus 3 is 8. These patterns aid the child in developing the concept of the number property of a set, and they also build readiness for addition.

Why is it so easy for you to add 5 to a number whose name in base 10 has a zero or 5 in the ones position? Probably because when you were a child you played games like hide-and-go-seek in which you would count 5, 10, 15, and so on. Now, when you encounter a situation in which you are required to add 5 to 65, you automatically think 70, because of this counting experience when you were a child. Having the child count (by twos through tens) beginning at various starting points provides him with excellent readiness experiences. For example, if you count by fives, starting at 1, you get 1, 6, 11, 16, 21, and so on. If you start at 7, you get 7, 12, 17, 22, 27, 32, 37, 42, 47. It will be easy for the child later to add 5 to numbers such as 27 or 16 because of these prior counting experiences.

Some pattern-counting experiences are important not only for counting by fives but also for counting by twos, threes, fours, sixes, sevens, eights, nines, and tens. When the child counts 9, 18, 27, 36, 45, 54, 63, is there a pattern that he can discover? What is the pattern in the tens position and in the ones position? Would this pattern hold if a person were to start counting at 7 by nines? How does the pattern change?

When asking a child to determine the number of a set through counting, encourage him to count by a number other than 1. For example, in Figure 6.3 the child could be requested to count the dots in the array by threes or twos.

. . .

. . .

Figure 6.3

6.4 TEACHING THE BASIC ADDITION FACTS USING MODELS

Such aids as a flannel board, a magnetic board, blocks, tongue depressors, buttons, a hundred board, a place-value chart, an abacus, charts, and a peg board are all useful in teaching the concept of addition. The procedure for getting a child to discover sums is essentially the same for all of these aids. Each is designed so that the child is an active participant.

A typical dialogue that might be used with these aids is as follows.*

Sample Dialogue

Teacher: Here we have 3 rabbits (blocks, sticks, strips of paper, cards, buttons, beads, boxes, spools, etc.).

(Point to the set of 5 objects.) We join the set of 3 and the set of 5. Who can tell me how many objects are in our new set? (8) We can tell what has happened by writing $3 + 5 = 8$. We read this as three and five is eight. (Later you will teach the children many other ways to read this mathematical sentence.) If I had put a set of 3 rabbits together with a set of 4 rabbits, how many objects would have been in our new set? (7)

John, come up and show us how we find out what 3 and 4 is. Mary, come to the board and write down an addition sentence that tells us that 3 and 4 is 7.

Let's record the addition facts that we have discovered in our addition table.

* Normally, a teacher does not write a dialogue and then use it with his class. A good teacher, knowing both the content and organization of his subject, develops his dialogue spontaneously and then modifies his presentation as his students react. The dialogues in this book, which were transcribed from demonstration lessons given by the author and which developed spontaneously, are not suggested as ideal models but are presented to acquaint the prospective teacher with the techniques of getting responses for the skill being taught. If a dialogue at times seems artificial, it is because numerous side trips, incorrect responses, and questions were omitted from the transcription of the tapes for the sake of brevity.

An aid to teaching addition of whole numbers, and one that needs special attention, is the number-line segment. Figure 6.4 shows how $3 + 5 = 8$ can be shown on the number-line segment. (The teacher is cautioned against introducing a child to a number line before he has a fairly firm grasp of the idea of the cardinality of a set, because the number line lends itself more to ordinality than to cardinality).*

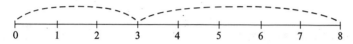

Figure 6.4

A dialogue that might be used with the construction of the example in Figure 6.4 follows:

Sample Dialogue

Teacher: We take a jump of 3. (After making the loop on the number-line segment, write the symbolic expression of this—that is, 3.) We keep going the same way. (Write a $+$ to the right of the 3, so that you now have written $3 +$.)

We take a jump of 5 more. (Write 5 to the right of the 3, so that you now have written $3 + 5$.)

Where are we after we have taken a jump of 3 and a jump of 5? (When someone answers 8, write $= 8$.) We have seen that 3 and 5 is 8. (Point to the mathematical sentence.)

6.5 USING PATTERNS TO TEACH ADDITION

Although it is essential to teach children sets models that suggest addition, many other methods can be used to supplement sets models. Among the most useful is the method of patterns.

There exists a special set of patterns for addition called structural properties. In the following chart we see instances of these structural properties:

* When a number line is used as a "measurement line" it is often associated with the concept of "how long" rather than "how many."

	Instance of	Reasons Taught
$3 + 2 = 2 + 3$	Commutative property: $n + m = m + n$	Cuts down on physical manipulations which must be used by the child to discover each fact.
$3 + 0 = 3$	Identity property: $n + 0 = n$	Cuts down on the number of facts the child has to memorize individually.
$2 + (3 + 4) =$ $(2 + 3) + 4$	Associative property: $n + (m + r) =$ $(n + m) + r$	Used in column addition, later analysis explanations and the technique of $9 + 8 = 9 + (1 + 7)$ $= (9 + 1) + 7$ $= 10 + 7$ $= 17$

The commutative property is a comparatively easy concept to develop. Let us examine how one might use models, an analogy, and a discovery method to develop this concept:

Sample Dialogue

Teacher: Place 3 washers on the right corner of your desk. Place 2 washers on the left corner of your desk. Put your sets together. One equation suggested by this activity is $3 + 2 = 5$.

Teacher: Now put a set of 2 on the right corner of your desk and a set of 3 on the left corner of your desk. Put your sets together. This suggests that $2 + 3$ is equal to what? Do we get the same answer when we add 2 and 3 as when we added 3 and 2? (This situation should not be interpreted by the reader as being the only addition equation you can derive from the activity. There is nothing sacrosanct about a set on the left corresponding to the first numeral in an equation.) The teacher repeats this activity several times, letting children suggest combinations to try. After each activity, the equations that are suggested by putting the sets together are recorded.

The teacher wants the children to reach the point where they will answer the following question negatively.

Teacher: Did changing the order of the addends change our sum?

The teacher could use an analogy to develop the same concept for which models have just been used.

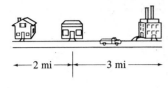

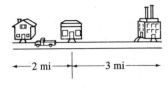

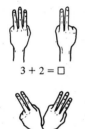

For example:

On Monday morning Mr. Jones drives to work. He leaves home and travels 2 miles to a store where he picks up the morning paper. He then travels 3 miles from the store to the place where he works. How many miles does he travel from his home until he gets to work? (After the children respond, the teacher writes the equation $2 + 3 = 5$ on the board.)

In the evening Mr. Jones drives home. He leaves work and travels 3 miles to a store where he picks up an evening paper. He then travels 2 miles to his home. How many miles does he travel from work to his home? (After the children respond, the teacher writes the equation $3 + 2 = 5$ on the board.) Does he travel the same number of miles from home to work as he does from work to home?

Variations of this analogy are then developed by the teacher using several instances of the commutative property.

Teacher: Did we change the number of fingers that were up? How are the equations different? Do we get the same sum in both equations?

$3 + 2 = \square$

$2 + 3 = \square$

The first step in teaching the child to discover the commutative property may consist of your pairing each addition problem with a corresponding commuted problem. For example, when asking a child to find the sum of 3 and 5 by putting a set of 3 objects together with a set of 5 objects, and thus finding the number property of the new set, the teacher could ask the child to find the sum of 5 and 3 using models.

When you place the symbolism for this problem on the board, or when the child writes the symbolism, the first request ("Find the sum of 3 and 5.") could be represented as $3 + 5 = \square$; the second request could be represented by $5 + 3 = \square$. In Figure 6.5 we see examples of pairs of problems that might be presented.

(1a) $3 + 6 = \square$ (2a) $4 + 5 = \square$ (3a) $1 + 8 = \square$
(1b) $6 + 3 = \square$ (2b) $5 + 4 = \square$ (3b) $8 + 1 = \square$

Figure 6.5

After the child has discovered the commutative pattern, he can be given problems requiring a knowledge of this pattern for finding a solution. Problems such as $6 + \square = 5 + 6$ and $3 + 8 = \square + 3$ are examples. The only requirement for a child's solving this problem is his recognizing that when we add two numbers in either possible order the sum is the same.

At this point, it should be emphasized that the words "commutative," "identity," and so on, are not as important for the child to acquire as the meaning of the words. As a matter of fact, you probably should make an effort to delay the children's verbalizing of these concepts until they have had some experiences with them.

In general, if an elementary mathematics series does not begin with problems of the discovery stage illustrated in Figure 6.5, it will give problems of the second stage illustrated here. If an elementary series fails to introduce a situation for the child's discovery of the commutative property, you will probably want to structure a situation to promote this discovery.

Problems can be structured to lead the child to a generalization. In this stage, you can present problems with multiple solutions. You can expect and encourage such answers as, "Teacher, any number will work!" Examples of problems in this stage are $3 + \square = \square + 3$, and $\square + 9 = 9 + \square$.

If no student makes the observation that any number could be named, you might single out one person's answer and tell the class that *this* is the correct answer. This designation of one answer as being correct will meet with objections from the class. Someone will say, "Any number would work," which is the generalization you want the children to make. Although no number of such problems will prove the commutative property, it is desirable that the child accept the reasonableness of the commutative property through work with many instances of it.

In the final stage, the student can be given a pattern such as $\square + \triangle = \triangle + \square$ and can be asked to create problems that would be true sentences using it. This type of activity is probably best delayed until the child has reached the intermediate grades at least.

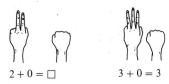

$2 + 0 = \square$ $3 + 0 = 3$

Figure 6.6

Figure 6.6 illustrates one method of introducing children to the identity concept $(n + 0 = n)$ using fingers for models. An analogy can also be used to develop this concept. For example:

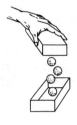

John was carrying two boxes. One box had 4 golf balls. John poured the box of 4 golf balls into the box of zero golf balls. How many balls were in the box with zero balls and 4 balls?

Children should be taught the identity property so that they can automatically give the sum when one of two addends is zero. One way of accomplishing this is to extend the child's conceptual level by going outside the numbers he normally would be studying. For example, note how in the following dialogue the child is led into number concepts he would only have the slightest conceptual knowledge of at the first-grade level. This is done primarily to promote the generalized nature of the concept:

$3 + 0 = \square$ Teacher: 3 plus 0 equals what?
               Child: 3.

$8 + 0 = \square$ Teacher: 8 plus 0 equals what?
               Child: 8.

$50 + 0 = \square$ Teacher: 50 plus 0 equals what?
               Child: 50.

$1000 + 0 = \square$ Teacher: 1000 plus 0 equals what?
               Child: 1000.

A third property that plays an important role in the child's learning his facts is the associative property for addition: for all whole numbers $(a + b) + c = a + (b + c)$ is an important idea finding many uses in the development of addition on the set of whole numbers. The associative property of addition plays a significant role not only in permitting column addition involving 3 or more addends from top to bottom or bottom to top but also in extending a child's concept of addition beyond the basic facts. For example, $8 + 5$ can be renamed $8 + (2 + 3)$, and by making use of the associative property, we get $(8 + 2) + 3$, which names $10 + 3$ or 13.

The first stage in teaching the associative property probably will involve your presenting pairs of problems just as was done in teaching the commutative property (see Figure 6.7). For example, asking the child to

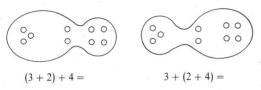

$(3 + 2) + 4 =$ $3 + (2 + 4) =$

Figure 6.7

find the sum of $(3 + 2) + 4$, finding first the sum of 3 and 2 and then adding the 4 to the 5, could be followed by a request for him to find the sum of $3 + (2 + 4)$, finding first the sum of 2 and 4 and then adding the 6 to the 3. This is an example of a pair of problems being used to show the child that the final sum is not affected by the choice of which pair of

(1a) $(4 + 9) + 3 = \square$	(3a) $(3 + 2) + 5 = \square$
(1b) $4 + (9 + 3) = \square$	(3b) $3 + (2 + 5) = \square$
(2a) $6 + (1 + 9) = \square$	(4a) $8 + (3 + 4) = \square$
(2b) $(6 + 1) + 9 = \square$	(4b) $(8 + 3) + 4 = \square$

Figure 6.8

numbers is added first. In Figure 6.8, we can see several pairs of problems that could be used to guide the child in discovering the associative property.

After the child has discovered the associative pattern, he can be given problems requiring a knowledge of this pattern for finding solutions. In

this stage, he can be asked to identify which numerals are missing in a mathematical sentence. Here his ability to identify the missing numeral is dependent upon his recognizing an instance of the associative property. Notice that this type of experience tests a child's operational ability with a pattern rather than his ability to say "associative pattern." Several examples of problems for this stage can be seen in Figure 6.9.

(a) $(4 + 9) + 6 = 4 + (\square + 6)$
(b) $3 + (\square + 2) = (3 + 5) + 2$
(c) $5 + (6 + 7) = (\square + 6) + 7$

Figure 6.9

The chief characteristic of the next stage is that any given problem has more than one correct solution. Typical examples of these multiple-solution problems are presented in Figure 6.10.

(a) $(3 + 4) + \square = 3 + (4 + \square)$
(b) $(9 + \square) + \triangle = 9 + (\square + \triangle)$
(c) $\square + (7 + 1) = (\square + 7) + 1$

Figure 6.10

The final stage in the child's learning the associative property of addition consists of creating instances of this property. The student can be given a pattern such as $(\square + \triangle) + \bigcirc = \square + (\triangle + \bigcirc)$ and be asked to create problems that would be true sentences using it.

Many patterns beside the structural properties can be used for developing addition facts. The following illustrate a few of the more common patterns used in teaching addition facts.

$3 + 3 = 6$	**Working off doubles pattern.** Children master their
$3 + 4 = 7$	doubles $(n + n = m)$ very early in their study of addition.
	This mastery can be used with the pattern that develops
$6 + 6 = 12$	just off a double $n + (n + 1) = r$ to teach some of the harder
$6 + 7 = 13$	facts such as $3 + 4, 4 + 5, 5 + 6, 6 + 7, 7 + 8,$ and $8 + 9.$
$3 + 9 = 12$	**The nine's addend pattern.** This is a useful pattern in
$5 + 9 = 14$	developing facts where one addend is a 9. The children,
$8 + 9 = 17$	through a discovery method, are led to see the relationship
	between the non-9 addend and the 1's digit in the sum (e.g.,
	the 3 and the 2 in 12, the 5 and the 4 in 14, and the 8
	and the 7 in 17).

The following table summarizes some of the methods a teacher has of getting his children to discover sums:

Problem	Method	Solution
$1 + 1 =$	Putting sets together. $\{\triangle\} \cup \{\square\} = \{\triangle, \square\}$	$1 + 1 = 2$
$3 + 2 =$	Using a number line.	$3 + 2 = 5$
$7 + 6 =$	Renaming, regrouping. $7 + 6 = 7 + (3 + 3) = (7 + 3) + 3 = 10 + 3 = 13$	$7 + 6 = 13$
$4 + 5 =$	Working from doubles. Since $4 + 4 = 8$ and 5 is 1 more than 4, then . . .	$4 + 5 = 9$
$9 + 6 =$	Using the commutative property. Since $6 + 9 = 15$, then . . .	$9 + 6 = 15$
$6 + 4 =$	Using patterns. Since $6 + 1 = 7$ and $6 + 2 = 8$ and $6 + 3 = 9$, then . . .	$6 + 4 = 10$
$9 + 0 =$	Generalization. Since $n + 0 = n$, then . . .	$9 + 0 = 9$

(For the $3 + 2$ row, number line:)

0 1 2 3 4 5 6 7

6.6 MEMORIZATION OF THE ADDITION FACTS

After a child has been introduced to some of the basic addition facts in a meaningful way, and after the child can solve equations without guidance by putting together sets with the correct number property, the child is ready to begin memorizing his facts.

The child will have memorized some of the facts before you begin an organized program to accomplish the task. (For example, some children will know 1 and 1 is 2, and 2 and 2 is 4 even before you formally introduce addition.)

It is essential that you identify the facts that each child knows before proceeding with activities promoting memorization, because you do not wish to expend either your effort or the child's with redundant practice.

The following three activities might be used to evaluate which facts a child knows:

1. Flash cards
2. Show me
3. Beat-the-bounce

The first two activities are nontimed activities, whereas beat-the-bounce is designed to test both the child's accuracy and speed of recall.

In using flash cards, show the child each card and allow him a reasonable length of time to answer. Don't permit him sufficient time to count on his fingers or use some other crutch. After the child has missed three to five facts, stop evaluating and have the child memorize the facts he has missed. You may wish to group the facts you display, using the flash cards, from easiest to hard, before beginning the evaluation.

In show-me type activities, the teacher calls out facts orally. When she says "show me," the children hold up a numeral showing what they believe to be the correct response. The teacher notes on a chart which children missed a particular fact. When she completes calling out the facts she assigns each child up to five facts to memorize.

A third activity that can be used to test not only fact knowledge but speed of recall is called "beat-the-bounce." In its usual form it takes on the characteristics of a game with the randomness of the facts called being the chance element and the required knowledge of the fact being the element of skill.

Four or more children participate in the game of beat-the-bounce. One child takes a ball and holds it at shoulder height. The child with the ball calls out an addition expression (e.g., $4 + 5$). Then the child calls out the first name of another child in the group. As the name is called, the child lets the ball drop. The child whose name was called has to respond with the correct answer before the ball hits the ground. If he does respond correctly, he wins and gets to be the questioner. If he misses, the original person gets to continue dropping the ball. Either the teacher or a monitor records the facts that are missed by individual children. When the game is concluded each child works on memorizing the facts he has missed.

In this chapter, we will examine a writing technique that has proved useful in helping children in a remedial clinic situation memorize facts. If you wish to verify its effectiveness, select any three symbols found on typewriter keys and use the following technique to memorize these three keys in relation to each other.

Before we examine the technique, let us review some basic don'ts of practice:

1. Don't specify the number of times the child should practice a fact, because he will be constantly interrupting his concentration on the fact by counting to see if he has written it enough times.
2. Don't include the plus sign or the bar in the practice since these are not involved in the mental process when the child is recalling the fact.
3. Don't have the child practice facts in the vertical form where the facts are placed one beside another. (For example, if the child were practicing 4 and 3 is 7 in the vertical form, the tendency would be for the child to write 4, 4, 4, etc., then 3, 3, 3, etc., then plus, plus, plus, etc., then bar, bar, bar, bar, etc., then 7, 7, 7, etc., and miss the association he is trying to make.)

A practice technique which avoids these don'ts is as follows:

Have each child start with an unlined piece of paper. Assume the child is trying to memorize 3 and 4 is 7. Have him start at the top of the paper and write a 3; under the 3 a 4; and under the 4 a 7. Have him continue in this manner until he reaches the bottom of the page. Have him write another column beginning with a 4, under the 4 a 3, and under the 3 a 7. Have him continue in this manner until he reaches the bottom. (As he practices a column, he should be thinking the fact; e.g., 4 and 3 is 7, 4 and 3 is 7, etc., or 4 plus 3 equals 7, etc.)

Some teachers prefer to have children also practice the related subtraction facts at the same time. Here the teacher would have the child start at the top of the paper and write 7, 4, 3, 7, 4, 3, and so on, thinking 7 minus 4 is 3, 7 minus 4 is 3. Figure 6.11 illustrates how this practice

3	4	7	7
4	3	4	3
7	7	3	4
3	4	7	7
4	3	4	3
7	7	3	4
3	4	7	7
4	3	4	3
7	7	3	4
3	4	7	7
4	3	4	3
7	7	3	4
3	4	7	7
4	3	4	3
7	7	3	4

Figure 6.11

might look on paper. This type of practice can also be used for multiplication and division facts.

There are many other ways of practicing facts. One of the most common techniques is to use an oral activity. Each school day has some unused moments that can be used as short practice periods for memorizing facts (e.g., the few moments after the class lines up to go to the lunchroom or go home).

Some teachers have found it useful to play "pass-a-fact along." The first child in the line whispers a fact to the second, and it is in turn relayed down the line; two or more facts can then be sent rippling down the line in this manner, with the teacher placing herself at the other end of the line to verify that the correct fact made it down the line.

Another device is to appoint a fact captain of the day. When the children leave the room they must whisper the passwords, which consist of two or more facts, to the fact captain.

It may be helpful to find additional techniques for promoting the mastery of basic facts in other texts.

6.7 EXPANDED NOTATION

Before teaching a child how to add ones to tens and ones (e.g., $34 + 2 = \square$), you will need to teach the child how to express a standard numeral in expanded form and how to express numerals in expanded form as standard numerals. In some elementary mathematics series, this concept of expanded notation is developed at the same time that the names for standard numerals are developed. In other series, it is taught just before the introduction of adding ones to tens and ones.

Teaching a child expanded notation can be accomplished by teaching children how to work exercises similar to the following:

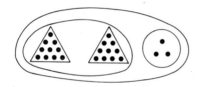

a. 2 tens 3 ones =

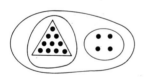

b. 1 ten $\square$ ones = 14
c. 4 tens 5 ones =
d. $\square$ tens 8 ones = 78
e. $20 + 6 = \square$ h. $22 = 20 + \square$
f. $30 + 7 = \square$ i. $82 = \square + 2$
g. $10 + 8 = \square$ j. $99 = 90 + \square$

Statement e can be read as 2 tens and 6 ones equals 26. Or it can be read as 20 and 6 equals 26.

One of the purposes of teaching the child expanded notation is to force him to focus on the place value inherent in the digits.

There are many activities and devices (place-value charts, toy money, etc.) that can be used in conjunction with the exercises described in this section to help establish meaning.

6.8 ADDITION ALGORITHM SEQUENCE

After the child has mastered some or all of his basic addition facts he will begin learning how to use these facts in computational schemes called addition algorithms. In the next sections we will explore several methods of developing one of the algorithm sequences. In this section you will be shown one of the more common sequences found in elementary mathematics series.

Instance	Type
a. 23 +4	Addition of ones to tens and ones. (No regrouping.)
b. 30 +40	Addition of tens to tens.
c. 34 +24	Addition of tens and ones to tens and ones. (No regrouping.)
d. 34 +8	Addition of ones to tens and ones with regrouping.
e. 48 +27	Addition of tens and ones to tens and ones with regrouping into the tens place.
f. 51 +93	Addition of tens and ones to tens and ones with regrouping into the hundreds place.

All other two-addend addition problems merely represent extensions of the concepts developed by this sequence. There are slight variations to this sequence in some elementary series. For example, some series teach the f-type situation earlier in the sequence.

In the following sections we will explore one method or model for each type of situation. However, in almost every instance each method and model is interchangeable with any other method or model depending on a teacher's preference and skill.

6.9 USING ANALYSIS TO TEACH ADDITION OF ONES TO TENS AND ONES (WITHOUT REGROUPING TENS)

Figure 6.12 is a step-by-step symbolic presentation by the teacher depicting the steps used in learning to add ones to tens and ones.*

* Although analysis has been chosen for emphasis in this section, in actual practice a teacher would begin the introduction with models.

In step 1, the teacher renames the 14, making it $(10 + 4)$, since the only skills related to this problem that the students know at this point are how to add ones to ones (basic facts) and how to add tens to ones (expanded notation). In step 2, the associative property for addition is used to associate the 4 with the 5 so that the ones can be added to the ones. In step 3, the 4 and 5 are added to give 9. In step 4, the skill developed working with expanded notation is used to rewrite $10 + 9$ as 19.

$$14 + 5$$
$$\downarrow$$
Step 1 $(10 + 4) + 5$
$$\downarrow$$
Step 2 $10 + (4 + 5)$
$$\downarrow$$
Step 3 $10 + 9$
$$\downarrow$$
Step 4 19

Figure 6.12

The children need an opportunity to *see* several similar step-by-step explanations. Even though you may not elicit from your students the reasons and/or justifications for each step, student responses should not be discouraged.

After you have developed the justification for adding ones to ones to obtain a sum that is combined with the tens (expanded notation skill), the child is ready to work similar problems using vertical notation. A typical problem in the early stages of this development can be seen in Figure 6.13.

$20 + 1$ Standard
$\underline{+ 8}$ numeral
$\qquad\qquad\downarrow$
$\square + \triangle = \bigcirc$

Figure 6.13

After the students have solved similar problems through the expanded form, they can be given exercises like those depicted in Figure 6.14. These exercises will provide for a smooth transition to the final stages of mastering the algorithm.

Phase 1   **Phase 2**
$60 + 4$ 64 64
$\underline{+ 3}$ $\underline{+ 3}$ $\underline{+ 3}$
$\square + \triangle \rightarrow \bigcirc$ $\square$

Figure 6.14

In the early stages of teaching the children to add using this notation, you can use expressions such as "6 tens" and "4 tens." This terminology can then give way to calling the 6 tens "60" and the 4 tens "40."

When the children are able to solve addition problems in the expanded form, you can phase out the expanded form for the more efficient numeral form. In Figure 6.15, we see examples representing typical exercises that could be used to phase out the expanded notation.

Phase 1		Phase 2
30 + 8	38	38
40 + 1	41	+41
□ + △ → ○		○

Figure 6.15

Some teachers prefer to use the word form of the expanded notation rather than the form with the plus sign. There is probably some merit to using the word form of analysis at this stage of conceptual development; however, the form that has just been developed will prove useful in concept areas other than operations on numbers. Figure 6.16 shows the word form of expanded notation in the vertical form.

3 tens 2 ones	32
+3 ones	+ 3
3 tens 5 ones	35

Figure 6.16

In practice, the preceding analysis method would be used in conjunction with other methods. Models would be needed from the beginning to reduce the level of abstraction for the child. It has been used in isolation in this section only to emphasize its nature as a teaching technique.

EXERCISES (1)

1. "10, 21, 32, 43, 54, etc." What does the sequence tell us we are counting by? Describe the pattern found in the tens place. Describe the pattern found in the ones place.
2. Describe a purpose for having the child perform a counting exercise as in Exercise 1.
3. In the following array, name two numbers greater than 1 that could be used to count the set of dots.

    .   .   .   .   .   .

    .   .   .   .   .   .

    .   .   .   .   .   .

4. Look in a teachers' edition of an elementary school textbook and find how you use either a place-value chart or a hundred board to teach the basic facts. Draw a series of pictures that would depict the steps for teaching a child that $6 + 9 = 15$, using either a place-value chart or a hundred board.

5. Make up six equations similar to those in Section 6.7 that could be used to introduce the child to the concept of expanded notation.

6. Identify the skill or the property for each of the steps in the following presentation:

$$47 + 2$$
$$\downarrow$$
Step 1 $(40 + 7) + 2$
$$\downarrow$$
Step 2 $40 + (7 + 2)$
$$\downarrow$$
Step 3 $40 + 9$
$$\downarrow$$
Step 4 49

7. Use the definition of sum to illustrate how you would show a child that the sum of 4 and 5 is 9.

8. List five ways you could read $6 + 7 = 13$.

9. Identify the addends and the sum in each of the following problems:

$$3 + 9 = 12 \qquad \begin{array}{r} 7 \\ +4 \\ \hline 11 \end{array}$$

10. Solve the following problem: $6 + \square = 6$. What property for addition does this represent?

11. Make up sample problems for each of the following stages in teaching the commutative property for addition: paired problems requiring knowledge of the property for solution; multiple-solution problems.

12. Make up sample problems for each of the following stages in teaching the associative property for addition: paired problems for discovering the property; single-solution problems requiring knowledge of the property for solution; multiple-solution problems.

6.10   USING A NUMBER-LINE MODEL AND TRANSLATION TO TEACH ADDITION OF TENS TO TENS

A skill that must be developed before the children are taught addition involving "regrouping the tens" is the skill of adding tens to tens.

The techniques and aids used in teaching the concept of adding tens to tens are similar to those used in teaching the addition of ones to ones. One of the techniques used in teaching these sums is to have the child recognize that when he learned the basic facts for ones he was also learning relationships that would help him to learn the addition of tens.

Some activities that will focus the child's attention on the close relationship between the addition of ones and the addition of tens can be seen in Figure 6.17.

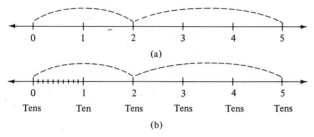

(a)

(b)

Figure 6.17

A typical dialogue that might be used to talk to children about addition of tens that would focus on the relation between adding ones and adding tens is as follows.

Sample Dialogue

Draw Figure 6.17 on the board.	Teacher: The a number line suggests $2 + 3 = 5$. The b number line suggests 2 tens plus 3 tens is equal to what?
	Child: 5 tens.
	Teacher: What is another name for 2 tens?
	Child: 20.
	Teacher: For 3 tens?
	Child: 30.
	Teacher: For 5 tens?
	Child: 50.
	Teacher: Therefore, 20 plus 30 equals what?

The technique illustrated in using addition of ones (which the children have mastered) to teach addition of tens is an example of the translation method of teaching.

By using a similar dialogue the teacher could at this point extend the child's conceptual level to addition of hundreds, addition of thousands, and so on.

6.11 USING A MONEY MODEL TO TEACH ADDITION OF TENS AND ONES TO TENS AND ONES (WITHOUT REGROUPING)

Toy money or real money is a very useful model for developing mathematical concepts. Children readily relate to the money since they recognize its importance in their daily lives. Using money as a model is generally regarded as a high-interest device. It seems that disadvantaged children will maintain a higher interest level when money is used as a model than when other models are used.

Ideally, real money should be used (dimes and pennies or ten dollar bills and one dollar bills), because one of the transfer benefits of using real money is the conceptual understanding the child gains from the discussions of the comparative worth of various denominations.

Let us examine a sample dialogue that might be used to develop the addition of tens and ones to tens and ones without regrouping.

Sample Dialogue

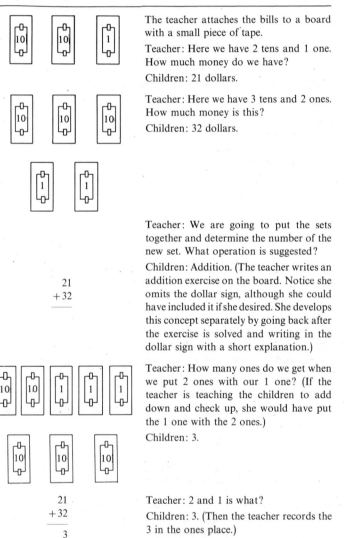

The teacher attaches the bills to a board with a small piece of tape.

Teacher: Here we have 2 tens and 1 one. How much money do we have?

Children: 21 dollars.

Teacher: Here we have 3 tens and 2 ones. How much money is this?

Children: 32 dollars.

Teacher: We are going to put the sets together and determine the number of the new set. What operation is suggested?

Children: Addition. (The teacher writes an addition exercise on the board. Notice she omits the dollar sign, although she could have included it if she desired. She develops this concept separately by going back after the exercise is solved and writing in the dollar sign with a short explanation.)

Teacher: How many ones do we get when we put 2 ones with our 1 one? (If the teacher is teaching the children to add down and check up, she would have put the 1 one with the 2 ones.)

Children: 3.

Teacher: 2 and 1 is what?

Children: 3. (Then the teacher records the 3 in the ones place.)

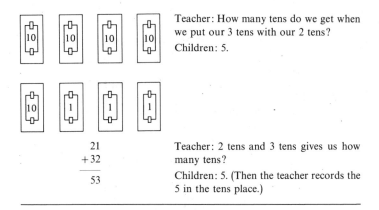

Teacher: How many tens do we get when we put our 3 tens with our 2 tens?

Children: 5.

21
+32
———
53

Teacher: 2 tens and 3 tens gives us how many tens?

Children: 5. (Then the teacher records the 5 in the tens place.)

6.12 **ADDITION OF ONES TO TENS AND ONES (WITH REGROUPING)**

Before we examine how a place-value chart can be used to teach this skill, let us examine the analysis of addition of ones to tens and ones with regrouping.

Figure 6.18 is a step-by-step symbolic presentation that might be placed on the board by the teacher. This presentation depicts the steps in learning to add ones to tens and ones when it is necessary to regroup after adding the ones.

In step 1, we have renamed 23, changing it to $(20 + 3)$. We have done this renaming because the skills the student has at this point to help him find the sum are those of adding ones to ones and tens to tens, and so on.

$$23 + 9$$
$$\downarrow$$
Step 1 $(20 + 3) + 9$
$$\downarrow$$
Step 2 $20 + (3 + 9)$
$$\downarrow$$
Step 3 $20 + 12$
$$\downarrow$$
Step 4 $20 + (10 + 2)$
$$\downarrow$$
Step 5 $(20 + 10) + 2$
$$\downarrow$$
Step 6 $30 + 2$
$$\downarrow$$
Step 7 32

Figure 6.18

Let us examine how a place-value chart (model) can be used to teach addition of ones to tens and ones (with regrouping).

Sample Dialogue

Tens	Ones
〖〗	〖〗
	〖〗〖〗〖〗〖〗〖〗〖〗〖〗〖〗〖〗

$$\begin{array}{r} 22 \\ +\ 9 \\ \hline \end{array}$$

Tens	Ones
〖〗	〗

Tens	Ones
〖〗〗	〗

$$\begin{array}{r} 1 \\ 22 \\ +\ 9 \\ \hline 1 \end{array}$$

$$\begin{array}{r} 1 \\ 22 \\ +\ 9 \\ \hline 31 \end{array}$$

Teacher: Here we have 2 tens and 2 ones. What number is represented?

Children: 22.

Teacher: Here we have 9 represented by 9 ones. We are going to combine our sets and find the number represented. What operation is suggested?

Children: Addition.

(The teacher places the addition exercise on the board.)

Teacher: I have placed the 9 ones with the 2 ones; how many ones do I have?

Children: 11.

Teacher: When I get more than 9 ones, I must bundle 10 of the ones up and exchange it for 1 ten. How many ones will I have left?

Children: 1 one.

We then trade in our 10 ones for 1 ten and place it with our other tens.

The teacher then records a 1 in the tens place.

Teacher: Now how many tens do we have?

Children: 3.

The 3 is recorded.

Teacher: What is another name for 3 tens and 1 one?

Children: 31.

Teaching addition with regrouping takes considerably more time and skill than nongrouping situations. It is very likely, although not desirable, that children could easily master addition without regrouping in the absence of any explanation of why you do what you do.

Adding tens and ones to tens and ones will be reserved for development in the exercises.

6.13 TEACHING COLUMN ADDITION

Before introducing children to the concept of column addition, you will find it useful to have them discover the associative property (see Section 6.5). The first problems of column addition a child should encounter are those in which the final sum is less than 10. A typical problem of this type can be seen in Figure 6.19.

$(4 + 2) + 1 = \square$
$$
\begin{array}{r}
4 \\
2 \\
+1 \\
\hline
\square
\end{array}
$$

Figure 6.19

A dialogue to accompany the vertical notation in Figure 6.19 might be as follows.

Sample Dialogue

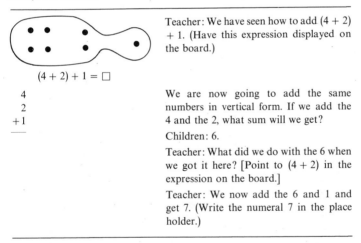

$(4 + 2) + 1 = \square$

$$
\begin{array}{r}
4 \\
2 \\
+1 \\
\hline
\end{array}
$$

Teacher: We have seen how to add $(4 + 2)$ + 1. (Have this expression displayed on the board.)

We are now going to add the same numbers in vertical form. If we add the 4 and the 2, what sum will we get?

Children: 6.

Teacher: What did we do with the 6 when we got it here? [Point to $(4 + 2)$ in the expression on the board.]

Teacher: We now add the 6 and 1 and get 7. (Write the numeral 7 in the place holder.)

The second type of problem the child should encounter is one with three addends arranged so that the first sum obtained is less than 10. Good examples of this type of problem are contrasted with unsatisfactory examples in Figure 6.20.

$$
\begin{array}{cccc}
3 & 2 & 7 & 8 \\
6 & 5 & 4 & 9 \\
+3 & +3 & +8 & +3 \\
\hline
\square & \square & \square & \square
\end{array}
$$
Acceptable   Unacceptable

Figure 6.20

After the concept of adding ones to tens and ones has been taught, the students should be ready to perform column addition involving a first sum greater than 9, so that the next addend will not force a regrouping situation.

After the concept of adding ones to tens and ones involving regrouping has been taught, the child is ready for any single-column addition following essentially the same sequence of steps. They are:

1. Column addition with no regrouping
2. Column addition with sums of ones greater than 9
3. Column addition with sums of tens greater than 90
4. Any two-digit column addition

Extension of the skill of regrouping tens, hundreds, thousands, and so on, follows the same basic sequence developed for the ones to tens and ones. Techniques used in the introduction of these concepts follow the procedure developed up to this point and will be further developed as exercises for you to work.

6.14   COLUMN ADDITION WITH LIMITED REGROUPING

Most of our emphasis to this point has been on developing the child's understanding of addition. However, if the child is to make addition an effective tool, he must not only understand how the tool functions but also be able to perform with the tool efficiently. Let us now examine how we might develop this efficiency.

$$\begin{array}{r} 27 \\ 49 \\ 68 \\ +83 \\ \hline \end{array}$$

In adding from top to bottom in the example at the left, it is necessary, if we desire efficiency, to be able automatically to identify sums associated with $7 + 9$, $16 + 8$, $24 + 3$, $2 + 2$, $4 + 4$, $8 + 6$, and $14 + 8$.

Even more efficiency could be obtained by being able to identify sums associated with the pairs of numbers $(7, 9)$, $(16, 8)$, $(24, 3)$, $(2, 2)$, $(4, 4)$, $(8, 6)$, and $(14, 8)$.

We have already discussed how automatic recall for sums involving the basic facts is developed. Let us now study a possible learning sequence that may help the child acquire the skills necessary for rapid higher-decade addition.

Until now we have had the child reason that $27 + 8 = 20 + 15 = 30 + 5$. However, this type of analysis is not efficient when we begin performing column addition. It is now more important for the child to begin to perform a pattern analysis similar to the following:

$8 + 7 = 15$, $18 + 7 = 25$, $28 + 7 = 35$,   etc.

This type of analysis points out that the general "effect" of adding 7 to x tens and 8 ones always results in $(x + 1)$ tens and 5 ones.

Once the child has mastered the basic facts, you should extend his skill level to the automatic mastery of adding ones to tens and ones.

One way this can be accomplished is through finding sums and then studying their pattern. The following set of exercises might represent such a typical set of problems:

$$
\begin{array}{cccc}
9 & 19 & 29 & 39 \\
+6 & +\ 6 & +\ 6 & +\ 6
\end{array}
$$

$$
\begin{array}{llll}
5 + 8 = \square & 15 + 8 = \square & 25 + 8 = \square & 35 + 8 = \square \\
7 + 2 = \square & 17 + 2 = \square & 27 + 2 = \square & 37 + 2 = \square
\end{array}
$$

After the children have mastered the skill of adding ones to tens and ones automatically, they can apply this skill to column-addition problems such as the following:

$$
\begin{array}{cccc}
8 & 35 & 346 & \$7.89 \\
9 & 68 & 288 & .98 \\
7 & 74 & 997 & .64 \\
+4 & +26 & +645 & +\ 8.29
\end{array}
$$

EXERCISES (2)

1. Illustrate with pictures of sets how you would establish for children the relationship between 7 ones plus 8 ones equals 15 ones and 7 tens plus 8 tens equals 15 tens.
2. Illustrate on a number-line segment how you would establish for children the relationship between 6 ones plus 7 ones equals 13 ones and 6 tens plus 7 tens equals 13 tens.
3. Make up a dialogue that could be used to introduce the following vertical notation. Use either money or a place-value chart.

$$
\begin{array}{l}
45 \quad \text{Standard} \\
+31 \quad \text{numeral}
\end{array}
$$

(Pretend that you have a class and try to anticipate its answers. The purpose of this exercise is to focus your attention on the basic structure of a presentation and not to have you develop "canned" dialogues to use with your students. Remember, the dialogues you will use later will develop spontaneously in a classroom, and the skill of your presentation will depend on your insight into what you are teaching.)

4. Justify or identify the skill involved in each of the following steps:

$$
35 + 8 \xrightarrow{\text{Step 1}} (30 + 5) + 8 \xrightarrow{\text{Step 2}} 30 + (5 + 8) \xrightarrow{\text{Step 3}}
$$

$$
30 + 13 \xrightarrow{\text{Step 4}} 30 + (10 + 3) \xrightarrow{\text{Step 5}} (30 + 10) + 3 \xrightarrow{\text{Step 6}}
$$

$$
40 + 3 \xrightarrow{\text{Step 7}} 43
$$

5. Write a dialogue that could be used to introduce vertical notation with regrouping, through the following example. Use either money or analysis.

$$
\begin{array}{l}
89 \\
+\ 8
\end{array}
$$

6. Work out a step-by-step presentation that could be used to justify and identify the skills needed to teach 38 + 47.

7. Sequence the following exercises from the first taught to the last:

16	23	40	8	33
+ 9	+ 3	+30	+7	+29

8. Sequence the following exercises from the first taught to the last:

3	2	1
5	2	9
+6	+5	+4

9. Sequence the following exercises from the first taught to the last:

31	21	48
52	32	16
+63	+45	+29

6.15   ADDITION "STORY PROBLEMS"

Problem solving involving *word problems* or *story problems* can be thought of as the process of extracting the basic information of the problem, translating this basic information into a mathematical sentence, and then applying previously learned concepts to derive a "solution" to the mathematical sentence. Although this is a greatly oversimplified interpretation of problem solving, it will provide us with a base from which to discuss techniques of developing problem-solving skills involving word and story problems.

Some of the basic principles we shall want to have to accompany our techniques of developing problem-solving skills are as follows:

1. A flexible framework should be provided to facilitate the child's ability to translate and solve new problems. Children should not be discouraged from using novel approaches that are valid to problem solving.
2. Problems should be within the realm of the child's experience. Experiences such as field trips, exhibits, visual aids, dramatizations, and speakers can be employed to fill in the experiential gaps.
3. The relationships that exist between various elements of the problem must be a part of the child's repertoire of concepts before his attempting to solve the problem.
4. Development of reading skills applicable to problem solving should parallel or precede problem solving involving word problems.

5. Children should be encouraged to create problems from mathematical data. This principle cannot be overstressed. The essence of true mathematical problem solving often involves the accumulation of data via experimentation or compilation, followed by the construction of a mathematical model to fit the data and then the testing of the validity of this model with future events or experiments.
6. Children should be instructed in techniques of estimation and verification.
7. After the children have had extensive experience with certain types of problems, the development of a generalization should be undertaken.

Although in this book techniques of teaching children to solve word problems that apply to specific computational skills—such as addition of whole number and subtraction of whole number—are isolated and analyzed in the specific chapters in which the operation is discussed, in actual practice, giving the child a large number of problems involving one operation will dull his flexibility for attacking unrelated problems. The inclusion of problem solving within each chapter emphasizes another element of problem solving: since computation and problem solving are highly interrelated, computation is not an end in itself but a facet of the larger goal of problem solving.

It is important to note that the problems found in elementary textbook series should represent only a small portion of the types of problem-solving situations to which a child can be exposed. Even though these problems serve as a useful base from which to extend problem-solving skills, the very nature of how these problems came to be included in these texts has eliminated the "unique-now" type of problem. Publishers and authors cannot include problems dealing with recent events, because this type of problem dates a book. As a consequence, problems of an immediate concern are omitted, leaving those problems of a yesterday, today, and tomorrow nature.

It is the specific responsibility of the teacher to provide children with them. It is also important that the development of problem-solving skills be oriented so that even the child with weak reading skills can develop skill in attacking problems of a quantitative nature. Such devices as a taped series of problems, problems displayed as picture situations on film strips, and loop films depicting problems in picture form can serve as good substitutes for textbook problems for the "nonreader," to develop his skill for attacking problems.

Although there are many studies in the area of problem solving, there are few, if any, "truths" that can be derived from research in this area. Experimental evidence suggests that requiring a group of children to conform to a particular pattern is not as effective as allowing them some flexibility in attacking problems. This is not to say that some individuals may not actually thrive under the more rigid regime, nor is it to say that we should not search for the basic structure of the problem and attempt to translate it into one or more mathematical sentences. Let us examine an "addition problem."

> John had 3 marbles. Mary gave him 2 more.
> John is 5 years old. How many marbles does John have now?

The child's first step is one of examination. If the problem is communicated in writing, then this examination takes the form of reading the problem until he feels that he understands it. If it is given orally, the examination takes the form of his listening and asking for the problem to be restated until he understands it.

A useful technique at this point is to request the student to restate the problem. Failure in problem solving often is due not to a lack of problem-solving ability but to the failure of the teacher to communicate the problem to the child. Requesting a restatement of the problem will help to identify this breakdown in communication.

As the problem is examined, have the child identify what we want to find out. In everyday situations, this represents a complex skill. Even though the problem is identified with a question or a missing word or phrase in a sentence in the typical elementary textbook, in an everyday situation the problem is identified spontaneously within the context of the quantitative situation. Frequently the problem precedes the collection of quantitative data that will be used to find a solution to the problem. For the problem given here we are concerned with finding, "How many marbles does John have now?"

Following the identification of the problem, the student has the task of identifying those quantitative aspects of the ideas communicated to him that will relate to the problem to be solved. Obviously, John's age will not relate to the number of marbles he has. The teacher should introduce extraneous information frequently to promote the child's ability to identify the structure of a problem within a larger context. This ability to discriminate the essential from the nonessential is an aspect of everyday problem solving that we must interject continually into the problems we present to our students. This interjection of nonessential data into a problem will have the following effects:

1. It will reduce the tendency of a child to interpret a problem as addition whenever he sees several names for numbers in the problem.
2. It will cause the child to examine each problem with greater care, knowing that some data may be extraneous.
3. The problems will be better models of those problems the child meets in everyday situations.

After the child has extracted the basic structure of the problem, he should do the following:

1. If he recognizes how to translate the problem into a mathematical sentence, he does so. The problem about John and Mary translates to $3 + 2 = \square$. [The teacher may want to relate the problem to the mathematical model of putting together sets (union) and the concept of addition.]
2. The child proceeds to derive a solution for the mathematical sentence he has constructed.

Other phases of developing problem-attack skills involving addition will be developed through the exercises.

EXERCISES (3)

1. Using one or more of the following sources, construct five story problems of a current-events nature involving basic addition facts appropriate for a group of students in a second-grade class:
   a. Newspaper   b. *World Almanac*   c. Magazine
2. Using the same sources, construct five story problems of a current-events nature involving column addition appropriate for a group of students in a third-grade class.
3. Using the same sources, construct five story problems of a current-events nature requiring the child to use addition and either subtraction, multiplication, division, or addition again to get the answer. These problems should be appropriate for a group in a fifth-grade class.
4. Using the same sources, construct five story problems of a current-events nature requiring the child to use addition and two other operations. These problems should be appropriate for a group in a fifth-grade class.
5. Make up a word problem for each of the following mathematical sentences:

   a. $3 + 10 = \square$ c. $30¢ + 40¢ + 10¢ = \square$
   b. $15 + 15 + 15 = \square$ d. $4567 + 3487 = \square$

BIBLIOGRAPHY

Ashlock, R. B. "Teaching the Basic Facts: Three Classes of Activities," *The Arithmetic Teacher* (October 1971), pp. 359–364.

Golden, S. R. "Fostering Enthusiasm Through Child-Created Games," *The Arithmetic Teacher* (February 1970), pp. 111–115.

Heddens, J. W. *Today's Mathematics* (Palo Alto, Calif.: Science Research Associates), 1971, pp. 153–156.

May, L. J. "Patterns and Properties in Addition and Subtraction," *Grade Teacher* (October 1967), pp. 41, 44, 46, 48, 50.

National Council of Teachers of Mathematics, *29th Yearbook* (Washington, D.C.), 1964, pp. 53–58, 65–70, 140–146.

National Council of Teachers of Mathematics. *30th Yearbook* (Washington, D.C.), 1965, pp. 19–21.

Sanders, W. K. "Let's Go One Step Farther in Addition," *The Arithmetic Teacher* (October 1971), pp. 413–415.

7

Teaching subtraction on the set of whole numbers

BEHAVIORAL OBJECTIVES

Student can . . .

Give a working definition of subtraction.

List five ways of reading a subtraction equation.

Illustrate four sets models for subtraction.

Identify by examples three patterns that can be used to teach subtraction facts.

Describe a readiness activity for subtraction.

Sequence a set of exercises in the order they are taught.

Describe how to use each of the following in teaching the subtraction algorithm involving regrouping:

    Place-value chart
    Money
    Balloons
    Analysis

Describe how translation is used in teaching subtraction of tens.

Develop an alternate subtraction algorithm using compensation.

7.1 INTRODUCTION

Subtraction presents a more complex teaching situation than does addition. The child must learn to interpret such varying problems as, "John has 4 marbles and Jim has 3. How many more marbles has John than Jim?" or, "If John had 4 marbles and lost 3, how many would he have left?" Both situations require subtraction for their solutions.

Subtraction on the set of whole numbers has a set of properties distinctly different from those the child encounters when studying addition. For example, the compensation property for subtraction, which employs the patterns

$$(\square + \triangle) - (\square + \triangle) = \square - \square \quad \text{and} \quad (\square - \triangle) - (\square - \triangle) = \square - \square$$

or, specifically

$$(8 + 2) - (6 + 2) = 8 - 6 \quad \text{and} \quad (8 - 3) - (6 - 3) = 8 - 6$$

utilizes the idea that if the same number is to be added to or subtracted from both the minuend and the subtrahend, the difference will be the same as if no number were added to or subtracted from the minuend and subtrahend.

The closure property does not hold for subtraction on the set of whole numbers (e.g., $4 - 8$ does not name a whole number). Neither the commutative property nor the associative property holds for subtraction. Although there exists an identity element for subtraction, its employment must be modified due to the noncommutative nature of subtraction. Even though the properties of subtraction will be new to the child, it is important to establish the close relationship existing between addition sentences and subtraction sentences.

7.2 DEFINITION, TERMINOLOGY, AND SYMBOLISM

The definition, terminology, and symbolism that we use in communicating the concepts of subtraction play a very significant role in teaching. Whereas faulty language, such as "3 is added to 2," when referring to "$3 + 2$," causes only minimal interference with the child's ability to master the concepts of addition, similar faulty language use for subtraction will greatly interfere with his mastery of subtraction. An incorrect statement such as "We always subtract the smallest from the largest," will lead the child to develop a misconception, because he later will learn subtraction with the set of integers where it is possible to subtract a larger number from a smaller number. "We can't subtract a larger number from a smaller number" is an incorrect statement that will lead the child to modify a problem so that he can follow directions. For example, in the problem $48 - 19 = \square$, if the child thinks that he cannot subtract 9 ones from 8 ones, he will subtract 8 ones from 9 ones. Careful attention to precise use of definition, terminology, and symbolism should be given special emphasis when subtraction is being taught.

Let us examine two working definitions of subtraction derived from such interpretations of subtraction as *set separation* and *set comparison*. (We also have a *missing addend* interpretation that is extremely important in relating addition and subtraction. For example, we can say $7 - 3 = 4$ because $4 + 3 = 7$.)

A working definition using the idea of *set separation* might be stated as follows:

Suppose we wanted to find the difference of two whole numbers $\square$ and $\triangle$. We would take the following steps:

Obtain a set, the number of which is $\square$.
Take away $\triangle$ objects from the set.
Determine the number property of the set remaining.

The number property of the set remaining is designated the difference of $\square$ and $\triangle$.

A working definition employing the idea of *set comparison* might be stated as follows:

Suppose we wanted to find the difference of two whole numbers $\square$ and $\triangle$. We would take the following steps:

Obtain a set, the number of which is $\square$.
Obtain a set, the number of which is $\triangle$.
Attempt to pair the elements of the sets.
Determine the number property of the unmatched subset of the set whose number property was $\square$.

The number property of the unmatched subset is designated the difference of $\square$ and $\triangle$.

$$6 - 2 = \square \qquad \begin{array}{r} 6 \\ -2 \\ \hline \square \end{array} \qquad \square + 2 = 6$$

Figure 7.1

There are three basic notations that you, as the elementary teacher, must teach your students (see Figure 7.1). Notice that $\square + 2 = 6$ is identified as a notation for subtraction. It is important that the child learn to think of this as a subtractive situation, because he will be translating some story problems to this mathematical sentence. Viewing this sentence as a subtractive sentence will facilitate his obtaining a solution to this type of problem.

There are many ways the mathematical sentences depicted in Figure 7.1 might be read. Some of these follow:

6 minus 2 is 4.
6 minus 2 equals 4.
6 subtract 2 equals 4.
2 subtracted from 6 equals 4.
2 from 6 is 4.
2 from 6 equals 4.

In Figure 7.2, the terminology applied to the subtraction notations is depicted. Note that there are two sets of terminology for every mathematical sentence except one. A teacher should exercise caution not to mix terms. For example, it would not be proper to say "minuend 6 and known addend 2." When we use the term minuend, we must be consistent and refer to the other numeral as the subtrahend.

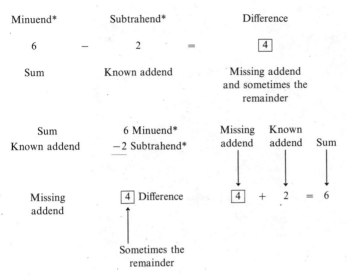

* Traditional vocabulary.

Figure 7.2

7.3 READINESS EXPERIENCES FOR SUBTRACTION

When you have your children attempt to pair sets and then ask how many items have not been paired, you are building readiness for subtraction. In the early phase of teaching addition, when you have the child find a missing addend without calling his attention to the fact that he is learning subtraction, you are preparing him for the concept that subtraction is the inverse of addition.

Other readiness activities consist of having the child count backward, starting at various points. For example, counting backward by twos starting at 21 prepares the child for subtracting 2 from a number whose name in the one's place is either 1, 3, 5, 7, or 9. The child should be given pattern-counting experiences with twos, threes, fours, fives, sixes, sevens, eights, and nines. He should be asked to start at various numbers less than 100 and count backward by twos, threes, and so on. For example, a dialogue for a counting experience involving threes starting with a set of 11 might proceed as follows:

"I have 11 objects and I take away 3 objects. I now have 8 objects. I take away 3 more objects and I now have 5 objects. I take away 3 more objects and I have 2 objects."

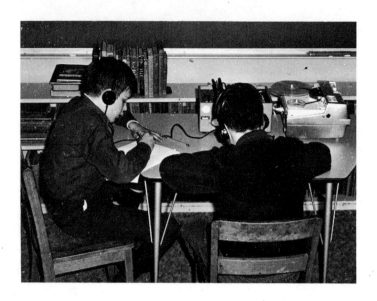

7.4 TEACHING THE BASIC SUBTRACTION FACTS USING MODELS

Those aids that proved useful in teaching the addition facts will also prove useful in teaching the subtraction facts. Flannel boards, magnetic boards, place-value charts, charts, and peg boards are a few of the aids that will help in teaching the concept of subtraction. Note that all of them are constructed to permit the active involvement of the child.

A typical dialogue that might be used with these aids to teach subtraction as the inverse of addition is as follows:

Sample Dialogue

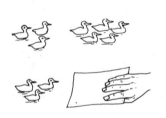

Teacher: Here we see 8 ducks (blocks, sticks, strips of paper, stones, buttons, beads, spools, pegs, etc.). (Point to the set of 8 objects.)

Teacher: I am covering some up. (Cover some of the objects—say 5—with a cardboard or your hand.)

Teacher: How many can we see now?

Child: 3.

Teacher: When we put these 3 together with the ones I am covering up, we get 8. How many am I covering up?

Child: 5.

Teacher: Yes, 3 and 5 is 8.

A typical dialogue that might be used to teach subtraction as the comparison of two sets is as follows:

Sample Dialogue

Teacher: Here we see some cats and some dishes. How many cats are there?

Child: 5.

Teacher: How many dishes are there?

Child 3.

Teacher: Mary, would you try to pair the dishes with the cats? How many cats do not have dishes?

Child: 2.

Teacher: How many more cats than dishes are there?

Child: 2.

A typical dialogue that might be used to teach subtraction as the partitioning of a subset from a set might be as follows:

Sample Dialogue

Teacher: Here we have 7 stars. If I take 3 stars away, how many do I have left?

The last common model for subtraction is the subset model. In the subset model you know something about the whole set and about part of the set and you wish to find out something about the rest of the set. Let us examine a sample story problem to see how this concept might be represented. Figure 7.3 summarizes the four basic sets models.

Mary has 5 bulbs. 2 of them are striped. How many are not striped?

Model	Suggests	Type of Model
0 0 0⟨0 0⟩	5 − 2 =	Take away
0 0 0 0 0 ↕ ↕ 0 0	5 − 2 =	Comparison
⟨0 0⟩ ⟨?⟩ ⟨0 0 0 0 0⟩	2 + □ = 5 or 5 − 2 =	Missing addend
0 0 0 ● ●	5 − 2 =	Subset

Figure 7.3

The number-line segment is another useful model in teaching subtraction. In Figure 7.4, we can see how $8 - 6 = 2$ would be shown on the number-

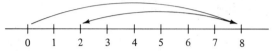

Figure 7.4

line segment. Notice that we are starting this number line at 0 so that a jump of 8 units to the right will put us at 8. The dialogue that might be used with this example is as follows:

Sample Dialogue

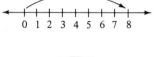

$8 - 6 = 2$

Teacher: We take a jump of 8. (After the loop on the number-line segment write the symbolic expression of this: 8.)

We turn around. (Write a minus sign to right of the 8 so that you have written $8 -$.) We take a jump of 6. (Write 6 to the right of the $8 -$ so that you now have written $8 - 6$.)

Teacher: Where are we after we have taken a jump of 8 and turned around and jumped 6? (After someone answers 2, write $= 2$.)

Teacher: We have seen that 8 less 6 is 2. (Point to the mathematical sentence.)

7.5   TEACHING SUBTRACTION FACTS USING PATTERNS

As with addition there are many useful patterns for supplementing the introduction of subtraction concepts. The following two patterns are taught primarily to reduce the number of facts the child has to memorize.

Pattern	Generalization
$4 - 0 = 4$	
$6 - 0 = 6$	
$10 - 0 = 10$	$n - 0 = n$
$805 - 0 = \square$	
$5 - 5 = 0$	
$7 - 7 = 0$	
$12 - 12 = 0$	$n - n = 0$
$864 - 864 = \square$	

By working with sets of objects, these concepts can be conveyed so that the child can easily understand them. Analogies such as the following will be useful in teaching this concept:

"Johnny carried 5 cents into a store. He didn't spend any money. How much money does he have left?" Or, "Beth has 3 dolls. Mary has 0 dolls. How many more dolls has Beth than Mary?"
"Bill had 3 pennies. He spent all 3 pennies. How much money did he have left?"

Related addition and subtraction facts form a useful pattern around which to develop facts. For example, $3 + 4 = 7$, $4 + 3 = 7$, $7 - 3 = 4$, and $7 - 4 = 3$ are related facts.

The following table gives instances of other patterns that are useful in developing subtraction facts.

	Type of Pattern
$7 - 4 = 3$	
$8 - 5 = 3$	Compensation
$9 - 6 = 3$	
$7 - 1 = 6$	
$7 - 2 = 5$	7 minuend
$7 - 3 = 4$	
$3 - 2 = 1$	
$4 - 2 = 2$	2 subtrahend
$5 - 2 = 3$	
$7 - 4 = (7 - 2) - 2$	
$\quad = 5 - 2$	Subtraction by parts pattern
$\quad = 3$	

The following table summarizes some of the ways we have of teaching the basic subtraction facts:

Problem	Method	Solution
$5 - 2 = \square$	Partitioning sets: $\cdot \cdot \cdot \odot \cdot$	$5 - 2 = 3$
$8 - 6 = \square$	Comparing sets:	$8 - 6 = 2$
$11 - 5 = \square$	Related addition sentence: $5 + 6 = 11$	$11 - 5 = 6$
$14 - 6 = \square$	Related subtraction sentence: $14 - 8 = 6$	$14 - 6 = 8$
$15 - 9 = \square$	Subtraction by parts: $15 - 5 = 10$; $10 - 4 = 6$	$15 - 9 = 6$
$12 - 3 = \square$	By patterns: $12 - 1 = 11$; $12 - 2 = 10$	$12 - 3 = 9$
$15 - 7 = \square$	By compensation: $15 - 7 = (15 + 3) - (7 + 3) = 18 - 10$	$15 - 7 = 8$
$7 - 4 = \square$	By the number line:	$7 - 4 = 3$
$9 - 6 = \square$	By relating to other facts: $8 - 6 = 2$	$9 - 6 = 3$

7.6 MEMORIZATION OF THE BASIC FACTS

At predesignated places in the child's discovery of the basic subtraction facts (such as after the subtraction facts with minuends through 5 have been discovered), the student should be encouraged to memorize the facts discovered.

"Show and tell," using flash cards, nonspeed and speed tests, and "beat the bounce" are some useful activities that will motivate the child to memorize the subtraction facts. Experiences with patterns of interrelated facts will facilitate memory and mastery of the basic facts. The exercises depicted in Figure 7.5 have been designed to promote recall through the exploration of familiar patterns.

(a) $6 - 4 = \square$ (e) $8 - \square = 2$
(b) $6 - \square = 4$ (f) $8 - \square = 6$
(c) $5 - 3 = \square$ (g) $\square - 5 = 3$
(d) $5 - 2 = \square$ (h) $\square - 3 = 5$

Figure 7.5

7.7 SUBTRACTION ALGORITHM SEQUENCE

After the child has mastered some or.all of the basic subtraction facts, he will begin learning how to use these facts in computational schemes called subtraction algorithms. In the next sections we will explore several methods of developing one of these algorithm sequences. In this section we discuss one of the more common sequences found in elementary school mathematics series.

The following types of subtraction exercises with one exception are complementary to the addition sequence (e.g., addition with regrouping $19 + 5 = 24$ equivalent to subtraction with regrouping $24 - 5 = 19$).

Instance	Type
25 − 3	Subtraction of ones from tens and ones. (No regrouping).
30 −20	Subtraction of tens from tens.
34 −12	Subtraction of tens and ones from tens and ones. (No regrouping.)

Instance	Type
23 − 4	Subtraction of ones from tens and ones. (Regrouping.)
35 −19	Subtraction of tens and ones from tens and ones. (Regrouping.) There are essentially no new skills represented by this type of exercise and its development will be left as an exercise.
405 −128	Zero case. (Child is unable to regroup from the next place. New skills must be taught at this point.)

All other whole number cases represent extensions of the previously mentioned types.

7.8 SUBTRACTION OF ONES FROM TENS AND ONES (NO REGROUPING) USING MONEY MODEL

Teaching children to subtract ones from tens and ones (with no regrouping) is comparatively easy. This ease is due to the closely parallel inverse skill of adding ones to tens and ones, which the children have been taught before this subtraction skill is introduced. Many of the problems you would encounter if addition had not been introduced first (such as lining up the ones and tens in the answer or learning to use appropriate devices) have been either solved or identified as areas for remediation.

Let us examine a method that uses money as the model. (Any of the methods that follow in the next several sections are interchangeable if the teacher uses care and skill.)

One of the distinct differences between the use of money as a model working with addition and working with subtraction is that in subtraction only the minuend is represented by the model.

Sample Dialogue

10 10 1 1 1 1 1

25
− 3

Teacher: How many tens do we have?
Children: 2.
Teacher: How many ones do we have?
Children: 5.
Teacher: What is the total value of our money?
Children: 25 dollars.
Teacher: How many ones does our exercise tell us we have to give up to someone?
Children: 3.
Teacher: John come up and take 3 ones back to your seat.

|10| |10| |1| |1|

```
   25
 -  3
 ────
    2
```

Teacher: How many ones are left?
Children: 2. (The teacher writes a 2 in the ones place.)

```
   25
 -  3
 ────
   22
```

Teacher: How many tens are left?
Children: 2. (The teacher writes a 2 in the tens place.)

Teacher: If we have 25 dollars and give 3 of the dollars to someone, how many dollars will we have left?

7.9 SUBTRACTION OF TENS FROM TENS USING NUMBER-LINE MODEL AND TRANSLATION

Subtraction of tens from tens can be developed shortly after the basic subtraction facts are mastered, if this sequence is desired. Since the concepts represented in subtraction of tens from tens, hundreds from hundreds, and so on, closely parallel the subtraction of ones from ones, the translation approach is probably the best method for development.

Sample Dialogue

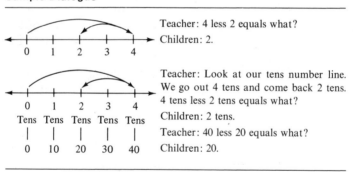

Teacher: 4 less 2 equals what?
Children: 2.

Teacher: Look at our tens number line. We go out 4 tens and come back 2 tens. 4 tens less 2 tens equals what?
Children: 2 tens.
Teacher: 40 less 20 equals what?
Children: 20.

It is a simple matter to extend the subtraction of tens to subtraction of hundreds, thousands, and so on.

7.10 SUBTRACTION OF TENS AND ONES FROM TENS AND ONES (NO REGROUPING) USING ABACUS-TYPE MODEL

Subtraction of tens and ones from tens and ones can be taught at any point after subtraction of tens is taught. Let us examine how a modified abacus model might be used to teach this skill.

Sample Dialogue

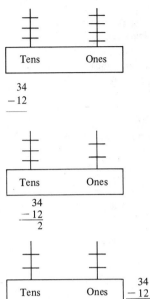

Teacher: What number is represented when we have 3 tens disks and 4 ones disks?

Children: 34.

Teacher: How many ones does our example tell us to remove from our 4 ones?

Children: Two ones.

Two of the ones disks are removed and a 2 is recorded in the ones place.

Teacher: How many tens disks are we asked to remove?

Children: 1.

One of the tens disks is removed and a 2 is recorded in the tens place.

All nonregrouping situations represent extensions of the concepts developed in this and the previous two sections.

7.11 SUBTRACTION OF ONES FROM TENS AND ONES (REGROUPING) USING BALLOON MODELS

In this section we will examine how balloons can be used as a model to teach regrouping.

Sample Dialogue

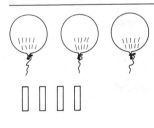

(The teacher takes 3 balloons and places 10 small strips of colored paper in each balloon. The balloons are then inflated and tied off. The 3 balloons and 4 single strips of paper are taped to a board.)

Teacher: In each balloon we have 10 strips and here beside the balloons we have 4 single strips. How many strips do we have if we have 3 tens and 4 ones?

Children: 34.

Teacher: In our example how many ones are we asked to subtract?

Children: 5.

34
− 5
_____

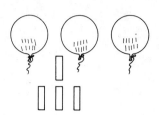

Teacher: Mary would you come to the board and get 5 strips?

Mary: I can't, there are only 4.

Teacher: Can someone suggest a way that Mary can get some more single strips?

Children: Break a balloon. (One of the children comes to the board and pops a balloon with a pin.)

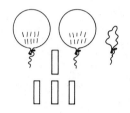

Teacher: How many tens do we have now?

Children: 2.

(Teacher crosses out the 3 and records a 2.)

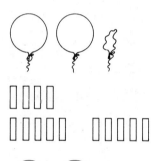

Teacher: We had 4 ones, then we got 10 more when we broke a balloon. How many ones do we have in all?

Children: 14.

(The teacher records a 1 by the 4 making the numeral 14. The 10 ones are placed by the 4 ones.)

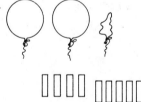

(Mary now removes 5 ones.)

Teacher: How many ones do we have left?

Children: 9.

(A 9 is recorded in the ones place.)

$$\begin{array}{r} 2 \\ \cancel{3}4 \\ -\ 5 \\ \hline 29 \end{array}$$

Teacher: How many tens do we have left?

Children: 2.

(A 2 is recorded in the tens place.)

With the exception of the zero case (which follows in the next section), all regrouping situations represent extensions of the concept presented in this section.

7.12 ZERO CASE SUBTRACTION ALGORITHM USING ANALYSIS

The zero cases are probably the most difficult to teach of all subtraction concepts. We will examine the nature of a zero case by analysis. Although the approach that is presented is not the only possible one, it is a very satisfactory approach.

Sample Dialogue

304
− 7

Teacher: How many ones do we have?

Children: 4.

Teacher: How many ones do we want to subtract?

Children: 7.

Teacher: Do we have any tens in the tens place to regroup?

Children: No.

Teacher: What does the 30 name?

Children: 30 tens.

Teacher: If we regroup one of the 30 tens as 10 ones, how many tens will we have left?

Children: 29.

29
3̸0̸4
− 7

(The teacher crosses out the 30 and records a 29.)

29₁
3̸0̸4
− 7

Teacher: We had 4 ones and we got 10 more by regrouping 1 of the tens. How many ones do we have now?

Children: 14.

(The teacher records the 1 in front of the 4, making a 14.)

29₁
3̸0̸4
− 7
───
297

(From this point the subtraction algorithm proceeds normally.)

Notice that before this concept can be developed you would have had to develop the concept of 30 in 304 representing 30 tens.

7.13 AN ALTERNATE SUBTRACTION ALGORITHM

The following assumptions are made in this presentation:

1. The pattern to be discussed will be new to you.
2. You will best understand a discovery technique if you are involved in a discovery technique.

3. This is just one of many approaches that can be used to get a student to discover this number pattern.

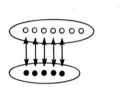 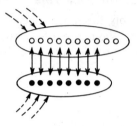

John has 7 marbles. Bill has 5 marbles. How many more marbles has John than Bill?

Write the equation that could be used to solve this problem. If you wrote $7 - 5 = \square$, you are correct.

Now suppose John and Bill each got 3 more marbles. How many more marbles does John have than Bill?

Does the equation $(7 + 3) - (5 + 3) = \square$ describe the situation where John and Bill have each received 3 marbles and the marbles are again compared to see how many more marbles John has than Bill?

Does John now have more marbles than he did before?

Notice how we have constructed a pair of problems to explore the pattern $7 - 5 = \square$:

$$(7 + 3) - (5 + 3) = \square$$

Would John have more marbles than Bill if we added 8 marbles to both sets, or 10 to both, or 64 to both?

Find the differences of the following problems. Study the pairs of problems that yield the same differences. Make up other problems that seem to follow the pattern you have discovered:

(1a) $65 - 37 = \square$	(3a) $16 - 5 = \square$	(5a) $187 - 29 = \square$
(1b) $68 - 40 = \square$	(3b) $18 - 7 = \square$	(5b) $207 - 49 = \square$
(2a) $10 - 7 = \square$	(4a) $29 - 15 = \square$	(6a) $647 - 296 = \square$
(2b) $9 - 6 = \square$	(4b) $30 - 14 = \square$	(6b) $341 - 290 = \square$

The pattern $a - b = (a + c) - (b + c) = (a - d) - (b - d)$ is called the compensation property for subtraction.

The compensation property for subtraction is useful in the modification of subtraction problems requiring some type of regrouping before use of the subtraction algorithm. The following sequence of steps shows how we might use the compensation property to restructure the problem to permit subtraction of tens from tens:

237	$(237 + 40)$	277
$- 164$	$-(164 + 40)$	$- 204$

The first stage in teaching the compensation property for subtraction is to construct pairs of problems for which the child can discover a pattern similar to the one just illustrated in the discussion of the marbles. Figure 7.6 shows several representative problems from this stage.

(1a) $13 - 7 = \square$ (2a) $14 - 5 = \square$
(1b) $(13 - 2) - (7 - 2) = \square$ (2b) $(14 + 3) - (5 + 3) = \square$
                 (3a) $35 - 17 = \square$
                 (3b) $(35 - 7) - (17 - 7) = \square$

Figure 7.6

In the second stage, you may want to give the child problems similar to those shown in Figure 7.7. These problems will require him to make use of the recently discovered pattern.

(a) $25 - 12 = (25 - 2) - (12 - \square)$ (c) $15 - 6 = 12 - \square$
(b) $27 - 8 = (27 + \square) - (8 + 3)$ (d) $26 - 12 = 28 - \square$

Figure 7.7

The third stage in teaching the compensation property for subtraction is to present problems having multiple solutions. It is a good idea to display some of the many solutions for each of these problems so that the student can begin to be guided toward a generalization. Representative problems from this stage are shown in Figure 7.8.

(a) $30 - 6 = (30 + \square) - (6 + \square)$ (c) $15 - 3 = (15 + \square) - (3 + \square)$
(b) $27 - 13 = (27 - \square) - (13 - \square)$ (d) $45 - \square = (45 - 2) - (\square - 2)$

Figure 7.8

In the last stage, you can give the students patterns as $\square - \triangle = (\square - \bigcirc) - (\triangle - \bigcirc)$ and $\square - \triangle = (\square + \bigcirc) - (\triangle + \bigcirc)$ and ask them to create true sentences using them.

A subtraction algorithm involving an approach different from the previously discussed techniques of regrouping the minuend is the compensation algorithm. In this algorithm, when the child encounters a situation that would otherwise require regrouping, he adds a number to both the minuend and subtrahend. For example, in $305 - 132$, he could add 70 or 80 or 90 to both the minuend and the subtrahend, restructuring the problem to $375 - 202$, or $385 - 212$, or $395 - 222$. However, for this example, 70 would probably be selected, because it would result in a zero in the subtrahend's tens position, and subtraction by zero is the easiest type of subtraction problem since zero is the identity element. In Figure 7.9 we can see how several problems are restructured using the compensation property. Notice in those instances having more than one situation requiring regrouping that the compensation property is used to alleviate each need for regrouping.

400	(400 + 1)	(401 + 90)	491
− 209	− (209 + 1)	− (210 + 90)	− 300

			191

1645	(1645 + 200)	1845
− 842	− (842 + 200)	− 1042

		803

384	(384 + 4)	388
− 196	− (196 + 4)	− 200

		188

Figure 7.9

Most elementary textbook series concentrate on developing the regrouping method as an integral part of the algorithm development. However, whichever method the series you use employs, it is probably best to give each child a wide variety of algorithms after he has mastered one.

EXERCISES (1)

1. By using pictures of sets, illustrate how you would make use of the set separation definition of difference (Section 7.2) to teach the child that $9 - 4 = 5$.
2. Using the definition of difference from Section 7.2 called set comparison, illustrate how you would teach a child that $9 - 4 = 5$.
3. Write five ways that one could read $6 - 5 = 1$.
4. For each of the following notations, when possible, identify the minuend, subtrahend, difference, sum, known addend, and unknown addend:

$$\begin{array}{c} 7 \\ -3 \\ \hline \boxed{4} \end{array} \qquad 8 - 2 = \boxed{6} \qquad 3 + \boxed{4} = 7$$

5. Count backward by nines, starting at 53. What pattern develops that will help the child learn to subtract 9 from a number?
6. Make up a specific matching activity that could be used to teach some fact giving a difference of 3.
7. Illustrate $8 - 5 = 3$ on a number-line segment.
8. Using the partitioning-out interpretation of subtraction, illustrate how you would teach $11 - 2 = 9$.
9. What are two related addition sentences and one related subtraction sentence for the sentence $13 - 7 = 6$?
10. Make up a dialogue to explain the following problem. Use either a money model or a modified abacus model.

$$\begin{array}{r} 89 \\ -6 \\ \hline \end{array}$$

11. Using number-line segments, illustrate the relation between subtracting 6 from 14 and 60 from 140.

12. Make up a dialogue to explain the following problem. Illustrate your dialogue with a sequence of pictures of a place-value chart.

$$98$$
$$-36$$

13. Make up a dialogue that will explain how to handle the need for regrouping in each of the following problems. (Use analysis.)

a. 372 b. 2004 c. 1240
 −246   −913   −330

14. Make up a dialogue that will explain how to handle the need for regrouping in each of the following problems. Use the compensation algorithm.

a. 372 b. 2004 c. 1240
 −246   −913   −330

15. A student mentally works the following problem in the described manner:

32 − 14.   4 from 2 equals a negative 2. A negative 2 and 30 is 28. 10 from 28 is 18.

 a. Did he get the right answer?
 b. Would this method always give him the correct answer?
 c. Would you discourage the child from working problems in this manner, or would you compliment him on his ingenuity?
 d. Would his algorithm be one you could teach all third-graders? Why or why not?

16. Give an example that will show that the associative property does not hold for subtraction.

17. Make up a set of problems for each of the first three stages in teaching the compensation property for subtraction.

18. Given the pattern $\square - (\triangle + \bigcirc) = (\square - \triangle) - \bigcirc$, make up sample problems for the first three stages of teaching this property.

19. Given the pattern $(\square + \triangle) - (\bigcirc + \bigcirc) = (\square - \bigcirc) + (\triangle - \bigcirc)$, make up sample problems for each of the first three stages in teaching this property.

20. Given the pattern $(\square + \triangle) - \bigcirc = \square + (\triangle - \bigcirc)$, make up sample problems for each of the first three stages in teaching this property.

21. Identify the patterns depicted in Exercises 18, 19, and 20 that are employed in each of the following algorithms:

    35   30   30 + 4   20 + 8
   − 7   − 2   − 2   −(10 + 6)

7.14   SUBTRACTION STORY PROBLEMS

Teaching a child to become proficient in solving subtraction story problems is complicated by the fact that the subtraction situation has many guises. The three most common ways of viewing subtraction in a social situation are as partitioning out, or "take away" (given a set, after part of the set is removed, the child determines the number property of the remaining subset), as comparison (given two sets, after the attempt to pair the elements of the sets, the child derives the number property of the unpaired subset), and as a missing addend (in which the union of two sets is taken and the number property of the resultant set and one of the original sets is known, after which the number property of the other original set is determined).

The first type of subtraction story that a child encounters generally is the take-away form. Let us first study some techniques of presenting such problems. Early work with it should concern stories that are easily depicted with concrete materials. For example, consider the following problem:

> John has 11 pencils.
> He gives Mary 7 of his pencils.
> How many pencils does he have then?

One technique that might be used to present this problem to children is to allow a child to take the part of John and another child to take the part of Mary. (Whenever possible, prepare problems the children can identify with.) A possible dialogue that might be used to accompany the action is as follows.

Sample Dialogue

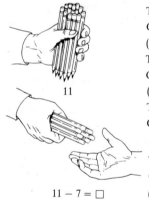

11

11 − 7 = □

Teacher: How many pencils does John have?
Children: 11.
(Write an 11 on the board.)
Teacher: What is he doing?
Children: He is giving some pencils to Mary.
(Write the − to the right of the 11.)
Teacher: How many does he give to Mary?
Children: 7.

(Write a 7 to the right of the 11 −.)
Teacher: What are we asked to find?
Children: How many John has left now.
(Write = □ to the right of 11 − 7.)

Teacher: We have learned that 11 less 7 is what?
Children: 4.

Teacher: How many pencils do you have left?
Children: 4.

Teacher: As you see, we find the answer to our problem by acting it out, or by working it mathematically.

You will want to contrast the take-away subtraction problems with the previously studied addition problems. A useful technique at this point is to start with John having 4 pencils and to have Mary return the 7 pencils, thus establishing the equation $4 + 7 = \square$.

Viewing subtraction in its social situation as comparison is more complex than the take-away situation. Whereas physical action is generally characteristic of the take-away situation, the comparison situation may or may not involve a physical action. Comparison involves two sets that may or may not be equivalent in number. For example, note the following problem:

John has 6 marbles.
Mary has 2 marbles.
How many more marbles does John have than Mary?

Let us discuss how we might use a flannel board to present the essential aspect of this problem. A possible dialogue that could be used to accompany this action is as follows.

Sample Dialogue

Teacher: Let's use these red disks as the marbles that John has. How many marbles does the problem tell us John had?

Children: 6.

(Write a 6 on the board. Place 6 disks on the flannel board.) (See Figure 7.10.)

Teacher: Let's use these blue disks for the marbles that Mary has. How many marbles does the problem tell us Mary has?

6   Children: 2.

(Write a 2 to the right of the 6.)

Teacher: If we pair Mary's 2 marbles with 2 of John's, how many are not paired?

Children: 4.

(Do this pairing with the disks.)

Teacher: Do the 4 unpaired disks tell us how many more marbles John has than Mary?

6   2   Children: Yes.

(Write = 4 to the right of 6   2.)

Teacher: What operation symbol should I put between the 6 and the 2?

Children: The subtraction symbol.

Teacher: As we have seen, when we are interested in finding out how many more members one set has than another, we can attempt to pair the sets to find out the answer, or we can find the answer using subtraction.

6   2 = 4

$6 - 2 = 4$

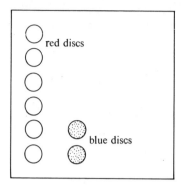

Figure 7.10. Flannel board.

Children should be given many opportunities to translate problems involving set comparison into subtraction equations. In Figure 7.11, we see the three variations of problems of a comparative nature.

Problems that can be translated into an equation with a missing addend can be referred to as missing addend problems. By the time the student reaches the point of analyzing missing addend story problems, he has already learned to retranslate problems such as $3 + \square = 8$ into $8 - 3 = \square$.

Number of set A: Number of set B: Number of unmatched subset:	Known Known Unknown	Known Unknown Known	Unknown Known Known
Some possible translations.	$a - b = \square$ or $a = \square + b$	$a - \square = c$ or $a - c = \square$ or $a = c + \square$	$\square - b = c$ or $\square = c + b$ or $\square - c = b$

Figure 7.11

Let us discuss a direct approach that could be used to lead the students to translate the problem into an equation

John has 5 marbles.
Mary gives him some more.
He now has 9 marbles.
How many marbles did Mary give him?

A possible dialogue that could accompany this problem is as follows.

Sample Dialogue

5

5 + □

Teacher: How many marbles does the problem tell us John started with?

Children: 5.

(Write a 5 on the board.)

Teacher: What happended next?

Children: Mary gave him some marbles.

Teacher: What symbol do you think we could use to translate the "giving to John"?

Children: The addition symbol.

Teacher: Does the sentence tell us how many she gave him?

Children: No.

Teacher: How can we show that we don't know this yet?

(Draw a square. The children may sometimes refer to this square as a box.)

Teacher: How can we show he now has 9 marbles?

(Write = 9 to the right of 5 + □.)

Teacher: What is another mathematical sentence that would ask the same question?

Children: 9 − 5 = □.

Some children may immediately recognize the subtractive nature of the preceding problem and translate it directly to 9 − 5 = □. Others may translate it first to 5 + □ = 9 and then to 9 − 5 = □ before solving. Some children may solve the problem directly from the 5 + □ = 9 translation. You probably will not want to discourage this flexibility in their methods of arriving at a solution of problems.

In summary, subtraction takes many forms. You will want to give each child a broad perspective of the many ways he may encounter subtractive situations in his environment. You also will need to contrast subtraction problems with addition problems by reconstructing subtraction problems into addition problems.

EXERCISES (2)

1. Using one or more of the following sources, construct five story problems of a current events nature involving take-away situations appropriate for a third-grade class:

   a. Newspaper   b. *World Almanac*   c. Magazine

2. Using the same sources, construct five story problems of a current events nature involving comparison situations appropriate for a third-grade class.
3. Using the same sources, construct five story problems about current events involving missing addend situations appropriate for a third-grade class.
4. Using the same sources, construct five story problems of a current events nature involving subtraction and another operation, for a third-grade class.
5. Make up a word problem for each of the following mathematical sentences:

a. $27 - 9 = \square$
d. $88 - \square = 34$
b. $32 - 25 = \square$
e. $\square + 45 = 68$
c. $35\cent - \square = 28\cent$
f. $91 + \square = 165$

BIBLIOGRAPHY

Deans, E. "Practice in Renaming Numbers—An Aid to Subtraction," *The Arithmetic Teacher* (February 1965), p. 142.

Hamilton, E. W. "Subtraction by the "Dribble" Method," *The Arithmetic Teacher* (May 1971), pp. 346–347.

Marion, C. F. "How to Get Subtraction into the Game," *The Arithmetic Teacher* (February 1970), pp. 169–170.

May, L. J. "Patterns and Properties in Addition and Subtraction" *Grade Teacher* (October 1967), pp. 41, 44, 46, 48, 50.

National Council of Teachers of Mathematics. *29th Yearbook* (Washington, D.C.), 1964, pp. 80–83, 88–89, 146–153.

Smith, C. W. "Subtraction Steps," *The Arithmetic Teacher* (May 1968), pp. 458–460.

Smith, C. W. "The Witch's Best Game," *The Arithmetic Teacher* (December 1966), pp. 683–684.

8

Teaching multiplication on the set of whole numbers

BEHAVIORAL OBJECTIVES

Student can . . .

Illustrate a multiplication fact using a sets model.

Illustrate a multiplication fact using an array model.

Illustrate a multiplication fact using a cross-product model.

List five ways to read a multiplication equation.

Identify two readiness activities for multiplication.

Illustrate a multiplication fact using a number-line model.

Determine why each of the structural properties of multiplication is taught.

Describe using models how each of the structural properties of multiplication is taught.

Identity three nonstructural properties that can be used to teach basic multiplication facts.

Sequence a given set of exercises in the order they would be taught.

Create a dialogue (complete with models) to explain how to teach some aspect of the multiplication algorithm.

Write an analysis of the "why" of some aspect of the multiplication algorithm.

Present an analogy for introducing the multiplication algorithm.

8.1 INTRODUCTION

The concepts relating to multiplication, like the concepts of addition, are closely intertwined with many concepts in arithmetic. It is important, therefore, for the teacher to build a sound foundation of understanding multiplication before other processes and concepts can be understood.

Mastery of such concepts as the division algorithm, "reduction of fractions," least common denominator, and the compensation property for division have as a prerequisite the mastery of multiplication concepts.

8.2   DEFINITION, TERMINOLOGY, AND SYMBOLISM

There are three definitions of multiplication being used in elementary school textbooks: *set*, *array*, and *cross-product* definitions. We will now illustrate how each of these definitions could be used to teach a child that the product of the factors 3 and 2 is 6.

In using the set definition, we would present 3 disjoint sets to the child, in which each set contains 2 objects. Then we would have him determine the number of items in the 3 sets. (In many instances, before the child is asked to determine the number of objects in the three sets, the union of the sets would be made.) The number he obtains, 6, would then be designated the product of 3 and 2 (see Figure 8.1).

Figure 8.1

In using the array definition, we would present the child with an array consisting of 3 rows of dots with 2 dots in each row (see Figure 8.2). He

$$3 \times 2 = \quad 3 \; \cdot\cdot$$

$$2$$

Figure 8.2

would then be asked to determine the number property of the array. The 6 that he would obtain would then be designated the product of 3 and 2.

There are several approaches that might be taken in presenting the cross-product definition. One of these is to describe a natural pairing situation. For example, if a girl had 3 blouses and 2 skirts, how many different ways could she dress? (See Figure 8.3.) The number 6 would be designated the product of 3 and 2.

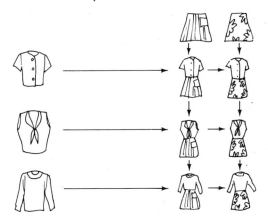

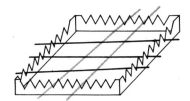

Figure 8.3

A similar approach is to use a frame and colored sticks. To find the product of 3 and 2, the child would select 3 sticks of one color (say black) and 2 sticks of a different color (gray). The child would lay one color horizontally and the other color vertically in his frame. (see Figure 8.4).

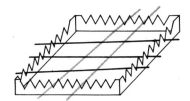

Figure 8.4

He would then be asked to determine the number of crosspoints. Because there are 6 points where the gray sticks cross the black sticks, we say the product of 3 and 2 is 6.

There are two notations you teach your students. In the horizontal form we are assuming a left-to-right reading. In the vertical form, we are assuming a bottom-to-top reading.

$$\begin{array}{r} 5 \\ \times 6 \\ \hline 30 \end{array}$$ Vertical form $6 \times 5 = 30$ Horizontal form

Figure 8.5

There are many ways that the mathematical sentences illustrated in Figure 8.5 can be read. A few of them follow:

6 sets of 5 balls are 30 balls.
6 times 5 equals 30.
6 times 5 is 30.
6 fives equal 30.
The product of the factors 6 and 5 is 30.
The product of the factors 6 and 5 equals 30.
5 multiplied by 6 is 30.
5 multiplied by 6 equals 30.

In Figure 8.6, the terminology applied to the various numerals in multiplication sentences is identified. Note that there are two sets of terms for each mathematical sentence. As a teacher, you should use care not to mix these terms in an explanation. For example, it would not be proper to say, "Factor 6 and multiplicand 5." When using the word *factor*, be consistent and use factor for the other number.

Factor	Factor	Product	Multiplicand*	5 Factor
6	× 5	= 30	Multiplier*	× 6 Factor
Multiplier*	Multiplicand*	Product	Product	30 Product

* Traditional vocabulary

Figure 8.6

8.3 READINESS EXPERIENCES FOR MULTIPLICATION

One of the earliest readiness exercises for multiplication is the counting activity conducted to develop readiness for addition. These counting activities build readiness for multiplication when the child starts counting at a multiple of the number he is counting by. For example, he might start counting by twos, starting at 8.

Another readiness exercise consists of having a child find the sums of doubles, triples, quadruples, and so on, by working with equal sets, for example, $4 + 4$, $6 + 6$, $3 + 3 + 3 + 3$.

The teacher can provide activities, even at the first-grade level, that will prepare the child for multiplication. Such questions as, "How many shoes do we have if we have two pairs of shoes?" and "How many people do we have if we have two sets of twins?" represent readiness questions.

8.4   TEACHING THE BASIC MULTIPLICATION FACTS
USING MODELS

The flannel board, magnetic board, stick frame with sticks, place-value chart, blocks for arrays, buttons, bottle tops, disks, spool board, peg board are all useful aids in teaching the concept of multiplication.

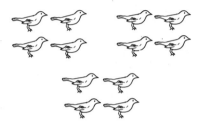

Figure 8.7. Three sets of four equal 12.

The flannel board and magnetic board, along with accompanying objects, will be useful when the set definition is used for teaching multiplication facts. Figure 8.7 shows one arrangement a teacher can use in preparing to teach that 3 sets of 4 are equal to 12.

Sample Dialogue

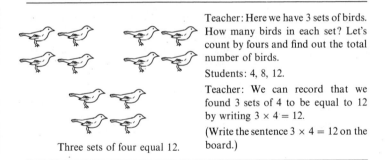

Three sets of four equal 12.

Teacher: Here we have 3 sets of birds. How many birds in each set? Let's count by fours and find out the total number of birds.

Students: 4, 8, 12.

Teacher: We can record that we found 3 sets of 4 to be equal to 12 by writing $3 \times 4 = 12$.

(Write the sentence $3 \times 4 = 12$ on the board.)

A similar technique can be used with the magnetic board. The peg board, spool board, and blocks will be useful when the array definition is used for teaching the multiplication facts. Figure 8.8 shows the arrangement a teacher might use on a spool board in preparing to teach that 3 rows of 4 are equal to 12. An accompanying dialogue might be as follows:

Sample Dialogue

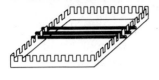

Teacher: Place 3 black sticks in your stick frame (step 1). (Demonstrate this on a large stick frame so that the children can see how you want the sticks placed.)

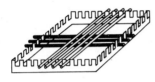

Teacher: Place 4 gray sticks in the frame so that they cross the black sticks (step 2). (Be demonstrating this.)

Teacher: Let's find out in how many places the black sticks cross the gray sticks by counting by fours. (4, 8, 12.)

Teacher: We can show that there are 3 sets of 4 crosspoints by writing the sentence $3 \times 4 = 12$.

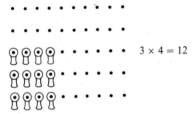

$3 \times 4 = 12$

Figure 8.8

Although the number line is not especially useful in introducing the basic facts, it will prove to be a very useful aid in teaching later multiplication skills: therefore, it may be advantageous to introduce it in teaching some basic multiplication facts, to familiarize the students with it. Figure 8.9 represents $3 \times 4 = 12$ on a number line.

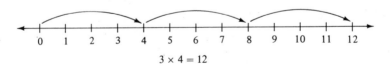

$3 \times 4 = 12$

Figure 8.9

"Let's take a jump of 4, and another jump of 4, and another jump of 4. How many jumps of 4 did we take?" (3.)

"Where did we begin jumping?" (At zero.)

"Where did we end our jumping?" (At 12.)

"We could tell this by writing the sentence $3 \times 4 = 12$."

8.5 TEACHING MULTIPLICATION FACTS USING PATTERNS

Although it is essential to use sets, arrays, and cross-product models (stick frame), patterns are also essential in the teaching of multiplication.

Just as there existed a special set of patterns for addition, called structural properties, there are special patterns called structural properties for multiplication. In the following chart we see instances of these structural properties:

	Instance of	Reasons Taught
$3 \times 2 = 2 \times 3$	Commutative property: $n \times m = m \times n$	Cuts down on physical manipulations needed by the child to discover each fact.
$2 \times 1 = 2$	Identity property: $n \times 1 = n$	Cuts down on the number of facts a child has to memorize individually.
$(2 \times 3) \times 4 = 2 \times (3 \times 4)$	Associative property: $(n \times m) \times r = n \times (m \times r)$	Used in later analysis.
$3 \times (4 + 2) = (3 \times 4) + (3 \times 2)$	Distributive property: $n \times (m + r)$ $= (n \times m) + (n \times r)$	Used in multiplication algorithms and by better student's to discover facts.
$5 \times 0 = 0$	Zero property (not a structural property): $n \times 0 = 0$	Cuts down on the number of facts a child has to memorize individually.

The identity property for multiplication is taught soon after the child begins to discover the multiplication facts. It is a comparatively easy property to teach. Let us examine how this property can be developed by using models and a pattern.

Sample Dialogue

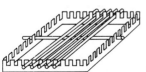

Here we have 1 stick crossed by 3 sticks. What multiplication equation is suggested? $(1 \times 3 = 3.)$

(Placing 2 more sticks in the frame,) Now we have 1 stick crossed by 5 sticks. What multiplication equation is suggested now? $(1 \times 5 = 5.)$

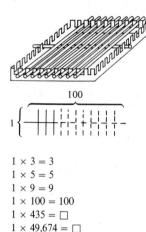

(Placing 4 more sticks in the frame.)
Now we have 1 stick crossed by 9 sticks.
What multiplication equation is suggested
now? $(1 \times 9 = 9.)$

If we placed 100 sticks one way and 1
stick the other way, what multiplication
equation would be suggested? $(1 \times 100 =$
$100.)$

$1 \times 3 = 3$
$1 \times 5 = 5$
$1 \times 9 = 9$
$1 \times 100 = 100$
$1 \times 435 = \square$
$1 \times 49,674 = \square$

(The equations forming the pattern are
placed on the board and equations to
extend the pattern are displayed.)

The commutative property for multiplication is also introduced early in
the child's experience with multiplication. If the child can discover this
property (i.e., $n \times m = m \times n$) early in his work with multiplication, it will
cut down on the amount of manipulation that the child must do in order
to discover the multiplication facts. (This is not to be construed as meaning
that the child will not have to memorize all the facts.) In the first stage,
you should present pairs of problems that will lead to the discovery.
Figure 8.10 shows how we might use an array to get the child to discover
the commutative property. (The rows running left and right are identified
with the first factor.)

As an array model is used the teacher should get the child to see that
the number of objects represented in the array is not changed by rotating
the array around. He can guide the children to this conclusion by a question
such as, "Did the number of stars change when I turned the array?"
Similarly guide the children to see how the equation suggested by the newly
oriented array is different from the previous equation.

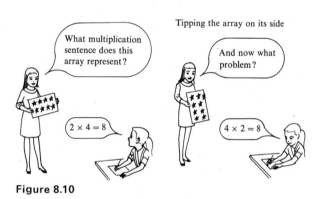

Figure 8.10

In Figure 8.11, we can see several pairs of equations that can be used to guide the child in discovering the commutative property of multiplication using patterns.

(1a) $3 \times 4 = \square$ (2a) $6 \times 9 = \square$ (3a) $2 \times 5 = \square$

(1b) $4 \times 3 = \square$ (2b) $9 \times 6 = \square$ (3b) $5 \times 2 = \square$

Figure 8.11

In the second stage the child should be given an opportunity to use this newly discovered concept in equations requiring single solutions. Before presenting students with equations from this stage, the teacher should be sure that they have discovered the commutative property by the array technique, patterning, or some other technique. The following equations are representative of this second stage: $7 \times \square = 9 \times 7$ and $4 \times 5 = 5 \times \square$.

In general, if an elementary mathematics series does not begin with the discovery stage, it will pick up the teaching of the commutative property at this stage. If the discovery stage is not the first stage presented, it is the teacher's responsibility to provide exercises to guide the child in discovering the commutative property of multiplication.

At this point a teacher would begin to extend the child's concept toward a generalization. He may employ equations with multiple solutions such as $3 \times \square = \square \times 3$. A student's typical reaction to problems of this type is, "Teacher, any number will work!" This is precisely the degree of generalization you are striving for at this point.

In the last stage for getting children to generalize, teachers often give the children an equation similar to the following and ask the children to construct a certain number of equations that would be true sentences using the pattern: $\triangle \times \square = \square \times \triangle$.

In Figure 8.12, we can see how the associative property for multiplication is used in teaching the child to multiply ones times tens by analysis. Notice how the associative property is used in going from the first to second line.

$3 \times 40 = 3 \times (4 \times 10)$
$\qquad = (3 \times 4) \times 10$
$\qquad = 12 \times 10 = 120$

Figure 8.12

In the first stage of teaching the associative property you can give the child pairs of equations, used in conjunction with models, that will lead the child to discover the property. Figure 8.13 shows how we might use a block array to guide a child in discovering the associative property.

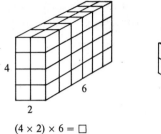
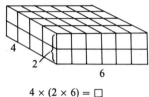

(4 × 2) × 6 = ☐   4 × (2 × 6) = ☐

Figure 8.13

As the array model is used, the teacher can get the child to observe that the number property does not change by changing the array by a question similar to the following: "Did we change the number of blocks by changing the position of the array?" By following this question with, "How did the equation suggested by the array change, when the array was changed?" the teacher can focus on the nature of the associative property.

Figure 8.14 presents several pairs of equations that can be used to guide the child in discovering the associative property for multiplication.

(1a) (3 × 7) × 6 = ☐   (2a) 4 × (5 × 6) = ☐   (3a) (2 × 3) × 2 = ☐
(1b) 3 × (7 × 6) = ☐   (2b) (4 × 5) × 6 = ☐   (3b) 2 × (3 × 2) = ☐

Figure 8.14

In the second stage, presented after the associative property has been discovered, the child is often given equations requiring a single solution. Several equations representative of this stage can be seen in Figure 8.15.

(a) 3 × (5 × 4) = (3 × ☐) × 4
(b) (8 × ☐) × 6 = 8 × (11 × 6)
(c) 5 × (1 × 2) = (5 × 1) × ☐

Figure 8.15

The third stage in teaching the associative property of multiplication is the multiple solution type of equation, which is designed to lead the child toward the generalization. Typical equations of this type are presented in Figure 8.16.

(a) (3 × 8) × ☐ = 3 × (8 × ☐)
(b) 6 × (☐ × △) = (6 × ☐) × △
(c) (☐ × 1) × 9 = ☐ × (1 × 9)

Figure 8.16

In the final stage of learning the associative property of multiplication, you can give your students patterns such as $(a \times b) \times c = a \times (b \times c)$ and ask them to create equations that are true sentences using this pattern.

A third structural property that bridges the concept of multiplication and addition is the distributive property of multiplication over addition [i.e., $a \times (b + c) = (a \times b) + (a \times c)$]. It is one of the most useful of the structural properties. It provides flexibility in teaching the basic multiplication facts and plays a significant role in the teaching of the multiplication algorithm.

Let us look at how this property provides flexibility in discovering the basic facts when used by the better student. Let us assume a student knows $7 \times 1 = 7$, $7 \times 2 = 14$, $7 \times 3 = 21$, $7 \times 4 = 28$, and $7 \times 5 = 35$. Assume also that he knows the multiplication over addition. When he is faced with the problem of determining the product of the factors 7 and 7, he could find the product in any one of the following ways:

$$7 \times (5 + 2) = (7 \times 5) + (7 \times 2) = 35 + 14 = 49$$
$$7 \times (3 + 4) = (7 \times 3) + (7 \times 4) = 21 + 28 = 49$$

In working the exercise shown in Figure 8.17, we make use of the distributive property in multiplying the 3 and 2 ones, and the 3 and 1 ten, and then by adding the 30 and 6 to get 36.

$$
\begin{array}{ccc}
12 \rightarrow & 12 \rightarrow & 12 \\
\times\ 3 & \times\ 3 & \times\ 3 \\
\hline
& 6 & 36
\end{array}
$$

Figure 8.17

The first stage in teaching the distributive property leads the child to discover the property and can be developed by patterning pairs of equations. Some teachers introduce children to the distributive property after they have developed through the fives tables; they begin working on the facts with 6 as a factor, so that the more able student can begin discovering the new facts through independent study.

In Figure 8.18 we have depicted array models which suggest two equations that could be used in the pattern for the distributive property of multiplication over addition. In Figure 8.18a, the rows are united to form a single array before the product is determined. In Figure 8.18b, the child is instructed to find the product of each array and then to determine the sum.

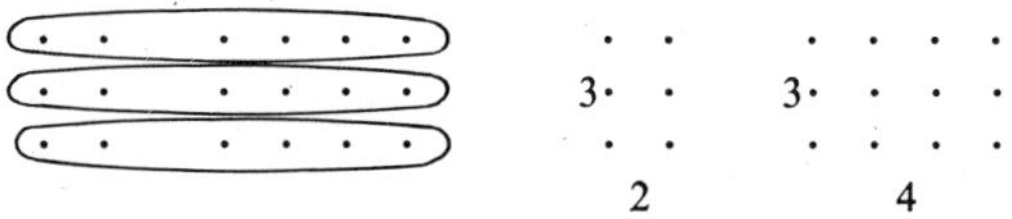

$3 \times (2 + 4) = \square$

$(3 \times 2) + (3 \times 4) = \square$

Figure 8.18

In Figure 8.19, we see several pairs of equations that can be used to guide the child in discovering the distributive property of multiplication over addition.

(1a) $2 \times (1 + 2) = \square$ (2a) $3 \times (4 + 2) = \square$ (3a) $4 \times (4 + 1) = \square$
(1b) $(2 \times 1) + (2 \times 2) = \square$ (2b) $(3 \times 4) + (3 \times 2) = \square$ (3b) $(4 \times 4) + (4 \times 1) = \square$

Figure 8.19

In the second stage the child is expected to identify the missing factor or missing addend, based on the previously learned pattern of the distributive property. Figure 8.20 presents representative equations of this stage.

(a) $3 \times (\square + 8) = (3 \times 5) + (3 \times 8)$
(b) $4 \times (8 + 7) = (\square \times 8) + (\square \times 7)$
(c) $3 \times (2 + 5) = (3 \times \square) + (3 \times 5)$

Figure 8.20

In the third stage, the child is pointed toward the generalization that "any three whole numbers can be used in the distributive pattern." Examples of equations in this stage are depicted in Figure 8.21.

(a) $\square \times (4 + 8) = (\square \times 4) + (\square \times 8)$
(b) $7 \times (\square + 2) = (7 \times \square) + (7 \times 2)$
(c) $3 \times (\square + \triangle) = (3 \times \square) + (3 \times \triangle)$

Figure 8.21

In the final stage of teaching the distributive property of multiplication over addition, the student is asked to create true mathematical sentences using the pattern

$$\square \times (\triangle + \bigcirc) = (\square \times \triangle) + (\square \times \bigcirc).$$

There are many patterns beside the structural properties that are useful in developing the multiplication facts, including the following.

Pattern

Examples	Description	How Used
(1a) $3 \times 3 = 9$	$(n - 1) \times (n + 1) =$	Helps develop the harder multi-
(1b) $2 \times 4 = 8$	$n^2 - 1$	plication facts which involve
(2a) $4 \times 4 = 16$	Similarly, a teacher	factors one more and one less
(2b) $3 \times 5 = 15$	can develop	than a double. For example, if
(3a) $5 \times 5 = 25$	$(n - 2) \times (n + 2) =$	a child knows 5 times 5 equals
(3b) $4 \times 6 = 24$	$n^2 - 4$	25, then he could figure out
	and	$4 \times 6 = 25 - 1 = 24$.
	$(n - 3) \times (n + 3) =$	
	$n^2 - 9$	
	etc.	
$9 \times 2 = 18$	The tens in the	Helps in the memorization of the
$9 \times 5 = 45$	product equals 1	nines facts.
$9 \times 8 = 72$	less than the non-9	
	factor. The ones in	
	the product plus the	
	tens digit make a	
	sum of 9.	
$5 \times 0 = 0$	$n \times (2 \times m) = m0$	Useful in the development of 5
$5 \times 2 = 10$		times an even number.
$5 \times 4 = 20$		
etc.		
$5 \times 1 = 5$	$n \times (2 \times m + 1) =$	Useful in the development of 5
$5 \times 3 = 15$	$m5$	times an odd number.
$5 \times 5 = 25$		
etc.		

The distributive property of multiplication over subtraction can be developed in a similar manner. This property also has several useful applications in elementary school mathematics because it is useful in discovering the multiplication facts. For example, if a child knows this property and his fives facts and ones facts, he could discover all of the fours facts as follows:

$$1 \times (5 - 1) = (1 \times 5) - (1 \times 1) = 4$$
$$2 \times (5 - 1) = (2 \times 5) - (2 \times 1) = 8$$
$$9 \times (5 - 1) = (9 \times 5) - (9 \times 1) = 36$$

This property is also useful for developing multiplication-speed skills. For example, to multiply 8×19, the child thinks, "$8 \times 20 = 160$, and $8 \times 1 = 8$, and $160 - 8 = 152$." Thus he finds the product of 8×19 by making use of this distributive property. In Figure 8.22, we see several pairs of problems that can be used to guide the child in making his initial discovery of this distributive property.

(1a) $3 \times (7 - 2) = \square$ (2a) $2 \times (9 - 5) = \square$ (3a) $5 \times (3 - 1) = \square$
(1b) $(3 \times 7) - (3 \times 2) = \square$ (2b) $(2 \times 9) - (2 \times 5) = \square$ (3b) $(5 \times 3) - (5 \times 1) = \square$

Figure 8.22

After the child has discovered the pattern, he should be given an opportunity to use this concept in problems requiring single solutions. A short review of problems from the paired-problem stage will be good background for problems from this stage. Figure 8.23 depicts several typical problems from this stage.

(a) $3 \times (5 - 2) = (3 \times \square) - (3 \times 2)$ (c) $3 \times (6 - 4) = (\square \times 6) - (\square \times 4)$
(b) $4 \times (\square - 6) = (4 \times 9) - (4 \times 6)$ (d) $\square \times (3 - 1) = (8 \times 3) - (8 \times 1)$

Figure 8.23

You should gradually extend the child's concepts toward the generalization. Problems having multiple solutions will help you toward this goal. Figure 8.24 presents typical problems from this stage.

(a) $\square \times (8 - 6) = (\square \times 8) - (\square \times 6)$ (c) $8 \times (\square - 1) = (8 \times \square) - (8 \times 1)$
(b) $4 \times (9 - \square) = (4 \times 9) - (4 \times \square)$ (d) $3 \times (\square - \square) = (3 \times \square) - (3 \times \square)$

Figure 8.24

In the final stage of getting the child to generalize this property, you can give him a pattern such as $a \times (b - c) = (a \times b) - (a \times c)$ and ask him to create problems that are true sentences using this pattern.

The following table summarizes some methods for teaching the basic multiplication facts:

Problem	Method	Solution
$2 \times 3 = \square$	Using arrays	$2 \times 3 = 6$
$3 \times 2 = \square$	Using sets	$3 \times 2 = 6$
$2 \times 4 = \square$	Using a number line	$2 \times 4 = 8$
$7 \times 5 = \square$	Using the commutative property: Since $5 \times 7 = 35$, then ...	$7 \times 5 = 35$
$8 \times 9 = \square$	Using the distributive property: $8 \times (4 + 5) = (8 \times 4) + (8 \times 5) = 32 + 40$	$8 \times 9 = 72$
$7 \times 1 = \square$	Using the identity property: Since $n \times 1 = n$, then ...	$7 \times 1 = 7$
$4 \times 2 = \square$	Cross-product	$4 \times 2 = 8$
$9 \times 5 = \square$	Using patterns: $9 \times 1 = 9, 9 \times 2 = 18, 9 \times 3 = 27, 9 \times 4 = 36$	$9 \times 5 = 45$
$7 \times 9 = \square$	Using generalizations: Since $(n - 1) \times (n + 1) = n^2 - 1, 8 \times 8 = 64$, then ...	$7 \times 9 = 63$
$3 \times 5 = \square$	Repeated addition: $5 + 5 + 5 = 15$	$3 \times 5 = 15$

8.6 MEMORIZATION OF THE BASIC FACTS

After the child has discovered various products—for example, after he has discovered all the products 25 or less—he should be encouraged to memorize these facts. Some previously mentioned activities are teaming up to use flash cards; nontimed and timed tests followed by practice on or rediscovery of missed facts; "beat the bounce," vertical writing practice, games, and relays.

8.7 THE PRODUCT OF ONES AND TENS

Before teaching a child how to multiply ones and tens and ones, it is necessary to establish the skill of finding the product of ones and tens. There are essentially two approaches that can be used to help the child establish the relationship between "ones times ones."

In the first of these approaches, called the *skip-counting method*, the child establishes the product through counting by multiples of 10 on a "tens number line." Figure 8.25 depicts how to discover that $3 \times 40 = 120$ by using the tens number line.

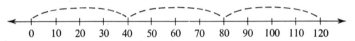

0   10   20   30   40   50   60   70   80   90   100 110 120

Figure 8.25

The following dialogue might accompany this presentation:

"How many tens are named by 40?" (4.) "If we take 3 jumps of 4 tens, we have jumped how far?" (Either 120 or 12 tens. Stress the 12 tens aspect, because you want the child to establish the relationship between multiplying ones and ones, and ones and tens.)
"We could record this by writing the sentence $3 \times 40 = 120$." (Write this on the board.)

The second approach to teaching ones times tens we shall call the *renaming-associative technique*. In teaching the child to multiply 3×40, you can first teach him to multiply ones times 10 by skip counting. He would then learn to rename 40 as 4×10. His problem would thus appear $3 \times (4 \times 10)$, the name 4×10 having been substituted for the name 40. The associative property is used to associate the 3 and the 4 and this product is determined. The final step consists of renaming 12×10, making it 120.

After a child has mastered the basic facts and the skill of multiplying ones and tens, he is ready to learn the one-digit–two-digit multiplication algorithm.

8.8   MULTIPLICATION ALGORITHM SEQUENCE

Ideally a child should have mastered his multiplication facts before he begins studying a multiplication algorithm. Practically, some children will be introduced to the multiplication algorithm before they have completed their mastery of the multiplication facts.

The multiplication exercises in the following table are representative of the exercises a child will encounter in the multiplication algorithm sequence.

Instance	Type
$3 \times 30 =$	Ones times tens
14	Ones times tens and ones
$\times\ 4$	
$40 \times 6 =$	Tens times ones (Sometimes taught at the same time ones times tens is taught.)
$40 \times 60 =$	Tens times tens
41	Tens and ones times tens and ones
$\times 32$	The algorithm development beyond this point is merely an extension of previously developed concepts.

8.9 MULTIPLICATION OF ONES TIMES TENS AND ONES

In Figure 8.26, we see an analysis presentation by the teacher depicting the steps used in learning to multiply ones times tens and ones.

	5×17
Step 1	$5 \times (10 + 7)$
Step 2	$(5 \times 10) + (5 \times 7)$
Step 3	$50 + 35$
Step 4	$50 + (30 + 5)$
Step 5	$(50 + 30) + 5$
Step 6	$80 + 5$
Step 7	85

Figure 8.26

In step 1 we have renamed 17, making it $(10 + 7)$. We have done this because the only multiplication skills the student has are how to multiply ones and ones, and ones and tens. In step 2, the distributive property has been used. In step 3, the teacher has used the two multiplication skills the children have been taught. In step 4, the 35 has been renamed $(30 + 5)$ because of the need to add the 3 tens to the 5 tens. In step 5, the associative property of addition has been applied. Addition of tens to tens has been made in step 6. In step 7, $(80 + 5)$ has been renamed 85.

The teacher should emphasize the explanation for step 5. At the end, he should go back to this step and ask, "What did we do with the 3 tens that we got by multiplying 5 and 7?"

Let us examine how an analogy might be used to develop the concept of ones times tens and ones.

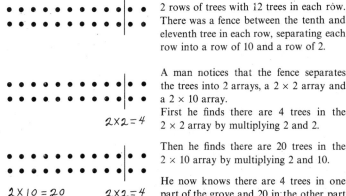

Once there was a grove of trees which had 2 rows of trees with 12 trees in each row. There was a fence between the tenth and eleventh tree in each row, separating each row into a row of 10 and a row of 2.

A man notices that the fence separates the trees into 2 arrays, a 2×2 array and a 2×10 array.

First he finds there are 4 trees in the 2×2 array by multiplying 2 and 2.

Then he finds there are 20 trees in the 2×10 array by multiplying 2 and 10.

He now knows there are 4 trees in one part of the grove and 20 in the other part of the grove.

$20 \times 4 = 24$

$$\begin{array}{r} 12 \\ \times\ 2 \\ \hline 4 \\ 20 \\ \hline 24 \end{array}$$

He adds the 4 and 20 to find the total number of trees.

Thus he finds there are 24 trees in the grove.

EXERCISES (1)

1. Name a readiness activity that would prepare a child for multiplication by 9.
2. Explain how you would use a magnetic board to teach $5 \times 7 = 35$. Use illustrations. Make up a dialogue.
3. Explain how you would use a peg board to teach $8 \times 6 = 48$. Use illustrations. Make up a dialogue.
4. Explain how you would use a stick frame to teach $8 \times 7 = 56$. Use illustrations. Make up a dialogue.
5. Explain, using a number line, how you would teach $3 \times 5 = 15$. Use illustrations. Make up a dialogue.
6. Explain how you would use a number line to teach $9 \times 20 = 180$. Use illustrations. Make up a dialogue.
7. Explain how you would teach 8×90 by the renaming-associative technique.
8. Make up a step-by-step presentation, with dialogue, explaining how you would introduce 8×28, using horizontal notation.
9. Make up an analogy that could be used to introduce the following problem:

   $$\begin{array}{r} 23 \\ \times\ 4 \\ \hline \end{array}$$

10. Use the set definition of product to illustrate how you would show a child that the product of the factors 4 and 5 is 20.
11. Use the array definition of product to illustrate how you would show a child that the product of the factors 3 and 7 is 21.
12. Use the cross-product definition to illustrate how you would show a child that the product of the factors 1 and 1 is 1.
13. List six ways you could read $5 \times 9 = 45$.
14. Identify each of the following in the mathematical sentences: factor, product.

   a. $8 \times 9 = 72$ b.
   $$\begin{array}{r} 6 \\ \times 3 \\ \hline 18 \end{array}$$

15. Solve the following problem: $88 \times \square = 88$. What property for multiplication is illustrated?
16. Make up sample problems for each of the first three stages in teaching the commutative property for multiplication.
17. Make up sample problems for each of the first three stages in teaching the associative property for multiplication.

18. Make up sample problems for each of the first three stages in teaching the distributive property of multiplication over addition.
19. Make up sample problems for each of the first three stages in teaching the distributive property of multiplication over subtraction.

8.10 INTRODUCING A STANDARD VERTICAL FORM FOR MULTIPLYING ONES AND TENS AND ONES

After the student has developed his ability to multiply ones and tens and understands that the tens obtained by multiplying ones and ones are added to the tens obtained by multiplying ones and tens, he is ready to learn the standard form of the multiplication algorithm. Figure 8.27 depicts the sequencing for introducing the standard form. Dialogue to accompany this presentation might be as follows:

Phase 1   **Phase 2**

$$
\begin{array}{r} 28 \\ \times\ 7 \\ \hline 56 \\ 140 \\ \hline 196 \end{array}
\qquad
\begin{array}{r} 28 \\ \times\ 7 \\ \hline 196 \end{array}
$$

Figure 8.27

"Let's now learn a new way to work this problem." (Write

$$
\begin{array}{r} 28 \\ \times\ 7 \\ \hline \end{array}
$$

on the board.)
"When we multiply 7 and 8, what product do we get?" (56.)
"Place the 56 here." (Place as shown in Phase 1.)
"What does the 2 stand for in 28?" (2 tens.)
"If we multiply 7 and 2 tens, what will the product be?" (14 tens, or 140.)
"Place the 140 here." (Place as shown in Phase 1.)
"Can anyone tell me why we have placed the 140 directly below the 56?"
    (Because it will be easy for us to add the 140 and the 56 in this form.)
"We now add the 140 and the 56 and obtain 196."

Some of your students of minimal ability may never progress to the next phase. It is possible that these children would have been the same students who, without the simplified algorithm depicted in Phase 1, would remain at the basic facts stage of development.

In Phase 2, the child is directed to write the numeral he obtains for the 6 ones when he multiplies 7 and 8, and to mentally retain the 5 tens, which will be added to the tens obtained when he multiplies 7 and 20.

8.11   MULTIPLICATION OF TENS AND TENS

The first activity in developing the skill of multiplying tens and tens is that of having a student learn that 10 times 10 is equal to 100. This can be done either through the previously discussed skip-counting technique, or by relating the concept of $10 \times 10 = 100$ to the concept of 10 dimes is as much as 100 pennies.

Many textbooks employ the renaming-associative technique to teach the product of tens and tens. Figure 8.28 gives a step-by-step presentation using this technique. In step 1, the 40 and 50 have been renamed 4×10 and 5×10, respectively. Step 2 makes use of the associative property, because the desire is to multiply the ones and ones, and the tens and tens. Step 5 makes use of the basic multiplication facts skill and the skill of multiplying 10 and 10. In step 6, 20×100 has been renamed 2000.

	40×50
Step 1	$(4 \times 10) \times (5 \times 10)$
Step 2	$4 \times (10 \times 5) \times 10$
Step 3	$4 \times (5 \times 10) \times 10$
Step 4	$(4 \times 5) \times (10 \times 10)$
Step 5	20×100
Step 6	2000

Figure 8.28

8.12   MULTIPLICATION OF TENS AND ONES BY TENS AND ONES

Although you will employ a detailed step-by-step presentation for introducing the skill of multiplying tens and ones by tens and ones, the student will start at a stage comparable to Phase 1 (see Section 8.10). Figure 8.29

27×35
   Renaming
$(20 + 7) \times 35$
   Distributive property of multiplication over addition
$(20 \times 35) + (7 \times 35)$
   Renaming
$[20 \times (30 + 5)] + [7 \times (30 + 5)]$
   Distributive property of multiplication over addition
$[(20 \times 30) + (20 \times 5)] + [(7 \times 30) + (7 \times 5)]$
   Multiplication skills
$600 + 100 + 210 + 35$
   Renaming
$600 + 100 + 200 + 10 + 30 + 5$
   Addition skills
$900 + 40 + 5$
   Renaming
945

Figure 8.29

shows such a step-by-step presentation by the teacher. The justification or
skill required for each step is given above it. The teacher should give
special emphasis to the step $(20 \times 30) + (20 \times 5) + (7 \times 30) + (7 \times 5)$. He
should focus the child's attention on what is being multiplied by the 7 in
27 and what is being multiplied by the 20 in 27.

In introducing the standard algorithm, the phasing-in starts at Phase 1
(see Section 8.10). Figure 8.30 depicts the phasing-in stages. An accompanying dialogue might be as follows:

Phase 1 Phase 2

35	35
× 27	× 27
35	245
210	700
100	945
600	
945	

Figure 8.30

"We have seen that in order to find the product of 27 and 35, we multiply
the 7 and 5, and the 7 and 3 tens, the 2 tens and 5, and finally the
2 tens and 3 tens. We then find the sum of these four products.
Notice where I have placed these four products."

"Why have I placed the numerals like this?" (Because we wish to find the
sum, and this is the most convenient form for adding these numbers.)

"We add and find the product of the factors 27 and 35, which is 945."

You may have some students of low aptitude who will stay at this phase
in the development of the multiplication algorithm. Do not be overly concerned that they do not progress beyond it; be pleased that they at least
have mastered a means of finding the product of two whole numbers. This
phase is slightly less efficient than the next phase, but we occasionally
must sacrifice the more efficient algorithm for one that is simpler to
understand.

In the next phase, the child is taught to remember those numbers that
will go into the regrouping upon the next multiplication. The teacher should
show the child that the sum of the partial products, 35 and 210 in the
first form, is the partial product 245 in the second phase. It should also
be pointed out that the sum of the partial products, 100 and 600 in the
first phase, forms the partial product 700 in the second phase.

In essence, the child has all the essential background at this point to
extend the algorithm with a minimum of new technique. Further development of the multiplication algorithm is left for the exercises. In summary,
the following are prerequisites for the mastery of the previously discussed
multiplication algorithm:

1. The child must know the basic multiplication facts.
2. He needs to understand his decimal system to the extent that he knows
   $1 \times 1 = 1, 1 \times 10 = 10, 10 \times 10 = 100, 10 \times 100 = 1000$.
3. He also needs to know:

ones times ones = ones	Example:

   ones times ones = ones   7 ones × 8 ones = 56 ones
   ones times ten = tens   7 ones × 8 tens = 56 tens or 560
   tens times tens = hundreds   7 tens × 8 tens = 56 hundreds or 5600

   and so on.
4. He needs to know and be able to use the distributive property of multiplication over addition.

EXERCISES (2)

1. Make a dialogue that could be used to introduce

$$\begin{array}{r} 92 \\ \times\ 8 \\ \hline 16 \\ 720 \\ \hline 736 \end{array}$$

2. Make up a dialogue that could be used to introduce

$$\begin{array}{r} 92 \\ \times\ 8 \\ \hline 736 \end{array}$$

3. Give a step-by-step explanation using the renaming-associative technique to explain $300 \times 4000 = 1,200,000$.
4. Give a step-by-step explanation in horizontal form of how the product of 35 and 182 is determined.
5. Work the following problem by using partial products requiring no mental regrouping:

$$\begin{array}{r} 237 \\ \times\ 46 \\ \hline \end{array}$$

6. Make up a dialogue that will explain how each of the partial products is obtained in the following problem:

$$\begin{array}{r} 237 \\ \times\ 46 \\ \hline 1422 \\ 9480 \\ \hline 10902 \end{array}$$

8.13 MULTIPLICATION STORY PROBLEMS

One of the first awarenesses that a child needs to acquire is that the request
to determine the number of a set formed by the unions of a number of
sets equal in number signals a multiplicative operation. He also has to
recognize that these sets, equal in number, can occur in an array, in a
measurement situation (such as a set of 4 nickels), or in a situation
where he is expected to extract the equal sets. For example, if items are
bought costing 5 cents, 12 cents, 5 cents, 12 cents, and 12 cents, the total
cost is obtained by $(2 \times 5) + (3 \times 12)$.

Let us examine some problems that involve translation into multiplication
sentences.

> John bought 3 pencils.
> Each pencil cost 5 cents.
> What was the total cost of the pencils?

Let us examine how a chart can be employed to broaden the child's
problem-solving skills. Let us assume that you have constructed a chart
similar to the one shown in Figure 8.31.

Number of pencils	Cost of each pencil	Total cost
1	5¢	
2	5¢	
3	5¢	
4	5¢	
5	5¢	

Figure 8.31

The following dialogue might be used to accompany this chart:

"If we bought 1 pencil for 5 cents, we would pay 5 cents for the pencil."
(Record 5 cents in the total-cost column.)
"If we bought 2 pencils, how much would we have to pay?" (10 cents.
Discuss the different ways we could have found the total cost. Add
5 cents and 5 cents, or say that $2 \times 5 = 10$.)
"If we bought 3 pencils, how much would we have to pay?" (15 cents.
Discuss the different ways we could have found this total cost. Add
10 cents and 5 cents.) "Knowing that 2 pencils cost 10 cents helps us
find the cost of 3 pencils." ($5 + 5 + 5 = 15$ and $3 \times 5 = 15$.)

After completing the table, place the following equations on the board:

1 ? 5 = 5
2 ? 5 = 10
3 ? 5 = 15
4 ? 5 = 20
5 ? 5 = 25

"What operation are we using if the pair of numbers 1, 5 gives us 5, the pair of 2, 5 gives us 10, and so on?" (Multiplication.)

Analyze similar problems, always pointing out the fact that when we find that we have many sets equal in number, the operation of multiplication will help us find the total number of members of the sets.

The child should be given some activities in solving problems that involve nothing other than the experience of translating a story problem into a mathematical sentence. When multiplication is involved, we can request the child to see how many ways he could translate a given problem. For example, the following problem can be translated in several ways:

Mary has 5 bags of cookies.
Each bag contains 6 cookies.
How many cookies does Mary have?

Translations are

$5 \times 6 = \square$ $\qquad$ $6 + 6 + 6 + 6 + 6 = \square$
$(2 \times 6) + (3 \times 6) = \square$ $\qquad$ $(1 \times 6) + (4 \times 6) = \square$

and so on.

EXERCISES (3)

1. Using one of the following sources, construct five story problems of a current events nature involving basic multiplication facts appropriate for a group of students in a third-grade class.

    a. Newspaper   b. *World Almanac*   c. Magazine

2. Using the same sources, construct five story problems of a current events nature involving a factor using one digit and a factor using two digits appropriate for fourth-grade students.

3. Using the same sources, construct five story problems of a current events nature involving two steps in which one of the operations is multiplication. These problems should be appropriate for fourth-grade students.

4. Using the same sources, construct five story problems of a current events nature requiring the children to use multiplication and two other operations appropriate for sixth-grade students.

5. Make up a word problem for each of the following mathematical sentences:

    a. $3 \times .17 = \square$ c. $(2 \times 5) + (3 \times 6) = \square$
    b. $3 \times 17 = \square$ d. $34 \times 67 = \square$

BIBLIOGRAPHY

Ando, M., and H. Ikeda. "Learning Multiplication Facts—More Than a Drill," *The Arithmetic Teacher* (October 1971), pp. 366–369.

Bechtel, R. D., and L. J. Dixon. "Multiplication—Repeated Addition?" *The Arithmetic Teacher* (May 1967), pp. 373–376.

Callahan, L. C. "A Romantic Excursion into the Multiplication Table," *The Arithmetic Teacher* (December 1969), pp. 609–613.

Herold, J. "Patterns for Multiplication," *The Arithmetic Teacher* (October 1969), pp. 498–499.

Hervery, M. A., and B. H. Litwiller. "A Graphical Representation of Multiples of the Whole Numbers," *The Arithmetic Teacher* (January 1971), pp. 47–48.

Hullihan, W. F. "Multiplication Unlimited," *The Arithmetic Teacher* (May 1968), pp. 460–461.

Junge, C. W. "Now Try This—In Multiplication," *The Arithmetic Teacher* (February 1967), pp. 134–135.

Knigge, W. "Effortless Multiplication," *The Arithmetic Teacher* (April 1967), p. 307.

National Council of Teachers of Mathematics. *29th Yearbook* (Washington, D.C.), 1964, pp. 59–65, 70–78, 153–157.

Schrage, M. "Presenting Multiplication of Counting Numbers on an Array Matrix," *The Arithmetic Teacher* (December 1969), pp. 615–616.

Shafer, D. M. "Multiplication Mastery Via the Tape Recorder," *The Arithmetic Teacher* (November 1970), pp. 581–582.

Traub, R. G. "Napier's Rods: Practice with Multiplication," *The Arithmetic Teacher* (May 1969), pp. 363–364.

Weaver, J. F. "Multiplication Within the Set of Counting Numbers," *School Science and Mathematics* (March 1967), pp. 252–270.

9

Teaching division on the set of whole numbers

BEHAVIORAL OBJECTIVES

Student can . . .

State a working definition of division.

List five ways of reading a division equation.

Identify a readiness activity for division.

Describe how to develop division facts using measurement models.

Describe how to develop division facts using partition.

Describe two patterns that can be used to teach division facts.

Cite an analogy that can be used to develop the repeated-subtraction division algorithm.

Give a step-by-step analysis of the repeated-subtraction division algorithm.

State an analogy that can be used to develop the standard division algorithm.

Give a step-by-step analysis of the standard division algorithm.

9.1 INTRODUCTION

The concepts related to division on the set of whole numbers play a crucial role in the concepts to be developed next—the concepts relating to the fractional numbers and the set of rational numbers.

The compensation property for division will not only facilitate the mastery of the decimal division algorithm but will also serve as a basis for determining equivalence classes for fractional numbers. It also will be an integral part of the development of and justification for the division algorithm for fractional numbers.

The right identity element for division of whole numbers will also play a leading role in the development of division on the set of fractional numbers. The right distributive properties of division over addition and division over subtraction will provide the bridging concepts for a smooth transition into addition and subtraction of fractional numbers. Careful development of these distributive properties will eliminate much of the mystery of why we do not add the denominators, or why it is important that the denominators name the same number.

9.2 DEFINITION, TERMINOLOGY, AND SYMBOLISM

Before exploring the techniques of teaching division, it will be helpful to review the symbolism, terminology, and definitions used to communicate our ideas.

First, we define quotient as follows:

The *quotient* of two whole numbers x and y ($y \neq 0$) will be the whole number z if $y \times z = x$.

For example, the quotient of 8 and 2 is 4, because $4 \times 2 = 8$ (or because $2 \times 4 = 8$). This definition of quotient will suffice if the first whole number is divisible by the second whole number. A whole number x is said to be *divisible* by a whole number y ($y \neq 0$) if there exists a whole number z such that $x = z \times y$.

The preceding definition of quotient is not adequate when we are concerned with division situations accompanied by remainders. In these cases, the quotient and remainder are defined as follows:

Let x and y be whole numbers such that y is not equal to zero. The *quotient and remainder* of x and y are w and z, respectively, if $x = (y \times w) + z$.

This definition is needed for cases like the quotient of 14 and 3, which is 4 with a remainder of 2, because $14 = (3 \times 4) + 2$.

Although we use the previous definitions for quotients, when we are interested in an efficient process to find this quotient, we "interpret" division in terms of repeated subtraction. A generalized form of this interpretation follows:

The quotient of two whole numbers x and y ($y \neq 0$) is the number of times y must be subtracted from x in order to get a remainder r, and $0 \leq r < y$.

An algorithm that uses this interpretation is called a *repeated-subtraction division algorithm*. There are four basic notations that represent division (see Figure 9.1).

(a) $12 \div 3 = 4$ (c) $\frac{12}{3} = 4$

$$3\overline{)12}$$

$$\begin{array}{r} 4 \\ \hline 12 \, | \, 4 \end{array}$$

(b) $12/3 = 4$ (d) $3\overline{)12}$ or $\quad 0 \, | \, 4$

Figure 9.1

An elementary teacher often has the tendency to stress the notation in Figure 9.1d at the expense of the other notations. Notation 9.1a is an important form permitting natural left-to-right reading; it is also a useful method of recording the basic division facts. It is important that students become familiar with notation 9.1c, which points out the fact that fractions can be thought of as denoting the quotient of two whole numbers.

There are many ways that the mathematical sentences illustrated in Figure 9.1 can be read. A few of them follow:

The quotient of 12 and 3 is 4.
The quotient of 12 and 3 equals 4.
12 divided by 3 is equal to 4.
12 divided by 3 is 4.
3 divides 12, 4 times.

In Figure 9.2, the terminology applied to the division notation and sentences relative to the definitions is identified. Note that there are two sets of terminology for every division sentence except one. For example, it would not be best to say "product 1 and divisor 3." When you use the term product, you should be consistent and refer to the other numbers as known factor, unknown factor, and remainder.

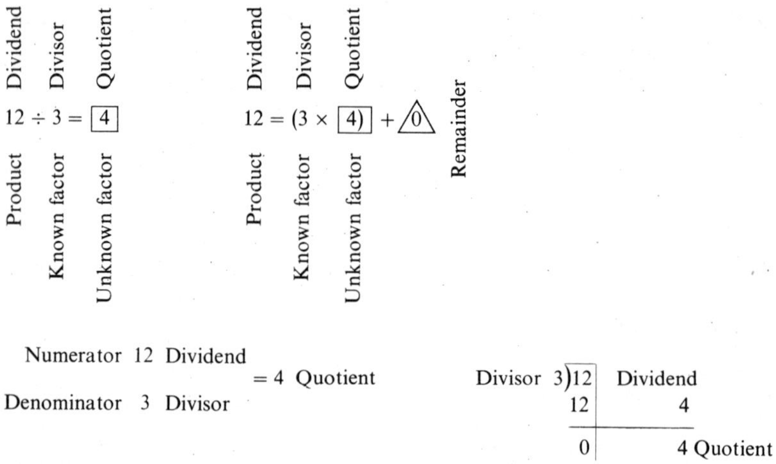

Figure 9.2

9.3 READINESS EXPERIENCES FOR DIVISION

A readiness activity for division as early as the first-grade level involves having the children actually construct sets, equal in number, from a given set. For example, given a set of 8 objects, see how many sets of 2 can be constructed. Another example might consist of having the children distribute

12 cards or buttons to the 4 corners of their desks so that they have the same number of cards in each corner. When the children are ready, the teacher asks, "How many are in each corner of your desk?" Then he says, "You have 4 sets. How many are in each set?"

9.4 MISSING FACTORS AND DIVISION

A child encounters division when he is asked to find a missing factor in a multiplication sentence. For example, in presenting the equation $\square \times 3 = 12$, the teacher asks, "What number is multiplied by 3 in order to get a product of 12?" The child's first encounter with the division symbol probably occurs in conjunction with the related mathematical sentence. For example, $\square \times 5 = 15$ is shown together with the problem $15 \div 5 = \square$. The teacher will tell the class that these mathematical sentences are asking exactly the same question, and that this second sentence is just another way of writing the first sentence.

9.5 TEACHING THE BASIC DIVISION FACTS USING MODELS

There are two basic sets models for teaching division facts. The most common sets model to introduce a child to division facts is the *measurement model*. In the measurement model the child measures out the number of objects suggested by the divisor. Figure 9.3 illustrates how this model can be introduced.

Figure 9.3

The other basic sets model is the *partitioning model*. In the partitioning model the child forms sets equal in number. Figure 9.4 illustrates how this model can be introduced.

Figure 9.4

Another useful teaching aid for exploring the division facts is the number-line model. This gives the teacher a good device for interpreting division as repeated subtraction. In Figure 9.5, we see a cartoon depicting a child finding out how many jumps of 3 it takes to go from 12 to 0. Even though the number of jumps of a given length will correspond to the quotient, the numbers corresponding to the various stopping points will be the remainders obtained when the student is using the repeated-subtraction interpretation of division. For example, when finding the number of sets

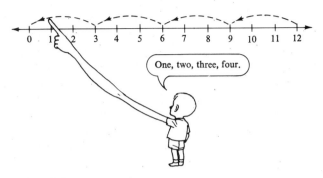

Figure 9.5

of 3 that can be partitioned out of a set of 12, we will have 9 left when we have partitioned out 1 set of 3, 6 of 12 left when we have partitioned out 2 sets of 3, and so on.

9.6 TEACHING DIVISION FACTS BY PATTERNS

The right identity element for division is taught soon after the child begins to learn his division facts. It is called the *right identity element* because in the mathematical sence $n \div 1 = n$, the 1 is placed to the right of the division symbol, as in $16 \div 1 = 16$, and this relation does not hold if the 1 is placed to the left of the division symbol $(1 \div 16 \neq 16)$.

This is a comparatively easy concept to teach. If you present a few examples in which the divisor refers to the number of sets you have and the dividend refers to the total number of objects that will be distributed to the one set, it is relatively easy to see that the resulting set contains the same number as represented by the dividend. You should extend this concept beyond numbers for which the n (in $n \div 1 = n$) is greater than 10. For example, if we have 354 apples and put them in 1 set, how many apples would be in the 1 set, or $354 \div 1 = \square$?

Another property you may want to have your students discover in their early experiences with basic division facts is the *right distributive property* of division over addition. This property will permit them to explore and discover division facts based on facts they already know. For example, suppose a child knows $30 \div 5 = 6$, and $15 \div 5 = 3$. He could be asked to discover what $45 \div 5$ is equal to as follows:

"$(30 + 15) \div 5 = \square$. What number is named by $(30 + 15)$?" (45.) "Let us discover what $45 \div 5$ is equal to by using our right distributive property. We rewrite the equation as $(30 \div 5) + (15 \div 5) = \square$. Find each of the quotients and add them. Who has discovered what $45 \div 5$ is equal to?"

Now you can give the students problems in which they are asked to discover some facts. For example:

$$36 \div 9 = (18 + 18) \div 9 = \square$$
$$63 \div 9 = (27 + 36) \div 9 = \square$$
$$40 \div 5 = (20 + 20) \div 5 = \square$$

The first step in getting children to discover the right distributive property of division over addition is to give them paired problems that will lead them to the discovery. Figure 9.6 presents several pairs of problems that can be used to guide children in discovering the right distributive property of division.

(1a) $(12 + 6) \div 3 = \square$ (2a) $(6 \div 2) + (4 \div 2) = \square$
(1b) $(12 \div 3) + (6 \div 3) = \square$ (2b) $(6 + 4) \div 2 = \square$
            (3a) $(8 + 4) \div 2 = \square$
            (3b) $(8 \div 2) + (4 \div 2) = \square$

Figure 9.6

Before presenting students with examples for the second stage, the teacher should be certain that the students have discovered the property. Then problems such as those shown in Figure 9.7 can be given. These problems require a single solution only.

(a) $(30 + 10) \div 5 = (\square \div 5) + (10 \div 5)$
(b) $(10 + 4) \div 2 = (10 \div \square) + (4 \div \square)$
(c) $(\square + 15) \div 3 = (6 \div 3) + (15 \div 3)$

Figure 9.7

In the third stage, the teacher can elicit multiple correct responses so that the children can see many solutions. Figure 9.8 shows typical problems.

(a) $(12 + 24) \div \square = (12 \div \square) + (24 \div \square)$
(b) $(30 + 15) \div \square = (30 \div \square) + (15 \div \square)$
(c) $(12 + \square) \div 2 = (12 \div 2) + (\square \div 2)$

Figure 9.8

The last stage is usually taught at the junior high level and should guide the students to make a generalization. They are given a pattern such as $(a + b) \div c = (a \div c) + (b \div c)$ and asked to create problems that would be true sentences using this pattern.

Teaching the right distributive property of division over subtraction uses exactly the same techniques as the right distributive property of division over addition. Development of this property will be treated as an exercise. A child's acquaintance with the right distributive property of division over addition also will be useful to him in phasing in addition of fractional numbers.

A third property you may want to introduce concurrently with the teaching of the basic division facts is the *compensation property* of division. It is one of the most useful division properties. It has application in establishing equivalent classes of fractions, simplifying division problems, simplifying division of fractional numbers using decimal notation, and exploring the fractional-number division algorithm (see Figure 9.9).

Finding equivalent names:

$\frac{1}{2} = \frac{1 \times 3}{2 \times 3} = \frac{3}{6}$

Simplification of division problems:

$.17\overline{)16.4}$ $.17 \times 100\overline{)16.4 \times 100}$ $17\overline{)1640}$

$24\overline{)216}$ $24 \div 4\overline{)216 \div 4}$ $6\overline{)54}$

Obtaining a common divisor for addition and subtraction of fractional numbers:

$\frac{2}{3} + \frac{2}{4} = \frac{2 \times 4}{3 \times 4} + \frac{2 \times 3}{4 \times 3}$ $\frac{3}{5} - \frac{1}{7} = \frac{3 \times 7}{5 \times 7} - \frac{1 \times 5}{7 \times 5}$

Obtaining a divisor of 1 when dividing by fractional numbers:

$\frac{3}{4} \div \frac{2}{7} = (\frac{3}{4} \times \frac{7}{2}) \div (\frac{2}{7} \times \frac{7}{2})$

Figure 9.9

The method of teaching this property proceeds a little differently from methods previously discussed. It is not begun by using the pairs of problems to lead to the discovery. It is better to start with a series of problems such as those shown in Figure 9.10. A typical dialogue to accompany the problems in Figure 9.10 (after the students have solved the equations) might be as follows:

(Column A) "Did we get the same quotient as a solution for each equation in Column A?" (Yes.) "What must we have done to the 5 and 1 in $5 \div 1$ to get the equation $10 \div 2 = \square$?" (Multiplied the dividend and divisor by 2.) "What must we have done to the 5 and 1 in $5 \div 1$ to get the equation $30 \div 6 = \square$?" (Multiplied the dividend and divisor by 6.) "When we multiplied the divisor and dividend by the same nonzero number, did our quotient change?" (No.)

Column A	Column B
$5 \div 1 = \square$	$60 \div 30 = \square$
$10 \div 2 = \square$	$30 \div 15 = \square$
$15 \div 3 = \square$	$10 \div 5 = \square$
$30 \div 6 = \square$	$2 \div 1 = \square$

Figure 9.10

(Column B) "Did we get the same quotient as a solution for each equation in Column B?" (Yes.) "What must we have done to the 60 and 30 in $60 \div 30$ to get the equation $30 \div 15 = \square$?" (Divided the dividend and divisor by 2.) "What must we have done to the 60 and 30 in $60 \div 30$ to get the equation $10 \div 5 = \square$?" (Divided the 60 and 30 by 6.) "When we divided the divisor and dividend by the same nonzero number, did our quotient remain the same?" (Yes.)

After the child's attention has been focused on the results of multiplying the dividend and divisor by a nonzero number, and of dividing the dividend and divisor by a nonzero number, he is ready to explore this concept further by working with pairs of problems. Figure 9.11 depicts problems typical of this stage.

(1a) $16 \div 8 = \square$	(2a) $14 \div 2 = \square$	(3a) $28 \div 14 = \square$
(1b) $32 \div 16 = \square$	(2b) $42 \div 6 = \square$	(3b) $4 \div 2 = \square$

Figure 9.11

In the third stage, problems requiring single solutions are given. Representative problems for this stage are $30 \div 10 = (30 \div \square) \div (10 \div 5)$; $6 \div 3 = (6 \times 4) \div (3 \times \square)$; and $12 \div 4 = (\square \div 2) \div (4 \div 2)$.

Then problems requiring multiple solutions are posed to the children. Typical problems for this stage are $24 \div 6 = (24 \div \square) \div (6 \div \square)$; $8 \div 4 = (8 \times \square) \div (4 \times \square)$; and $49 \div \square = (49 \times 3) \div (\square \times 3)$.

In the fifth and last stage, the students are given two patterns, such as $a \div b = (a \div c) \div (b \div c)$ and $(a \times c) \div (b \times c)$. They are then asked to create sentences for each of the patterns that would be true sentences using these patterns.

Some of the many methods we have of teaching the basic division facts are summarized in the following table:

Problem	Method	Solution
$6 \div 2 = \square$	Using sets (partition)	$6 \div 2 = 3$

(measurement)

Problem	Method	Solution
$4 \div 2 = \square$	Using arrays	$4 \div 2 = 2$

Problem	Method	Solution
$8 \div 2 = \square$	Using a number line	$8 \div 2 = 4$

$36 \div 6 = \square$	Using the right distributive property $(30 + 6) \div 6 = (30 \div 6) + (6 \div 6) =$ 5 + 1	$36 \div 6 = 6$
$8 \div 1 = \square$	Using properties: Since $n \div 1 = n, \ldots$	$8 \div 1 = 8$
$8 \div 8 = \square$	Since $n \div n = 1, \ldots$	$8 \div 8 = 1$
$12 \div 3 = \square$	Using repeated subtraction $12 - 3 = 9, 9 - 3 = 6,$ $6 - 3 = 3, 3 - 3 = 0$	$12 \div 3 = 4$

EXERCISES (1)

1. Using the definition of quotient (without remainder), show that the quotient of 144 and 6 is 24.
2. Explain why 72 is divisible by 9.
3. Using the definition of quotient and remainder, show that the quotient of 16 and 5 is 3 with a remainder of 1.
4. Write four basic division notations for: The quotient of 15 and 3 is 5.
5. List four ways of reading the following: $6 \div 2 = 3$.
6. Where possible, identify each of the following: dividend, divisor, quotient, remainder, product, known factor, unknown factor.

$$20 = (4 \times 5) + 0 \qquad 16 \div 2 = 8 \qquad \begin{array}{r} 5 \\ 3\overline{)15} \\ 15 \\ \hline 0 \end{array}$$

7. Make up sample problems for each of the first three stages in teaching the right distributive property of division over subtraction.
8. Make up sample problems for the second, third, and fourth stages for teaching the compensation property for division.

9.7 A REPEATED-SUBTRACTION DIVISION ALGORITHM

Before we begin an analysis approach for developing this division algorithm, let us examine how an analogy might be used to develop this algorithm.

305

John took to the bank a piggy bank filled with 305 pennies.

1 nickel = 5 pennies

He wanted to trade his pennies in for nickels.
He knew he could get 1 nickel for each set of 5 pennies he gave the teller.

$5 \times 10 = \square$
$5 \times 20 = \square$
$5 \times 30 = \square$

How many pennies would he have to trade in to get 10 nickels? 20 nickels? 30 nickels?

$5)\overline{305}$

He wrote down the symbols at the left.

$$5)\overline{305}\ \big|\ 60$$

He then wrote down a 60 because he thought he could get 60 nickels.

He multiplied 60 and 5 to find out how many pennies he would have to give up to get 60 nickels.

$$5)\overline{305}\ \big|\ 60$$
$$300$$

He wrote 300 down to note how many pennies he would have to give up.

He gave the teller 300 pennies in order to get 60 nickels.

$$5)\overline{305}\ \big|\ 60$$
$$300$$
$$5$$

He subtracted 300 from 305 to see how many pennies he had left.

He wrote a 1 down because he knew he could get 1 nickel for the 5 pennies.

```
5)305
  300 │60
  ───
    5 │
      │1·
```

He wrote down 5 to note how many pennies he would have to give up.

```
5)305
  300 │60
  ───
    5 │
    5 │1
```

He gave the teller 5 pennies and got a nickel.

He subtracted the 5 from the 5 to indicate how many pennies he had left.

```
5)305
  300 │60
  ───
    5 │
    5 │1
  ───
    0 │
```

First he got 60 nickels, then, more nickels. He adds the 60 and 1 to find the total number of nickels he got.

```
5)305
  300 │60
  ───
    5 │
    5 │1
  ───
    0 │61
```

He notes he got 61 nickels for 305 pennies.

You would naturally not start this algorithm with a dividend as large as 305. It was done here only to illustrate the usefulness of an analogy for teaching this algorithm.

The first stage in teaching the repeated-subtraction division algorithm involves introducing the child to the notation he will use. The mechanics of using this notation should be introduced through some basic fact for which the child already knows the quotient. This known fact can be used so that he can focus on the mechanics of handling the notation without the distraction of also searching for the quotient of two numbers involving new division situations. For example:

"We have discovered that the quotient of 15 and 3 is 5. Let's learn a new method of finding the quotient of two whole numbers." (Place on the board the notation depicted in Stage 1 of Figure 9.12.)

"This is another way of asking, '15 divided by 3 equals what number?'"
(Place a set of 15 objects on a flannel board.) "Johnny, will you come
up and get some sets of 3?" (He may get 1, 2, 3, 4, or 5 sets of 3.)
"How many sets of 3 did you take?" (Let us assume that he took 4 sets
of 3.)

Stage 1	Stage 2	Stage 3	Stage 4
3)15	3)15 12 | 4	3)15 12 | 4 3 |	3)15 12 | 4 3 3 | 1 0 | 5

Figure 9.12

"How do we find out how many objects Johnny took, if we know that
he took 4 sets of 3?" (We multiply 4 and 3.)

"Let's put our 4 here (Stage 2) to show that Johnny took 4 sets, and
let's put our 12 here (Stage 2) to show how many objects Johnny took.
How do we find out how many objects are left on the board, if we use
arithmetic to find our answer?" (We subtract the 12 from the 15;
Stage 3.)

"How many sets of 3 are left on the board?" (1.) "Mary, will you take this
1 set of 3 from the board? Let's put our 1 here (Stage 4) to show
that Mary took 1 set of 3, and let's put out 3 here (Stage 4) to
show how many objects Mary took from the board."

"How do we find, by using arithmetic, how many we have left on the
board?" (We subtract the 3 from the 3.)

"We have taken 4 sets of 3 and 1 set of 3 from the board. How do we
find, by using arithmetic, the total number of sets of 3 taken from the
board?" (Add the 4 and the 1, as in Stage 4.)

Use this problem again considering other possible ways of removing the
sets of 3. For example, consider the case in which the sets of 3 are
removed 1 set at a time. Call the children's attention to the fact that there
are many ways in which we can arrive at the answer. Emphasize that in
spite of the different approaches we can take in arriving at the answer, in
each case the quotient is the same.

Write on the board all of the possible ways of finding that the quotient
of 15 and 3 is 5. Ask what specific numerals in the algorithms mean. Check
each stage of the development of the algorithm to see that the children
understand the mechanics of recording the number of sets removed, the total
number of objects removed, and the number of objects remaining on the
board. After the children have developed a familiarity with the mechanics of

the repeated-subtraction algorithm using familiar facts, they are ready to attack complex division situations. Let's explore a typical complex situation with an example and accompanying dialogue.

"In the problem $72 \div 4 = \square$, we are asked to find how many sets of 4 are in 72." (In Stage 1, Figure 9.13, we see how we will write the symbols so that we can compute the answer.)

Stage 1   Stage 2   Stage 3

```
4)72      4)72          4)72
            28 | 7        28 | 7
                          44
```

Figure 9.13

"Will someone take a guess at how many sets of 4 can be taken from the 72?" (Assume that someone says 7, although any number less than or equal to 18 will be correct.)

"How do we find out how many we are taking if we take 7 sets of 4?" (Multiply 7 and 4 to get 28.) "Let's put the 28 here (Stage 2) to show how many have been taken from 72. How do we find out how many are left after we take 28 from 72?" (We subtract.) "We now have 44 left." (Stage 3.)

Repeat this process until all of the sets of 4 have been removed from the set of 72. Each time sets of 4 are removed, call the children's attention to how we find out how many objects are left. When all sets of 4 have been removed, ask, "How do we find the total number of sets of 4 which have been removed?" (By adding.)

Have the children rework this problem in a different way. Call their attention to the fact that although there are many ways to work the problem, some of the ways are faster than others.

After they have mastered the basic idea that we can find the quotient of two whole numbers by the technique of using repeated subtraction, the teacher should guide each child in the refinement of this algorithm. The child should constantly be asked to improve his solution of current problems in the light of his experience with previous problems. He should constantly examine and compare the effects of removing various numbers of sets of a given number.

Questions similar to the following are appropriate for guiding the child in refining his division algorithm:

"Did taking 6 sets of 6 from 354 reduce 354 very much?" (No.) (See Figure 9.14a.) "Why don't you try removing a larger number of sets of 6?"

```
6)354          6)126          6)252
  36 6           60 10
 318             66
                 66 11
                  0 21
  (a)            (b)            (c)
```

Figure 9.14

"We have seen that there are 21 sets of 6 in 126." (See Figure 9.14b.) "Will 252 have more or less sets of 6 than 126?" (More.) "Can we use this information to help us find how many sets of 6 there are in 252?"

9.8 ACTIVITIES TO PROMOTE EFFICIENCY

There are certain activities the teacher can structure for the child that will promote efficiency with the repeated-subtraction algorithm. The first involves having the child discover the relationship existing between multiplication of multiples of 10 and division of multiples of 10. For example, notice how the following problems would promote the child's discovery of this relationship:

If	then	and
$6 \times 4 = 24$	$6 \times 40 =$ _____	$6 \times 400 =$ _____
$24 \div 6 = 4$	$240 \div 6 =$ _____	$2400 \div 6 =$ _____ .

A second activity to promote the child's efficiency is to have him find sets of factors that can serve as a replacement in making a true sentence in an inequality. Problems of this type can be seen in Figure 9.15, along with the sets of factors.

Replacement set: counting numbers

Set of factors
$8 \times \square < 100$ $\{1, 2, 3, 4, 5, 6, 7, 8, 9, 10, 11, 12\}$
$11 \times \square < 100$ $\{1, 2, 3, 4, 5, 6, 7, 8, 9\}$

Replacement set: multiples of 10

Set of factors
$8 \times \square < 1000$ $\{10, 20, 30, 40, 50, 60, 70, 80, 90, 100, 110, 120\}$
$11 \times \square < 1000$ $\{10, 20, 30, 40, 50, 60, 70, 80, 90\}$

Replacement set: multiples of 100

Set of factors
$8 \times \square < 10,000$ $\{100, 200, 300, 400, 500, 600, 700, 800, 900, 1000, 1100, 1200\}$
$11 \times \square < 10,000$ $\{100, 200, 300, 400, 500, 600, 700, 800, 900\}$

Replacement set: counting numbers

Set of factors
$82 \times \square < 384$ $\{1, 2, 3, 4\}$
$147 \times \square < 1874$ $\{1, 2, 3, 4, 5, 6, 7, 8, 9, 10, 11, 12\}$

Figure 9.15

A third activity involves having the child develop skill in ascertaining the largest multiple of 1000, 100, 10, or 1 that can be subtracted each time. A typical dialogue to develop this concept might be as follows:

"Could we subtract 1000 sets of 16 in this problem?" (See Figure 9.16.) (The answer is yes, because $1000 \times 16 = 16,000$, and 16,000 can be subtracted from 42,645.) "Can we subtract 3000 sets of 16?" (No, because $3000 \times 16 = 48,000$, and we do not have 48,000 things.)

$$16\overline{)42,645}$$

Figure 9.16

This process is repeated, asking how many hundred sets of 16 can be removed, and then tens, and then ones.

The child should be given the opportunity to see that the removal of sets by multiples of thousands, hundreds, tens, and ones offers a distinct advantage in terms of efficiency and ease of subtraction over removal of multiples of sets representing intermediate numbers, such as the removal of 137 sets of 16 and then 228 sets of 16, and so on. He should be given the opportunity to discover that a knowledge of the place-value system aids in deciding how many of a given set can be removed. For example, in the preceding problem we were concerned only with how many sets of 16 were in 42,000; 645 did not contribute any essential information to our determining how many sets to remove initially. The child should be led to focus on that part of the numeral that will help him decide how many multiples of thousands, hundreds, tens, or ones can be removed.

Further extensions of this algorithm to include removal of multiples of ten thousands, hundred thousands, millions, and so on, follow the same developmental lines as has the preceding discussion. This algorithm will be discussed further in Chapter 13 where we shall be concerned with division in which a decimal notation is used in the algorithm.

9.9 AN ALTERNATE DIVISION ALGORITHM

Before beginning an analysis approach of the standard division algorithm, let us examine how an analogy coupled with involvement might be used to introduce this algorithm.

A paymaster had to distribute 402 dollars equally to 6 workmen.

hundreds	tens	ones
4		2

The paymaster went to the bank and got 4 100-dollar bills and 2 1-dollar bills, making a total of 402 dollars. But when the paymaster got back to his pay window he was very disappointed:

Teacher: Why was he dissappointed?

Child: Because he could not distribute 4 100-dollar bills to 6 people.

hundreds	tens	ones
	40	2

He went back to the bank and traded in his 4 100-dollar bills for 10 1-dollar bills.

Teacher: How many tens could he get for 4 100-dollar bills?

Children: 40 10-dollar bills.

Teacher: What is the largest number of tens that each of the 6 workmen can get if they must each receive the same number of tens?

Children: 6 10-dollar bills.

$$\begin{array}{r} 6 \\ 6\overline{)402} \end{array}$$

Teacher: Since each person is getting 6 tens we place the 6 in the tens place. 6 sets of 6 tens is how many tens?

Children: 36 tens.

$$\begin{array}{r} 6 \\ 6\overline{)402} \\ 36 \end{array}$$

(The 36 is recorded under the 40 tens.)

Teacher: How many of the 40 tens does he have left after he gives out 36 of them?

Children: 4.

$$\begin{array}{r} 6 \\ 6\overline{)402} \\ 36 \\ \hline 4 \end{array}$$

(The 4 is recorded under the 6 tens.)

The paymaster goes back to the bank and trades in his 4 tens for ones.

$$\begin{array}{r} 6 \\ 6\overline{)402} \\ 36 \\ \hline 42 \end{array}$$

Teacher: How many ones will he get for his 4 tens?

Children: 40.

Teacher: How many ones did he have altogether?

Children: 42. (42 is recorded.)

$$\begin{array}{r} 67 \\ 6\overline{)402} \\ 36 \\ \hline 42 \end{array}$$

Teacher: What is the largest number of ones that each of the 6 workmen can receive equally?

Children: 7 ones.

Teacher: We place the 7 in the ones place.

```
     Teacher: 6 sets of 7 ones is how many?
 67  Children: 42. (The 42 is recorded.)
6)402 Teacher: How many ones are left?
 36  Children: Zero.
 ‾‾
 42
 42
 ‾‾
  0
```

(The zero is recorded.) Each workman
received 67 dollars.

The following presentation probably will be familiar to you in that it illustrates the type of division algorithm you undoubtedly were taught. The problem illustrates how the quotient of 32 was obtained using this algorithm:

```
    32
65)2080
   195
   ‾‾‾
   130
   130
   ‾‾‾
     0
```

The skills needed for the mastery of this algorithm are similar to those required for the repeated-subtraction division algorithm. They are multiplication skills, subtraction skills, and inequality relationships such as $65 \times \square \leq 2000$. However, because it is a more refined algorithm, the inherent meaning behind each step is often masked by the refinement. For example, here the 195 is in reality 1950, but in simplifying the recording process, the zero has been omitted.

Let us begin with a one-digit divisor and explore a possible sequence that might be employed in teaching this algorithm.

3)963 In the example at the left, what is named by the 9? By the 6? By the 3? (900, 60, and 3; or 9 hundreds, 6 tens, and 3 ones.)

This illustration shows us how we might represent the dividend on a place-value chart:

Hundreds	Tens	Ones
⬚ ⬚ ⬚ ⬚ ⬚ ⬚ ⬚ ⬚ ⬚	⬚ ⬚ ⬚ ⬚ ⬚ ⬚	⬚ ⬚ ⬚ → 3)9 hundreds + 6 tens + 3 ones

Beginning at the left, we can partition our hundreds into 3 sets of 3 hundreds. The following illustration and symbolism describes what we did:

Hundreds	Tens	Ones	3 hundreds
⬚ ⬚ ⬚	⬚ ⬚ ⬚ ⬚ ⬚ ⬚	⬚ ⬚ ⬚ → 3)9 hundreds + 6 tens + 3 ones	
⬚ ⬚ ⬚			
⬚ ⬚ ⬚			

We can similarly partition the tens and ones as indicated by the following illustration and symbolism:

Hundreds	Tens	Ones	
□ □ □ □ □ □ □ □ □	□ □ □ □ □ □	□ □ □ →	3 hundreds + 2 tens + 1 one 3$\overline{)}$9 hundreds + 6 tens + 3 ones

Let us now examine a more complex situation in which regrouping must precede our partitioning. Consider this problem: divide 153 by 3. Let us analyze this situation by the following illustration of a place-value chart:

Hundreds	Tens	Ones
□	□ □ □ □ □	□ □ □

It becomes immediately obvious that the 1 set of 100 cannot be partitioned into sets of 3. However, if the 1 set of 100 is regrouped into 10 tens, we can partition the resulting set of 15 tens into 5 sets of 3 tens. This is illustrated by the following picture and symbolism:

Hundreds	Tens	Ones	
	□ □ □ □ □ □ □ □ □ □ □ □ □ □ □	□ □ □ →	5 tens + 1 one 3$\overline{)}$15 tens + 3 ones

Let us now look at an example in which a partial remainder is obtained after regrouping. Consider 420 divided by 3. The following illustration of a place-value chart depicts how 420 would be represented:

Hundreds	Tens	Ones	
□ □ □ □	□ □	→	3$\overline{)}$4 hundreds + 2 tens + 0 ones

After we have partitioned out sets of 3 hundreds, we note we have 1 set of 100 remaining:

Hundreds	Tens	Ones	
□ □ □ □	□ □	→	1 hundred 3$\overline{)}$4 hundreds + 2 tens + 0 ones 3 hundreds 1 hundred

By regrouping this 1 hundred into 10 tens, we obtain 12 tens, which can be partitioned into 4 sets of 3 tens. This is illustrated and symbolized as follows:

Hundreds	Tens	Ones
▯ ▯	▯ ▯ ▯ ▯ ▯ ▯ ▯ ▯ ▯ ▯ ▯ ▯	

$$
\begin{array}{l}
\quad\quad\quad\quad 1\ \text{hundred} + 4\ \text{tens} \\
\hline
\rightarrow 3\overline{)4\ \text{hundreds} + 2\ \text{tens} + 0\ \text{ones}} \rightarrow \\
\quad\quad 3\ \text{hundreds} \\
\quad\quad \overline{\quad\quad\quad\quad} \ 12\ \text{tens} \\
\quad\quad\quad\quad\quad\quad 12\ \text{tens} \\
\quad\quad\quad\quad\quad\quad \overline{\quad\quad\quad} \\
\quad\quad\quad\quad\quad\quad\ 0\ \text{tens}
\end{array}
$$

$$
\begin{array}{r}
140 \\
\rightarrow 3\overline{)420} \\
3 \\
\hline
12 \\
12 \\
\hline
0 \\
0
\end{array}
$$

Finally, we find that 0 sets of ones can be partitioned into sets of 3, zero times. Thus we see that $420 \div 3 = 140$.

By similar investigations you can help the child understand how to cope with situations such as the following:

$$
\begin{array}{l}
\quad\quad 1\ \text{hundred} + 0\ \text{tens} \\
\hline
3\overline{)3\ \text{hundreds} + 2\ \text{tens} + 1\ \text{one}} \rightarrow \\
\quad 3\ \text{hundreds} \\
\quad \overline{\quad\quad\quad} \\
\quad\quad\quad\quad 2\ \text{tens}
\end{array}
\quad
\begin{array}{l}
\quad\quad 1\ \text{hundred} + 0\ \text{tens} + 7\ \text{ones} \\
\hline
3\overline{)3\ \text{hundreds} + 2\ \text{tens} + 1\ \text{one}} \rightarrow \\
\quad 3\ \text{hundreds} \\
\quad \overline{\quad\quad\quad\quad} \\
\quad\quad\quad\quad 21\ \text{ones} \\
\quad\quad\quad\quad 21\ \text{ones} \\
\quad\quad\quad\quad \overline{\quad\quad} \\
\quad\quad\quad\quad\quad 0
\end{array}
$$

$$
\begin{array}{r}
107 \\
\rightarrow 3\overline{)321} \\
3 \\
\hline
21 \\
21 \\
\hline
\end{array}
$$

Notice that there are special cases, such as the 0 tens that was obtained in the quotient 107, that do not have to be taught as special cases with the repeated-subtraction algorithm. For example, in the following algorithm the question of how many sets of 3 in 2 tens does not arise:

$$
\begin{array}{r|l}
3\overline{)321} \\
300 & 100 \\
\hline
21 \\
21 & 7 \\
\hline
0 & 107
\end{array}
$$

Gradually, the "types" of divisive cases are extended to two-digit divisors such as the following:

$$20\overline{)640} \qquad 30\overline{)960} \qquad 32\overline{)6496} \qquad 85\overline{)1356}$$

Educators have studied the relative efficiency of rounding numbers "up" or "down" in order to arrive at a trial divisor when a problem contains a two-digit divisor. Morton* reports that rounding all "two-figure" divisors ending in 6, 7, 8, or 9 upward and all "two-figure" divisors ending in 1, 2, 3, 4, or 5 downward results in estimates being correct 73.2 percent of the time.

Although it is statistically impractical for the child to perform an analysis such as the one Morton describes in his article, it is feasible to have a child become aware of the relative "weight" of the ones digit to the tens digit in a two-digit divisor. It is also important that the child be aware of the comparative weight of the various ones. For example, the 2 in 32 can be compared to the 9 in 39 when 32 and 39 are divisors.

There is no new skill involved in teaching children to use divisors greater than two digits. For example, in the analysis required to obtain the trial quotient for 7896 ÷ 372, we would use 40 tens as a trial divisor.

EXERCISES (2)

1. What division facts could be discovered if a child had a deck of 12 cards?
2. Illustrate, using a number line, how you could direct a child to discover that $16 \div 2 = 8$.
3. Explain, using an illustration on a flannel board, together with a dialogue, how you could help a child discover that $30 \div 6 = 5$.
4. Illustrate four or more possible stages that a child might go through (see Figure 9.12) in using the repeated-subtraction division algorithm to find that $6 \div 2 = 3$.
5. Which of the following problems might be the first problem a child would encounter using the repeated-subtraction division algorithm? Justify your answer.

   $36 \div 4 = \square \qquad 100 \div 10 = \square \qquad 20 \div 2 = \square$

6. Make up some exercises that would be useful in helping a child develop skill in partitioning multiples of 100 from a number.
7. Make up some exercises that would be useful in helping a child develop skill in partitioning multiples of 10 from a number.
8. Study each of the following problems. Make up a dialogue for each problem that would aid the child in increasing his efficiency.

$$
\begin{array}{r}
24\overline{)3424} \\
24 \;\big|\; 1 \\
\hline
3400
\end{array}
\qquad
\begin{array}{r}
24\overline{)100} \\
\big|\; 5 \\
\end{array}
\qquad
\begin{array}{r}
24\overline{)480} \\
240 \;\big|\; 10 \\
\end{array}
$$

---

* R. L. Morton, "Estimating Quotient Figures When Dividing by Two-Place Numbers," *Elementary School Journal* (November 1947), vol. 48, pp. 141–148.

9. Explain the meaning of the 39 in each of the following:

$$
\begin{array}{r}
2196 \\
2)\overline{4392}
\end{array}
\qquad
\begin{array}{r}
40)\overline{7964} \\
40 \\
\hline
39
\end{array}
\qquad
\begin{array}{r}
40)\overline{40386} \\
40 \\
\hline
39
\end{array}
$$

9.10   DIVISION STORY PROBLEMS

Just as the teaching of subtraction story problems was complicated, so is the teaching of division story problems complicated. The three most common types of story problems may be described as the partitive situation, the measurement situation, and the missing-factor situation.

In *the partitive situation*, the number property of a set is known and the equivalent sets into which the set is to be partitioned are known. It is not known how many will be in each set. The following problem depicts a typical partitive situation.

John has 12 cards.
He is to deal out the cards equally to 3 people.
How many cards will each person get?

This problem translates to the mathematical sentence $12 \div 3 = \square$.

In *the measurement situation*, the number of the set is known, and the number of each equal set that is removed from the set is known, but the number of sets is not known. The following problem depicts a typical measurement situation:

John has 12 cards.
He gives each person 3 cards.
How many people can get cards?

This problem translates to the mathematical sentence $12 \div 3 = \square$. Notice that both problems translate to the same sentence, even though the physical situations are different.

In developing the child's attack skills for either of the preceding problems, the teacher should either demonstrate the problem or allow the child to act out the situation. You will want to "compare" partitive situations with measurement situations and discuss how the numerals in the mathematical sentences are derived. For example, given the sentence $35 \div 5 = \square$, if the sentence has been derived from a partitive situation, the 5 tells us how many sets there are; but if the sentence has been derived from a measurement situation, the 5 tells us how many are in each set.

The third type of division story problem, *the missing-factor situation,* is depicted in the following problem:

Mary gave John some bags of cookies.
Each bag held 5 cookies.
There was a total of 30 cookies in the bags.
How many bags did Mary give John?

Let us use this problem to discuss another technique for developing problem-solving skills. This type of problem provides an excellent opportunity for developing the skill of making a reasonable "guess."

"Would 1 bag be a good guess of how many bags Mary gave John?" (No.)
"Why?" (Because 1 bag would contain only 5 cookies and not 30 cookies. We wouldn't have enough cookies.)
"If each bag contained 1 cookie, how many bags would we need to get 30 cookies?" (30 bags.) "If Mary had 5 cookies in each bag, would 30 bags be a good guess of how many bags it would take to get 30 cookies?" (No.)
"Why?" (We would have too many cookies with 30 bags.)
"We have found that 1 bag gives us too few cookies and that 30 bags give us too many cookies. If we had to guess another number, where should we guess our number?" (We should guess a number between 1 and 30, because it is between those numbers.)

It is important to continue exploring techniques for determining the reasonableness of answers. The preceding technique of finding boundaries that would give us too few and too many is just one technique. Probably the most common technique is rounding off the numbers in our problem, coupled with a "mental" calculation utilizing these rounded-off numbers.

For example, consider the following problem:

If the total bill for a certain number of items is 136 cents, and if each item cost 17 cents, how many items were purchased?

We can obtain a quick estimate by rounding off 136 cents to 140 cents, and 17 cents to 20 cents; then a quick mental calculation will give us the answer 7. Knowing the answer is somewhere close to 7 will make us suspicious if upon dividing 136 by 17, we obtain an answer such as 18. Some children use this "feel" for the relative size of the answer as a clue in deciding which operation is a reasonable one to employ in the solution of a problem. The technique is not unlike that used by the mathematician in searching for a mathematical model to fit a set of data.

EXERCISES (3)

1. Using one or more of the following sources, construct five story problems of a current events nature involving partitive situations appropriate for a fourth-grade class.

    a. Newspaper   b. *World Almanac*   c. Magazine

2. Using the same sources, construct five story problems about current events involving measurement situations appropriate for a fourth-grade class.

3. Using the same sources, construct five story problems of a current events nature involving division and one other operation appropriate for a sixth-grade class.

4. Using the same sources, construct five story problems about current events involving missing-factor situations appropriate for a sixth-grade class.

5. Make up a word problem for each of the following mathematical sentences:

   a. $394 \div 6 = \square$ d. $(16 + 4) \div 5 = \square$

   b. $4.94 \div 6 = \square$ e. $900 \div 3 = \square$

   c. $(36 + 40) \div 4 = \square$ f. $(80 \div 5) + (60 \div 10) = \square$

BIBLIOGRAPHY

Connelly, R. and J. Heddens. "'Remainders' That Shouldn't Remain," *The Arithmetic Teacher* (October 1971), pp. 379–380.

DiSpigno, J. "Division Isn't That Hard," *The Arithmetic Teacher* (October 1971), pp. 373–377.

Duncan, H. F. "Division by Zero," *The Arithmetic Teacher* (October 1971), pp. 381–382.

Jarosh, S. C. "The Number Line and Division," *The Arithmetic Teacher* (November 1970), pp. 617–618.

McLean, R. C. "Estimating Quotients for the New Long Division Algorithm," *The Arithmetic Teacher* (May 1969), pp. 398–400.

National Council of Teachers of Mathematics. *29th Yearbook* (Washington, D.C.), 1964, pp. 78–83, 89–92, 157–164, 177–186.

Reeve, O. R. "The Missing Factor in Division," *The Arithmetic Teacher* (March 1968), pp. 275–277.

Swart, W. L. "Teaching Division-by-Subtraction Process," *The Arithmetic Teacher* (January 1972), pp. 71–75.

10

Teaching the fractional numbers

BEHAVIORAL OBJECTIVES

Student can . . .

Illustrate, given a fractional number, the number suggested by using a discrete set, or partitioning of a continuous set, or a ratio sets model.

Define a fractional number.

Define equivalent fractions.

Illustrate two models that can be used for determining equivalence.

Identify one circumstance in which un-reduced fractions may be the best form to leave the answer to a problem.

List three applications of mixed numerals.

Explain by analysis a property of fractional numbers that is not a property of whole numbers.

Identify two properties of fractional numbers that are also properties of the set of whole numbers.

10.1 INTRODUCTION

The idea of a fractional number is a sophisticated concept that requires more maturity and background on the part of the child than the concept of a whole number. Whereas a whole number is the property of a discrete set, a fractional number can be associated with

1. The partitioning of a discrete set
2. The ratio of the number properties of two sets
3. A number associated with the partitioning of a continuous set
4. A number representing the quotient of two whole numbers (the divisor never being zero)

The quotient idea will prove most useful in terms of bridging the concept of whole numbers and the concept of fractional numbers, whereas the partitioning of a continuous set and the idea of subsets of a discrete set will provide a less abstract mathematical model to use in teaching children an intuitive concept of a fractional number.

In the primary grades, the main emphasis will be on developing an intuitive concept of fractional numbers, and the child will work with such models as polygonal regions, line segments, lines, and discrete sets. A second emphasis will be on developing an intuitive concept of equivalent names for the same fractional number through work with congruent regions and congruent segments.

In the intermediate grades, the main emphasis will be on extending the concept of the fractional number and equivalent fractions and on developing the operations of addition and multiplication along with their respective inverses.

This chapter is concerned with the teaching of fractional numbers and equivalent fractions. In Chapter 14 the concept of fractional numbers will be broadened to include the study of decimal notation and the concepts of ratio and percent.

10.2 TECHNIQUES OF PARTITIONING CONTINUOUS SETS

Before we undertake the presentation techniques of teaching specific fractional numbers, it will be useful to review techniques of partitioning a set.

It will facilitate the child's understanding if you select geometric regions that can be partitioned into the desired "fractional parts" simply by folding the figure over (in order to obtain the partitioning). Notice in Figure 10.1 that if a circle with its interior region is cut out and folded over

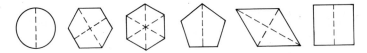

Figure 10.1

so that the boundary is superimposed on itself, the crease obtained will partition the region into halves. If we were to repeat this process, utilizing the crease as a boundary, we could partition the circle's region into fourths. Figure 10.1 also depicts how we could obtain fourths and sixths using a hexagonal region, halves using pentagonal and square regions, and fourths using a rhombus. You will want to experiment with these regions to see what other fractional parts can be derived by paper folding.

10.3 DEFINITION, TERMINOLOGY, AND SYMBOLISM

Even though we do not introduce the child to the definition of fractional numbers in his early intuitive explorations, the basic definition should always play a role in the teacher's presentation.

A *fractional number* is defined as the quotient of two whole numbers, such that the divisor is never zero; in other words, a fractional number is any number that can be named by $\frac{a}{b}$ where a and b are whole numbers and $b \neq 0$.

A *fraction* is defined as the symbol or name for a fractional number and is of the form $\frac{a}{b}$ where a and b name whole numbers.

It is not only important to know that a fraction is a name for a fractional number, but it is also important to know when two fractions name the same fractional number.

Two fractions $\frac{a}{b}$ and $\frac{c}{d}$ name the same fractional number if and only if $a \times d = b \times c$. We say that $\frac{2}{3}$ and $\frac{4}{6}$ name the same fractional number because $2 \times 6 = 3 \times 4$. This concept will be developed further when the method for teaching equivalent fractions is discussed. When two fractions name the same fractional number, we say that they are *equivalent fractions*.

In Figure 10.2, we see various numerals and fractions naming fractional numbers. Note that the whole numbers are a subset of the set of fractional numbers. This is a consequence of the way a fractional number has been defined. It is important that the child, at an early point in his exploration of fractional numbers, become aware of the fact that all whole numbers are also fractional numbers.

In this text, we shall use the terms *numerator* and *denominator* in reference to the numbers named by the numerals in the notation $\frac{a}{b}$. The number

Simplest name	Fraction names	Decimal fraction names
3	$\dfrac{3}{1}, \dfrac{6}{2}, \dfrac{9}{3}, \ldots$	$2.99\overline{9}$ or $3.00\overline{0}$ or 3
$\dfrac{1}{3}$	$\dfrac{1}{3}, \dfrac{2}{6}, \dfrac{3}{9}, \ldots$	$.33\overline{3}$
$\dfrac{11^*}{9}$	$\dfrac{11}{9}, \dfrac{22}{18}, \dfrac{33}{27}, \ldots$	$1.22\overline{2}$

Figure 10.2

named by b is referred to as the *denominator* and the number named by a referred to as the *numerator*. Since the fractional number named by $\dfrac{a}{b}$ is defined as the quotient of two whole numbers ($b \neq 0$), it is also possible to refer to b as a *divisor* and a as a *dividend*.

When using the notation $\dfrac{a}{b}$ to name a fractional number, we read the b with an ordinal designation (with the exceptions of $b = 2$, in which case it is called halves, or $b = 1$, in which case it is called ones) and the a with a cardinal designation. It is for this reason that both the cardinal and the ordinal names should be explored before introducing very many fractional numbers and their names. Some fractions and the method of reading them are as follows:

$\dfrac{3}{4}$ three-fourths $\dfrac{5}{2}$ five-halves $\dfrac{2}{8}$ two-eighths

(Note that the word names for fractional numbers are hyphenated.)

10.4 EARLY EXPERIENCES WITH FRACTIONAL NUMBERS

Children come to school with vague, often misconceived, ideas about fractional numbers. Parents have permitted and encouraged work with imperfect models. To a preschool child, to take one-half of a cookie often means nothing more than not taking all of the cookie. The child's early preschool experiences seldom involve work with congruent partitioning of sets. It is only when a brother or sister points out the fact that he or she did not get the same amount that there is concern for "halfness" or "thirdness." The preschool child's method of partitioning a set into equal parts is most often done on a visual basis with only a cursory attempt made to establish real congruence.

One of the first concepts that must be developed by the teacher is this concept of congruence. In other words, we cannot have a model we refer

---

* We can also express this fraction as the sum of a whole number and a fractional number as $1 + \frac{2}{9}$ or the shortened form $1\frac{2}{9}$. The second notation is often referred to as a *mixed numeral*.

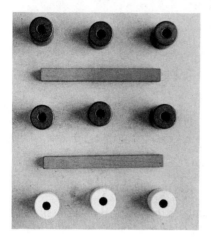

to as halves or thirds or fourths, and so on, until we have satisfied the requirement of congruent measures.

This checking of congruent measures can be accomplished physically by many techniques. The first and most common is that of visually checking something that has been partitioned around points or lines of symmetry, where it is clear that the partitioning has formed congruent parts.

Another common technique, which is useful in conveying the idea that fractional numbers have many equivalent names, is to cut out one of the partitioned regions or partitioned segments and check by overlaying to see if it is congruent with other partitioned regions or segments.

When the mathematical model is a discrete set, such as that depicted in Figure 10.3, we check the set to see that its number is divisible by the number of the subset.

●   ●   ●   ●

0   0   0   0 $\frac{1}{3}$

0   0   0   0

Figure 10.3

The children should be given opportunities to partition models into congruent parts. The teacher should select models for them that are easy to partition. For example, a circle does not lend itself to easy partitioning by the child, whereas most regular polygons do. Notice in Figure 10.4 that the square and the hexagon lend themselves readily to partitioning.

Partitioning should not be restricted to two-dimensional figures. Experiences such as sawing a board into equal pieces, partitioning a set of cookies into sets equal in number, and cutting up a cake or pie so that

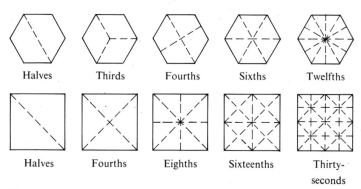

Figure 10.4

everyone gets the same sized piece offer opportunities to extend the concept of fractional numbers through three-dimensional models.

Not only should the child be given experiences with mathematical models that have been partitioned into congruent parts, but he also should have experiences with noncongruent partitioning. In Figure 10.5, two figures are depicted that have been partitioned into noncongruent parts.

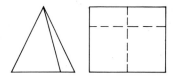

Figure 10.5

Some typical questions that might be asked by the teacher, and the responses of the children, are as follows:

Sample Dialogue

(See Figure 10.5.) Teacher: Has the triangle been partitioned into halves?
Children: No.
Teacher: How do you know?
Children: Because all of the parts are not of equal size.

After partitioning polygons into halves, thirds, fourths, and so on, and after the children realize the necessity for congruent regions, it is then time to introduce the concept of a subset of the partitioned pieces. It is only through the children's awareness of the relation of the subset to the set that they can gain a complete understanding of fractional numbers. For example, consider this typical dialogue that can be used to introduce the concept:

Sample Dialogue

(See Figure 10.6.)   Teacher: Into how many pieces has the square been partitioned?

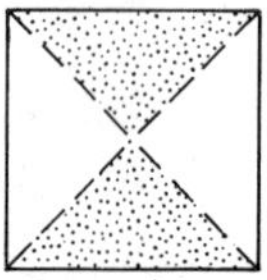

Children: 4.

Teacher: Are they congruent to each other?

Children: Yes.

Teacher: What can we say that each piece represents?

Children: Fourths.

Teacher: We can tell that two-fourths is shaded by writing $\frac{2}{4}$.

Figure 10.6

The child's first experiences with fractional numbers will be with numbers less than or equal to 1. When the concept of fractional numbers is extended to include numbers greater than one, the most appropriate teaching aid is the number-line segment. However, a careful effort must be made, when the number-line segment is introduced, to relate the concept of division of whole numbers to the definition of a fractional number as the quotient of two whole numbers (the divisor $\neq 0$). For example, $6 \div 2$ can be interpreted on the number-line segment as two backward jumps of equal length from 6 to 0 (see Figure 10.7).

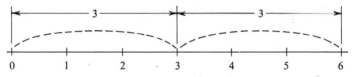

Figure 10.7

Such questions as the following should be asked when bridging the concepts between whole numbers and fractional numbers:

Sample Dialogue

(See Figure 10.7.)   Teacher: What is the length of each of our jumps?

Children: 3 units.

Teacher: What is the quotient of 6 and 2?

Children: 3.

Teacher: When we are jumping, where do we find our answer named?

Children: At the point we start our last jump.

The children should have many experiences finding the quotient of two whole numbers by manipulations on a number line. These early experiences should involve pairs of numbers where the dividend is divisible by the divisor. The teacher should continually focus the child's attention on the following:

1. The quotient can be associated with the distance of each jump.
2. The point where the last jump is started is always the name of the quotient.

After a child becomes familiar with the technique of finding a whole-number quotient by manipulations on a number-line segment, this technique can be used to introduce the concept of a fractional number as the quotient of any two whole numbers. For example, suppose that we want to find the quotient of 3 and 4. We would start with a number-line segment 3 units in length. We would then take 4 jumps of equal length from 3 to 0. The starting point of our last jump is named $\frac{3}{4}$. To check our answer, we count by $\frac{3}{4}$s, starting at zero: $\{0, \frac{3}{4}, \frac{6}{4}, \frac{9}{4}, \frac{12}{4}\}$. Since $\frac{12}{4}$ is another name for 3, we can see that we have the correct quotient of 3 and 4 (see Figure 10.8.).

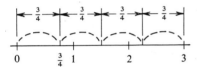

Figure 10.8

Such questions as, "Is $\frac{3}{4}$ more or less than 1?" and "Is $\frac{3}{4}$ more or less than $\frac{1}{2}$?" should be asked at this stage.

The number-line segment is well suited as a model for fractional numbers greater than 1. For example, consider the representation of $9 \div 4$ on a number-line segment as depicted in Figure 10.9.

The child can readily see that $\frac{9}{4}$ is greater than 2 and less than 3. He can also check his work by the process of counting by $\frac{9}{4}$s to discover that $\frac{36}{4}$ is another name for 9.

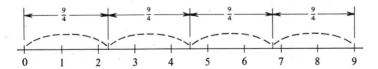

Figure 10.9

EXERCISES (1)

1. What partitionings do each of the following polygons lend themselves to?
   a. Regular pentagon   b. Regular octagon

2. How does a child check to see if a discrete set has been partitioned into sixths?

3. Illustrate each of the following, using a different polygon for each: $\frac{2}{5}$, $\frac{2}{3}$, $\frac{5}{8}$.

4. Illustrate $12 \div 4$ on a number-line segment.
5. Illustrate $4 \div 12$ on a number-line segment.
6. Illustrate $1 \div 2$ on a number-line segment.
7. Illustrate $9 \div 7$ on a number-line segment.

10.5 EQUIVALENT FRACTIONS

Shortly after introducing the children to the concept of fractional numbers, you should structure situations so they will discover that each fractional number has many names. Questions such as, "Mary has $\frac{2}{4}$ of a candy bar and John has $\frac{1}{2}$ of the same candy bar; who has more?" will promote this discovery.

The children should be given many experiences that establish the equivalence of fractional names through subset comparisons before they are introduced to the formal techniques of generating names for fractional numbers. In working with polygons, this experience takes the form of mentally "seeing" that one partition can be transformed into another partitioning (see Figure 10.10) or of cutting and fitting regions to determine that two methods of partitioning yield the same area.

In checking whether two names are equivalent, using discrete sets, we must be sure that the same discrete set can be partitioned into the subsets named by the two numbers. For example, if we were interested in knowing whether $\frac{2}{7}$ and $\frac{1}{3}$ name the same fractional number and, if not, which one

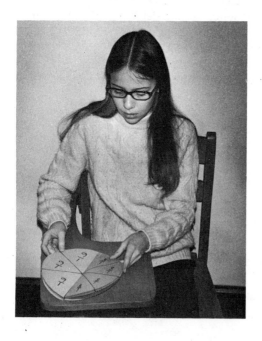

Yes, $\frac{2}{4}$ names $\frac{1}{2}$.

Figure 10.10

names the larger fractional number, we would need a discrete set that could be partitioned into thirds and sevenths. The most readily constructed set consists of a set with 3 rows of 7 items in each row, or 7 rows with 3 items in each row. It is easy to see in Figure 10.11 that $\frac{1}{3}$ names a larger fractional number than $\frac{2}{7}$, because $\frac{1}{3}$ of this set is 7, and $\frac{2}{7}$ is only 6. (Construction of a model of this type is useful to show a child why one can tell whether $\dfrac{a}{b}$ is equal to, greater than, or less than $\dfrac{c}{d}$, depending on the relationship of "a times d" to "b times c.")

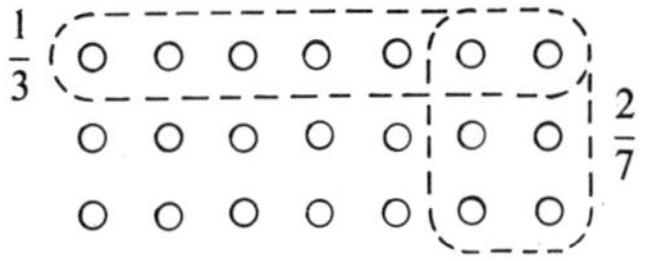

$\frac{1}{3}$ ⬭⬭⬭⬭⬭⬭⬭⬭⬭
⬭⬭⬭⬭⬭⬭⬭⬭⬭ $\frac{2}{7}$
⬭⬭⬭⬭⬭⬭⬭⬭⬭

Figure 10.11

A rectangular region that has been partitioned into various fractional parts is a very useful aid in getting children to discover equivalent fractions. Figure 10.12 depicts a common form of this aid. The child can

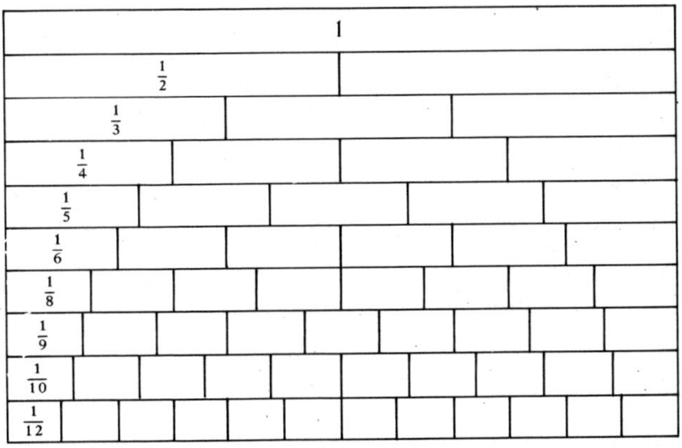

Figure 10.12

easily check for congruence between various partitions. The most common technique for checking congruence is to move a sheet of paper (with a straightedge running from top to bottom) from left to right across the partitioned region. The child will find which partitioning segments are common to various types of partitioning.

Another useful aid for helping children discover equivalent fractions is to use many number-line segments that have been partitioned in a manner similar to the partitioning of the rectangular region in Figure 10.12. However, the manner in which the children use this aid is different, for they mark off the length of one type of fractional partitioning on the edge of a second sheet of paper and see if other line segments have partitions that correspond to the length. Figure 10.13 depicts a typical model of this teaching aid.

Figure 10.13

Using the "multinumber-line segment" pictured in Figure 10.13, the children could discover the following sets of equivalent fractions:

$$\left\{\frac{1}{2}, \frac{2}{4}, \frac{3}{6}\right\}, \left\{\frac{2}{2}, \frac{3}{3}, \frac{4}{4}, \frac{6}{6}\right\}, \left\{\frac{4}{3}, \frac{8}{6}\right\}, \left\{\frac{3}{2}, \frac{6}{4}, \frac{9}{6}\right\}, \left\{\frac{5}{3}, \frac{10}{6}\right\}, \left\{\frac{4}{2}, \frac{6}{3}, \frac{8}{4}, \frac{12}{6}\right\}.$$

When you are developing the concept of quotients of whole numbers through the use of the number-line segments, it is possible to begin developing the idea of equivalent *division expressions*. For example, in Figure 10.14 we see the expressions $12 \div 4$, $9 \div 3$, $6 \div 2$, and $3 \div 1$ represented on different number-line segments.

A dialogue that could accompany this type of exercise, which would introduce the child to equivalent division expressions, might be as follows:

Sample Dialogue

(See Figure 10.14.)   Teacher: You can see that 3 has many division names. Can someone tell me some more division names for 3?

Child: $\frac{15}{5}, \frac{18}{6}, \frac{21}{7}$.

Teacher: If we started with the division name $3 \div 1$, what would we have to do to both the 3 and the 1 to get 6 and 2?

Child: Multiply both numbers by 2.

Teacher: How could we get 12 and 4 from 3 and 1?

Child: Multiply the 3 and the 1 by 4.

Teacher [Write on the board $(3 \times \square) \div (1 \times \square)$.]: Can someone use this pattern to get a division name for 3 that has a 9 for the divisor?

Child: 27 divided by 9.

Teacher: Can someone use this pattern to get a ~~divisor~~ *division* name for 3 that has a 10 for the divisor?

Child: 30 divided by 10.

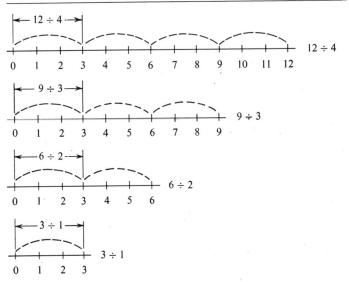

Figure 10.14

After the child has used the number-line segment to construct mathematical models of fractional numbers, his concept can be extended with this type of model to include the concept of equivalent fractions. Figure 10.15

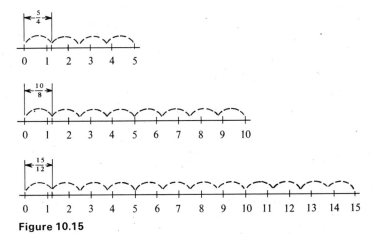

Figure 10.15

depicts how equivalent names for $\frac{3}{4}$ can be discovered by using number-line segments.

Sometimes it is advantageous to think of the fraction $\frac{a}{b}$ as $a \times \frac{1}{b}$. For example, in the child's early fractional number experiences, he is asked to determine equivalent fractions by comparing two partitioned polygonal regions. When considering $\frac{a}{b}$ as representing $a \times \frac{1}{b}$ on a number-line segment, it will be important for the child to construct the $\frac{1}{b}$ partition first, and then make a repetition of this type of partition. Figure 10.16 illustrates the steps we must take in showing $\frac{8}{3}$ on a number-line segment when $\frac{8}{3}$ is viewed as $8 \times \frac{1}{3}$.

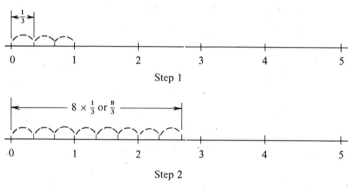

Figure 10.16

Although it is true that every equivalent fraction is a suitable name for a fractional number, there are times when one name may be more convenient to use than another. For example, the fraction referred to as being in the *simplest form* is often the most useful to employ in an operation such as the multiplication of fractions. (A fraction $\frac{a}{b}$ is said to be in the simplest form of a set of equivalent fractions if the only whole number that both a and b are divisible by is 1.)

During the premodern mathematics period, only those fractions "reduced" to lowest terms were deemed acceptable answers to a problem. The teacher should make the child aware that the fraction chosen to express the answer to a problem depends on the problem's context, as well as on the concepts the student is being prepared for. For example, if we are building readiness for decimal notation, $\frac{4}{10}$ may be a much more acceptable form in which to leave the answer than the form $\frac{2}{5}$. Or, if a child is going to have to utilize the idea of $\frac{1}{3}$ with respect to a dozen, the $\frac{4}{12}$ conveys much more meaning when viewed as the ratio of 4 to 12. Later, when the students study precision of measurements, they will note that $\frac{4}{8}$ tells us that the measurement was made to the nearest $\frac{1}{8}$ inch and that changing the answer to $\frac{1}{2}$ inch would mislead us as to how precise the measurement was.

Even though you should teach your students to find many names for fractional numbers, you should also encourage them to choose the most appropriate name for the situation.

10.6 MIXED NUMERALS

There are many occasions in the everyday affairs of people when a whole-number name is used in conjunction with the name of a fractional number less than 1. Such expressions as " $3\frac{1}{4}$ feet of rope," " $4\frac{1}{2}$ million dollars," " $10\frac{2}{5}$ seconds," " $29\frac{8}{10}$ inches of mercury," " $2\frac{3}{8}$ yards of cloth," and " $7\frac{1}{2}$ revolutions per second" are just a few of the mixed numeral expressions that confront us. The first concept can be developed either through the use of a set of discrete polygonal regions or on a number-line segment. Figure 10.17 depicts a representation of $2\frac{3}{4}$ with sets of square regions and on a number-line segment.

The concept of translating mixed numerals to fraction form will be discussed when the concept of addition of fractional numbers is introduced.

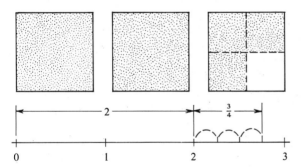

Figure 10.17

10.7 PROPERTIES OF THE SET OF FRACTIONAL NUMBERS

The first property that the children will learn is that zero is the smallest fractional number. The set of fractions for the fractional number zero is the set $\{\frac{0}{1}, \frac{0}{2}, \frac{0}{3}, \ldots\}$. Note that $\frac{0}{0}$ is not a name for zero, because division by zero is undetermined.

One of the most important properties of the set of fractional numbers is that between any two fractional numbers there exists an infinite set of fractional numbers. Suppose you want to demonstrate that we could find as many fractional numbers between $\frac{1}{3}$ and $\frac{1}{2}$ as we desired. Express both fractional numbers as $\frac{2}{6}$ and $\frac{3}{6}$ and ask the students if they multiply the divisor and dividend by the same number. (The answer is "no"; this is merely using the compensation property for division.)

Then suggest multiplying the numerator and denominator of both fractional numbers by 1 billion. We obtain $\frac{2,000,000,000}{6,000,000,000}$ and $\frac{3,000,000,000}{6,000,000,000}$.

It will be easy for the children to see that the set of fractional numbers $\left\{\frac{2,000,000,001}{6,000,000,000}, \frac{2,000,000,002}{6,000,000,000}, \ldots, \frac{2,999,999,999}{6,000,000,000}\right\}$ are all fractional numbers that are between $\frac{1}{3}$ and $\frac{1}{2}$. By multiplying by 1 billion, we obtained 999,999,999 numbers between the numbers $\frac{1}{3}$ and $\frac{1}{2}$. If we had multiplied by a larger number, we would have obtained more numbers between $\frac{1}{3}$ and $\frac{1}{2}$. By choosing a number sufficiently large, we could find as many fractional numbers between $\frac{1}{3}$ and $\frac{1}{2}$ as we would choose.

An alternate approach for showing a child that there exists an infinite set of fractional numbers between any two numbers is called the *averaging technique*. This technique involves finding a fractional number between two fractional numbers by averaging. Demonstrate that we could always use this technique to find a new fractional number between the last found fractional number and one of the earlier found fractional numbers or one of the original fractional numbers. For example, take $\frac{1}{2}$ and $\frac{1}{3}$. We average these two fractional numbers by adding $\frac{1}{2}$ and $\frac{1}{3}$ and dividing by 2. Thus we obtain the number $\frac{5}{12}$. We demonstrate that this is between $\frac{1}{2}$ and $\frac{1}{3}$ by expressing $\frac{1}{2}$ and $\frac{1}{3}$ in terms of twelfths. We then proceed to find a fractional number either between $\frac{1}{2}$ and $\frac{5}{12}$ or between $\frac{1}{3}$ and $\frac{5}{12}$ by the averaging method. The children will soon see that this averaging method could be used as many times as necessary to find as many fractional numbers between $\frac{1}{2}$ and $\frac{1}{3}$ as desired.

A third property of the set of fractional numbers, which is also a property of the set of whole numbers, is the trichotomy property. Given two fractional numbers $\frac{a}{b}$ and $\frac{c}{d}$, it is always true that either $\frac{a}{b} < \frac{c}{d}$ or $\frac{a}{b} = \frac{c}{d}$ or $\frac{a}{b} > \frac{c}{d}$.

EXERCISES (2)

1. Demonstrate that $\frac{3}{8}$ and $\frac{6}{16}$ are equivalent fractions by constructing suitable mathematical models of polygons.
2. Demonstrate that $\frac{3}{5}$ and $\frac{6}{10}$ are equivalent fractions by constructing a suitable mathematical model using an array.
3. Make up a partitioned fractional-number bar that could be used to show that $\frac{2}{7}$ and $\frac{4}{14}$ name the same fractional number.

4. Make up a multinumber-line segment to show that $\frac{7}{4}$ and $\frac{21}{12}$ are equivalent fractions.

5. Illustrate each of the following quotients on a number-line segment:

$$\frac{15}{5}, \frac{30}{10} \qquad \frac{3}{4}, \frac{6}{8}, \frac{12}{16} \qquad \frac{4}{3}, \frac{8}{6}, \frac{16}{12}$$

6. Illustrate $\frac{13}{4}$ on a number-line segment where $\frac{13}{4}$ is thought of as $13 \times \frac{1}{4}$.

7. Show that $3\frac{1}{2}$ and $\frac{7}{2}$ are equivalent names by representing both on number-line segments.

8. A child wrote the following:

$$\frac{3}{4} \times \frac{9}{7} = \frac{0}{13}$$

   a. Has the child written the proper product?

   b. Justify your answer.

9. Give a step-by-step explanation to show that there is an infinite set of fractional numbers between $\frac{9}{7}$ and $\frac{9}{8}$, using each of the following techniques:

   a. Compensation property for division.

   b. Averaging.

BIBLIOGRAPHY

Bohan, H. "Paper Folding and Equivalent Fractions," *The Arithmetic Teacher* (April 1971), pp. 245–249.

Collier, C. C., and H. H. Lerch. *Teaching Mathematics in the Modern Elementary School* (New York: Macmillan), 1969, pp. 202–220.

Cunningham, G. S., and D. Raskin. "The Pegboard as a Fraction Maker," *The Arithmetic Teacher* (March 1968), pp. 224–227.

Drizigacker, R. "FRIO, or Fractions in Order," *The Arithmetic Teacher* (December 1966), pp. 684–685.

Gibb, E. G. "Fractions," *Grade Teacher* (April 1962), pp. 54, 95–97.

Heddens, James W. *Today's Mathematics* (Palo Alto, Calif.: Science Research Associates), 1971, pp. 206–229.

National Council of Teachers of Mathematics. *29th Yearbook* (Washington, D.C.), 1964, pp. 215–238.

Rode, J. "Make a Whole—A Game Using Simple Fractions," *The Arithmetic Teacher* (February 1971), pp. 116–118.

11
Teaching addition and subtraction of fractional numbers

BEHAVIORAL OBJECTIVES
Student can . . .

Define addition and subtraction of fractional numbers in terms of the right distributive property of division over addition and subtraction, respectively.

Illustrate, using a number-line model, an addition equation.

Illustrate, using polygonal models, an addition equation.

List five ways of reading an addition equation.

List five ways of reading a subtraction equation.

Construct a dialogue to teach a structural property of addition by a discovery activity.

Describe a readiness activity for addition (subtraction).

Describe a technique for developing a common denominator intuitively.

Construct a dialogue for teaching the divisibility method of finding the least common denominator.

Construct a dialogue for teaching the factor method for finding the least common denominator.

Give a step-by-step analysis of the factor method of finding the least common denominator.

State a step-by-step analysis of the greatest common factor method of finding a least common denominator.

Illustrate, using a number-line model, a subtraction equation.

Illustrate, using polygonal models, a subtraction equation.

Give a step-by-step analysis of the addition algorithm involving mixed numerals.

Give a step-by-step analysis of the subtraction algorithm involving mixed numerals.

11.1 INTRODUCTION

Instruction in addition and subtraction of fractional numbers during the premodern period was a fragmented approach in which students learned the handling of a series of specific cases. In Figure 11.1, we can see all of the various combinations of problems that were taught as distinct learning experiences. One studied how to add proper fractions and proper fractions, proper fractions and improper fractions, proper fractions and mixed numerals. The various other combinations that were treated as special skills requiring specialized instruction can also be traced.

One of the effects of this type of presentation was the student's inability to tie together the general relationships existing for addition and subtraction on the set of whole numbers as well as fractional numbers. A child taught by this technique would view the solution of problems such as $\frac{1}{7} + \frac{3}{7} = \square$ and $\frac{14}{7} + \frac{21}{7} = \square$ as requiring distinct processes in solution. Some reacted to being asked to solve the second problem by saying, "We haven't learned how to add that kind of 'fraction' yet." But these same children could solve the first problem with ease and could solve the second problem if it were written as $(14 \div 7) + (21 \div 7) = \square$. To many students of this period, the term fraction was synonymous with those fractional numbers between zero and 1, rather than with the set of all quotients of two whole numbers (divisor not zero) greater than or equal to zero. Addition of fractions became to these students addition of numbers between zero and 1.

A modern approach to teaching a child addition and subtraction of fractional numbers is to allow those properties he has learned about the set of whole numbers to serve in aiding his mastery of further concepts. As an example of how whole-number concepts can be utilized to teach fractional-number concepts, consider how the exploration of the right distributive property of division over addition in this problem—$(6 \div 2) + (4 \div 2) = (6 + 4) \div 2$—leads naturally into situations such as the following: $(1 \div 2) + (1 \div 2) = (1 + 1) \div 2 = 2 \div 2 = 1$, or, in fraction form, $\frac{1}{2} + \frac{1}{2} = \frac{2}{2} = 1$. In the premodern era, whole-number concepts were set aside while the "new" concepts of fractional numbers were mastered.

11.2 DEFINITION, TERMINOLOGY, AND SYMBOLISM

Before presenting the techniques of teaching addition and subtraction, we shall discuss the basic ideas and symbolism that are employed in our methods of teaching fractional numbers.

Fundamental to all of our discussions will be this question: What, specifically, do we mean by "addition" and "subtraction"? We defined the concept of sum in terms of the number property associated with the union

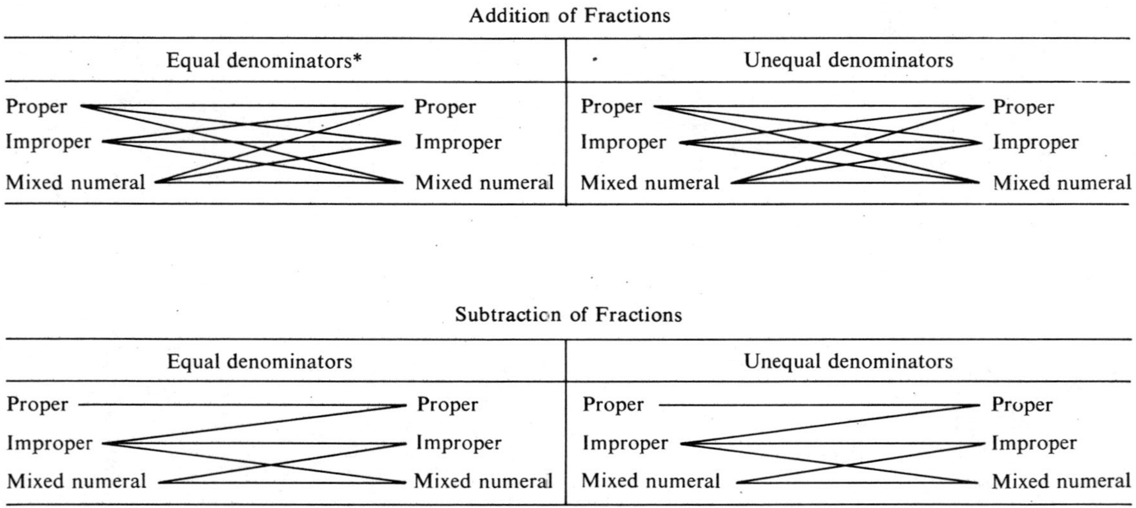

Addition of Fractions

Equal denominators*

Proper
Improper
Mixed numeral

Unequal denominators

Proper
Improper
Mixed numeral

Subtraction of Fractions

Equal denominators

Proper
Improper
Mixed numeral

Unequal denominators

Proper
Improper
Mixed numeral

* Denominators have been defined as the number named by the numeral b in $\frac{a}{b}$.

Figure 11.1

of two discrete sets. To maintain a smooth transition from the addition of whole numbers to the addition of fractional numbers, and to employ a mathematical model that will exhibit properties consistent with the quotient definition of fractional numbers, we shall view the sum of two fractional numbers as the number associated with the union of certain partitioned continuous or discrete sets. A working definition for the sum of two fractional numbers follows:

Let $\dfrac{a}{b}$ and $\dfrac{c}{d}$ be two fractional numbers represented on a number line by segments of measure AB and CD, respectively. The sum of $\dfrac{a}{b}$ and $\dfrac{c}{d}$ is the number associated with the measure of the union of $\overline{AB}$ and $\overline{CD}$.*

Figure 11.2 depicts how this working definition can be used to establish that $\frac{3}{2} + \frac{6}{2} = \frac{9}{2}$.

The utilization of a number line in the definition offers the advantage over most other models we might choose in that it is readily adapted for sums of fractional numbers less than or equal to 1, as well as for sums greater than 1. (For example, if one finds the sum of $\frac{2}{3}$ and $\frac{2}{3}$ by using regions of a rectangle, the tendency is to view the sum as being $1 + \frac{1}{3}$, rather than as $\frac{4}{3}$.) This idea is illustrated in Figure 11.3.

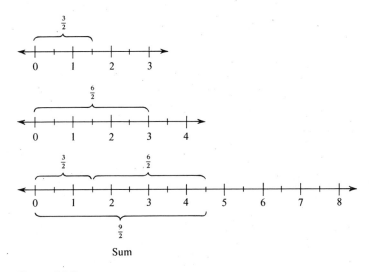

Sum

Figure 11.2

* The line segment pictured here can be named by the two endpoints A and B. We use these letters to refer to the line segment as $\overline{AB}$ (read line segment AB).

A————————————————————B

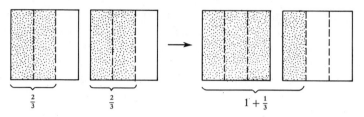

Figure 11.3

Note that the working definition requires us to add only those fractional numbers that have the same divisor named in the fraction form. This is an artificial requirement simplifying our determining the number associated with the union of segments *AB* and *CD*. Our definition is suitable whether or not the divisors named are the same, provided we have some way of determining the number property of the union of *AB* and *CD*. It would be possible to omit this requirement if we were always permitted the luxury of working with a number line. For example, we could measure off $\frac{1}{2}$ and $\frac{1}{4}$ on a number line and determine the number property of the line segment formed by the union by measuring out segments of this length enough times to measure *n* units. Figure 11.4 illustrates this idea.

In the interest of having the child develop the most efficient algorithm for the addition and subtraction of fractional numbers, we shall require that the divisors named in the fractions name the same number. In those cases in which this requirement is not met, we shall teach the child how to select for substitution equivalent names for the same fractional number.

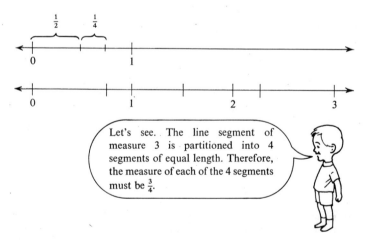

Figure 11.4

The *sum* of two fractional numbers $\frac{a}{b}$ and $\frac{c}{b}$ is defined as $\frac{a+c}{b}$.

The *difference* of two fractional numbers $\frac{a}{b}$ and $\frac{c}{b}$, where $\frac{a}{b} \neq \frac{c}{b}$, is defined as $\frac{e}{b}$

if and only if $\frac{a}{b} = \frac{c}{b} + \frac{e}{b}$.

Although the difference of two fractional numbers is defined in this manner, and the child will use this definition to check his work, subtraction will be interpreted concretely in the same manner as it was for the set of whole numbers. This will involve relating subtraction to set separation, set comparison, and excluded subset (missing addend) of a union of joining of sets.

There are several conventional notations for fractional numbers that you will need to teach your students. Figure 11.5 depicts some of the types of notation used in teaching addition and subtraction of fractional numbers.

$$(4 \div 2) + (3 \div 2) = \square \div \triangle$$

$$\frac{4}{2} + \frac{3}{2} = \frac{\square}{\triangle} \rightarrow \quad \frac{4}{2} \rightarrow \quad 2 \rightarrow \quad 2$$
$$\underline{+\frac{3}{2}} \quad \underline{+1\frac{1}{2}} \quad \underline{+1+\frac{1}{2}}$$

$$(4 \div 2) - (3 \div 2) = \square \div \triangle$$

$$\frac{4}{2} - \frac{3}{2} = \frac{\square}{\triangle} \rightarrow \quad \frac{4}{2} \rightarrow \quad 2 \rightarrow \quad 2$$
$$\underline{-\frac{3}{2}} \quad \underline{-1\frac{1}{2}} \quad \underline{-(1+\frac{1}{2})}$$

$$\frac{3}{2} + \frac{\square}{\triangle} = \frac{4}{2} \rightarrow \quad \frac{3}{2} \rightarrow \quad 1\frac{1}{2} \rightarrow \quad 1+\frac{1}{2}$$
$$\underline{+\frac{\square}{\triangle}} \quad \underline{+\frac{\square}{\triangle}} \quad \underline{+\frac{\square}{\triangle}}$$
$$\frac{4}{2} \qquad 2 \qquad 2$$

Figure 11.5

The notation "$\frac{3}{4} + \frac{5}{4} = \frac{8}{4}$" can be read in many ways, a few of which follow:

Three-fourths and five-fourths is eight-fourths.
Three-fourths and five-fourths equals eight-fourths.
The sum of three-fourths and five-fourths is eight-fourths.
The sum of three-fourths and five-fourths equals eight-fourths.
Five-fourths added to three-fourths is eight-fourths.

Similarly, the notation "$\frac{6}{7} - \frac{2}{7} = \frac{4}{7}$" can be read in many ways, a few of which follow:

Two-sevenths subtracted from six-sevenths is four-sevenths.
Two-sevenths subtracted from six-sevenths equals four-sevenths.
Six-sevenths less two-sevenths is four-sevenths.

Six-sevenths less two-sevenths equals four-sevenths.
Six-sevenths subtract two-sevenths is four-sevenths.
Six-sevenths subtract two-sevenths equals four-sevenths.

The terminology used with fraction addition and subtraction sentences and notations is identical to that used for whole-number addition and subtraction sentences. This terminology is depicted in Figure 11.6.

Addend	Addend	Sum			
$\frac{3}{4}$ $+$	$\frac{6}{4}$ $=$	$\frac{9}{4}$		$\frac{3}{4}$	Addend
				$+\frac{6}{4}$	Addend
				$\frac{9}{4}$	Sum

Minuend	Subtrahend	Difference			
$\frac{5}{4}$ $-$	$\frac{3}{4}$ $=$	$\frac{2}{4}$	Sum	$\frac{5}{4}$	Minuend
Sum	Known addend	Missing addend	Known addend	$-\frac{3}{4}$	Subtrahend
			Missing addend	$\frac{2}{4}$	Difference

Known addend	Unknown addend	Sum
$\frac{3}{4}$ $+$	$\boxed{\frac{2}{4}}$ $=$	$\frac{5}{4}$

Figure 11.6

11.3   TEACHING THE STRUCTURAL PROPERTIES OF ADDITION

Before investigating methods of teaching addition and subtraction of fractional numbers, we shall investigate the techniques of presenting the structural properties of addition and subtraction. When these properties are mentioned later, in methods of teaching addition and subtraction to children, it will be understood that they were introduced to the children prior to that point.

One of the first properties that a child discovers is the identity element for addition. In presenting properties for the fractional numbers, you should motivate him to search for those properties that he discovered for the set of whole numbers and that are also properties of the set of fractional numbers. Statements such as the following will serve to motivate him to look for a number: "We have seen that zero is the identity element for the set of whole numbers. Let's see if the fractional numbers have an identity element." Structuring problems to help the child discover the commutative and associative properties of addition for fractional numbers requires certain subtleties not employed for the same whole-number properties. Notice in Figure 11.7 that the paired problems utilize equivalent names, which adds the distraction of equivalence to the search for commutativity and associativity.

(1a) $\frac{2}{4} + \frac{3}{2} = \square$ (2a) $(\frac{2}{3} + \frac{1}{6}) + \frac{5}{12} = \square$

(1b) $\frac{6}{4} + \frac{2}{4} = \square$ (2b) $\frac{4}{6} + (\frac{2}{12} + \frac{5}{12}) = \square$

Figure 11.7

Whereas the commutative property for the set of whole numbers has a mathematical use* and a functional use as well, the commutative and associative properties for the set of fractional numbers have mainly a mathematical use. For example, knowledge of the commutative property for addition for the set of whole numbers decreases the number of explorations the child needs to make in order to discover the basic addition facts. Since there are no basic fractional facts the child must memorize, the commutative property does not serve to minimize effort when he is mastering addition on the set of fractional numbers.

The techniques for teaching the child to discover these mathematical patterns are similar to those used for discovering the same patterns for the set of whole numbers. The first stage consists of a structured learning experience where the child is given pairs of problems employing these patterns. After he has discovered the pattern, its reinforcement is established by problems requiring a single solution. To focus his mind on the general nature of the pattern he has discovered, problems requiring multiple solutions are introduced next. At this stage, a number of the many solutions for each problem should be elicited. The final stage in this learning process consists of giving the child the patterns

$$\frac{a}{b} + \frac{c}{d} = \frac{c}{d} + \frac{a}{b}$$

and

$$\left(\frac{a}{b} + \frac{c}{d}\right) + \frac{e}{f} = \frac{a}{b} + \left(\frac{c}{d} + \frac{e}{f}\right)$$

and asking him to create true mathematical sentences using these patterns.

---

* Structural properties have an inherent mathematical use in providing a means to compare and contrast various number systems.

Problems leading to discovery	(1a) $\frac{3}{4} + \frac{4}{7} = \frac{\triangle}{\square}$ (1b) $\frac{4}{7} + \frac{21}{28} = \frac{\triangle}{\square}$	(1a) $(\frac{1}{2} + \frac{1}{3}) + \frac{2}{5} = \frac{\triangle}{\square}$ (1b) $\frac{2}{4} + (\frac{2}{6} + \frac{4}{10}) = \frac{\triangle}{\square}$
Problems requiring single solutions	$\frac{3}{4} + \frac{4}{5} = \frac{\triangle}{\square} + \frac{21}{28}$	$(\frac{1}{2} + \frac{1}{3}) + \frac{\triangle}{\square} = \frac{1}{2} + (\frac{1}{3} + \frac{2}{9})$
Problems requiring multiple solutions	$\frac{\triangle}{\square} + \frac{3}{8} = \frac{6}{16} + \frac{\triangle}{\square}$	$(\frac{1}{5} + \frac{3}{4}) + \frac{\triangle}{\square} = \frac{2}{10} + (\frac{3}{4} + \frac{\triangle}{\square})$

Figure 11.8

In Figure 11.8, we have representative problems from the first three stages of teaching the commutative and associative properties for addition of fractional numbers.

EXERCISES (1)

1. Using the working definition for sum and the number line as a mathematical model, illustrate $\frac{2}{3} + \frac{3}{3} = \frac{7}{3}$.
2. Using a hexagon as a model, illustrate $\frac{1}{6} + \frac{2}{6} = \frac{3}{6}$.
3. Based on the definition of difference, name an addition sentence that would be equivalent to $\frac{7}{3} - \frac{4}{3} = \frac{\square}{\triangle}$.
4. Write four ways that each of the following mathematical sentences can be read:
   a. $\frac{2}{5} + \frac{5}{5} = \frac{7}{5}$ b. $\frac{7}{8} - \frac{3}{8} = \frac{4}{8}$
5. Identify the addends and sum in the following:
   a. $\frac{3}{4} + \frac{5}{4} = \frac{8}{4}$ b. $\begin{array}{r} \frac{3}{4} \\ +\frac{5}{4} \\ \hline \frac{8}{4} \end{array}$
6. Identify the minuend, subtrahend, difference, known addend, missing addend, and sum for each of the following, if applicable:
   a. $\frac{3}{4} + \frac{1}{4} = \frac{4}{4}$ b. $\frac{4}{4} - \frac{1}{4} = \frac{3}{4}$
7. Make up sample problems for each of the first three stages for teaching the commutative property for addition on the set of fractional numbers.
8. Make up sample problems for each of the first three stages for teaching the associative property for addition on the set of fractional numbers.

11.4 TEACHING THE STRUCTURAL PROPERTIES OF SUBTRACTION

One of the first structural properties for fractional numbers that a child encounters is the right identity element. Leading him to generalize the concept that $\frac{a}{b} - \frac{0}{f} = \frac{a}{b}$ is accomplished in the straightforward manner of presenting him with problems such as $\frac{3}{4} - \frac{0}{5} =$ ___ and $\frac{6}{7} - \frac{0}{7} =$ ___. It takes only a few problems of this type for the child to realize the generalization.

The compensation property for subtraction of fractional numbers, although not representing a highly functional property, does represent a mathematically interesting property that you may want to have your students investigate. Problems typically encountered at each stage in the learning process are depicted in Figure 11.9.

Problems leading to discovery	$\begin{cases} \text{(1a)}\ (\frac{3}{4} + \frac{2}{7}) - (\frac{1}{4} + \frac{2}{7}) = \frac{\triangle}{\square} \\ \text{(1b)}\ \frac{3}{4} - \frac{1}{4} = \frac{\triangle}{\square} \\ \text{(2a)}\ (\frac{9}{7} - \frac{2}{3}) - (\frac{6}{7} - \frac{2}{3}) = \frac{\triangle}{\square} \\ \text{(2b)}\ \frac{9}{7} - \frac{6}{7} = \frac{\triangle}{\square} \end{cases}$
Problems requiring single solutions	$\begin{cases} \frac{3}{4} - \frac{1}{2} = (\frac{3}{4} + \frac{\triangle}{\square}) - (\frac{1}{2} + \frac{3}{5}) \\ \frac{16}{7} - \frac{8}{7} = (\frac{16}{7} - \frac{3}{6}) - (\frac{8}{7} - \frac{\triangle}{\square}) \end{cases}$
Problems requiring multiple solutions	$\begin{cases} \frac{6}{8} - \frac{3}{8} = (\frac{6}{8} + \frac{\triangle}{\square}) - (\frac{3}{8} + \frac{\triangle}{\square}) \\ \frac{13}{4} - \frac{7}{4} = (\frac{13}{4} - \frac{\triangle}{\square}) - (\frac{7}{4} - \frac{\triangle}{\square}) \end{cases}$

Figure 11.9

The final stage in presenting this concept is to have the student make up mathematical sentences using both of these patterns:

$$\frac{a}{b} - \frac{c}{d} = \left(\frac{a}{b} + \frac{e}{f}\right) - \left(\frac{c}{d} + \frac{e}{f}\right),$$

and

$$\frac{a}{b} - \frac{c}{d} = \left(\frac{a}{b} - \frac{e}{f}\right) - \left(\frac{c}{d} - \frac{e}{f}\right).$$

11.5 READINESS ACTIVITIES FOR ADDITION AND SUBTRACTION OF FRACTIONAL NUMBERS

There are many activities that can be conducted to promote a readiness for addition and subtraction of fractional numbers. Among the most useful of these activities is that of counting by fractional numbers. For example, you might start around the room having each successive child count by two-thirds. The first child says $\frac{2}{3}$, the second $\frac{4}{3}$, the third $\frac{6}{3}$, and so on. Stop the counting at some point (e.g., $\frac{12}{3}$) and say 2 more thirds would be what? (The next child would respond $\frac{14}{3}$.) Repeat this procedure with several stopping points.

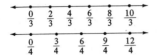

Figure 11.10

When using this type of counting activity as a readiness for addition of fractional numbers, choose numerators that are easily counted. For example, twos, threes, fours, fives, nines, tens, and multiples of tens.

Readiness for subtraction also can be developed by counting backward. For example, $\frac{20}{5}$, $\frac{18}{5}$, $\frac{16}{5}$, less 2 more fifths would be what?

This counting activity can be accompanied by the concurrent use of a number-line model. Notice in Figure 11.10 number-line models that could be used for counting by two-thirds and three-fourths.

You may wish to examine some elementary mathematics series for other methods of developing readiness for addition and subtraction of fractional numbers.

11.6 TEACHING THE ADDITION ALGORITHM

In the early stages of teaching the addition algorithm, the child encounters only situations where the divisors named in the fraction sentence are the same. His first experiences consist of manipulating sets and translating the results of this manipulation into the sum. Figure 11.11 presents two types of manipulation that aid the child in finding a sum.

At some stage in the child's early experiences, you should tie together the concepts of the right distributive property of division over addition and the addition of fractional numbers. This should be accomplished after the child has had an opportunity to find sums by manipulating various types of sets.

A typical dialogue that might be used to tie these concepts together is as follows:

"When we were studying division of whole numbers, what other way did we have for finding the answer to $(16 \div 4) + (8 \div 4) = \square$?" (We could add the 16 and 8 and then divide by the 4.) "What are some other notations we could use to show $(16 \div 4) + (8 \div 4) = \square$?" $\left(\frac{16}{4} + \frac{8}{4} = \square.\right)$

"How could we rewrite $(16 + 8) \div 4 = \square$ in a fraction form?"

$$\left(\frac{16 + 8}{4} = \square.\right)$$

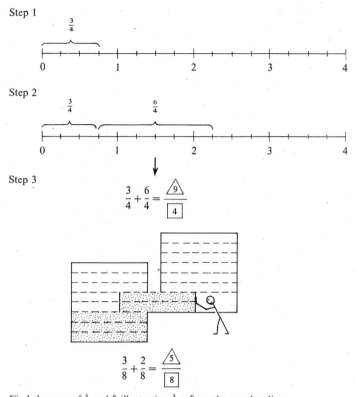

Find the sum of $\frac{3}{4}$ and $\frac{6}{4}$ illustrating $\frac{3}{4} + \frac{6}{4}$ on the number line:

Figure 11.11

"Let's see if we can use this method to find our sum when we are adding fractional numbers. What have we found is the sum of $\frac{2}{4}$ and $\frac{1}{4}$?" ($\frac{3}{4}$. The assumption is that the students have discovered this sum by working with manipulative devices.) "We can write this as $\frac{2}{4} + \frac{1}{4} = \frac{3}{4}$. How would we write our problem if we were going to solve it by first finding a sum and then dividing?"

$$\left(\frac{2+1}{4} = \square. \right)$$

"Will we get the same answer?" (Yes.) "Let's work a series of problems by rewriting them and working them by finding the sum first and then dividing. This, you remember, is an alternate way for solving $(a \div c) + (b \div c) = \square$."

Step 1

The child marks off the length $\frac{1}{2}$ on the edge of a strip of paper, using a halves number-line segment as a guide.

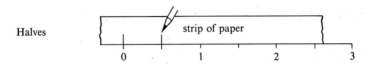

Step 2

He then places the strip of paper on a thirds number-line segment, placing the mark designating the right end of the $\frac{1}{2}$ length he has just made above the zero mark on the thirds scale. He then marks off a segment $\frac{4}{3}$ in length.

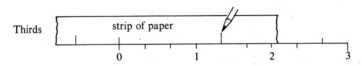

Step 3

The child now looks for the next number-line segment below halves and thirds that has both halves and thirds marked off on it. He then places the left mark over the zero mark and reads off the number corresponding to the right mark on his strip of paper.

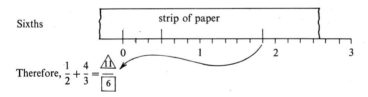

Therefore, $\frac{1}{2} + \frac{4}{3} = \frac{\triangle}{\boxed{6}}$

Figure 11.12

11.7 DEVELOPING A COMMON DENOMINATOR INTUITIVELY USING MODELS

Teaching children to add and subtract fractional numbers with common denominators are simple tasks when compared to teaching children to add fractional numbers with unlike denominators, which is probably one of the most complex mathematics skills that must be taught at the elementary school level.

The first procedure discussed is designed to ease the child into developing an understanding of how common denominators originate. It will not substitute for the "why" and "how" least common denominators are derived. Different methods of developing least common denominators will be presented in the next section.

The following method is one way of giving a child an intuitive "feel" for common denominators:

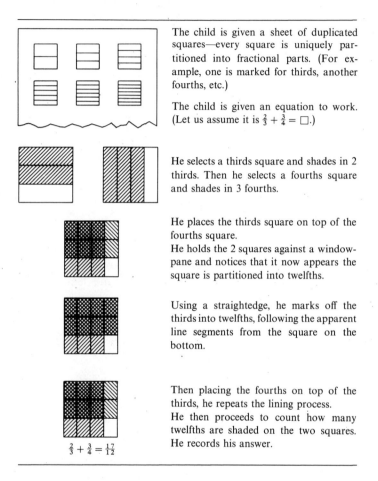

The child is given a sheet of duplicated squares—every square is uniquely partitioned into fractional parts. (For example, one is marked for thirds, another fourths, etc.)

The child is given an equation to work. (Let us assume it is $\frac{2}{3} + \frac{3}{4} = \square$.)

He selects a thirds square and shades in 2 thirds. Then he selects a fourths square and shades in 3 fourths.

He places the thirds square on top of the fourths square.
He holds the 2 squares against a window-pane and notices that it now appears the square is partitioned into twelfths.

Using a straightedge, he marks off the thirds into twelfths, following the apparent line segments from the square on the bottom.

Then placing the fourths on top of the thirds, he repeats the lining process.
He then proceeds to count how many twelfths are shaded on the two squares. He records his answer.

$$\frac{2}{3} + \frac{3}{4} = \frac{17}{12}$$

By repeating similar activities a child will discover that a common denominator can be derived by using the product of the denominators. He will also discover the effect of the new denominator on the numerator. Some teachers prefer to add a part to the equations where the newly partitioned squares are suggested. For example,

$$\frac{2}{3} + \frac{3}{4} = \frac{8}{12} + \frac{9}{12} = \frac{17}{12}$$

A multinumber-line-segment chart and a partitioned fractional-number-bar chart are other devices that can be used to build readiness for finding a least common denominator.

11.8 DIVISIBILITY METHOD OF FINDING LEAST COMMON DENOMINATOR

One of the most widely used methods of finding the least common denominator, and probably the easiest to use when small denominators are involved, is a method that uses the concept of divisibility. Note the reasoning involved in the following example:

$\frac{2}{3} + \frac{3}{4} = \square$ Thought: What is the smallest number that can be divided by both a 3 and a 4 and still give a zero remainder? Answer: 12.

$\frac{2}{3} + \frac{3}{4} = \square$ Thought: I will have to multiply the $\frac{2}{3}$ by $\frac{4}{4}$ (a name for 1) in order to get a denominator of 12. I will have to multiply the $\frac{3}{4}$ by $\frac{3}{3}$ (a name for 1) to get a denominator of 12.

11.9 FACTOR METHOD OF FINDING LEAST COMMON DENOMINATOR

Although the factor method is not an easy method and requires a high factoring skill level on the part of the child, it is a basic method for finding least common denominators which has direct application in the child's later study of algebra. The development of prime factorization is presented in Chapter 15. The following simple example should suffice here:

$\frac{1}{6} + \frac{3}{4}$ Thought: 6 factors into 2 and 3. 4 factors into 2 and 2.

$\dfrac{1}{2 \times 3} + \dfrac{3}{2 \times 2}$ Thought: I need one more 2 to go with the 2 and 3 so it will have as many twos as the denominator on the right. I need a 3 to go with the 2 and 2 so this denominator will have as many threes as the denominator on the left.

$(\frac{1}{6} \times \frac{2}{2}) + (\frac{3}{4} \times \frac{3}{3}) = \frac{2}{12} + \frac{9}{12} = \frac{11}{12}$ I will choose the following names for 1 to get rid of the deficient denominators: $\frac{2}{2}$ and $\frac{3}{3}$.

11.10 GREATEST COMMON FACTOR METHOD OF FINDING LEAST COMMON DENOMINATOR

The greatest common factor method of finding the least common denominator is similar to the prime factorization method of the previous section. The chief difference is the degree to which a number is factored. In prime factorization several factors can be derived. In the greatest common

factor method only two factors are derived. Let us examine how this method
is developed:

$\frac{1}{12} + \frac{5}{18}$	Thought: The greatest common factor of 12 and 18 is 6.
$\dfrac{1}{2 \times 6} + \dfrac{5}{3 \times 6}$	Thought: I need a factor of 3 to go with the 2 and 6. I need a factor of 2 to go with the 3 and 6. Therefore, I will choose $\frac{3}{3}$ and $\frac{2}{2}$, respectively.
$\dfrac{1 \times 3}{2 \times 6 \times 3} + \dfrac{5 \times 2}{3 \times 6 \times 2}$	

After a child develops competence in finding the sum of two fractional
numbers, it is the teacher's responsibility to help him refine his answers
so that the forms he chooses for those answers will suit the use he
plans for the answers. Frequently, the simplest form of the fraction is
desirable. For example, if the sum $\frac{3}{12}$ is obtained, and if we are interested
in using $\frac{3}{12}$ of a pound of butter in a recipe, the $\frac{1}{4}$ form would be more
convenient, because butter can be obtained in quarter-pound sticks.
However, if we are to measure something, and the $\frac{3}{12}$ refers to part of a
foot, the $\frac{3}{12}$ form might be the best equivalent name for the answer.

Sometimes a mixed-numeral name is preferable to a fraction name. For
example, suppose we have found, using addition, that we need $\frac{9}{2}$ yards
of material to make a coat. When we get ready to order this, we will
specify $4\frac{1}{2}$ yards. However, if we are told that we are going to be paid
1 dollar for each quarter-bushel of berries we pick, knowing that we
picked $\frac{19}{4}$ bushels is more useful to us than knowing that we picked $4\frac{3}{4}$
bushels of berries.

11.11 MIXED NUMERALS AND ADDITION

From the very beginning of a child's work with mixed numerals, he should
be made aware of the fact that they name fractional numbers and that a
number expressed as a mixed numeral can also be expressed as a fraction.
Before he learns to add fractional numbers using only the mixed-numeral
form, the teacher should make him aware of the fact that he already
knows how to find the sum using the fraction form. For example, he would
be able to find the sum of $2\frac{1}{4}$ and $3\frac{1}{7}$ as follows:

$$2\frac{1}{4} + 3\frac{1}{7} = \frac{9}{4} + \frac{22}{7} = \frac{63}{28} + \frac{88}{28} = \frac{151}{28} = 5\frac{11}{28}$$

He can now refine his technique for finding the sum by remembering
that $2\frac{1}{4} = 2 + \frac{1}{4}$ and $3\frac{1}{7} = 3 + \frac{1}{7}$. This is illustrated in the following sequence
of steps:

$(2 + \frac{1}{4}) + (3 + \frac{1}{7})$

      Repeated use of associative and commutative properties

$(2 + 3) + (\frac{1}{4} + \frac{1}{7})$

      Addition of whole numbers

$5 + (\frac{7}{28} + \frac{4}{28})$

      Addition of fractional numbers

$5 + \frac{11}{28}$

      Definition of mixed numeral

$5\frac{11}{28}$

Similarly, the vertical form for the algorithm can be introduced using this expanded form of the mixed numeral. This sequencing is illustrated in Figure 11.13.

$$\begin{array}{ccc} 3\frac{1}{4} & 3 + \frac{1}{4} & 3 + \frac{3}{12} \\ +2\frac{1}{3} & +2 + \frac{1}{3} & +2 + \frac{4}{12} \\ \hline & & 5 + \frac{7}{12} = 5\frac{7}{12} \end{array}$$

Figure 11.13

This work with the expanded form builds readiness for later work with addition using decimal notation.

11.12 TEACHING SUBTRACTION OF FRACTIONAL NUMBERS

Teaching subtraction on the set of fractional numbers is accomplished by techniques identical to those encountered when teaching addition. The child is first taught to find differences of fractional numbers involving fractions with the same divisor named in the minuend and subtrahend. This early exploration is accomplished using manipulative devices similar to those employed for addition of fractional numbers. In Figure 11.14, we see two types of manipulations that aid the child in finding a difference.

The subtraction algorithm for fractional numbers can be introduced by the right distributive property of division over subtraction. The development of this algorithm will be left for the exercises.

Before teaching the child how to utilize the least-common-denominator method to find the difference of two fractional numbers, you should show him how to obtain the difference by working with devices such as the multinumber-line segment. Figure 11.15 shows how a child can use a multinumber-line segment to find the difference of $\frac{4}{3}$ and $\frac{1}{2}$.

Find the difference of $\frac{6}{2} - \frac{1}{2}$:

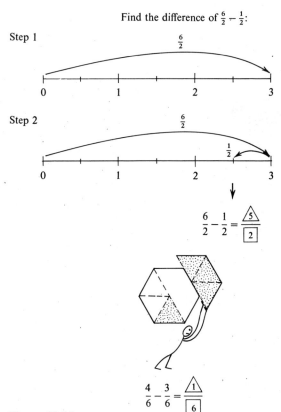

$$\frac{6}{2} - \frac{1}{2} = \frac{\boxed{5}}{\boxed{2}}$$

$$\frac{4}{6} - \frac{3}{6} = \frac{\boxed{1}}{\boxed{6}}$$

Figure 11.14

Step 1

The child marks off the length $\frac{4}{3}$ on the edge of a strip of paper, using a thirds number-line segment as a guide.

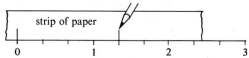

Step 2

He then places the strip of paper on a halves number-line segment, placing the right end of the $\frac{4}{3}$ length he has just made directly above the $\frac{1}{2}$ mark on the halves scale. He then marks off the length $\frac{1}{2}$, as shown in the illustration.

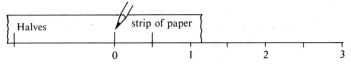

Step 3

The child now looks for the next number-line segment below halves and thirds that has both halves and thirds marked off on it. He then places the left mark over the zero mark and reads off the number corresponding to the middle mark on his strip of paper.

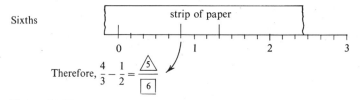

Sixths

Therefore, $\dfrac{4}{3} - \dfrac{1}{2} = \dfrac{\boxed{5}}{\boxed{6}}$

Figure 11.15

After the child develops competence in finding the difference of two fractional numbers using the multinumber-line segment, he should be taught the mathematical technique for obtaining the difference by first finding the least common denominator. This is accomplished by having him rewrite the original problem in the form used when he is finding a solution by using the number-line segment. After the subtraction expression is rewritten in a form using the least common denominator obtained from the multi-number-line segments, the expression should be written in the completely factored form. The child will be able to focus on the pattern that unfolds if this activity is conducted on a chart as in Figure 11.16.

	Form obtained from multinumber line	Completely factored form
$\frac{3}{5} - \frac{1}{3}$	$\frac{9}{15} - \frac{5}{15}$	$\frac{3 \times 3}{5 \times 3} - \frac{1 \times 5}{3 \times 5}$
$\frac{7}{4} - \frac{3}{2}$	$\frac{7}{4} - \frac{6}{4}$	$\frac{7}{4} - \frac{3 \times 2}{2 \times 2}$

Figure 11.16

Ask the children to discover the pattern that tells how to find two fractions with the same divisor named. Have them try more examples using their newly found pattern. Have them check their answers by using the multinumber-line segments. They should be taught to refine their answers in the same way that they did when learning addition of fractional numbers.

11.13 MIXED NUMERALS AND SUBTRACTION

Teaching subtraction where the numbers involved are expressed as mixed numerals should be viewed as a preparation for teaching the child decimal notation. Expanded notation should be stressed, so that he can see the close relationship between what he has already learned and this new skill.

$$
\begin{array}{cccc}
23\frac{1}{3} & 20 + 3 + \frac{1}{3} & 10 + 12 + \frac{4}{3} & 10 + 12 + \frac{20}{15} \\
- 7\frac{4}{5} \rightarrow & - \quad (7 + \frac{4}{5}) \rightarrow & - \quad (7 + \frac{4}{5}) \rightarrow & - \quad (7 + \frac{12}{15}) \\
\hline
& & & 10 + 5 + \frac{8}{15} \\
& & & \downarrow \\
& & & 15\frac{8}{15}
\end{array}
$$

Figure 11.17

The vertical notation lends itself to subtraction where the numbers involved are expressed as mixed numerals. The sequencing used in teaching this concept is illustrated in Figure 11.17.

EXERCISES (2)

1. Make up sample problems for each of the first three stages in teaching the compensation property for subtraction.
2. Illustrate each of the following:
   a. $\frac{3}{5} + \frac{6}{5} = \frac{9}{5}$ on a number line
   b. $\frac{1}{4} + \frac{2}{4} = \frac{3}{4}$ using square regions
   c. $\frac{6}{7} - \frac{3}{7} = \frac{3}{7}$ using a number line
3. For each of the following, write a corresponding sentence using fraction notation:
   a. $(6 \div 2) + (8 \div 2) = (6 + 8) \div 2$
   b. $(12 \div 5) + (4 \div 5) = (12 + 4) \div 5$
   c. $(4 \div 7) - (2 \div 7) = (4 - 2) \div 7$
   d. $(30 \div 6) - (12 \div 6) = (30 - 12) \div 6$
4. Illustrate how a child could find the sum of $\frac{3}{4}$ and $\frac{2}{3}$ using a multinumber-line segment.
5. Make up methods similar to the methods in sections 11.8, 11.9, and 11.10 that could be used for finding the least common denominator mathematically.
6. Using vertical notation and the expanded form, give step-by-step sequencing showing how to add $3\frac{4}{7}$ and $2\frac{9}{11}$.
7. Illustrate $\frac{6}{5} - \frac{1}{2} = \frac{7}{10}$ using multinumber-line segments.

8. Using vertical notation and the expanded form, give a step-by-step sequence showing how to subtract $2\frac{9}{11}$ from $3\frac{4}{7}$.

9. Find a circumstance when each of the following sums might be the most desirable form in which to leave an answer:

a. $\frac{1}{5} + \frac{4}{10} = \frac{6}{10}$ d. $\frac{3}{4} + \frac{3}{4} = \frac{6}{4}$

b. $\frac{1}{2} + \frac{1}{4} = \frac{75}{100}$ e. $\frac{3}{4} + \frac{3}{4} = 1\frac{1}{2}$

c. $\frac{4}{2} + \frac{6}{2} = \frac{10}{2}$

11.14   EXTENDING THE CHILD'S PROBLEM-SOLVING SKILL

Children need continuous experience in relating the study of numbers to their environment. The study of numbers in the absence of its relationship to the everyday world is not satisfactory. By the time the child begins to work with problems involving fractional numbers, he has matured to the point where he is ready to learn or discover the more subtle aspects of problem solving, including the following:

1. How problems arise in his environment
   a. In the experimental setting
   b. In the consumer setting
   c. In the social setting in a more complex type of experience than has been discussed previously
2. How problem solving often involves identifying not only the problem but also those aspects of the data that will lead to a reasonable solution
3. How numerical data are collected, organized, and reported

Let us examine how the first two of these have implications for the teaching of problem solving by relating each to the study of problems involving fractional numbers. The third aspect listed will be studied when we explore the techniques of teaching graphing.

What are some elementary science experiences that will motivate problem solving? Almost any scientific experiment will offer many opportunities for relating problem solving to mathematical models. For example, concepts relative to fractional numbers can be associated with data collected about plant growth, rainfall, temperature, animal growth, and so on. Concepts about operations on fractional numbers can be associated with such experimental areas as the biological, physical, and earth sciences.

For example, Flat A planted with beans receives $\frac{1}{4}$ of an ounce of superphosphate each week for 5 weeks. Flat B planted in the same way receives $\frac{1}{8}$ of an ounce of superphosphate each week for 5 weeks. Flat A yields $6\frac{1}{2}$ ounces of beans; Flat B yields $6\frac{1}{3}$ ounces of beans. Problems such as the following could be posted from this situation (although not all could be solved with the given data):

How much more superphosphate was used in Flat A than Flat B? How much more crop was grown in Flat A than Flat B?

Can we decide whether it would be worthwhile for a farmer with similar soil to decrease his administration of phosphate from the $\frac{1}{4}$ per flat to the $\frac{1}{8}$ per flat rate?

Students should be given many opportunities to collect data, to devise problems using these data, and then to solve their problems. To nurture their ability to arrive at creative solutions, encourage them to search for several ways in which a given problem can be solved. For example, consider the following problem:

Mary needs 7 strips of paper. Each strip must be $2\frac{1}{2}$ inches in length and $\frac{1}{2}$ inch wide. What would be the minimum length of a rectangular piece of paper from which Mary could cut her strips for the following cases:

1. If the paper she cuts can be of any width or length?
2. If the paper she uses is $\frac{1}{2}$-inch wide?

Consider the following mathematical models, which could lead to solutions.

Length $2\frac{1}{2}''$

1 strip $\frac{1}{2}''$ wide	7 strips $17\frac{1}{2}'' \times \frac{1}{2}''$
2 strips $1''$ wide	4 strips $10'' \times 1''$
3 strips $1\frac{1}{2}''$ wide	3 strips $7\frac{1}{2}'' \times 1\frac{1}{2}''$
4 strips $2''$ wide	2 strips $5'' \times 2''$
5 strips $2\frac{1}{2}''$ wide	2 strips $5'' \times 2\frac{1}{2}''$
6 strips $3\frac{1}{2}''$ wide	2 strips $5'' \times 3''$
7 strips $3\frac{1}{2}''$ wide	1 strip $2\frac{1}{2}'' \times 3\frac{1}{2}''$

Paper $\frac{1}{2}$ inch wide

$7 \times 2\frac{1}{2} = \square$
$2\frac{1}{2} + 2\frac{1}{2} + 2\frac{1}{2} + 2\frac{1}{2} + 2\frac{1}{2} + 2\frac{1}{2} + 2\frac{1}{2} = \square$
$14 + (7 \times \frac{1}{2}) = \square$
$(7 \times 2) + (7 \times \frac{1}{2}) = \square$
$7 \times \frac{5}{2} = \square$
$(8 \times 2\frac{1}{2}) - 2\frac{1}{2} = \square$
$5 + 5 + 5 + 2\frac{1}{2} = \square$
Etc.

This can be visualized via the geometric models in Figure 11.18.

The child should be encouraged to examine his problem solving in terms of answering two questions: (1) Which way that I solved this problem was the most efficient? and (2) Can I describe other types of problems that could be solved in a similar manner?

Although the problems arising from the technical side of our society represent an important area of concern, of equal concern should be the problems arising from consumer experiences. It is important that the child have experiences that will enable him to answer such questions as:

1. Which of two items is the "best buy" in terms of a per-item cost?
2. To what extent do we equate durability, quality, and design in determining the best buy?
3. How does volume buying affect the per-unit cost of an item?

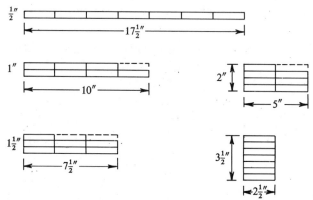

Figure 11.18

You may find one or more of the following activities useful in finding the answers to such questions:

1. Consumer surveys
   a. Item preference
   b. Why the item is preferred
   c. Which preferences have an emotional origin rather than a qualitative or quantitative origin
   (This sort of experience serves as a foundation on which a knowledge of the role of statistics in our society can be built.)
2. Quality-control experiments
   a. Durability (wearing, fading, tearing, etc.)
   b. Rate of consumption
   c. Quality comparison
   d. Sampling
   (This will serve as a foundation for learning about the role mathematics plays in the quality of goods that are on the market.)
3. Inventory of the hidden costs relative to the purchase of an item
   a. Transportation
   b. Handling
   c. Packaging
   d. Advertising
   e. Production
   (This will help build a foundation for such mathematical topics as linear and nonlinear algebra.)

BIBLIOGRAPHY

Adachi, M. "Addition of Unlike Fractions," *The Arithmetic Teacher* (March 1968), pp. 221–223.

Hannon, H. "Sets Aid in Adding Fractions," *The Arithmetic Teacher* (February, 1959), pp. 35–38.

Heddens, J. W. *Today's Mathematics* (Palo Alto, Calif.: Science Research Associates), 1971, pp. 232–255.

National Council of Teachers of Mathematics. *29th Yearbook* (Washington, D.C.), 1964, pp. 239–254.

Riedesel, C. A. *Guiding Discovery in Elementary School Mathematics* (New York: Appleton-Century-Crofts), 1967, pp. 213–227.

12

Teaching multiplication and division of fractional numbers

BEHAVIORAL OBJECTIVES
Student can . . .

Define multiplication of fractional numbers.

Illustrate an array model that would suggest a specific multiplication equation.

List four ways a multiplication equation can be read.

State four ways a division equation can be read.

Describe how children can be led to discover specific structural properties for multiplication.

Give a step-by-step analysis of a division algorithm.

Give a step-by-step analysis of a vertical form of the multiplication algorithm involving mixed numerals.

12.1 INTRODUCTION

Historically, multiplication of fractional numbers has not been in its proper sequence in the elementary school curriculum. Multiplication has been taught after the child learns addition and subtraction, in spite of the fact that he would find it a useful aid in defining equivalent names in terms of multiplication by 1. For example, $\frac{3}{7}$ and $\frac{6}{14}$ name the same number, because $\frac{2}{2}$ is a name for 1, and $\frac{3}{7} = \frac{3}{7} \times \frac{2}{2} = \frac{3 \times 2}{7 \times 2} = \frac{6}{14}$. Instead of using this logical approach to establishing equivalence, we must make use of the compensation property for division, which, although not mathematically incorrect, is considerably more awkward.

The teaching of the multiplication algorithm for whole numbers is dependent on the child's mastery of addition of whole numbers, whereas the teaching of the multiplication algorithm for fractional numbers is not dependent on addition of fractional numbers. Similarly, the successful mastery of the division algorithm for whole numbers is dependent upon one's ability to subtract whole numbers as well as to multiply. There exists no prerequisite of subtraction skills in order to learn the division algorithm for fractional numbers.

12.2 DEFINITION, TERMINOLOGY, AND SYMBOLISM

Before presenting the techniques of teaching multiplication and division of fractional numbers, we shall discuss the basic ideas and symbolism used in our methods of teaching these concepts.

We shall use the following definition, involving a mathematical model of a product, in our early discussions of product in an attempt to connect the semi-abstract to the abstract:

> The product of $\triangle$ and $\square$ is defined as the number property associated with a $\triangle$ by $\square$ rectangular array.

Figure 12.1 depicts how $\frac{5}{4} \times \frac{1}{2}$ can be shown using this array definition.

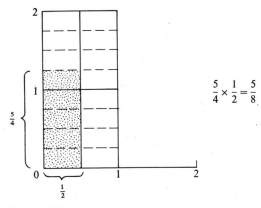

$$\frac{5}{4} \times \frac{1}{2} = \frac{5}{8}$$

Figure 12.1

Division is defined as the inverse of multiplication:

> The quotient of $\frac{a}{b}$ and $\frac{c}{d}$ is said to be $\frac{e}{f}$ if and only if $\frac{a}{b} = \frac{c}{d} \times \frac{e}{f}$.

For example, the quotient of $\frac{3}{4}$ and $\frac{7}{5}$ is $\frac{15}{28}$, because $\frac{3}{4} = \frac{7}{5} \times \frac{15}{28}$. Although this definition will be used to check the correctness of a quotient, the division algorithm for fractional numbers will be developed using the idea of division by 1, the compensation property for division, and the idea of a number's reciprocal (or multiplicative inverse). (We define $\frac{a}{b}$ as a *reciprocal* of $\frac{c}{d}$ if $\frac{a}{b} \times \frac{c}{d} = 1$; $\frac{c}{d}$ is said to be the *multiplicative inverse* of $\frac{a}{b}$ if $\frac{a}{b} \times \frac{c}{d} = 1$. For example, $\frac{3}{4} \times \frac{4}{3} = 1$.)

There are several notations and terminologies you must teach your students. Figure 12.2 depicts some representative types of notation that are used in teaching multiplication and division of fractional numbers. These are expressed in both fraction form and mixed-numeral form.

Multiplier	Multiplicand	Product
$\frac{3}{4}$ $\times$	$\frac{7}{8}$ $=$	$\frac{21}{32}$
Factor	Factor	Product

Multiplicand	$4\frac{3}{4}$	Factor
Multiplier	$\times 3\frac{1}{2}$	Factor

Dividend	Divisor	Quotient
$\frac{3}{4}$ $\div$	$\frac{7}{3}$ $=$	$\frac{9}{28}$
Product	Known factor	Unknown factor

$$\frac{3}{8}$$
$$2$$
$$\frac{9}{4}$$ } Partial products
$$12$$

Product $\qquad$ $16\frac{5}{8}$ Product

Figure 12.2

The sentence "$\frac{3}{2} \times \frac{7}{2} = \frac{21}{4}$" can be read in many ways. A few of them follow:

Three-halves times seven-halves is twenty-one-fourths.
Three-halves times seven-halves equals twenty-one-fourths.
The product of three-halves and seven-halves is twenty-one-fourths.
The product of three-halves and seven-halves equals twenty-one-fourths.
Seven-halves multiplied by three-halves is twenty-one-fourths.

Similarly, the sentence "$\frac{2}{3} \div \frac{1}{4} = \frac{8}{3}$" can be read in many ways:

Two-thirds divided by one-fourth equals eight-thirds.
Two-thirds divided by one-fourth is eight-thirds.
The quotient of two-thirds and one-fourth is eight-thirds.
The quotient of two-thirds and one-fourth equals eight-thirds.

12.3 TEACHING THE STRUCTURAL PROPERTIES OF MULTIPLICATION

Before investigating the methods of teaching multiplication or division on the set of fractional numbers, we shall investigate the properties that will play a central role in the presentation of these operations.

One of the most important properties for the child to become familiar with is the identity element for multiplication. It is important that he view the fraction of the form $\frac{\triangle}{\triangle}$ as a name for 1 and realize its implication as a factor. Several problems of the following type will lead the child toward discovering these relationships:

a. $\frac{3}{4} \times \frac{7}{7} = \frac{\triangle}{\square}$

b. $\frac{11}{11} \times \frac{6}{7} = \frac{\triangle}{\square}$

c. $\frac{6}{7} \times \frac{\triangle}{\square} = \frac{6}{7}$

d. $\frac{\triangle}{\square} \times \frac{9}{5} = \frac{9}{5}$

A new pattern, which was not present for whole numbers, appears for the first time as the reciprocal pattern or the idea of a multiplicative inverse. This property is extremely important in developing the division algorithm for fractional numbers. It takes only a few examples for the child to discover the pattern $\dfrac{a}{b} \times \dfrac{b}{a} = 1$. Some typical problems the teacher could give are as follows:

a. $\frac{3}{4} \times \frac{4}{3} = \frac{\triangle}{\square}$ c. $\frac{13}{3} \times \frac{3}{13} = \frac{\triangle}{\square}$

b. $\frac{2}{7} \times \frac{7}{2} = \frac{\triangle}{\square}$ d. $\frac{15}{6} \times \frac{\triangle}{\square} = 1$

Problems similar to that depicted by (d) are extremely important, because this skill is a prerequisite to the understanding of the division of fractional number algorithm. After the child has discovered the pattern, you should give him the pattern $\frac{\triangle}{\square} \times \frac{\square}{\triangle} = 1$, and ask him to make up true sentences using it.

Teaching the commutative and associative properties for multiplication of fractional numbers requires the same subtleties that were required for the corresponding properties for addition of fractional numbers. Notice in Figure 12.3 that the paired problems utilize equivalent names, adding the distraction of equivalence to the search for commutativity and associativity.

	Commutative multiplication	Associative multiplication
Problems leading to discovery	$\frac{3}{4} \times \frac{4}{7} = \square$ $\frac{8}{14} \times \frac{3}{4} = \square$	$\frac{3}{5} \times (\frac{4}{7} \times \frac{6}{9}) = \square$ $(\frac{6}{10} \times \frac{4}{7}) \times \frac{18}{27} = \square$
Problems requiring single solutions	$\frac{6}{7} \times \frac{2}{3} = \frac{4}{6} \times \frac{\triangle}{\square}$	$(\frac{3}{4} \times \frac{1}{3}) \times \frac{2}{4} = \frac{3}{4} \times (\frac{2}{6} \times \frac{\triangle}{\square})$
Problems requiring multiple solutions	$\frac{\triangle}{\square} \times \frac{3}{11} = \frac{3}{11} \times \frac{\triangle}{\square}$	$(\frac{3}{4} \times \frac{\triangle}{\square}) \times \frac{1}{6} = \frac{3}{4} \times (\frac{\triangle}{\square} \times \frac{1}{6})$

Figure 12.3

The last stage in teaching these properties consists of having the children make up true sentences using the commutative and associative patterns.

The distributive properties of multiplication over addition and multiplication over subtraction are taught by the same techniques used to teach the corresponding properties for the set of whole numbers. The stages for teaching these distributive properties are shown in Figure 12.4.

The last stage in teaching these properties consists of giving the students the following patterns and asking them to make up true sentences using them:

$$\frac{a}{b} \times \left(\frac{c}{d} + \frac{e}{f}\right) = \left(\frac{a}{b} \times \frac{c}{d}\right) + \left(\frac{a}{b} \times \frac{e}{f}\right) \quad \text{and} \quad \frac{a}{b} \times \left(\frac{c}{d} - \frac{e}{f}\right) = \left(\frac{a}{b} \times \frac{c}{d}\right) - \left(\frac{a}{b} \times \frac{e}{f}\right)$$

	Distributive property of multiplication over addition	Distributive property of multiplication over subtraction
Problems leading to discovery	$\frac{3}{4} \times (\frac{4}{7} + \frac{3}{5}) = \frac{\square}{\triangle}$ $(\frac{3}{4} \times \frac{4}{7}) + (\frac{3}{4} \times \frac{3}{5}) = \frac{\square}{\triangle}$	$(\frac{1}{3} \times \frac{6}{7}) - (\frac{1}{3} \times \frac{2}{5}) = \frac{\square}{\triangle}$ $\frac{1}{3} \times (\frac{6}{7} - \frac{2}{5}) = \frac{\square}{\triangle}$
Problems requiring single solutions	$\frac{2}{7} \times (\frac{8}{4} + \frac{6}{7})$ $= (\frac{\square}{\triangle} \times \frac{8}{4}) + (\frac{\square}{\triangle} \times \frac{6}{7})$	$\frac{3}{5} \times (\frac{3}{4} - \frac{4}{7})$ $= (\frac{3}{5} \times \frac{\triangle}{\square}) - (\frac{3}{5} \times \frac{4}{7})$
Problems requiring multiple solutions	$\frac{\triangle}{\square} \times (\frac{3}{10} + \frac{4}{5})$ $= (\frac{\triangle}{\square} \times \frac{3}{10}) + (\frac{\triangle}{\square} \times \frac{4}{5})$	$\frac{3}{2} \times (\frac{\triangle}{\square} - \frac{1}{7})$ $= (\frac{3}{2} \times \frac{\triangle}{\square}) - (\frac{3}{2} \times \frac{1}{7})$

Figure 12.4

EXERCISES (1)

1. Using the definition of multiplication of fractional numbers, and using Figure 12.1, construct an array that depicts $\frac{3}{4} \times \frac{5}{4}$.
2. Write the corresponding multiplication sentence for each of the following:
   a. $\frac{3}{8} \div \frac{7}{8} = \frac{\triangle}{\square}$ c. $\frac{2}{4} \div \frac{3}{4} = \frac{\triangle}{\square}$
   b. $\frac{9}{2} \div \frac{8}{3} = \frac{\triangle}{\square}$ d. $\frac{3}{4} \div \frac{4}{3} = \frac{\triangle}{\square}$
3. Write four ways that each of the following mathematical sentences can be read:
   a. $\frac{3}{7} \times \frac{9}{8} = \frac{\triangle}{\square}$ b. $\frac{3}{7} \div \frac{9}{8} = \frac{24}{63}$
4. Identify the factor, products, and partial products of each of the following, if applicable:
   a. $\frac{3}{5} \times \frac{8}{7} = \frac{24}{35}$ b. $\begin{array}{r} 3\frac{1}{2} \\ \times 3\frac{1}{2} \\ \hline \frac{1}{4} \\ \frac{3}{2} \\ 9\frac{3}{2} \\ \hline 12\frac{1}{4} \end{array}$
5. Identify the divisor, dividend, quotient, known factor, unknown factor, and product in the following, if applicable:
   a. $\frac{3}{7} \times \frac{2}{5} = \frac{6}{35}$ b. $\frac{16}{3} \div \frac{5}{2} = \frac{32}{15}$
6. Make up exercises that might lead a child to discover that each of the following may be a property which holds true for the set of fractional numbers:
   a. Commutative property for multiplication
   b. Associative property for multiplication
   c. Distributive property of multiplication over addition
   d. Distributive property of multiplication over subtraction
   e. Reciprocal property

12.4 TEACHING THE STRUCTURAL PROPERTIES OF DIVISION

The structural properties for division of fractional numbers play a crucial role in the development of the division algorithm for fractional numbers. The most important of these properties is the right identity for division. This is the first concept that should be taught when you are beginning division concepts.

The following dialogue illustrates how we can proceed from the concept of division of whole numbers to the concept of dividing a fractional number by 1:

"If we have 12 objects and partition them into 4 sets equal in number, how many will be in each set?" (3.)

"We could tell this with the sentence $12 \div 4 = 3$." (Write this mathematical sentence on the board.) "If we have 12 objects and distribute them to 1 set, how many will we have in that 1 set?" (12) "What would our mathematical sentence say in order to describe what we did?" ($12 \div 1 = 12$.)

"Suppose we have $\frac{3}{4}$ of someting and distributed it to 1 set. How much would be in that set?" (The $\frac{3}{4}$ of something that we had.). "What would be our mathematical sentence describing what we did?" ($\frac{3}{4} \div 1 = \frac{3}{4}$.)

Create other problems that have a divisor of 1, and have the children create the mathematical sentences. Use the definition of division to show that the quotient obtained is correct.

The compensation property for division of fractional numbers makes possible a variety of algorithms that can be developed for division of fractional numbers. In Figure 12.5, two different algorithms are depicted employing the compensation property for division.

$$\tfrac{8}{4} \div \tfrac{3}{7} = (\tfrac{8}{4} \times \tfrac{7}{3}) \div (\tfrac{3}{7} \times \tfrac{7}{3}) = \tfrac{56}{12} \div 1 = \tfrac{56}{12}$$

$$\tfrac{8}{4} \div \tfrac{3}{7} = (\tfrac{8}{4} \times \tfrac{7}{7}) \div (\tfrac{3}{7} \times \tfrac{4}{4}) = \tfrac{56}{28} \div \tfrac{12}{28} = (56 \times \tfrac{1}{28}) \div (12 \times \tfrac{1}{28}) = \tfrac{56}{12}$$

Figure 12.5

When the compensation property of division is used to teach the division algorithm, its employment will have to be taken on faith, since it is not possible to prove the reasonableness of the property without having first developed the division algorithm. This paradox leads some teachers to prefer the use of multiplicative identity rather than the compensation property as a part of the justification in the analysis. In Figure 12.6 we see this contrasting analysis.

Using compensation	Multiplicative identity
$\tfrac{1}{2} \div \tfrac{2}{3} = (\tfrac{1}{2} \times \tfrac{3}{2}) \div (\tfrac{2}{3} \times \tfrac{3}{2})$ $= \tfrac{3}{4} \div 1$ $= \tfrac{3}{4}$	$\dfrac{\tfrac{1}{2}}{\tfrac{2}{3}} \times \dfrac{\tfrac{3}{2}}{\tfrac{3}{2}} = \dfrac{\tfrac{3}{4}}{1} = \tfrac{3}{4}$

Figure 12.6

The distributive properties for division of fractional numbers are taught with the same stages as were those properties for whole numbers. Figure 12.7 depicts representative problems for these stages.

	Right distributive property of division over addition	Right distributive property of division over subtraction
Problems leading to discovery	$(\tfrac{3}{7} + \tfrac{1}{4}) \div \tfrac{4}{9} = \tfrac{\triangle}{\square}$ $(\tfrac{3}{7} \div \tfrac{4}{9}) + (\tfrac{1}{4} \div \tfrac{4}{9}) = \tfrac{\triangle}{\square}$	$(\tfrac{3}{8} - \tfrac{1}{7}) \div \tfrac{6}{5} = \tfrac{\triangle}{\square}$ $(\tfrac{3}{8} \div \tfrac{6}{5}) - (\tfrac{1}{7} \div \tfrac{6}{5}) = \tfrac{\triangle}{\square}$
Problems requiring single solutions	$(\tfrac{4}{5} + \tfrac{3}{8}) \div \tfrac{\triangle}{\square}$ $= (\tfrac{4}{5} \div \tfrac{6}{7}) + (\tfrac{3}{8} \div \tfrac{6}{7})$	$(\tfrac{2}{3} - \tfrac{1}{5}) \div \tfrac{1}{7})$ $= (\tfrac{\triangle}{\square} \div \tfrac{1}{7}) - (\tfrac{1}{5} \div \tfrac{1}{7})$
Problems requiring multiple solutions	$(\tfrac{3}{5} + \tfrac{2}{9}) \div \tfrac{\triangle}{\square}$ $= (\tfrac{3}{5} \div \tfrac{\triangle}{\square}) + (\tfrac{2}{9} \div \tfrac{\triangle}{\square})$	$(\tfrac{\triangle}{\square} - \tfrac{1}{7}) \div \tfrac{2}{8}$ $= (\tfrac{\triangle}{\square} \div \tfrac{2}{8}) - (\tfrac{1}{7} \div \tfrac{2}{8})$

Figure 12.7

The final stage in teaching the distributive property involves giving the child the following patterns and asking him to use these patterns to create true mathematical sentences:

$$\left(\frac{a}{b}+\frac{c}{d}\right)\div\frac{e}{f}=\left(\frac{a}{b}\div\frac{e}{f}\right)+\left(\frac{c}{d}\div\frac{e}{f}\right)$$

and

$$\left(\frac{a}{b}-\frac{c}{d}\right)\div\frac{e}{f}=\left(\frac{a}{b}\div\frac{e}{f}\right)-\left(\frac{c}{d}\div\frac{e}{f}\right).$$

12.5 TEACHING THE MULTIPLICATION ALGORITHM

A skill that is one of the easiest to teach children is the multiplication algorithm for fractional numbers. The ease of teaching is due not only to the naturalness of multiplying the numerators and the denominators but also to the availability of a concrete approach that closely parallels the approach used in teaching multiplication of whole numbers.

In the early stages of teaching this algorithm, it may be useful, although it is not necessary, to restrict your first examples to factors less than 1. For example, the product of $\frac{3}{5}$ and $\frac{2}{3}$ can be developed as follows:

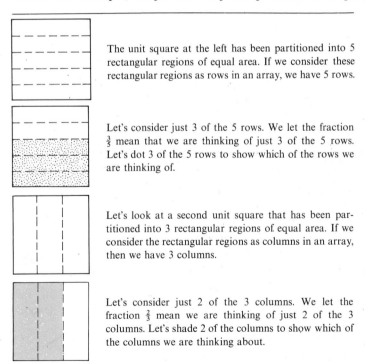

The unit square at the left has been partitioned into 5 rectangular regions of equal area. If we consider these rectangular regions as rows in an array, we have 5 rows.

Let's consider just 3 of the 5 rows. We let the fraction $\frac{3}{5}$ mean that we are thinking of just 3 of the 5 rows. Let's dot 3 of the 5 rows to show which of the rows we are thinking of.

Let's look at a second unit square that has been partitioned into 3 rectangular regions of equal area. If we consider the rectangular regions as columns in an array, then we have 3 columns.

Let's consider just 2 of the 3 columns. We let the fraction $\frac{2}{3}$ mean we are thinking of just 2 of the 3 columns. Let's shade 2 of the columns to show which of the columns we are thinking about.

At the left is an array that depicts a unit square that simultaneously considers $\frac{3}{5}$ and $\frac{2}{3}$. (This is equivalent to our simultaneously thinking of an array of 3 rows and 2 columns and saying the product is 6.) Notice that our unit is now partitioned into a 5-by-3 array, of which we are considering only 3 rows and 2 columns, or a 3-by-2 array. (Notice this corresponds to the intersection of the two sets.) Thus we see that when we think of a $\frac{3}{5}$-by-$\frac{2}{3}$ array, we are also thinking of an array of 6 together with a unit-square array of 15. Thus $\frac{3}{5} \times \frac{2}{3} = \frac{6}{15}$. Let's see how this idea can be extended to fractional numbers greater than 1.

The only modification (this is not really a modification but a highlight of the way we referred to our partitioning) is that the divisor always refers to the manner in which the unit squares are partitioned, and the dividend denotes the array under consideration.

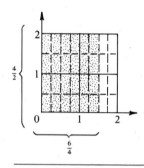

Thus $\frac{4}{2} \times \frac{6}{4}$ is interpreted by considering sufficient unit squares on unit squares partitioned into 2 rows by 4 columns such that we can observe an array of 4 rows by 6 columns. The intersection of the shaded area and the dotted area and the dotted area in the square gives a mathematical model for the product of $\frac{4}{2}$ and $\frac{6}{4}$.

12.6 TEACHING THE DIVISION ALGORITHM

The tendency in a traditional curriculum was to tell the child that in order to divide fractional numbers, we simply "inverted" the divisor and then multiplied. Giving him the rule without any justification often led to his forgetting the exact rule but remembering that something was to be inverted. Thus, to be doubly safe, he inverted both the divisor and the dividend. Some students, remembering that something was to be inverted, inverted the dividend rather than the divisor. To establish a bridge of reason over which the child can return to reconstruct his rule, we now help him understand "why."

The following dialogue is typical of one that might be used to establish the why of the division algorithm. The problem presented is $\frac{3}{4} \div \frac{4}{5} = \frac{\triangle}{\square}$.

"Instead of a divisor of $\frac{4}{5}$, what would be the ideal divisor for this problem?" (1.) "Why?" (Because we have seen that division by 1 yields a quotient equal to the dividend.)

"What pattern have we learned that could help us get a name for 1?" (The reciprocal pattern, or $\frac{\triangle}{\square} \times \frac{\square}{\triangle} = 1$.)

"What does the reciprocal pattern tell us we have to multiply $\frac{4}{5}$ by in order to get a product of 1?" ($\frac{5}{4}$.)

"When we had a quotient of two whole numbers and multiplied the divisor by a nonzero number, what did we have to do to the dividend so that our quotient did not change?" (We multiplied the dividend times the same number.) "Let's see if this same pattern works when the quotient is a fractional number. How will we be able to check to see if the quotient that we have found is correct?" (Multiply the divisor times the quotient and see if we get the dividend.)

Now place the following problem on the board: $\left(\frac{3}{4} \times \frac{5}{4}\right) \div \left(\frac{4}{5} \times \frac{5}{4}\right) =$. $\frac{15}{16} \div 1 = \frac{\triangle}{\square}$.

"We have seen that if the dividend is a fractional number and the divisor is 1, we will get what for a quotient?" (The quotient will be equal to the dividend.)

"Therefore, what is our quotient?" ($\frac{15}{16}$.)

"Let's check our quotient to see if it is the correct answer: $\frac{15}{16} \times \frac{4}{5} = \frac{60}{80} = \frac{3}{4}$. As we can see, $\frac{15}{16}$ is the correct answer."

Figure 12.8 depicts a possible step-by-step presentation of this algorithm.

$$\frac{5}{7} \div \frac{3}{4}$$
$$\downarrow - - - - - \text{ Compensation property}$$
$$\left(\frac{5}{7} \times \frac{4}{3}\right) \div \left(\frac{3}{4} \times \frac{4}{3}\right) \quad \text{The } \frac{4}{3} \text{ was selected because we want to use the reciprocal property}$$
$$\downarrow - - - - - \text{ Reciprocal property}$$
$$\left(\frac{5}{7} \times \frac{4}{3}\right) \div 1$$
$$\downarrow - - - - - \text{ Multiplication algorithm}$$
$$\frac{5 \times 4}{7 \times 3} \div 1$$
$$\downarrow - - - - - \text{ Multiplication}$$
$$\frac{20}{21} \div 1$$
$$\downarrow - - - - - \text{ Division by 1}$$
$$\frac{20}{21}$$

Figure 12.8

12.7 AN ALTERNATE DIVISION ALGORITHM

There are several fractional-number division algorithms. When division has been emphasized as the inverse of multiplication, then the following algorithm for division is appropriate:

$$\frac{3}{4} \div \frac{2}{3} = \frac{\triangle}{\square}$$

$$\frac{3}{4} = \frac{2}{3} \times \frac{\triangle}{\square} \qquad \text{Definition of division}$$

$$\frac{3}{4} \times \frac{3}{2} = \frac{2}{3} \times \frac{3}{2} \times \frac{\triangle}{\square} \qquad \text{If } a = c, \text{ then } b \times a = b \times c$$

$$\frac{3}{4} \times \frac{3}{2} = 1 \times \frac{\triangle}{\square} \qquad \text{Reciprocal property}$$

$$\frac{3}{4} \times \frac{3}{2} = \frac{\triangle}{\square} \qquad \text{Identity property}$$

$$\frac{9}{8} = \frac{\triangle}{\square} \qquad \text{Multiplication of fractional numbers}$$

12.8 MULTIPLICATION INVOLVING MIXED-NUMERAL ALGORITHMS

Multiplication involving mixed numerals has limited social application, because it is more convenient to represent the mixed numerals as either fractions or decimals; however, we shall see that work with the vertical form of the mixed-numeral algorithm will highlight the general nature of the multiplication algorithm. Having the students study this algorithm will also provide readiness for the decimal algorithm.

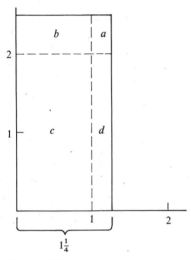

Figure 12.9

In Figure 12.9, we see a mathematical model depicting $2\frac{1}{2} \times 1\frac{1}{4}$. Notice that the following labeled fractions correspond to the similarly labeled areas in Figure 12.9:

a. $\frac{1}{8}$ c. 2
b. $\frac{1}{2}$ d. $\frac{2}{4}$

Notice further that numbers corresponding to the area regions are represented as partial products when we use the distributive property to multiply $(2 + \frac{1}{2})$ and $(1 + \frac{1}{4})$. In the expanded form we have

$$
\begin{array}{r}
1 + \frac{1}{4} \\
\times\, 2 + \frac{1}{2} \\
\hline
\frac{1}{8} \\
\frac{1}{2} \\
\frac{2}{4} \\
2 \\
\hline
2 + \frac{9}{8} = 3\frac{1}{8} \\
\end{array}
$$

Partial products

Product

In the standard form we have

$$
\begin{array}{r}
1\frac{1}{4} \\
\times 2\frac{1}{2} \\
\hline
\frac{1}{8} \\
\frac{1}{2} \\
\frac{2}{4} \\
2 \\
\hline
2\frac{9}{8} = 3\frac{1}{8}
\end{array}
$$

EXERCISES (2)

1. For the stage requiring single solutions and the stage requiring multiple solutions make up sample problems for teaching the compensation property for division of fractional numbers.
2. Make up sample problems for the first three stages for teaching the right distributive property of division over addition of fractional numbers.
3. Make up sample problems for the first three stages for teaching the right distributive property of division over subtraction of fractional numbers.
4. Construct a mathematical model that could be used to show $\frac{3}{2} \times \frac{1}{5} = \frac{3}{10}$.
5. Identify each step (a to e) taken in the following presentation:

$$\frac{3}{4} \div \frac{5}{7}$$
a. $\downarrow$
$$\left(\frac{3}{4} \times \frac{7}{5}\right) \div \left(\frac{5}{7} \times \frac{7}{5}\right)$$
b. $\downarrow$ c. $\downarrow$
$$\frac{3 \times 7}{4 \times 5} \div 1$$
d. $\downarrow$
$$\frac{21}{20} \div 1$$
e. $\downarrow$
$$\frac{21}{20}$$

6. Some elementary series present a common-denominator method of division. Identify each step in this algorithm:

$$\frac{1}{2} \div \frac{2}{3}$$
a. $\downarrow$
$$\left(\frac{1}{2} \times \frac{3}{3}\right) \div \left(\frac{2}{3} \times \frac{2}{2}\right)$$
b. $\downarrow$
$$\frac{1 \times 3}{2 \times 3} \div \frac{2 \times 2}{3 \times 2}$$
c. $\downarrow$
$$\frac{3}{6} \div \frac{4}{6}$$
d. $\downarrow$
$$\left(3 \times \frac{1}{6}\right) \div \left(4 \times \frac{1}{6}\right)$$
e. $\downarrow$
$$3 \div 4$$
f. $\downarrow$
$$\frac{3}{4}$$

7. Construct a mathematical model for teaching $2\frac{2}{3} \times 3\frac{1}{4}$.
8. Find the product of $2\frac{2}{3}$ and $3\frac{1}{4}$ using the vertical algorithm and the expanded form. Identify each partial product in terms of a region of your mathematical model in Exercise 7.

BIBLIOGRAPHY

Bausom, R. V. "Division of Fractions for Understanding," *School Science and Mathematics* (May 1965), pp. 432–435.

Freemen, W. W. K. "Mrs. Murphy's Pies—An Introduction of Division by Fractions," *The Arithmetic Teacher* (April 1967), pp. 310–311.

Hales, B. B., and M. N. Nelson. "Dividing Fractions with Fraction Wheels," *The Arithmetic Teacher* (November 1970), pp. 619–621.

Junge, C. W. "Now Try This—Division of Fractions," *The Arithmetic Teacher* (February 1968), pp. 177–178.

National Council of Teachers of Mathematics. *29th Yearbook* (Washington, D.C.), 1964, pp. 254–277.

Olberg, R. "Visual Aid for Multiplication and Division of Fractions," *The Arithmetic Teacher* (January 1967), pp. 44–46.

13

Teaching numeration systems

BEHAVIORAL OBJECTIVES

Student can . . .

Contrast the characteristics of the Hindu-Arabic numeration system with a specific ancient numeration system.

Create a numeration system with specific characteristics.

Identify characteristics of an artificial numeration system.

Construct an analogy that could be used to teach grouping, place value, base, and exponents.

Describe a translation approach that could be used to introduce an ancient numeration system.

Express in scientific notation a numeral given in standard form.

Express as a standard numeral a numeral given in scientific notation.

13.1 INTRODUCTION

In this chapter we shall study both ancient numeration systems and "modern" nondecimal systems. We shall discuss how to teach ancient numeration systems to provide the child with a better understanding of his own system. Although the comparative aspect of this system is stressed, you will also want to study each system with respect to its stage of evolution and to the role it played in its culture.

We shall look at certain properties of nondecimal systems that are characteristic of the system of numeration, rather than looking at properties of number systems per se. It is through this experience with nondecimal numeration systems that a child is able to isolate those properties relating to the numeration system. You will also want to examine with your students the role of these nondecimal systems in our modern society. The comparative aspect of the nondecimal systems will also be discussed, with the goal of giving the child a better understanding of his own system.

13.2 NUMERATION SYSTEMS OF EARLY CIVILIZATIONS

We can only speculate about man's first numeration system. Certainly the cave man's picture of deer being killed in a hunt was one of the first attempts to convey to others the number property of a set. It appears that notches cut in sticks found in the graves of these early men corresponded in number to the number of possessions (such as bone bracelets and pottery) placed in the grave with the body. If this interpretation is correct, we might say that this cave painting represented an early attempt by man to set up a one-to-one correspondence between a set of objects and a set of notches.

We can observe this type of matching among shepherds of the early Christian era who maintained a sack of pebbles whose number corresponded to the number of sheep in the flock. As the sheep were brought in each day, the shepherd matched his pebbles one-to-one with the sheep. If pebbles matched one-to-one, the shepherd knew that all the sheep were accounted for.

13.3 AN EGYPTIAN NUMERATION SYSTEM

The first numeration system we shall look at in great detail is that of the Egyptians. Five thousand years ago, Egypt was a prosperous country with well-developed numeration systems. The Egyptians used three numeration systems, the hieratic, demotic, and hieroglyphic. We shall be especially interested in the characteristics of the hieroglyphics, which were chiseled into stone and used to record historical data. If we were to travel to Egypt and visit the pyramids, we could see the accomplishments of the Pharaohs recorded on the walls of the pyramids. These recordings include such things as the number of prisoners taken, the number of bushels of wheat harvested, and the number of cattle raised. What makes the hieroglyphic system of special interest to the student of mathematics is the similarities and dissimilarities that exist between the Egyptian numeration system and our own. Let us look at their system and compare.

Figure 13.1 shows how the Egyptian stone mason depicted the numerals 1 through 9. Notice that the numeral 6 is created by 6 repetitions of the

Egyptian numerals	I	I I	I I I	I I I I	I I I I I	I I I I I I	I I I I I I I	I I I I I I I I	I I I I I I I I I
Our numerals	1	2	3	4	5	6	7	8	9

Figure 13.1

symbol for 1. When a symbol is used again to create a name for a number and names the same number each time it is used, we say that this system displays the characteristic of *repetition*. Thus we see that the Egyptian system possessed the characteristic of repetition.

Notice that the Egyptian numerals for numbers 1 through 9 are not unlike our tally system, which is occasionally used to denote the number of something being counted.

The Egyptians introduced a new symbol for 10, rather than employ a symbol using 10 ones. The symbol ∩ for 10 is often referred to as the heel-bone symbol. This radical change in symbolism upon reaching 10 helps us to identify what we call the *base* of the system. In our own base-10 system, the base is not signaled by the introduction of a new symbol, but rather by the process of going from the use of one digit to denote a number to the use of two digits to denote a number. Figure 13.2 shows

Egyptian numerals	∩	∩∩	∩∩∩	∩ ∩∩∩	∩∩ ∩∩∩	∩∩∩ ∩∩∩	∩ ∩∩∩ ∩∩∩	∩∩ ∩∩∩ ∩∩∩	∩∩∩ ∩∩∩ ∩∩∩
Our numerals	10	20	30	40	50	60	70	80	90

Figure 13.2

how the Egyptians could designate the tens—from 10 to 90. Notice that repetition is again employed.

With the set of numerals for ones and the set for tens, the Egyptians were able to name any number from 1 to 99. For example, 75 would be represented by ∩∩∩ ||||| , and 92 by ∩∩∩ ∩∩∩ ∩∩∩ || .

Note that if 92 were denoted || ∩∩∩ ∩∩∩ ∩∩∩ , it would still be possible to decipher the number to which the symbols refer. When the repositioning of the symbols does not change the meaning that we associate with each symbol, we say the system does not have the place value. This is in contrast to our system, in which the repositioning does affect the value that we associate with each symbol. For example, consider 34 and 43. In the first case, the 3 represents 3 tens and the 4 represents 4 ones; in the second case, the 3 represents 3 ones and the 4 represents 4 tens. Notice that we are saying that the value associated with an individual symbol is changed in order for place value to be represented. (We are not saying that just because a new value for the numeral is obtained by shifting the individual symbols that place value is necessarily present. For example, in the Roman numerals IX and XI, the I symbol means one, whether it is positioned on the left or the right, but the value represented by the whole numeral is changed by this repositioning. Therefore, we say that the Roman system does not have place value.)

The Egyptians changed symbols at 100, 1000, 10,000, 100,000, and

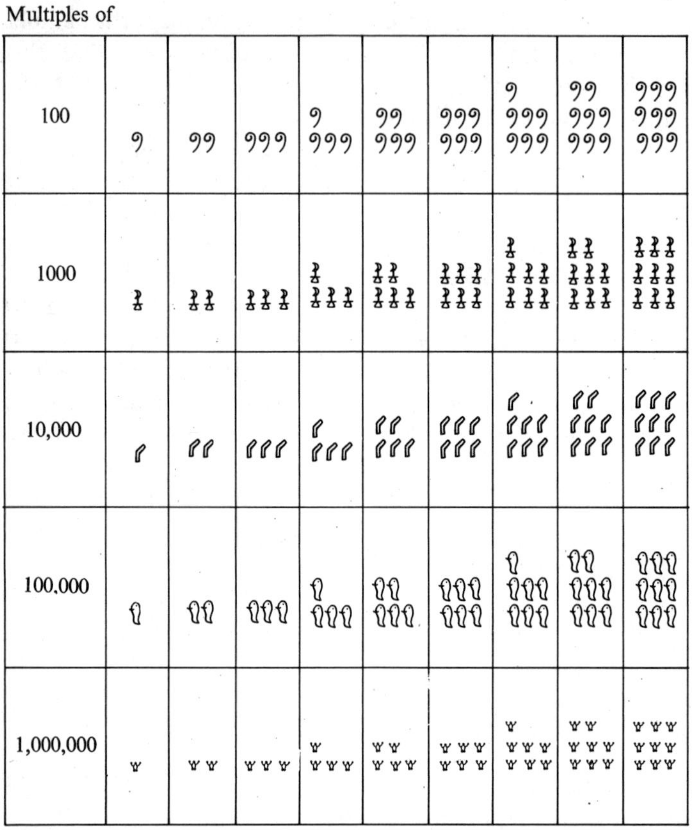

Multiples of

Figure 13.3

1,000,000. Figure 13.3 shows how multiples of each of these are depicted. With these symbols, the Egyptian could name any number from 1 to 9,999,999. For example, 2,000,035 could be represented by 𝄆. Notice that we do not need a zero symbol to represent the absence of a particular type of group. Since the Egyptians did not employ a zero symbol, we say that this characteristic was not present in their system. This is in contrast to our system, in which we need to indicate the absence of a particular type of group. For example, in 305 the 0 denotes zero groups of 10.

To determine the value of an Egyptian numeral, we simply add the numbers named by each symbol. For example, the value of 𝄆 is determined as follows: 1000 + 1000 + 1000 + 10 + 10 = 3020. Because of the technique of adding numbers to determine the number named, we say that the Egyptian system is an *additive system*. This characteristic is also possessed by our system, although the word names of the system mask this characteristic. For example, the value of 317 is obtained by adding 3 hundreds to 1 ten to 7 ones and obtaining 317.

We have seen that the Egyptian numeration system is repetitive, has base 10, has no place value, has no zero, and is an additive system. In contrast, we see that our system is not repetitive, has a zero, and has place value. Like the Egyptian system, it is additive and a base-10 system.

13.4 THE MAYAN NUMERATION SYSTEM

Let us look at still another numeration system that has several interesting characteristics. From about the beginning of the Christian era, the Mayan Indians on the Yucatan Peninsula in Central America had a highly efficient numeration system. What made this system especially remarkable was that it utilized a symbol for zero, a characteristic that was not present in the European version of our numeration system until the thirteenth century. With their system, the Mayans were able to develop a fairly complex society. They had a well-developed calendar consisting of a 360-day official year and a solar year of 365+ days.

Figure 13.4 depicts how the Mayans made their numerals for 1 to 20. The first characteristic we note is that repetition is very much in evidence in this system. Notice that 1 dot is used repetitively to denote 2, 3, and 4, and 1 bar is used repetitively to denote 10 and 15.

In detecting major changes in notation, we observe that a new symbol is introduced at both 5 and 20. We might say that there are two bases operable in this system except for the fact that the change of symbolism at the 5 does not represent a recurring pattern consistent with other changes that take place at 25, 125, 625, and so on. Since this change in symbolism is restricted to one instance, in contrast to the Egyptian system where at each power of 10 (10, 100, 1000, 10,000) a new symbol was introduced, we say that this is not a base-5 system, but this is a base-20 system, even though there will be exceptions to the scheme of having a new place value designated at every power of 20.

Let us see how other numbers were designated. Note that in Figure 13.5 digits occupying the second level in the numeral name sets of twenties. Since the positioning of the numeral changes the value of the individual symbol, we say that this system has place value. Note that the Mayan place-value system names ones on the bottom, twenties at the second level, and three-hundred and sixties at the third level.

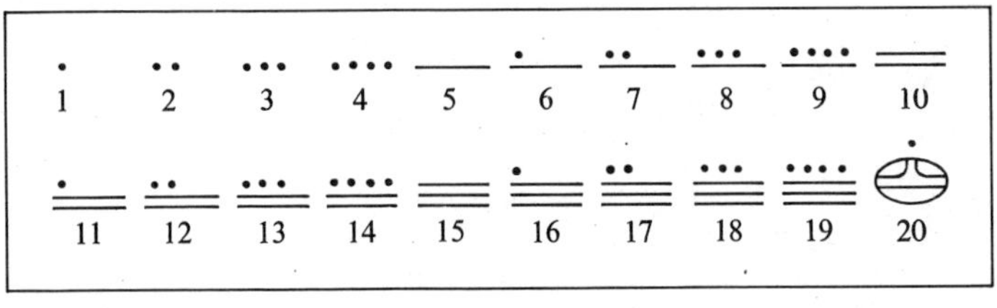

Figure 13.4

Second level   • •   Twenties   20 + 20 = 40

Bottom level   • • •   Ones   1 + 1 + 1 = 3
                                                    ──
                                                    43

Third level   • • •   360 + 360 + 360 = 1080

Second level   ⑩   0 =   0

Bottom level   ═══   5 + 5 = 10
                                               ────
                                               1090

Figure 13.5

The Mayan system, like our own system, is additive. Once the value of each level is determined, we simply add these numbers together to determine the number named by the numeral.

13.5 THE ROMAN NUMERATION SYSTEM TAUGHT BY TRANSLATION

Not only shall we examine the characteristics of the Roman system,* but we shall also discuss techniques of teaching this system, because it is the most frequently taught ancient numeration system. This is not to say that it has more intrinsic merits than either of the two previously discussed systems. It was, in fact, an awkward system that probably inhibited the Romans from making any significant contribution in the area of number theory. However, its continued maintenance probably stems from the continuing impact of the Roman culture and philosophy on our Western civilization. The Roman numerals served a "scholarly" purpose long after they were supplemented for practical applications by the more efficient Hindu-Arabic system.

Let us examine how we might utilize patterns to teach the Roman numerals. Notice in Figure 13.6 that we have partitioned the Roman numerals into three sets. First the child would learn to associate the numbers

Hundreds	Tens	Ones
C	X	I
CC	XX	II
CCC	XXX	III
CD	XL	IV
D	L	V
DC	LX	VI
DCC	LXX	VII
DCCC	LXXX	VIII
CM	XC	IX

Figure 13.6

* Actually, the system we shall discuss, and the one usually identified as the Roman system, represents a modification of the Roman system. This modification was made, to a large extent, during the Middle Ages.

from 1 to 10 with their corresponding Roman numerals. Then he would be asked to find the pattern that exists between the first column and the second and third columns. Notice that there is a very consistent pattern that is identical for ones, tens, and hundreds.

After the child has discovered the pattern that exists for ones, tens, and hundreds, we can give him experience in translating from our system to the Roman and from the Roman to our system. For example, we can write 247 by selecting the name for 200 from the hundreds column, the name for 40 from the tens column, and the name for 7 from the ones column. We thus see that CCXLVII is a name for 247. We can also translate DCCXLIV to our system by recognizing that DCC comes from the seventh position in the hundreds column, XL from the fourth position in the tens column, and IV from the fourth position in the ones column. Therefore, DCCXLIV names 744.

After many similar translating activities, if you want to have the children reach a skill level for which a table is not needed, you will have them memorize the pattern for 1 through 9 and the names for 10, 50, 100, and 500. With this information and their previous experiences with the development of the pattern, the children can easily recreate the table mentally and translate freely in either direction.

To further develop the children's competence, you will want to examine with them the characteristics of this system. In III and XXX we can see evidence of the characteristic of repetition. Like the Egyptian system, the Roman system does not have a zero numeral. Notice that there is a consistent change in numerals at 5, 50, and 500 and also at 10, 100, and 1000. Might we say that the Roman system has utilized aspects of both a base-5 and a base-10 system?

Certainly the additive property is one of the characteristics, as evidenced by LXVII being equal to $50 + 10 + 5 + 1 + 1 = 67$. But the system also has a subtractive characteristic, as can be evidenced by IX being equal to $10 - 1 = 9$, or XL being equal to $50 - 10 = 40$.

We might be tempted to say that the Roman system has place value, because it makes a difference whether we place a I to the left or the right of a X. However, remember that the value of this symbol must change as a prerequisite for the designation of place value. And because the value of I in IX and in XI remains a name for 1 regardless of its location, it does not show place value.

EXERCISES (1)

1. What are the characteristics?

Symbols	*a*	*aa*	*aaa*	*b*	*ba*	*baa*	*baaa*	*bb*
Corresponding number of dots	•	••	•••	••• •	••• ••	••• •••	••• ••• •	••• ••• ••

2. What are the characteristics?

Symbols	a	b	c	aa	ab	ac	ba	bb	bc	ca
Corresponding number of dots	•	• •	• • •	• • • •	• • • • •	• • • • • •	• • • • • • •	• • • • • • • •	• • • • • • • • •	• • • • • • • • • •

3. What are the characteristics?

Symbols	a	b	c	ak	aa	ab	ac	bk
Corresponding number of dots	•	• •	• • •	• • • •	• • • • •	• • • • • •	• • • • • • •	• • • • • • • •

4. What are the characteristics?

Symbols	a	b	c	ak	k	ka	kb	kc	kak
Corresponding number of dots	•	• •	• • •	• • • •	• • • • •	• • • • • •	• • • • • • •	• • • • • • • •	• • • • • • • • •

5. What are the characteristics?

Symbols	a	b	c	bb	d	bc	e	bbb	cc	bd
Corresponding number of dots	•	• •	• • •	• • • •	• • • • •	• • • • • •	• • • • • • •	• • • • • • • •	• • • • • • • • •	• • • • • • • • • •

6. What are the characteristics?

Symbols	a	aa	aaa	aa aa	b	a b	aa b	bbaa	aba aa	bb
Corresponding number of dots	•	• •	• • •	• • • •	• • • • •	• • • • • •	• • • • • • •	• • • • • • • •	• • • • • • • • •	• • • • • • • • • •

13.6 TEACHING EXPONENT NOTATION USING MODELS

In this section we will examine how models can be used to develop the concept of exponent notation. In the next section we will discuss an alternative approach using an analogy.

In working with exponent notation the base number identifies the type of grouping being done. For example, in 3^2 the 3 is the base number and tells us we are grouping by threes. The exponent tells us the hierarchy of grouping. Note in the following table how the hierarchy of grouping is conveyed by the models.

Exponent Name	Factor Name	A Model
3^2	3×3 3 sets of 3	
3^3	$3 \times (3 \times 3)$ 3 sets of (3 sets of 3)	

By definition 3^1 is equal to 3 and 3^0 is equal to 1. This idea can be generated from a pattern such as the following:

$4 \times 4 \times 4 \times 4 = 4^4 = 256$
$4 \times 4 \times 4 = 4^3 = 64$
$4 \times 4 = 4^2 = 16$
$4 = 4? = ?$
$4? = ?$

Teacher: To go from 256 to 64 what have we divided the 256 by?

Children: 4.

Teacher: To go from 64 to 16 what have we divided the 64 by?

Children: 4.

Teacher: If the pattern continues, what will we place under the 16?

Children: 4.

Teacher: Notice the pattern in your exponents goes 4, 3, 2. What do you think the next exponent will be?

Children: 1.

It is also possible to arrive at a rationale for the 0 and 1 exponents using models. For example, if we think of the 1 as telling us how many times we have grouped, then

$3^1 = 3$

and

$4^1 = 4$

Similarly, the 0 exponent can indicate an absence of grouping. For example, 4^0 would mean we are going to group by fours, but we have not yet begun the grouping so each object exists as a single entity and not in a group.

13.7   TEACHING GROUPING VIA AN ANALOGY

Let's examine how an analogy can be used to develop nondecimal numeration concepts. Pretend you work in a factory that makes paper cups. Each day the shipping room of this factory receives many orders specifying various types of packaging for the cups. The packaging foreman has discovered that by classifying these orders into the basic type of grouping that each order represents and by organizing his workers into teams that are responsible for handling a specific type of grouping, he can efficiently fill the orders with a minimum chance of error.

For example, suppose he reads an order and notices that the purchaser of the cups wants the cups packaged into various groups of 3, 9, 27, 81, and so on. Noticing that each of the groupings the purchaser has requested factors as 1×3, 3×3, $3 \times 3 \times 3$, $3 \times 3 \times 3 \times 3$, the foreman sends this order over to his "3-grouping" table. Each person sitting at the table has been given these directions: "Wait until you have 3 groups in front of you, then stack these groups into 1 stack of cups and pass them to the person on your right."

These cups drop out of a paper-cup-making machine one at a time. When the first person in the line gets 3 cups in front of him, he groups them into a stack of 3 and passes them on to the next person. This person waits until 3 stacks of 3 cups are in front of him and he then groups these into one stack of 3 threes and passes these on to the next person, and so on. The packaging foreman, by noting the progress of cups on the line at any given time, is able to tell how many cups have been packaged. Let us see how he does this.

Assume that you have had children acting out the various roles in our story, as in Figure 13.7. The foreman's reasoning to determine the number of cups on the table might go something like this: The cups in front of the girl near the machine are in groups of ones, because if she had grouped them, she would have passed them on. The stack in front of the boy is in a group of 3 and he is waiting for 2 more such stacks so that he can make a group of

Figure 13.7

3 threes and pass it on. Each stack in front of the second girl from the machine is in a group of 3 threes, because she received each of these stacks from the boy on her left. She is waiting for 1 more stack of 3 threes so that she can make a stack of 3 stacks of 3 threes.

The foreman finds that there are 23 cups on the table by the following reasoning: 2 cups in front of the first girl and 1 set of 3—or 3 cups—in front of the boy, and 2 sets of 3 threes—or 2 sets of 9, or 18 cups—in front of the second girl; thus $18 + 3 + 2 = 23$.

The foreman decides that if he labels each person in such a way as to tell how many times the sets have been grouped at that position, it will be easier for him to compute how many cups are on the table. Figure 13.8 shows how the people looked.

Figure 13.8

The 0 told him that the cups in front of this person had been grouped zero times—in other words, they were still in groups of ones just as they had come from the machine. The 1 tells him that the objects in front of the boy had been grouped one time by the girl to his left. The 2 tells him that the objects in front of the girl have been grouped twice—once by the girl near the machine and a second time by the boy.

Since the foreman had a great many tables to keep track of, he devised a system to keep track of what type of grouping was taking place at each table. He did it in such a way that he could look at any person at any table and tell what sort of grouping was taking place at that table. Figure 13.9 depicts how he placed the numerals 3 to the left and below the numeral that indicates the number of times the cups have been grouped.

Now when he looked at a table and noticed a 4^2, he knew that people were grouping by fours at this table, and that stacks in front of this person had been grouped two times before coming to that point. In other words, he knew that 4^2 meant that 4 ones had been grouped and then 4 sets of this 4 had been grouped to form a set of 4 fours, or 16 cups.

One day, the foreman was showing a visitor through his packaging plant. The visitor said that he understood what the numerals on the front of the

Figure 13.9

workers meant, but he did not understand why there were not more stacks in front of each worker. The foreman explained that at a table grouping by 3, no person could ever have more than 2 stacks left in front of him, because as soon as he got 3 of something, he would group them and pass them on.

The visitor said, "Oh, I see. That would mean that at a table grouping by fives, 4 stacks would be the largest number that could ever be left in front of a worker, because as soon as he got 5 stacks, he would group them and pass the new stack on. Why, that means that if you are grouping by tens, the most you could ever have left would be 9 stacks."

The visitor suggested that he should place another numeral on the front of the workers to show how many of a given group the worker had left in front of him. Figure 13.10 shows how the workers looked after he added the numerals to name the number of groups in front of each worker. From left to right, we can read 2×3^2 as 2 sets of 3 threes; 1×3^1 as 1 set of 3; and 2×3^0 as 2 sets of ones.

In constructing a story for use in presenting mathematical concepts, it is not necessary that each concept be developed fully. By carefully phrased questions during and following this story, you can extend the concepts

Figure 13.10

outlined in your story and develop other related concepts. For example:

"What is the smallest number of cups that could be left in front of a worker when the production is stopped?" (Zero.)

"Can any number of cups be grouped by threes if we have enough people?" (Yes.)

"How many people would we need to group 1025 cups if we grouped by twos?" (11. Let the children arrive at this number by considering the sequence 1, 2, 4, 8, 16, 32, 64, 128, 256, 512, 1024.)

Special vocabulary is probably taught best in a situation where these words can be focused on best. For example, the numeral that identifies the type of grouping being done is called the *base*. In 3^5, the 3 is identified as the base. The number that indicates the number of times that grouping has taken place by the base number is called the *exponent*. In 3^5, the 5 is identified as the exponent.

13.8   NONDECIMAL PLACE VALUE USING TRANSLATION

If we were to denote numbers in the manner of the last stage of development used by the foreman, there would be little trouble deciphering the number named. For example, let us consider how $4 \times 5^2 + 0 \times 5^1 + 2 \times 5^0$ immediately tells us that we are grouping by fives and that we have 4 groups of 5 fives, 0 groups of 5, and 2 ones. In other words, we are referring to 102 of something.

In our attempt to simplify the effort required to write the name of this number, we "strip" "$\times 5^2 + \times 5^1 + \times 5^0$" from our notation, leaving only 402. We place the 4 and 0 and 2 close together and affix the word five to let everyone know that we are grouping by fives (402_{five}). We leave to the reader the task of identifying the 2 as 2 ones, the 0 as 0 fives, and the 4 as 4 fives.

It is the teacher's responsibility to help the child reconstruct the inherent meaning in the nondecimal numeral by translation experience. Figure 13.11

$3201_{four} \xrightarrow{\text{translates to}} 3 \times 4^3 + 2 \times 4^2 + 0 \times 4^1 + 1 \times 4^0$

$2650_{seven} \xrightarrow{\text{translates to}} 2 \times 7^3 + 6 \times 7^2 + 5 \times 7^1 + 0 \times 7^0$

$3 \times 9^2 + 8 \times 9^1 + 0 \times 9^0 \xrightarrow{\text{translates to}} 380_{nine}$

$9 \times 10^2 + 3 \times 10^1 + 7 \times 10^0 \xrightarrow{\text{translates to}} 937_{ten}$

Figure 13.11

depicts sample translations. Note that these translations are made in both directions.

We can explore the meaning of this symbolism at this abstract level if we proceed from the type of explanation represented by the paper cup factory. We can also develop nondecimal numeration systems via a sequence of activities quite similar to those we used to develop the concepts relating to our place-value systems. Figure 13.12 depicts such a sequence of activities that could be used to develop the concepts relating to nondecimal notation.

The study of nondecimal systems can be motivated by making a study of how these systems are utilized in our culture. Such activities as relating dozen and gross to base 12, or nickels and quarters to base 5, or computer calculations to base 2 will motivate the study of these particular bases.

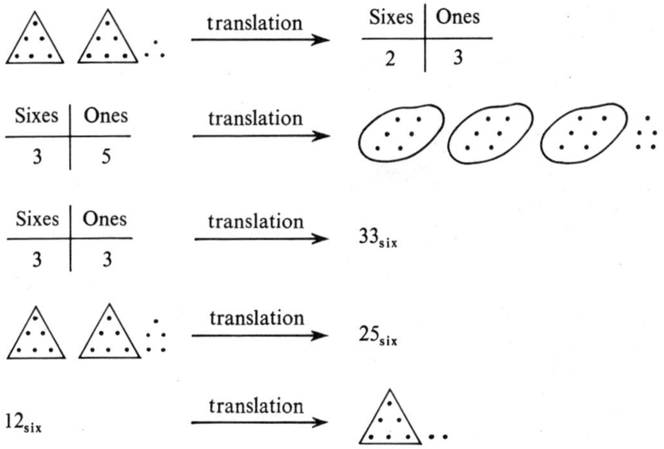

Figure 13.12

13.9 SCIENTIFIC NOTATION

The idea of the arbitrariness of grouping coupled with the idea of base and exponent can be utilized to develop the concept of scientific notation. You will want to tell your children that they are going to study a new system of notation used by scientists to simplify numerals that would normally require many digits to write. For example, 2,000,000 can be written as 2×10^6, which greatly reduces the number of symbols needed to name the number.

By convention, scientific notation always uses a base of 10. Also by convention, the numeral that names the number of the particular grouping of 10 to which you are referring is either 1 or a number between 1 and 10. For example, 3,500,000 is expressed as 3.5×10^6 in scientific notation, because 3.5 is between 1 and 10, and 10^6 indicates that a base of 10 has been used for grouping.

In the elementary school, almost all of the child's experiences with this notation involve translating large numbers to scientific notation. Figure 13.13 depicts some typical translations.

$3,000 \xrightarrow{\text{translates to}} 3 \times 10^3$

$30,000 \xrightarrow{\text{translates to}} 3 \times 10^4$

$36,000 \xrightarrow{\text{translates to}} 3.6 \times 10^4$

$36,400 \xrightarrow{\text{translates to}} 3.64 \times 10^4$

$1,000 \xrightarrow{\text{translates to}} 1 \times 10^3$

Figure 13.13

EXERCISES (2)

1. For each of the following illustrations describe the base, the number of cups in piles (a), (b), and (c), and the total number of cups pictured.

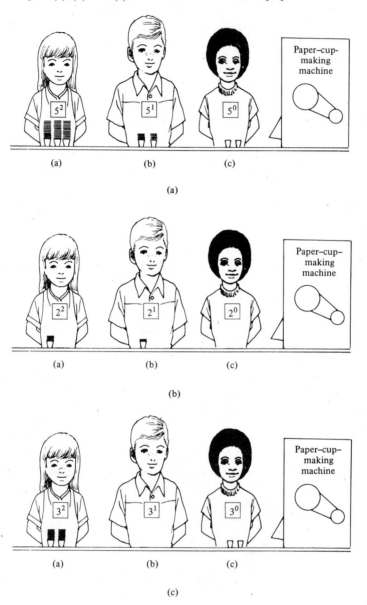

2. Construct a set of translation activities similar to Figure 13.11, which could be used to develop place value for a base-8 system.

3. Construct a sequence of activities similar to those depicted by Figure 13.12, which could be used to develop a base-2 (binary) system.
4. Construct an ordered sequence of translation activities that would aid the child in learning to convert from a standard numeral to scientific notation.

BIBLIOGRAPHY

Banks, J. Houston. *Learning and Teaching Arithmetic* (Boston: Allyn & Bacon), 1964, pp. 20–24.

Churchill, Eileen M. *Counting and Measuring* (London: Routledge & Kegan Paul), 1962, pp. 11–44.

Hamilton, E. W. " Number Systems, Fad or Foundation," *The Arithmetic Teacher* (May 1961), pp. 242–245.

Hollis, Loye Y. " Why Teach Numeration?" *The Arithmetic Teacher* (February 1964), pp. 94–95.

Johnson, Donovan A., and William H. Glenn. *Understanding Numeration Systems* (St Louis, Mo.: Webster), 1960, pp. 2–10.

National Council of Teachers of Mathematics. *Enrichment Mathematics for the Grades, 27th Yearbook* (Washington, D.C), 1963, pp. 234–244.

National Council of Teachers of Mathematics. *Instruction in Arithmetic, 25th Yearbook* (Washington, D.C), 1960, pp. 12–15, 277–278.

National Council of Teachers of Mathematics. *The Growth of Mathematical Ideas, Grades K-12, 24th Yearbook* (Washington, D.C.), 1959, pp. 17–19.

VanDerWaerden, B. L. *Science Awakening: Egyptian, Babylonian, Greek Mathematics* (New York: Oxford University Press), 1961.

14

Teaching decimal notation, ratio, and percentage

14.1 INTRODUCTION

Although there is evidence that decimal notation was used earlier, it "came of age" in the sixteenth century. Standardization of notation, however, was not immediate. As a matter of fact, the symbolism remains incompletely standardized to this date.* For example, in the United States we represent $2\frac{3}{10}$ as 2.3; in England, $2\frac{3}{10}$ is represented as 2·3. During the early use of decimal notation, a numeral that names a number less than 1 was distinguished from the part of the numeral that names a number 1 or greater than 1 in one of the following ways:

$$2.3 = 2_3 = 2\overline{3} = 2{\cdot}3$$

* David Eugene Smith, *History of Mathematics* (Boston: Ginn and Company), 1953, Vol. II, p. 246.

252

As can be easily seen, the dot that we refer to as the decimal point plays only a minor role in the decimal system, because the system of decimal notation can exist independent of this symbol.

Decimal notation represents an extension of our place-value notation, which makes possible the representation of all fractional numbers in terms of place-value notation.

14.2 DEFINITION, TERMINOLOGY, AND SYMBOLISM

These decimals, which we use for naming fractional numbers, are useful at the junior high level for extending the concepts of rational numbers (of which the fractional numbers constitute a subset) and irrational numbers. At the elementary level, we shall be especially interested in the types of decimal notation called terminating decimals and periodic (or repeating) decimals.

A *terminating decimal* is a decimal that contains a finite number of digits. All terminating decimals can be expressed in the form $\dfrac{c}{2^a \cdot 5^b}$, such that a, b, and c are elements of the set of whole numbers.

A *periodic decimal* is a decimal consisting of a finite series of digits that repeat infinitely. $.33\overline{3}$ and $3.2474\overline{747}$ are examples of periodic decimals. The bar over the digits indicates that this series of digits repeats infinitely. Every terminating decimal can be expressed as a periodic decimal simply by affixing 3 zeros with a bar over the last zero on the right. For example, .5 can be expressed as the periodic decimal $.500\overline{0}$.

Figure 14.1 depicts an analysis of a numeral in terms of the standard numeral form, the expanded form, and the fractional form. It also depicts the meaning of the place value.

14.3 TEACHING DECIMAL NOTATION BY TRANSLATION

The child's first encounter with decimal notation (other than its use with various types of measure) is its use as an alternate way of naming a fractional number. The teacher should establish certain relationships between concepts the child has mastered using fractions and the new decimal notation. Along with this establishment of parallel concepts, the teacher should help the child to see that decimal notation greatly simplifies the computational skills involving fractional numbers.

When money is not used as a vehicle to introduce decimal notation, it is common practice to begin a child's introduction to decimal notation with tenths, just as it is common technique to begin the study of enumerating the set of whole numbers with the ones. It is desirable at the beginning to employ mathematical models to which the child can make reference.

Ways of Reading Notations	five hundred	sixty -	four and	one	thousand seven	hundred	eighty-nine ten thousands	
	five,	six,	four point.	one,	seven,	eight,	nine	
	5	6	4	1	7	8	9	← Standard numeral
	500 +	60 +	4 +	$\frac{1}{10}$ +	$\frac{7}{100}$ +	$\frac{8}{1000}$ +	$\frac{9}{10,000}$	← Expanded form
	5×100 +	6×10 +	4 +	$1 \times \frac{1}{10}$ +	$7 \times \frac{1}{100}$ +	$8 \times \frac{1}{1000}$ +	$9 \times \frac{1}{10,000}$	
	5×10^{2} +	6×10^{1} +	4×10^{0} +	1×10^{-1} +	7×10^{-2} +	8×10^{-3} +	9×10^{-4}	Junior high level

Figure 14.1

Partitioned rectangular regions, pentagonal regions, circular regions, and unit line segments serve as useful models. Figure 14.2 depicts how each of these aids would be used to illustrate $\frac{3}{10}$ or 0.3 (or .3).

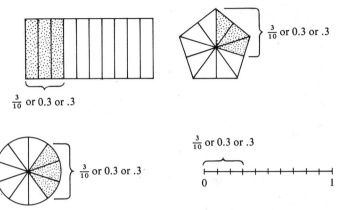

Figure 14.2

The teacher can make the child's practice in renaming a fractional number expressed as a fraction more meaningful by using complete mathematical sentences instead of simply having the child rewrite fractions in decimal form. The following examples illustrate how using complete sentences helps the child see the parallel between computations involving fraction notation and computations involving decimal notation:

The child's translation of the sentence:

$\frac{3}{10} + \frac{4}{10} = \frac{7}{10} \longrightarrow .3 + .4 = .7$

$\frac{8}{10} - \frac{3}{10} = \frac{5}{10} \longrightarrow .8 - .3 = .5$

At this early stage in mastering decimal notation, we should help the child see that 1.0 names both $\frac{10}{10}$ and 1. Translation of sentences in fraction form offers a convenient vehicle for conveying these concepts:

The child's translation of the fraction sentence:

$\frac{3}{10} + \frac{7}{10} = \frac{10}{10} = 1 + \frac{0}{10} \longrightarrow .3 + .7 = 1 = 1.0$

It is important to have the child master the many ways of interpreting the decimals. For example, 4.3 can be interpreted as 4 ones and 3 tenths, or as 43 tenths. Once he has mastered transcribing sentences involving tenths, his ability can be extended to translation involving mixed numerals. Following are some typical translation problems.

Solve and translate to decimal notation:

$4\frac{3}{10} + 5\frac{2}{10} = \square \rightarrow 4.3 + 5.2 = \square$

$6\frac{9}{10} + 8\frac{7}{10} = \square \rightarrow 6.9 + 8.7 = \square$

$4\frac{7}{10} - 2\frac{4}{10} = \square \rightarrow 4.7 - 2.4 = \square$

The concept of decimal notation for hundredths is introduced and developed in a manner similar to that employed for tenths. Figure 14.3 depicts a mathematical model that can be used to show $\frac{13}{100}$ or 0.13.

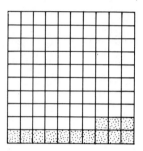

Figure 14.3

The process of translation from fractional hundredths to decimal hundredths again offers the teacher an opportunity to establish the relationship of the concepts for fractional numbers and the new decimal notation. For example:

$\frac{3}{100} + \frac{5}{100} = \frac{8}{100}$ $\xrightarrow{\text{translates to}}$ $.03 + .05 = .08$

$\frac{14}{100} + \frac{9}{100} = \frac{23}{100}$ $\xrightarrow{\text{translates to}}$ $.14 + .09 = .23$

$\frac{35}{100} - \frac{17}{100} = \frac{18}{100}$ $\xrightarrow{\text{translates to}}$ $.35 - .17 = .18$

This process of translation should include examples involving tenths and hundredths. For example:

$\frac{3}{10} + \frac{4}{100} = \frac{30}{100} + \frac{4}{100} = \square$

$.3 + .04 = .30 + .04 = \square$

$\frac{63}{100} - \frac{4}{10} = \frac{63}{100} - \frac{40}{100} = \square$

$.63 - .4 = .63 - .40 = \square$

These translations should progress to the vertical notation, because one of the advantages of our decimal notation is that it provides a smooth transition from the algorithms developed for whole numbers to the algorithms developed for fractional numbers. Some typical translations follow:

$$\begin{array}{cc} \frac{3}{10} & \frac{30}{100} \\ +\frac{9}{100} & +\frac{9}{100} \\ \hline \end{array} \xrightarrow{\text{translates to}} \begin{array}{cc} .3 & .30 \\ +.09 & +.09 \\ \hline \end{array}$$

$$\begin{array}{cc} \frac{63}{100} & \frac{63}{100} \\ -\frac{4}{10} & -\frac{40}{100} \\ \hline \end{array} \xrightarrow{\text{translates to}} \begin{array}{cc} .63 & .63 \\ -.4 & -.40 \\ \hline \end{array}$$

Figure 14.4 show how the translation technique can be used to give meaning to the development of the decimal subtraction algorithm.

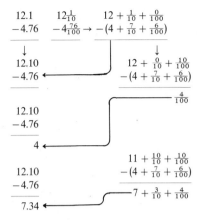

Figure 14.4

Extension of concepts involving thousandths, ten-thousandths, hundred-thousandths, and so on, parallels the development of the concepts for tenths and hundredths.

14.4 COMMON TERMINATING DECIMALS

The teacher should establish decimal names for halves, fourths, fifths, and twentieths at an early stage in presenting the decimal notation. At this early stage, the children will not have the advantage of the decimal division algorithm to derive the correct translation from fraction to decimal. Even though the child does not have the decimal division algorithm, he has other skills that can provide him with sufficient understanding to make this translation meaningful. For example, the compensation property of division provides a means of justifying such relationships as $\frac{1}{4} = .25$, $\frac{1}{5} = .20$, and $\frac{1}{2} = .50$. A series of questions and statements such as the following can be used to establish that .75 and $\frac{3}{4}$ are equivalent names:

"Let's see if we can find a decimal name for a fraction that is not expressed in tenths or hundredths or thousandths. Let's try to find a decimal name for $\frac{3}{4}$."

"What property have we studied that helps find other equivalent fractions?" (Compensation property for division.)

"Is there a whole number we can multiply times the divisor and the dividend in 3 divided by 4 such that we can get a divisor of 100?" (25.)

With the introduction of the decimal division algorithm, we can reestablish that $\frac{1}{2} = .5$, $\frac{1}{5} = .2$, $\frac{1}{4} = .25$, and so on. For example:

$$\begin{array}{r} .5 \\ 2\overline{)1.0} \\ \underline{1.0} \\ 0 \end{array} \quad \text{because} \quad .5 \times 2 = 1.0 \quad \text{or} \quad \begin{array}{r} .5 \\ 2\overline{)1.0} \\ \underline{1.0} \\ 0 \end{array}$$

14.5 PERIODIC DECIMALS

The repeating or periodic decimals are developed concurrently with the development of the decimal division algorithm. For example, consider the following algorithm depicting $1 \div 3$:

$$
\begin{array}{r|l}
3)\overline{1.000} & \\
.900 & .3 \\ \hline
.100 & \\
.090 & .03 \quad \text{or} \\ \hline
.010 & \\
.009 & .003 \\ \hline
.001 &
\end{array}
\qquad
\begin{array}{r}
.333 \\
3)\overline{1.000} \\
9 \\ \hline
10 \\
9 \\ \hline
10 \\
9 \\ \hline
1
\end{array}
$$

If we look at the quotients and remainders, it becomes evident why the quotient of 1 and 3 is named by a repeating decimal:

First division: $\quad 1 \div 3 = \frac{3}{10} + \frac{1}{30} = \frac{3}{10} + (\frac{1}{3} \times \frac{1}{10})$

Second division: $\quad 1 \div 3 = \frac{3}{10} + \frac{3}{100} + \frac{1}{300} = \frac{3}{10} + \frac{3}{100} + (\frac{1}{3} \times \frac{1}{100})$

Third division: $\quad 1 \div 3 = \frac{3}{10} + \frac{3}{100} + \frac{3}{1000} + \frac{1}{3000} = \frac{3}{10} + \frac{3}{100} + \frac{3}{1000} + (\frac{1}{3} \times \frac{1}{1000})$

Questions like the following will be useful for developing the concept of a repeating decimal:

"What will we obtain if we divide a fourth time?" $(1 \div 3 = \frac{3}{10} + \frac{3}{100} + \frac{3}{1000} + \frac{3}{10,000} + \frac{1}{300,000}.)$

"Our first remainder was $\frac{1}{3 \times 10}$, our second was $\frac{1}{3 \times 10 \times 10}$, our third was $\frac{1}{3 \times 10 \times 10 \times 10}$; what will our ninth remainder be?"

$(\frac{1}{3 \times 10 \times 10 \times 10 \times 10 \times 10 \times 10 \times 10 \times 10 \times 10}.)$

"Will we always get a remainder?" (Yes.) "Can we know what our remainder will be after we have divided 4,328,265 times?" (Yes.)

Concepts such as the following should be developed intuitively with many examples: If a number is divided by n, then the number of digits in the repeating series of digits cannot exceed n; if a divisor n is of the form $2^x \cdot 5^y$ (x and y being whole numbers), then the resulting decimal will be terminating; a recurrent digit signals a repeating series of digits when the recurrence has taken place after a series of zeros and there are no nonzero digits from that point on in the dividend.

The child should be asked to focus on these concepts by such well-designed questions as the following:

"John, the pattern of digits keeps repeating. Can you see anything that might tell you this would continue on and on?"

"Mary, your pattern of digits keeps repeating on and on. Can you notice anything about the remainders that might have told you that this would happen? When could you have first known this would happen?"

EXERCISES (1)

1. We can show that $\frac{7}{2 \times 2 \times 2 \times 5}$ can be named by a terminating decimal as follows: $\frac{7}{2 \times 2 \times 2 \times 5} \times \frac{5 \times 5}{5 \times 5} = \frac{7 \times 5 \times 5}{(2 \times 5) \times (2 \times 5) \times (2 \times 5)} = \frac{175}{1000} = .175$. Show that each of the following can be named by a terminating decimal by a similar technique:

a. $\frac{375}{2}$ b. $\frac{41}{5 \times 5}$ c. $\frac{3714}{2 \times 5 \times 5}$

2. Solve and then translate into decimal notation each of the following sentences:

a. $\frac{3}{10} + \frac{6}{10} = \frac{\triangle}{\square}$ c. $\frac{3}{10} - \frac{1}{10} = \frac{\triangle}{\square}$

b. $\frac{4}{10} + \frac{7}{100} = \frac{\triangle}{\square}$ d. $\frac{8}{10} - \frac{9}{100} = \frac{\triangle}{\square}$

3. Make up problems using fraction notation (to be translated to decimal notation) that could be used to illustrate the following:

a. $a + b = b + a$ d. $a - b = (a + d) - (b + d)$

b. $(a + b) + c = a + (b + c)$ e. $a + b = (a - c) + (b + c)$

c. $a - b = (a - d) - (b - d)$ f. $a + 0 = 0 + a = a$

4. If you were to divide by each of the following numbers, indicate the number of possible remainders you could obtain:

a. 17   b. 259   c. 371   d. 179,387,241

5. Derive decimal names for each of the following. (*Hint*: Give this problem some thought before working it.)

a. $\frac{1}{9}$ d. $\frac{4}{9}$ g. $\frac{1}{11}$ j. $\frac{100}{11}$

b. $\frac{2}{9}$ e. $\frac{5}{9}$ h. $\frac{2}{11}$ k. $\frac{10}{11}$

c. $\frac{1}{3}$ f. $\frac{2}{3}$ i. $\frac{3}{11}$ l. $\frac{121}{11}$

14.6 DECIMAL NOTATION FOR MULTIPLICATION AND DIVISION

The development of decimal notation for multiplication and division closely parallels our development of this notation for addition and subtraction. Early experiences involve the child in translating from fraction to decimal notation. Figure 14.5 depicts typical translations of multiplication.

Problem	Solution	Translation
$\frac{3}{10} \times \frac{4}{10} = \frac{\triangle}{\square}$	$\frac{12}{100}$	$.3 \times .4 = .12$
$\frac{2}{10} \times \frac{4}{10} = \frac{\triangle}{\square}$	$\frac{8}{100}$	$.2 \times .4 = .08$
$\frac{3}{10} \times \frac{8}{100} = \frac{\triangle}{\square}$	$\frac{24}{1000}$	$.3 \times .08 = .024$
$\frac{45}{10} \times \frac{2}{10} = \frac{\triangle}{\square}$	$\frac{90}{100}$	$4.5 \times .2 = .90$

Figure 14.5

It is hoped that in making the type of translation depicted in Figure 14.5, the child will begin to discover a rule for placing the decimal point in the name for the product. Such translations provide the child with readiness for extending the standard multiplication algorithm to the decimal-multiplication algorithm. Notice in Figure 14.6 how the multiplication algorithm is developed by relating the decimal partial products to those obtained using fraction names.

3.67
.014

$$.00028 \leftarrow \frac{4}{1000} \times \frac{7}{100} = \frac{28}{100,000} \qquad \frac{28}{100,000}$$

$$.0024 \leftarrow \frac{4}{1000} \times \frac{6}{10} = \frac{24}{10,000} \qquad \frac{240}{100,000}$$

$$.012 \leftarrow \frac{4}{1000} \times \frac{3}{1} = \frac{12}{1000} \qquad \frac{1200}{100,000}$$

$$.0007 \leftarrow \frac{1}{100} \times \frac{7}{100} = \frac{7}{10,000} \qquad \frac{70}{100,000}$$

$$.006 \leftarrow \frac{1}{100} \times \frac{6}{10} = \frac{6}{1000} \qquad \frac{600}{100,000}$$

$$.03 \leftarrow \frac{1}{100} \times \frac{3}{1} = \frac{3}{100} \qquad +\frac{3000}{100,000}$$

.05138 $\qquad \frac{5138}{100,000}$

Figure 14.6

The technique for refining this complete partial-products algorithm to the standard multiplication algorithm is the same as the one we used for relating the whole-number-multiplication algorithm.

3.2	3.2	3.2
× 2.4	2.4	2.4
.08	1.28	128
1.2	6.4	64
.4	7.68	7.68
6.		because tenths × tenths = hundredths
7.68		

Figure 14.7

The development of the division algorithm is closely related to the development of the multiplication algorithm. Although there exist many versions of the decimal-division algorithm, in this section we will take a careful look at the decimal-variable-subtraction-division algorithm.* The ease with which this algorithm is developed will be directly proportional to the depth of understanding the children have of the multiplication algorithm. Let us use the technique of tracing through a dialogue that might be associated with the development of this algorithm:

---

* The author has selected this less refined algorithm for development because he feels it will be an easier transition to the more complex algorithm for the teacher than if a more refined algorithm were used, and then the transition to the simpler algorithm were attempted.

$3 \times \square = 12$

In the sentence at the left, what are we asking? (We are asking, "3 times what number equals 12?") What is that number? (4.) What algorithm could we use to find our answer? (The division algorithm.)

$6 \times \square = 3$

In the sentence at the left, what are we asking? (We are asking, "6 times what number equals 3?")

Let us see if our division algorithm can be remodeled to help us find the quotient.

$6\overline{)3}$

If we had a set of 3 objects, would it be possible to take away 1 set of 6 objects, or 6 sets of 1 object? (No.) Suppose we took 1 set of 3 objects and partitioned each object into tenths. How many tenths would we get? (30.)

$6\overline{)3.0}$

At the left, we have indicated these 30 tenths by writing 3.0. If we take our set of 30 tenths and partition these into 6 equivalent sets, what would be in each set? (5 tenths.) If we remove 6 of these sets of 5 tenths, how many tenths would we have left? (Zero.)

$$\begin{array}{r} 6\overline{)3.0} \\ \underline{3.0} \ |.5 \\ 0 \ |.5 \end{array}$$

At the left, we have shown mathematically what we did.

$6 \times .5 = 3.0$

At the left, we see as we check our answer that .5 is the quotient of 3 and 6. Let us look at a more complex problem.

$.014\overline{)3.1244}$

Whenever our divisor is not a whole number, we can make use of the compensation property to restructure the problem in a manner that creates a divisor that is a whole number. For example, if we multiply the divisor and dividend in the problem at the left by 1000, we derive a new problem that will have the same quotient as our original problem.

$.014 \times 1000\overline{)3.1244 \times 1000}$

$14\overline{)3124.4}$ ⋅

The notation at the left depicts this process of using the compensation property.
(As you will see, all division problems can, by the use of the compensation property, be resolved to a division problem with a whole-number divisor. Thus, if the child is taught to master the use of an algorithm involving a whole-number divisor, he will be able to derive the quotient of any two fractional numbers.)

Let us specify that we are searching for a quotient to the nearest tenth. This will mean that we will compute our answer to hundredths and "round" the answer back to tenths. We will place a numeral 0 in the hundredths position to indicate that we are eventually going to be grouping sets of hundredths. Can we get 14 sets of 100 from 3124.40? (Or can we get 100 sets of 14 from 3124.40?) (Yes.) Can we get 14 sets of 200 from 3124.40? (Or 200 sets of 14?) (Yes.) If we take 14 sets of 200, or 2800, from 3124.40, how do we determine how much we will have left? (We subtract 2800 from 3124.40.) Can we get 14 sets of 10 from 324.40? (Or 10 sets of 14?) (Yes.) Can we get 14 sets of 20 from 324.40? (Or 20 sets or 14?) (Yes.) How much do we have left after we have taken 14 sets of 200 and 14 sets of 20 from 3124.40? (44.40.)

```
14)3124.40
           200

14)3124.40
   2800.00  200.
    324.40
    280.00   20.
     44.40
```

Are there 14 sets of 1 in 44.40? (Yes.)
14 sets of 2? (Yes.)
14 sets of 3? (Yes.)
14 sets of 4? (No.)

```
14)3124.40
   2800.00  200.
    324.40
    280.00   20.
     44.40
     42.00    3.
      2.40
```

Are there 14 sets of $\frac{1}{10}$ in 2.40? (Yes.)
Are there 14 sets of $\frac{2}{10}$ in 2.40? (No.)
Are there 14 sets of $\frac{1}{100}$ in 1.00? (Yes.)
Are there 14 sets of $\frac{7}{100}$? (Yes.)
Renaming $(200 + 20 + 3 + .1 + .07)$, we obtain 223.17 as the quotient of 3.1244 and .014.

```
14)3124.40
   2800.00  200.
    324.40
    280.00   20.
     44.40
     42.00    3.
      2.40
      1.40    .1
      1.00
       .98    .07
       .02
```

Even though this example depicts a problem a student will encounter in the later stages of mastering this algorithm, it contains all of the essential techniques he must master if he is to develop efficiency in using this algorithm.

14.7 TEACHING DECIMAL DIVISION USING A PLACE-VALUE CHART AND AN ANALOGY

Let us examine how a place-value chart model can be used in conjunction with an analogy to introduce the concept of annexing zeros in the dividend:

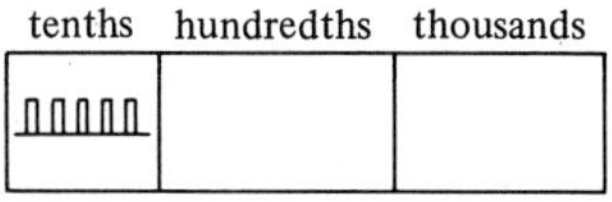

Let's assume you have 5 tenths and you want to distribute these among 4 people. What is the largest number of tenths each person can get if each person must receive the same number of tenths? (1.)

```
  .1
4).5
```

We place 1 in the tenths place to show that each person receives 1 tenth. We record a decimal point to denote the 1 as $\frac{1}{10}$.

```
  .1
4).5
   4
```

If you give each of 4 people 1 tenth, how many tenths are distributed? (4.) (The 4 is recorded.)

```
  .1
4).5
   4
   -
   1
```

You had 5 tenths and distributed 4 of them. How many do you have left? (1.) (A 1 is recorded.)

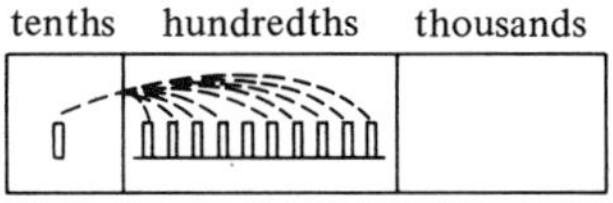

You trade in your 1 tenth for hundredths. How many hundredths can you get for 1 tenth? (10.)

```
   1
4).50
   4
   -
   10
```

Zeros are recorded in the hundredths place.

```
  .12
4).50
   4
   -
   10
    8
```

If you distribute the 10 hundredths to each of 4 people so that each person gets the same number of hundredths, how many hundredths will each person get? (2.) (A 2 is recorded in the hundredths place.)

```
  .12
4).50
   4
   -
   10
    8
    -
    2
```

You had 10 hundredths and passed 8 hundredths out. How many hundredths did you have left? (2.) (The 2 is recorded.)

tenths hundredths thousandths

If you trade in your 2 hundredths for thousandths, how many thousandths will you get? (20.)

```
  .12
4).500
  4
  __
  10
   8
  __
  20
```

(Zeros are recorded in the hundredths place.)

```
  .125
4).500
  4
  __
  10
   8
  __
  20
```

What is the largest number of thousandths each of the 4 people can get if each gets the same number of thousandths? (5.) (A 5 is recorded in the thousandths place.)

```
  .125
4).500
  4
  __
  10
   8
  __
  20
  20
  __
```

If you pass out 4 sets of 5 thousandths, how many thousandths do you pass out in all? (20.) (The 20 is recorded.)

```
  .125
4).500
  4
  __
  10
   8
  __
  20
  20
  __
   0
```

How many thousandths do you have left? (Zero.) (The 0 is recorded.)

14.8 TEACHING RATE PAIRS (RATIO)

There are many occasions in our society when we are interested in a many-to-many correspondence. For example, if apples are selling at 3 apples for 10 cents, then the following sets of ordered pairs represent this relationship: (3, 10), (6, 20), (9, 30), ... Commonly, we express these ordered pairs using fractional notation. When we use a pair of numbers under conditions of many-to-many in a social application we refer to this pair of numbers as a *rate pair*. We define two rate pairs $\frac{a}{b}$ and $\frac{c}{d}$ as being *equivalent* if and only if $a \times d = b \times c$. For example, $\frac{3}{4} = \frac{6}{8}$ because $3 \times 8 = 4 \times 6$.

At the elementary level, a student's main concern with rate pairs is that of finding a suitable equivalent name from a set of equivalent names or, possibly, of constructing equivalent names. For example, if 3 apples cost 10 cents, how many apples can be bought for 60 cents? This problem involves teaching the child how to proceed to obtain the equivalent name knowing $\frac{\square}{60}$ and $\frac{3}{10}$. Our definition of equivalent pairs helps us find the proper rate pair. We know that $\square \times 10 = 3 \times 60$, or $\square \times 10 = 180$ if $\frac{\square}{60}$ is to be a member of the same set of equivalent rate pairs to which $\frac{3}{10}$ belongs. Therefore we see that $\square = 18$ and that we could buy 18 apples for 60 cents if apples are being sold 3 for 10 cents.

The child's first experience with rate pairs should involve constructing many-to-many correspondence. Figure 14.8 represents a child's construction of sets matched 3 to 4.

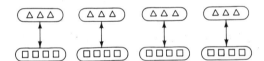

Figure 14.8

Questions such as the following, referring to Figure 14.8, will aid in developing the idea of rate pair:

"How many squares are matched with 6 triangles?" (8.) "When we have a 5-by-3 array of triangles, what array would we have for squares?" (5-by-4.) "How many triangles are matched with 16 squares?" (12.)

As children become competent in the construction of sets of equivalent rate pairs, the teacher should involve them in rate-pair applications. Some of the more common types of rate-pair situations from which the teacher can construct problems are as follows:

Length to time: miles per hour
Length to length: feet per mile
Area to area: square feet per acre
Volume to volume: pints per quart
Items to money: *n* cans per *m* cents
Money to weight: cents per pound
Money to money: dimes per dollar

Sometimes we are interested in comparing two rate pairs when the possibility exists that they are not from the same class. For example, in a supermarket, we notice that cans of beans are priced at 3 cans for 11 cents and 2 cans for 8 cents. We are interested in buying the brand that represents the greatest saving. We accomplish our comparison by finding equivalent rate pairs with the same cents named. We find that $\frac{3}{11} = \frac{24}{88}$ and $\frac{2}{8} = \frac{22}{88}$. Thus we can see that the beans selling at 3 cans for 11 cents represent the best buy.

Frequently we are interested in making relative comparisons of rate pairs. This relative comparison is accomplished by selecting rate pairs that have the same denominator named. When we select a denominator of 100 in order to make the comparison of rate pairs, we give this type of rate pair a special name. We refer to each of the numerators as so many percent. For example, in $\frac{30}{100}$, the 30 can be referred to as 30 percent.

14.9 TEACHING PERCENT

Percent notation is used extensively in our society. Since it is useful for reducing statistical data to an easily understood form and for conveying relationships in business applications of number, it will be important to develop not only the mathematical meaning of percent (that percent is another notation used to represent fractional numbers) but also its function as a "comparator."

Percent is not studied extensively at the elementary level. Only the foundation for working with percent notation is presented. In this section, we shall discuss only those aspects of percent that are applicable to the elementary school curriculum.

The first concern taught is that the "cent" in percent refers to a set of 100 and that when we talk about percent we are referring to so many items per hundred. For example, 23 percent means that we are comparing 23 elements of a set of the 100-element set. We introduce the symbol, %, which is read "percent," and which conveys the idea of "per hundred."

The child's early experiences should consist of direct translation experiences involving subsets of 100. This type of activity is illustrated by the table in Figure 14.9.

Because the concept of rate pair has preceded the development of percent, and because percent is being taught as a special case of the rate pair, it is important that once the concept of n per hundred is developed, sets of equivalent rate pairs are developed for percents. For example, not only should the students recognize that 50% is the rate pair $\frac{50}{100}$, but they also should know that there exists the infinite set of rate pairs $\frac{1}{2}, \frac{2}{4}, \frac{3}{6}, \ldots$, each element of which is equivalent to 50%.

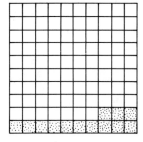

Fraction	Decimal	Percent
$\dfrac{13}{100}$	.13	13%

Figure 14.9

Finding the percent form when given a rate pair is accomplished with ease using our definition of equivalent rate pairs. For example, $\frac{3}{4}$ is equivalent to $\frac{\square}{100}$ if and only if $3 \times 100 = 4 \times \square$. Therefore $\square = 75$, and therefore $\frac{3}{4}$ is equivalent to 75%. Further concepts relating to percent will be developed in the exercises.

EXERCISES (2)

1. Solve and then translate each of the following to decimal notation:

   a. $\frac{3}{10} \times \frac{17}{100} = \frac{\triangle}{\square}$　　b. $\frac{4}{100} \times \frac{5}{100} = \frac{\triangle}{\square}$　　c. $\frac{42}{10} \times \frac{35}{100} = \frac{\triangle}{\square}$

2. Solve each of the following problems using the decimal-variable-subtraction-division algorithm.

   a. $471 \div 64$ (to the nearest tenth)
   b. $47.1 \div 64$ (to the nearest tenth)
   c. $47.1 \div 6.4$ (to the nearest hundredth)
   d. $471 \div .064$ (to the nearest tenth)
   e. $47.1 \div .64$ (to the nearest tenth)

3. Using the definition $\frac{a}{b} = \frac{c}{d}$, if, and only if, $a \times d = b \times c$, find the missing information:

   a. $\frac{30}{1} = \frac{\triangle}{4}$　　*Situation:* If John travels 30 miles per hour, how many miles can he travel in 4 hours?

   b. $\frac{12}{1} = \frac{144}{\triangle}$　　*Situation:* If there are 12 inches in 1 foot, how many feet are there in 144 inches?

   c. $\frac{3}{4} = \frac{\triangle}{36}$　　*Situation:* If 3 pieces of candy cost 4 cents, how many pieces can be bought for 36 cents?

4. Find five "rate pairs" equivalent to $\frac{3}{7}$.

5. Find the equivalent rate pairs that would enable you to compare the following:

   $\frac{4}{7}$　to　$\frac{9}{16}$

6. % can be interpreted as $\times \frac{1}{100}$ (read "times one hundredth"). Using this interpretation, find the fraction names for each of the following:

   a. 3%　　b. 130%

7. % can be interpreted as × .01 (read "times one hundredth"). Using this interpretation, find the decimal names for each of the following:

a. 22%   b. 4%   c. 1%

BIBLIOGRAPHY

Amstutz, M. G. "Let's 'Place' the Decimal Point, Not Move It," *The Arithmetic Teacher* (April 1963), pp. 205–207.

Davis, Philip J. *The Lore of Large Numbers* (New Haven, Conn.: Yale University Press), 1961, pp. 5–46, 115–143.

Honer, Wendall W. "Jimmy's Equivalents for the Sevenths," *The Arithmetic Teacher* (April 1963), pp. 197–198.

Rappaport, D. "Percentage—Noun or Adjective," *The Arithmetic Teacher* (January 1961), pp. 25–26.

School Mathematics Study Group. *Studies in Mathematics*, Vol. IX: *A Brief Course in Mathematics for Elementary School Teachers* (Stanford, Calif.: Stanford University Press), 1963, pp. 293–325.

Van Engen, Henry. "Rate Pairs, Fractions and Rational Numbers," *The Arithmetic Teacher* (December 1960), pp. 389–399.

Wendt, A. "Per Cent Without Cases," *The Arithmetic Teacher* (October 1959), pp. 209–214.

15

Teaching elementary number theory via independent explorations

BEHAVIORAL OBJECTIVES

Student can . . .

Distinguish between primes and composite numbers.

Describe how array models can be used for independent explorations by children in studying primes and composites.

Identify two types of sieves that can be used independently by children for isolating prime numbers.

Identify how divisibility rules for 2, 3, 4, 5, 6, and 9 can be used in independent exploration activities.

Construct an independent activity involving perfect, deficient, and abundant numbers.

Construct an independent activity involving figurate models.

Construct independent practice activities involving factor trees for specific composite numbers.

Construct practice sheets using set intersection to find the least common multiple.

15.1 INTRODUCTION

There are some who believe that elementary number-theory experiences offer the teacher a good opportunity to convey to the child the essence of mathematics. Number-theory experiences can provide the child with the thrill of pursuit and discovery when he tries to unlock the secret of a number pattern and then follows up his speculation or conjecture by testing the conjecture.

The area of number theory is one of the frontiers in mathematics in which a persistent novice has a chance of making a new mathematical discovery. The basic tools required for discovery are neither elaborate nor highly abstract. Each discovery that the child makes (even those discoveries new only to that child) unlocks doors to rooms filled with other patterns and relationships beckoning to be discovered.

A very useful by-product of stimulating a child's interest in number theory is that the path to discovery requires him to make many calculations.

He is thus stimulated to practice calculating in a meaningful way—the calculations are directed toward the satisfaction of a goal, rather than used simply for the sake of practice.

A second useful by-product of the study of number theory is that it develops the child's "number sense" and provides information that enhances the child's computational skills, such as how to find a least common multiple, which has direct application in finding the least common denominator for adding fractional numbers.

15.2 PRIMES, COMPOSITES, AND UNIT

In this chapter, we are concerned with the set of counting numbers: The following designate the set of counting numbers: 1, 2, 3, 4, 5, ... Another way of describing the set of counting numbers is to say that it is the set of all whole numbers except zero.

We are interested in partitioning this subset of the whole numbers into three disjoint subsets. We shall perform our partition on the basis of some of the factor names of these counting numbers. Consider the factor names for the first six counting numbers presented in Figure 15.1.

As you can see, a person could use 1 as a factor as many times as he desired and get as many factor names as he wanted. In order to restrict the number of names that we get, we shall say that 1 cannot be used as a factor more than once. And, in order to restrict further the number of factor names we obtain, we shall say that if two names use exactly the same factors but in different order, those two names are the same. With the new restrictions, our original lists of factor names are reduced to the arrangement shown in Figure 15.2.

When a number has no factor names, it is called a *unit*; when it has only one factor name, it is called a *prime number*; and when it has two or more factor names, it is called a *composite number*. Thus we see that 1 is the only number that can be classified as a unit, because by using 1 and any other counting number we can always obtain one factor name for any number by 1.

---

1 $1 \times 1, 1 \times 1 \times 1, 1 \times 1 \times 1 \times 1$

2 $1 \times 2, 2 \times 1, 1 \times 1 \times 2$

3 $1 \times 3, 3 \times 1, 1 \times 1 \times 3$

4 $1 \times 4, 4 \times 1, 2 \times 2, 1 \times 1 \times 4$

5 $1 \times 5, 5 \times 1, 1 \times 1 \times 5$

6 $1 \times 6, 6 \times 1, 2 \times 3, 3 \times 2, 1 \times 1 \times 6$

Figure 15.1

1	No factor names
2	1×2
3	1×3
4	$1 \times 4, 2 \times 2$
5	1×5
6	$1 \times 6, 2 \times 3$

Figure 15.2

Now that we have defined how we partition the set of counting numbers, we shall explore different techniques children can use in independent activities to decide systematically when a number has only one factor name. To do this, let us review the meaning of such factor names as 1×4 and 2×2 based on the array definition:

1×4 means 1 row of 4 or $\cdots$
2×2 means 2 rows of 2 or ::

One way we can lead a child to discover if a number is a prime or composite is to have him start with a set of objects of that number and see if an array other than an array with 1 column or 1 row can be constructed. For example, the child could discover that 12 is not a prime number, because any of the following arrays could be constructed in addition to the 1×12 and the 12×1 array:

$$4 \times 3 \qquad 2 \times 6 \qquad 3 \times 4 \qquad 6 \times 2$$

You might structure your independent activity as follows: Each child is given a set of 30 or more objects. He is instructed to begin with 2 objects and find the maximum number of arrays that can be constructed with the 2 objects, then 3 objects, then 4 objects, and so on. He is instructed to record the number of possible arrays for each number of objects. Before beginning this exploratory activity you may wish to demonstrate the possibilities using one example.

As the child matures, more sophisticated procedures can be developed. The first of these involves noting the relationships that exist between primes and various sequences. In Figure 15.3, we note that the factor names of every number are multiples of 2. And notice that every number larger than 2 in this sequence has at least one name other than the name using the 1 as a factor. From this we can conclude that no number greater than 2 in our list can be a prime.

Explorations of possible arrays using two
blocks, three blocks, and four blocks.

2	4	6	8	10	12	14	16
1 × 2	2 × 2	3 × 2	4 × 2	5 × 2	6 × 2	7 × 2	8 × 2

Figure 15.3

The same logic can be applied to starting a sequence with a 3 and
considering every third number. In Figure 15.4 we see that every number
larger than 3 in this type of sequence has at least one name other than the
name using the 1 as a factor. Therefore no number greater than 3 in our list
in Figure 15.4 can be a prime.

3	6	9	12	15	18	21
1 × 3	2 × 3	3 × 3	4 × 3	5 × 3	6 × 3	7 × 3

Figure 15.4

We could set up similar sequences for 5, 7, 11, and so on, and study the
resulting tables to determine which of our counting numbers can be
established as composites. We can, however, help the children devise a more
efficient technique for discovering the primes, now that we have established
the logical reason why every second counting number after 2 is a
composite, why every third counting number after 3 is a composite, and so
forth.

Consider the table depicted in Figure 15.5. We have shaded in the 1 box, because the 1 has been identified as a unit. Now, if we mark every second number from 2, we shall have eliminated all the multiples of 2 that are composites. We have done this in Figure 15.6.

1	2	3	4	5	6	7	8	9	10
11	12	13	14	15	16	17	18	19	20
21	22	23	24	25	26	27	28	29	30

Figure 15.5

1	2	3	4	5	6	7	8	9	10
11	12	13	14	15	16	17	18	19	20
21	22	23	24	25	26	27	28	29	30

Figure 15.6

We notice that 3 is the next number after the 2 that is not marked. Since it obviously cannot be a multiple of 2, and it could not be a multiple of a number larger than itself, it must be a prime. We can eliminate all the multiples of this number that are composite by marking out every third number larger than 3. We have done this in Figure 15.7.

1	2	3	4	5	6	7	8	9	10
11	12	13	14	15	16	17	18	19	20
21	22	23	24	25	26	27	28	29	30

Figure 15.7

By a similar development, we can discover larger and larger primes. This process is called *sieving*. Once the basic idea of a sieve is developed the children can begin independent activities involving sieving to find not only primes but various types of composite numbers. The student can participate in more advanced sieving activities by building the concept that any counting number can be expressed as $6 \times \square + \triangle$, where the replacements for $\square$ and $\triangle$ come from the set $\{0, 1, 2, 3, 4, \ldots\}$. Consider the following pattern:

a. $6 \times 0 + 1 = 1$ $6 \times 1 + 1 = 7$ $6 \times 2 + 1 = 13$
b. $6 \times 0 + 2 = 2$ $6 \times 1 + 2 = 8$ $6 \times 2 + 2 = 14$
c. $6 \times 0 + 3 = 3$ $6 \times 1 + 3 = 9$ $6 \times 2 + 3 = 15$
d. $6 \times 0 + 4 = 4$ $6 \times 1 + 4 = 10$ $6 \times 2 + 4 = 16$
e. $6 \times 0 + 5 = 5$ $6 \times 1 + 5 = 11$ $6 \times 2 + 5 = 17$
f. $6 \times 0 + 6 = 6$ $6 \times 1 + 6 = 12$ $6 \times 2 + 6 = 18$

By having the child extend this pattern, you will help him to recognize that any counting number can be expressed by it.

Notice that the numbers named by (b), (d), and (f) are all even numbers and have multiples of 2. Notice that row (c) names multiples of 3. This means that, other than the primes 2 and 3, we shall find all other primes in rows (a) and (e). Figure 15.8 is a table that utilizes this information.

1	7	13	19	25	31	37
2	8	14	20	26	32	38
3	9	15	21	27	33	39
4	10	16	22	28	34	40
5	11	17	23	29	35	41
6	12	18	24	30	36	42

Figure 15.8

Even though this technique provides a convenient method of eliminating the multiples of 2 and 3 from consideration, it is still necessary to sieve out the multiples of 5, 7, 11, and so on. The technique of sieving is a useful technique for isolating the smaller primes, but it is not an efficient technique to use in deciding whether or not 4809 is a prime.

15.3 DIVISIBILITY RULES

Divisibility rules offer the teacher an excellent opportunity to promote meaningful practice on basic skills as well as acting as vehicles for independent exploration by the students. Before children can begin independent exploration, you will need to define the divisibility of two counting numbers in terms of a quotient and a remainder.

$\triangle$ is said to be *divisible by* $\square$ if the quotient of $\triangle$ and $\square$ is equal to a counting number and the remainder is zero.

For example, 8 will be said to be divisible by 2, because the quotient of 8 and 2 is 4, and the remainder is equal to zero.

Independent explorations using the right distributive property of division over addition can lead to the discovery of divisibility rules if the exercises are structured in such a way that relationships such as those between remainders are highlighted. Study the pattern in Figure 15.9 and see if you can generalize the relationships that exist between the remainders and the relationship between the quotients.

	Quotients	Remainders
$(35 + 23) \div 11$	5	3
$(35 \div 11) + (23 \div 11)$	3, 2	2, 1
$(24 + 25) \div 9$	5	4
$(24 \div 9) + (25 \div 9)$	2, 2	6, 7*
$(45 + 39) \div 4$	21	0
$(45 \div 4) + (39 \div 4)$	11, 9	1, 3

* *Hint*: $6 + 7 = 13$ and $13 \div 9$ gives a remainder of 4.

Figure 15.9

If we express the quotients as mixed numerals, the following relationship is seen:

$(35 + 23) \div 11 = 5\frac{3}{11}$
$(35 \div 11) + (23 \div 11) = 3\frac{2}{11} + 2\frac{1}{11} = 5\frac{2+1}{11} = 5\frac{3}{11}$

also

$(24 + 25) \div 9 = 5\frac{4}{9}$
$(24 \div 9) + (25 \div 9) = 2\frac{6}{9} + 2\frac{7}{9} = 4\frac{6+7}{9} = 4\frac{13}{9} = 5\frac{4}{9}$

also

$(45 + 39) \div 4 = 21\frac{0}{4}$
$(45 \div 4) + (39 \div 4) = 11\frac{1}{4} + 9\frac{3}{4} = 20\frac{1+3}{4} = 20\frac{4}{4} = 21$

As can be seen easily, it is possible to determine a remainder on division by considering the sequence of remainders obtained on division when the dividend is expressed as a sequence of addends.

Children who discover this idea through independent activities can explore extensions of this concept which result in rules of divisibility. Let us see how it will aid us in developing rules of divisibility for 2, 3, 5, and 9.

We have seen that the sum of the partial remainders can be used to identify what the remainder will be when the number is divided. Let us express our numerals in expanded notation and observe the partial remainders when the number is divided by 2. Figure 15.10 shows several numbers that have been divided by 2 and the remainders obtained.

By working a series of exercises of this type, the child will be ready to speculate that he need only observe the remainder from the ones to tell whether a number is divisible by 2. By structuring a similar set of

```
      300 + 35 + 1          3500 +  50 + 1          1500 + 100 + 3
  2)600 + 70 + 3        2)7000 + 100 + 2        2)3000 + 200 + 7
      600   70   1          7000   100   2          3000   200   6
      ─────────────          ─────────────          ─────────────
       0    0   1             0     0   0             0     0   1

0 + 0 + 1 = 1;         0 + 0 + 0 = 0;          0 + 0 + 1 = 1;
therefore             therefore              therefore
673 ÷ 2 gives us a     7102 ÷ 2 gives us a     3207 ÷ 2 gives us a
remainder of 1         remainder of 0         remainder of 1
```

Figure 15.10

exercises, we can lead children to discover the rules for divisibility by 3. Figure 15.11 depicts such a structured set of exercises. By completing such

Enter the remainder for each of the following:

	Remainder		Remainder		Remainder		Remainder
1 ÷ 3		10 ÷ 3		100 ÷ 3		1000 ÷ 3	
2 ÷ 3		20 ÷ 3		200 ÷ 3		2000 ÷ 3	
3 ÷ 3		30 ÷ 3		300 ÷ 3		3000 ÷ 3	
4 ÷ 3		40 ÷ 3		400 ÷ 3		4000 ÷ 3	
5 ÷ 3		50 ÷ 3		500 ÷ 3		5000 ÷ 3	
6 ÷ 3		60 ÷ 3		600 ÷ 3		6000 ÷ 3	
7 ÷ 3		70 ÷ 3		700 ÷ 3		7000 ÷ 3	
8 ÷ 3		80 ÷ 3		800 ÷ 3		8000 ÷ 3	
9 ÷ 3		90 ÷ 3		900 ÷ 3		9000 ÷ 3	

Figure 15.11

a table, the child may discover the relationship between the number being divided by 3 and its remainder. This discovery will facilitate the next step in his formation of the rule. The child should now be able to compute mentally the remainder of a number such as 6532 on division by 3. (His mental process will be something similar to the following: 6000 leaves a remainder of 0, 500 a remainder of 2, 30 a remainder of 0, and 2 a remainder of 2. Therefore, when 6532 is divided by 3, a remainder of 1 will be obtained.)

Similarly, the child can be led to generalize a rule for divisibility by 5 by similar independent exploration. Figure 15.12 illustrates some of the

```
      120 +  8 + 0          800 + 18 + 1          1800 + 120 + 1
  5)600 + 40 + 3        5)4000 + 90 + 6        5)9000 + 600 + 5
      600   40   0          4000   90   5          9000   600   5
      ─────────────          ─────────────          ─────────────
       0    0   3             0     0   1             0     0   0

0 + 0 + 3 = 3;         0 + 0 + 1 = 1;          0 + 0 + 0 = 0;
therefore             therefore              therefore
643 ÷ 5 gives us a     4096 ÷ 5 gives us a     9605 ÷ 5 gives us a
remainder of 3         remainder of 1         remainder of 0
```

Figure 15.12

exercises that might be constructed to lead the child to see that the ones digit, in a base-10 numeral, will identify whether a number is divisible by 5.

By structuring a set of exercises similar to those constructed for developing the rules of 3, we can have the child discover a rule of divisibility by 9. Figure 15.13 depicts such a table.

Enter the remainder for each of the following:

Remainder	Remainder	Remainder	Remainder
$1 \div 9$	$10 \div 9$	$100 \div 9$	$1000 \div 9$
$2 \div 9$	$20 \div 9$	$200 \div 9$	$2000 \div 9$
$3 \div 9$	$30 \div 9$	$300 \div 9$	$3000 \div 9$
$4 \div 9$	$40 \div 9$	$400 \div 9$	$4000 \div 9$
$5 \div 9$	$50 \div 9$	$500 \div 9$	$5000 \div 9$
$6 \div 9$	$60 \div 9$	$600 \div 9$	$6000 \div 9$
$7 \div 9$	$70 \div 9$	$700 \div 9$	$7000 \div 9$
$8 \div 9$	$80 \div 9$	$800 \div 9$	$8000 \div 9$
$9 \div 9$	$90 \div 9$	$900 \div 9$	$9000 \div 9$

Figure 15.13

From this table, the child can discover quickly that n tens divided by 9 gives a remainder of n, and that x hundreds divided by 9 gives a remainder of x, and so on. He should now be able, after a brief mental calculation, to give the remainder when any four-digit number is divided by 9.

EXERCISES (1)

1. Describe an activity involving blocks that could lead a child to the identification of prime numbers.
2. Describe an independent activity employing sieving that could be used to identify a certain type of multiple.
3. Construct a set of exercises using the right distributive property of division over addition that could have a reasonable probability of leading the child to discover a divisibility rule.

15.4 PERFECT NUMBERS

Prerequisite to the task of having the child classify various subsets of the set of counting numbers through independent activities is the skill of deriving the set of divisors of a given number.

In constructing the set of divisors, we find that 1 and the number itself are always members of this set. Our rules for divisibility will facilitate finding other divisors. For example, let us find the set of divisors of the number 276. Figure 15.14 illustrates how our analysis might proceed.

Number	Divisors	Reason
276	1 and 276	Every number is divisible by itself and the number 1
	2	Satisfies rule for divisibility by 2
	138	Because $276 \div 2 = 138$ implies $276 \div 138 = 2$
	3	Satisfies rule for divisibility by 3
	92	Because $276 \div 3 = 92$ implies $276 \div 92 = 3$
	4	Because 276 is divisible by 4
	69	Because $276 \div 4 = 69$ implies $276 \div 69 = 4$
	6	Because 6 is divisible by both 2 and 3
	46	Because $276 \div 6 = 46$ implies $276 \div 46 = 6$
	12	Because 12 is divisible by both 3 and 4
	23	Because $276 \div 12 = 23$ implies $276 \div 23 = 12$

Figure 15.14

Thus we have discovered the set of divisors of 276 is 1, 2, 3, 4, 6, 12, 23, 46, 69, 92, 138, 276. Sometimes we can eliminate a divisor on the basis of a divisibility rule; for example, we can eliminate 5 as a divisor of 276, because the ones place contains neither 5 nor 0. Other times, as in the case of 7 and 13 where a simple rule of divisibility is absent, we must perform the division. When we reach a point—in this case, 23—where we have tested all numbers up to one of the divisors in our descending sequence of divisors, we no longer have to test any larger numbers.

We refer to the set of all divisors of a number, except the number itself, as a *set of proper divisors*. This set of proper divisors will be very important in our effort to repartition the set of counting numbers. Figure 15.15 depicts several sets of proper divisors.

If a number is equal to the sum of its proper divisors, we call it a *perfect* number. If a number is less than the sum of its proper divisors, it

Set of proper divisors

1	$\emptyset$
2	{1}
3	{1}
30	{1, 2, 3, 5, 6, 10, 15}
36	{1, 2, 3, 4, 6, 9, 12, 18}

Figure 15.15

is called an *abundant* number. And if a number is neither an abundant nor a perfect number, we say it is a *deficient* number. For example, 12 is an abundant number, because $12 < 1 + 2 + 3 + 4 + 6$; 6 is a perfect number, because $6 = 1 + 2 + 3$; and 10 is a deficient number because $10 > 1 + 2 + 5$.

At this point exercises can be constructed to lead the child to independently search for perfect, deficient, and abundant numbers.

15.5 CONSTRUCTING FACTOR TREES

Our technique of either using divisibility tests or actually testing a trial divisor by division is an inefficient technique for obtaining the set of proper divisors. In this section, we shall examine sophisticated independent activities that determine the proper divisors of a number.

As we have seen, each number can have an infinite set of factor names if we allow 1 to be used as a factor. To restrict the number of factors a number can have, we shall restrict the use of ones to those numbers that would have no factor names if 1 were excluded. For example, $1 = 1 \times 1$, and $13 = 1 \times 13$. We shall further restrict the number that can serve as a factor by specifying that each factor must be either a prime or the number 1.

The following factor names satisfy our present restrictions: 3×1, 1×3, $2 \times 3 \times 5$, $7 \times 7 \times 2 \times 5$, $2 \times 5 \times 7 \times 7$, $2 \times 7 \times 5 \times 7$, $7 \times 2 \times 7 \times 5$.

Upon obtaining the product using these factor names, you would recognize that names with the same factors, regardless of order, name the same product. Because changing the order of the factors does not give us a new number, we shall by convention order our factor names from the smallest factor named on the left, and proceeding in a left-to-right manner, list the largest factor named always to the right of the smaller factors. For example, $2 \times 2 \times 3 \times 7 \times 13 \times 29$ follows this technique of ordering factors.

Let us examine how we can obtain systematically a factor name in this form. Consider the number 60: we find that 2 is a factor giving us 2×30; 2 is a factor of 30 giving us $2 \times 2 \times 15$; 3 is a factor of 15, giving us $2 \times 2 \times 3 \times 5$; and because 5 is a prime, we are finished. Figure 15.16 denotes this analysis using a factor tree. Note that our factors are located at the ends of the branches.

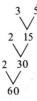

Figure 15.16

Figure 15.17 depicts several factors trees that have been derived by such analysis. (Note that when the original number is a prime, the branches consist of 1 and the prime.)

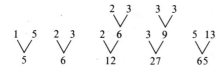

Figure 15.17

Since we shall have a need later to distinguish between the fact that 2 is a factor of a given number and 2 twos are factors of a given number, we identify our factors by subscripts. For example, 2_2 will indicate that this is the second 2. By using subscripts we can talk about the complete set of prime factors for a given number. For example, $2_1, 2_2, 3_1, 3_2$ is the complete set of prime factors of 36.

Let us examine how you can structure an independent exploration that would result in the child's learning the concept of prime factorization. For this activity the child is given a pack of cards naming prime numbers. There are several twos, threes, fives, and so on, in the pack. The child is given a duplicated paper similar to the following:

2	×	×	×	×
3	×	×	×	×
4	×	×	×	×
5	×	×	×	×
6	×	×	×	×
7	×	×	×	×
8	×	×	×	×
9	×	×	×	×
10	×	×	×	×
11	×	×	×	×
12	×	×	×	×

He is assigned the task of using only these cards and the operation of multiplication to name the specified numbers. Following is a partially completed task sheet:

2	2 ×	×	×	×
3	3 ×	×	×	×
4	2 ×	2 ×	×	×
5	5 ×	×	×	×
6	2 ×	3 ×	×	×
7	7 ×	×	×	×
8	2 ×	2 ×	2 ×	×
9	×	×	×	×
10	×	×	×	×
11	×	×	×	×
12	×	×	×	×

By varying the task requirements to include (1) having the child try to find two names for a number using different primes, and (2) having the primes displayed from smallest to greatest, the child will gain some insight into the uniqueness of prime factorization.

15.6 LEAST COMMON MULTIPLE

By obtaining the union of two complete sets of prime factors for two numbers, it is possible to find the least common multiple of these two numbers. Figure 15.18 depicts the derivation of several least common multiples by the union of complete sets of prime factors.

We use the least common multiple to obtain a common divisor when adding fractional numbers. For example, knowing that 8 is the least common multiple of 4 and 8 shows us how to modify $\frac{3}{4} + \frac{1}{8}$ to $\frac{3 \times 2}{4 \times 2} + \frac{1}{8} = \frac{6}{8} + \frac{1}{8}$, so that the right distributive property of division over addition can be used.

Set of numbers	Union of complete sets of prime factors	Least common multiple
35 and 25	$\{5_1, 7_1\} \cup \{5_1, 5_2\} = \{5_1, 5_2, 7_1\}$	$5 \times 5 \times 7 = 175$
6 and 8	$\{2_1, 3_1\} \cup \{2_1, 2_2, 2_3\} = \{2_1, 2_2, 2_3, 3_1\}$	$2 \times 2 \times 2 \times 3 = 24$
3 and 10	$\{3_1\} \cup \{2_1, 5_1\} = \{2_1, 3_1, 5_1\}$	$2 \times 3 \times 5 = 30$
4 and 8	$\{2_1, 2_2\} \cup \{2_1, 2_2, 2_3\} = \{2_1, 2_2, 2_3\}$	$2 \times 2 \times 2 = 8$

Figure 15.18

By working with a modification of the duplicated sheet described in the previous section, an independent activity can be constructed which will lead the child to discover how least common multiples are generated.

The prime pack this time consists of each type of prime being on a certain color card. For example, all the cards displaying 2 can be on blue cards and all the cards displaying 3 can be on orange cards.

The child's first task is to display the prime factorization of pairs of numbers. For example, 35 and 25 would be displayed as follows:

| 5 | × | 7 | × M × |

| 5 | × | 5 | × M × |

The child is assigned the task of transfering the primes from one card to the second card with the understanding that if a numeral already is displayed on the second card, then it may be covered by one identical numeral in the transfer.

After the task is completed the display would be as follows:

| × | M | × | M | × |

| 5 | × | 5 | × | 7 |

Thus the child would discover by this exploration that the least common multiple is 175.

15.7 GREATEST COMMON DIVISOR

By obtaining the intersection of two complete sets of prime factors for two numbers, it is possible to find the greatest common divisor of these two numbers. Figure 15.19 depicts the derivation of several greatest common divisors by the intersection of complete sets of prime factors.

Set of numbers	Intersection of complete sets of prime factors	Greatest common divisor
35 and 25	$\{5_1, 7_1\} \cap \{5_1, 5_2\} = \{5_1\}$	5
12 and 8	$\{2_1, 2_2, 3_1\} \cap \{2_1, 2_2, 2_3\} = \{2_1, 2_2\}$	$2 \times 2 = 4$
3 and 10	$\{3_1\} \cap \{2_1, 5_1\} = \{\quad\}$	1*
4 and 8	$\{2_1, 2_2\} \cap \{2_1, 2_2, 2_3\} = \{2_1, 2_2\}$	$2 \times 2 = 4$

* Because no common prime factor was obtained and because 1 is a factor of every number, the greatest common divisor must be 1.

Figure 15.19

We use the greatest common divisor to find the simplest form for a set of equivalent fractions. For example, given $\frac{18}{24}$, the intersection of the complete set of factors of 18 and 24 is $\{2_1, 3_1, 3_2\} \cap \{2_1, 2_2, 2_3, 3_1\} = \{2_1, 3_1\}$; therefore 6 is the greatest common divisor. Using the compensation property $\frac{18 \div 6}{24 \div 6}$, we obtain $\frac{3}{4}$, which is the simplest form in the set of equivalent fractions.

The same task materials used by the student for finding the least common multiple can be used to find the greatest common divisor. Instead of transferring the cards the student has to pair all matching cards that occur in both sets. For example, if we start with 8 and 12 displayed:

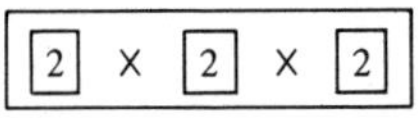

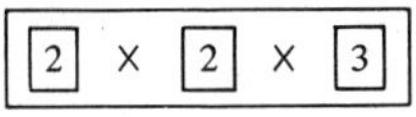

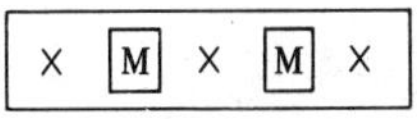

| 2 | × | 2 | × | 2 |

| 2 | × | 2 | × | 3 |

| × | M | × | M | × |

Then two of the 2's in the upper display can be paired with two of the 2's in the bottom display, resulting in

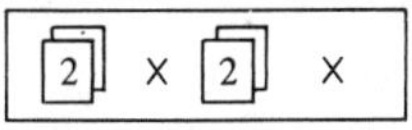

| 2 | × | 2 | × |

or 4 as being identified as the greatest common divisor.

15.8 FIGURATE "NUMBERS"

Figurate "numbers" get their name from the fact that the mathematical model of dots used to represent a set with a stated number property can be structured to depict triangles, squares, pentagons, and so forth. For example, 4 is said to be a square number because it can be depicted as ∶∵.

Of special importance in studying figurate numbers is not the model but the series that relates to this model. For example, consider the representations of triangular numbers shown in Figure 15.20. Notice that the series 1, $1 + 2, 1 + 2 + 3, 1 + 2 + 3 + 4$, and so forth, is suggested by these models.

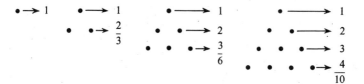

Figure 15.20

Of even greater interest is the series generated for square numbers. Notice in Figure 15.21 the remarkable relationship that exists between the sum of n consecutive odd numbers and n^2.

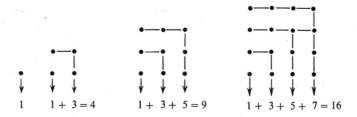

Figure 15.21

Such unusual relationships, which are found through exploration with number patterns, provide the child with a sense of discovery and achievement. The child who recognizes that any series of calculations may reveal a remarkable pattern views such calculations not as a task but as a vehicle to discovery. It is the teacher's responsibility to "unlock the door to the hallway of number theory" because through this hall many children gain their first glimpses and appreciation of the real beauty of mathematics. Number theory truly offers the child his first opportunity to explore mathematics on his own.

EXERCISES (2)

1. Construct a task activity that would result in the child finding a perfect number between 20 and 30.

2. Construct a task activity that would result in the finding of the prime factorization of 990.
3. Construct a task activity that would result in the child finding the least common multiple for 382 and 522.
4. The following dot patterns serve as models for pentagonal numbers. Identify the series a child might discover by studying these patterns.

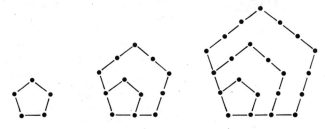

BIBLIOGRAPHY

Collier, C. C., and H. H. Lerch. *Teaching Mathematics in the Modern Elementary School* (New York: Macmillan), 1969, pp. 47–71.

Ferrer, Sister M. "Primes at the Primary Level," *Catholic School Journal* (November 1961), pp. 48–49.

Grossnickle, F. E., L. J. Brueckner, and J. Reckzeh. *Discovering Meanings in Elementary School Mathematics* (New York: Holt, Rinehart and Winston), 1968, pp. 205–212.

Heddens, J. W. *Today's Mathematics* (Palo Alto, Calif.: Science Research Associates), 1971, pp. 190–204.

Kennedy, R. E. "Divisibility by Integers Ending in 1, 3, 7, or 9," *Mathematics Teacher* (February 1971), pp. 137–138.

May, L. J. *Teaching Mathematics in the Elementary School* (New York: Free Press), 1970, pp. 141–164.

Spitzer, H. F. *Teaching Elementary School Mathematics* (Boston: Houghton Mifflin), 1967, pp. 13–30.

16

Teaching the integers

BEHAVIORAL OBJECTIVES

Student can . . .

Identify three ways that an elementary school child might be exposed to integer concepts in a nonschool situation.

State an analogy that can be used to introduce the concept of integers.

Describe addition of integers in terms of taking a trip "followed by" another trip.

Describe subtraction of integers in terms of taking a trip "followed by" the opposite of another trip.

Describe an analogy that could be used to introduce multiplication.

Describe a method of getting children to discover a property of an operation on the set of integers.

Define the "less than" relationship of integers in terms of equality and addition.

Describe a patterning technique that can be used to introduce negative exponents.

Describe how translation can be used to introduce scientific notation.

16.1 INTRODUCTION

Long before the child formally studies the set of directed numbers we call integers, he has been exposed to many instances of their application. For example, listening to reports of weather around the country he hears the announcer say that it is 20 degrees below zero in Bismarck, North Dakota. Listening to his father discuss his business affairs, he hears that the company went $1000 into the red that year. Watching a rocket being launched on television, he sees ..., -9, -8, -7, -6, -5, -4, -3, -2, -1, 0, 1, 2, 3, ..., flashed on the screen, one numeral at a time. Playing a game, he notes that he has gone 5 in the "hole" by landing on a disk that says to take 10 points from your score. He hears the teacher refer to "3 hours ago," or the football announcer say that the team made a "minus 34-yard gain in the first half."

Whereas a rigorous introduction of integers is postponed until the junior high, the basic properties of integers and operations on the set of integers

are developed intuitively at the elementary level. Although there exists an isomorphic relationship between the non-negative directed numbers and the set of whole numbers that the child has studied, these sets are quite distinct. For example, let a, b, c, and d be whole numbers and let a^1, b^1, c^1, and d^1 be the integers we associate with a, b, c, and d. We then say that there is an isomorphic relation between the set of whole numbers and the set of non-negative numbers, because when $a + b = c$, then $a^1 + b^1 = c^1$; and when $a \times b = d$, then $a^1 \times b^1 = d^1$. Even though both of these sets behave identically under the same operation, it is probably best to have the child make this discovery rather than have you make the statement that the non-negative numbers *are* the set of whole numbers.

16.2 ADDITION ON THE SET OF INTEGERS

It is a primary responsibility of the teacher to help the child recognize a need for integers. This need is not only mathematical—for example, we need a number that satisfies the equation $\square + 5 = 0$—but is also practical. For example, we have occasions when "5 being the number property of a set" does not fully convey the number property of the set. A bill for 5 dollars and a check for 5 dollars are entirely different uses of fiveness.

In grades after the elementary grades, it is a simple matter to define directed numbers and proceed to establish their place in the hierarchy of number systems. At the elementary level, we must proceed in a more intuitive manner in order to transit smoothly from the set of whole numbers to the set of integers.

Let us consider how one might intuitively introduce the integers through a map. Assume that John lived in the house labeled *a* in Figure 16.1. What

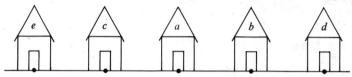

Figure 16.1

would the students immediately notice if you were to say that Mary lives in the second house from John's house? The children would immediately say that you could not tell which house Mary lives in from those directions. What you have done is create a need for conveying more information.

Discuss with the children various ways that we can communicate to someone which house Mary lives in if she lives in the house labeled *d*. For example, you might say that she lives in the second house to the right of John's house if you are facing John's house. Or you might write $\vec{2}$ where the arrow tells us which way to go from John's house and the 2 tells us how many houses from John's house. Or you might write *r2* where the *r* tells us to go right and the 2 tells us to go 2 houses, and so on. Let the children discuss how to symbolize directions for going to various houses from John's house.

Let us now settle on one type of symbolism and rename all of the houses in terms of their location with respect to John's house (see Figure 16.2).

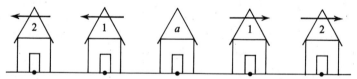

Figure 16.2

We are left with the problem of telling everyone where John's house is. Obviously, John's house is neither to the right nor left of John's house. Therefore we use neither a → symbol nor a ← to mark the location of John's house. This is a very important principle relating to what we shall come to call the zero of the set of integers. This zero is neither positive nor negative, although there will be times when it is desirable to define it either as positive or negative, as when programing a computer. Because we go zero houses from John's house to get to John's house, it is appropriate that we name the location of John's house zero.

Having established a zero and the sets of numbers that will be related to zero, we are at a point where we can explore operations on this new set of numbers.

Where would we be if we went to $\vec{2}$ and then went 3 houses to the right of this house? Symbolically, we might express this idea as $\vec{2}$ followed by $\vec{3} = \square$. Extending our map, we see that this would take us to house $\vec{5}$. Therefore we will say that $\vec{2}$ followed by $\vec{3} = \vec{5}$. Similarly, we could ask where we would be if we went to $\vec{2}$ and then went 3 houses to the left. Symbolically, we might express this idea as $\vec{2}$ followed by $\overleftarrow{3} = \square$. We see that this would take us to house $\overleftarrow{1}$. Therefore we say that $\vec{2}$ followed by $\overleftarrow{3} = \overleftarrow{1}$.

We are now at a position where we can explore certain properties attributable to the operation "followed by" on the set of directed numbers.

As you have probably surmised, the operation "followed by" is equivalent to addition. Therefore, let us replace the words "followed by" by the symbol $+$. Thus we have established the meaning behind an operation before we have introduced the symbol for it. This is consistent with the sequence we should employ generally in introducing symbolism.

After establishing the arbitrariness of the symbol chosen to depict our new set of numbers, we can proceed to the more standard symbols for integers. By convention we affix $-$ to all numerals to the left of zero on the number line and $+$ to all numerals to the right of zero on the number line. (Although some textbooks affix only the $-$, this author believes that in early activities with integers an effort should be made to distinguish the positive integers from the nonzero whole numbers. After the isomorphic relationship between the sets of non-negative integers and the set of whole numbers has been established, the $+$ may be dropped.) Thus we see that $\vec{3} + \vec{2}$ translates to $^{+}3 + {}^{-}2$ (read "positive three plus negative two").

16.3 SUBTRACTION ON THE SET OF INTEGERS

We can lay the groundwork for the development of subtraction by having the students investigate patterns such as $^{-}3 + {}^{+}3 = 0$, $^{+}7 + {}^{-}7 = 0$, and $^{-}2 + {}^{+}2 = 0$. Because of this relationship, we say that $^{-}3$ is the opposite of $^{+}3$, $^{+}7$ is the opposite of $^{-}7$, $^{-}2$ is the opposite of $^{+}2$, and so forth.

We are now ready to look at an operation we call "followed by the opposite of." We see that

$^{+}7$ followed by the opposite of $^{-}2$ means

$^{+}7$ followed by $^{+}2$, and

$^{-}3$ followed by the opposite of $^{+}4$ means

$^{-}3$ followed by $^{-}4$

Returning to our number line, we discover that

$^+7$ followed by the opposite of $^-2 = {}^+9$, and

$^-3$ followed by the opposite of $^+4 = {}^-7$

After having thus established the meaning behind our operation, we introduce the symbol — for "followed by the opposite of." We now explore the following related number sentences:

$^-3 - {}^-2 = {}^-1$ and $^-1 + {}^-2 = {}^-3$

$^-4 - {}^+2 = {}^-6$ and $^-6 + {}^+2 = {}^-4$

$^+8 - {}^+3 = {}^+5$ and $^+5 + {}^+3 = {}^+8$

$^+5 - {}^-3 = {}^+8$ and $^+8 + {}^-3 = {}^+5$

Thus we see that the operations of addition and subtraction for integers are related in the same way that addition and subtraction were related for the set of whole numbers. We can also explore the concept that for every integer x and y, $(x - y)$ equals an integer. In other words, the set of integers is closed under subtraction.

EXERCISES (1)

1. What property is being investigated by the following set of paired problems? What discovery do we hope the children will make by working these problems?

a. $^+6 - {}^+3 = \square$ c. $^-3 - {}^-2 = \square$ e. $^-4 - {}^+3 = \square$

b. $^+3 - {}^+6 = \square$ d. $^-2 - {}^-3 = \square$ f. $^+3 - {}^-4 = \square$

2. What conclusion would the child draw about the associative property for subtraction by working the following pairs of problems?

a. $(^+3 - {}^-2) - {}^+4 = \square$ c. $(^-5 - {}^+4) - {}^-1 = \square$

b. $^+3 - (^-2 - {}^+4) = \square$ d. $^-5 - (^+4 - {}^-1) = \square$

3. What relationship that we have previously discussed are we attempting to re-establish with the following sets of paired problems?

a. $^+6 - {}^+2 = \square$ c. $^-3 - {}^+2 = \square$ e. $^-4 - {}^-5 = \square$

b. $^+6 + {}^-2 = \square$ d. $^-3 + {}^-2 = \square$ f. $^-4 + {}^+5 = \square$

4. What property of subtraction on the set of whole numbers does the following pattern relate to?

a. $^+3 - {}^-6 = \square$ c. $^-3 - {}^-9 = \square$

b. $(^+3 - {}^-4) - (^-6 - {}^-4) = \square$ d. $(^-3 + {}^+7) - (^-9 + {}^+7) = \square$

16.4 TEACHING MULTIPLICATION AND DIVISION OF INTEGERS BY ANALYSIS AND DEFINITION

The topic of multiplication of integers is not developed extensively at the elementary school level. However, if we are ready to make a few assumptions about the isomorphic relationship that exists between operations on the set of non-negative integers and the operations on the set of whole numbers, the operation of multiplication on the set of integers offers the elementary teacher a good opportunity to introduce the child to mathematical proof.

In order to illustrate this, let us make the following assumption:

If a, b, and c are whole numbers, and a^1, b^1, and c^1 are their corresponding non-negative integers, then $a \times b = c$ implies $a^1 \times b^1 = c^1$. For example, if $3 \times 4 = 12$, then $^+3 \times {}^+4 = {}^+12$. The distributive property for multiplication over subtraction behaves in exactly the same manner for the set of integers as it does for the set of whole numbers. For example, if $6 \times (4 - 2) = (6 \times 4) - (6 \times 2)$, then $^+6 \times ({}^+4 - {}^+2) = ({}^+6 \times {}^+4) - ({}^+6 \times {}^+2)$.

With these assumptions, we can now proceed to establish that a positive integer times a negative integer gives a product that is a negative integer. Consider the following:

$^+6 \times {}^-3 = {}^+6 \times ({}^+1 - {}^+4)$	Renaming
$^+6 \times ({}^+1 - {}^+4) = ({}^+6 \times {}^+1) - ({}^+6 \times {}^+4)$	Distributive property of multiplication over subtraction
$({}^+6 \times {}^+1) - ({}^+6 \times {}^+4) = {}^+6 - {}^+24$	Multiplication of positive integers
$^+6 - {}^+24 = {}^-18$	

Thus we have established that $^+6 \times {}^-3 = {}^-18$. By a similar argument we could establish for each pair of integers (one negative and one positive) that the product is negative.

We can now proceed to "prove" that a negative integer times a negative integer is a positive integer. Consider the following:

$^-6 \times {}^-3 = {}^-6 \times ({}^+1 - {}^+4)$	Renaming
$^-6 \times ({}^+1 - {}^+4) = ({}^-6 \times {}^+1) - ({}^-6 \times {}^+4)$	Distributive property of multiplication over subtraction
$({}^-6 \times {}^+1) - ({}^-6 \times {}^+4) = {}^-6 - {}^-24$	Previously proved relationship (negative times positive equals negative)
$^-6 - {}^-24 = {}^+18$	

After the rules of multiplication have been established by the distributive property of multiplication over addition, the basic properties for the operation of multiplication can be explored. The following set of problems is typical of those you might use to get children to discover the commutative property of multiplication:

(1a) $^-3 \times {}^+5 = \square$ (2a) $^-7 \times {}^-6 = \square$ (3a) $^+2 \times {}^+4 = \square$
(1b) $^+5 \times {}^-3 = \square$ (2b) $^-6 \times {}^-7 = \square$ (3b) $^+4 \times {}^+2 = \square$

Notice that these problems have included each possible combination of negative and positive integers. It is not sufficient to structure the discovery exercises so that the child discovers that the commutative property holds for just one of the cases, such as a negative times a negative. All the combinations should be explored. In a like manner, the associative property can be explored with your class. The following problems are representative of the cases you may want to include in the exploration exercises:

$(^+6 \times {}^+4) \times {}^+5 = \square$ $^-2 \times (^-5 \times {}^+6) = \square$
$^+6 \times (^+4 \times {}^+5) = \square$ $(^-2 \times {}^-5) \times {}^+6 = \square$

$(^-3 \times {}^+2) \times {}^+6 = \square$ $(^-7 \times {}^+9) \times {}^-8 = \square$
$^-3 \times (^+2 \times {}^+6) = \square$ $^-7 \times (^+9 \times {}^-8) = \square$

$^+2 \times (^-4 \times {}^+7) = \square$ $(^+3 \times {}^-9) \times {}^-4 = \square$
$(^+2 \times {}^-4) \times {}^+7 = \square$ $^+3 \times (^-9 \times {}^-4) = \square$

$(^+3 \times {}^+5) \times {}^-2 = \square$ $^-2 \times (^-3 \times {}^-8) = \square$
$^+3 \times (^+5 \times {}^-2) = \square$ $(^-2 \times {}^-3) \times {}^-8 = \square$

After having established the multiplication of integers, it is a simple matter for you to define division as the inverse operation of multiplication and to proceed to establish the rules of signs for division. For example, $^+8 \div {}^-2 = {}^-4$, because $^-4 \times {}^-2 = {}^+8$.

16.5 TEACHING MULTIPLICATION BY AN ANALOGY

There are many common analogies used to teach operations on integers. We have examined one of these analogies for addition of integers which involves taking a trip.

Let us examine how you can use an analogy to develop the "how" but not the "why" we arrive at various signs for products.

Teacher: Our analogy will involve a messenger who delivers bills and checks to people and picks up bills and checks for people. We will be concerned with the effect of these deliveries on the person receiving them from the messenger, or the effect on the person giving them to the messenger.

Teacher: Would a person receiving checks be happy or sad?

Children: Happy.

Teacher: Would a person be happy or sad if he received bills?

Children: Sad.

Teacher: If a person gives the messenger checks, would he be happy or sad and why?

Children: Sad, because he has given up his money.

Teacher: If a person gives the messenger bills, would the person be happy or sad? Why?

Children: Happy, because he can look forward to receiving some money when people pay their bills.

Teacher: We will say being happy is positive and being sad is negative. The messenger giving will be positive and the messenger taking will be negative. Checks will be positive and bills will be negative.

Happy	+
Sad	−
Give	+
Receive	−
Checks	+
Bills	−

$^+3 \times {}^+5 = \square$

Teacher: The equation on the left tells us the messenger gave the person 3 checks, each of which was worth 5 dollars. What is the total value of the checks?

Children: 15 dollars.

$^+3 \times {}^+5 = {}^+15$

Teacher: Would the person receiving checks be happy or sad?

Children: Happy.

Teacher: Therefore we say our product is a positive 15.

$^+3 \times {}^-5 = \square$

Teacher: The equation at the left tells us the messenger is giving the person 3 bills, each of which is for 5 dollars. What is the total amount owed?

Children: 15 dollars.

$^+3 \times {}^-5 = {}^-15$

Teacher: Would the person receiving the bills be happy or sad?

Children: Sad.

Teacher: Therefore we say our product is a negative 15.

$^-3 \times {}^+5 = \square$

Teacher: The equation at the left tells us the messenger is receiving from the person 3 checks, each of which is worth 5 dollars. What is the total value of the checks?

Children: 15 dollars.

$-3 \times {}^+5 = {}^-15$

Teacher: Would the person giving up the checks be happy or sad?

Children: Sad.

Teacher: Therefore we say our product is negative 15.

$^-3 \times ^-5 = \square$

Teacher: The equation at the left tells us the messenger is receiving from the person 3 bills, each of which is worth 5 dollars. What is the total value of the bills?

Children: 15 dollars.

$^-3 \times ^-5 = ^+15$

Teacher: Would the person giving the bills up be happy or sad?

Children: Happy.

Teacher: Therefore we say our product is a positive 15.

Although extensive use of this analogy would enable children to remember the "rules" of multiplication of integers, it would not establish the "why." The "why" of multiplication of integers by proof is often delayed until junior high school or high school.

EXERCISES (2)

1. Assuming $a \div b = c$ if $b \times c = a$, establish the following:

a. $^+6 \div ^-3 = ^-2$ b. $^-6 \div ^-3 = ^+2$ · c. $^+6 \div ^+3 = ^+2$

2. Create pairs of problems that could be used to help the child discover the compensation property for division of integers.

3. Create pairs of problems that could be used to aid the child in discovering the right distributive property of division over addition of integers.

4. Create pairs of problems that could be used to help the child discover the right distributive property of division over subtraction of integers.

16.6   ORDERING THE INTEGERS

After introducing the child to integers, the teacher is in a position to develop several important inequality relationships. (We shall define an integer x as being less than an integer y if there exists a positive z such that $x + z = y$.)

We shall explore ways to develop intuitively some of the inequality relationships at the elementary level. The first of those we might develop is that for x, y, and z that are elements of the integers, if $x < y$, then $x + z < y + z$. This idea can be promoted by having the children explore the following types of problems.

Put a $<$ or $>$ in each of the following:

If $^+3 < ^+5$, then $^+3 + ^-2 \bigcirc ^+5 + ^-2$

If $^+3 < ^+5$, then $^+3 + ^+2 \bigcirc ^+5 + ^+2$

If $^+3 < ^+5$, then $^+3 + ^-2 \bigcirc ^+5 + ^-2$

If $^-3 < {}^+5$, then $^-3 + {}^+5 \bigcirc {}^+5 + {}^+5$
If $^-5 < {}^-3$, then $^-5 + {}^-2 \bigcirc {}^-3 + {}^-2$
If $^-5 < {}^-3$, then $^-5 + {}^+5 \bigcirc {}^-3 + {}^+5$

Although no number of such examples can prove the suspected relationship, it is sufficient in the elementary school to promote the suspicion that such a relationship exists for all integers.

Another relationship to which the children can be "exposed" is the following. For every x, y, and z that are elements of the integers, if $x < y$, then $x - z < y - z$. This idea can be promoted by having the children explore the following types of problems.

Put a $<$ or $>$ in each of the following:

If $^+3 < {}^+5$, then $^+3 - {}^+6 \bigcirc {}^+5 - {}^+6$
If $^+3 < {}^+5$, then $^+3 - {}^-6 \bigcirc {}^+5 - {}^-6$
If $^-3 < {}^+5$, then $^-3 - {}^+6 \bigcirc {}^+5 - {}^+6$
If $^-3 < {}^+5$, then $^-3 - {}^-6 \bigcirc {}^+5 - {}^-6$
If $^-5 < {}^-3$, then $^-5 - {}^+6 \bigcirc {}^-3 - {}^+6$
If $^-5 < {}^-3$, then $^-5 - {}^-6 \bigcirc {}^-3 - {}^-6$

16.7 NEGATIVE EXPONENTS AND SCIENTIFIC NOTATION

A useful technique for introducing the child to negative exponents is to do it via a pattern. For example, consider the following.

$1000 = 10^3$
$\frac{1000}{10} = 100 = 10^2$
$\frac{100}{10} = 10 = 10^1$
$\frac{10}{10} = 1 = 10^0$

Notice that in going from 1000 to 100 we have divided the 1000 by 10, and in going from 100 to 10 we have divided the 100 by 10, and so on. If we maintain this pattern to go from 1 to the next number, we shall have divided the 1 by 10, giving us a quotient of $\frac{1}{10}$. At this point, we could ask the children to study the pattern 10^3, 10^2, 10^1, 10^0 and see what might be a logical exponent to affix to the 10 in order to maintain the pattern. A negative 1 would be the logical choice.

Continuing in this manner, we can establish:

$1 \div 10 = \frac{1}{10} = 10^{-1} = .1$
$\frac{1}{10} \div 10 = \frac{1}{100} = 10^{-2} = .01$
$\frac{1}{100} \div 10 = \frac{1}{1000} = 10^{-3} = .001$
etc.

Having introduced scientific notation, you can have the children explore some simple translations into scientific notation where a negative exponent results.

Consider the following translations:

$.004 \rightarrow 4 \times \frac{1}{1000} \rightarrow 4 \times 10^{-3}$

$.00009 \rightarrow 9 \times \frac{1}{100,000} \rightarrow 9 \times 10^{-5}$

Notice that we have introduced an intermediate translation in order to emphasize the meaning behind the negative power of 10. These intermediate steps are especially useful when the translation involves problems such as the following:

$.014 \rightarrow 14 \times \frac{1}{1000} \rightarrow 1.4 \times 10 \times \frac{1}{1000} \rightarrow 1.4 \times 10^{-2}$

$.00127 \rightarrow 127 \times \frac{1}{100,000} \rightarrow 1.27 \times 100 \times \frac{1}{100,000} \rightarrow 1.27 \times \frac{1}{1000} \rightarrow 1.27 \times 10^{-3}$

EXERCISES (3)

1. Create a set of problems that would lead the child to suspect that the following relationships are true:

    a. If $x > 0$ and $y < z$, then $y \cdot x < z \cdot x$
    b. If $x < 0$ and $y < z$, then $y \cdot x > z \cdot x$.

2. Create a set of problems that would lead the child to suspect that the following relationships are true:

    a. If $x > 0$ and y and z are divisible by x, and $y < z$, then $y \div x < z \div x$.
    b. If $x < 0$ and y and z are divisible by x, and $y < z$, then $y \div x > z \div x$.

BIBLIOGRAPHY

Ashlock, R. B., and T. A. West. "Physical Representations for Signed-number Operations," *The Arithmetic Teacher* (November 1967), pp. 549–554.

Heddens, J. W. *Today's Mathematics* (Palo Alto, Calif.: Science Research Associates), 1971, pp. 320–335.

Hollis, L. Y. "Multiplication of Integers," *The Arithmetic Teacher* (November 1967), pp. 555–556.

National Council of Teachers of Mathematics. *30th Yearbook* (Washington, D.C.), 1969, pp. 1–66.

Newman, C. M. "The Importance of Definitions in Mathematics: Zero," *The Arithmetic Teacher* (May 1967), pp. 379–382.

Sherzer, L. "Adding Integers Using Only the Concepts of One-to-One Correspondence and Counting," *The Arithmetic Teacher* (May 1969), pp. 360–362.

17

Teaching geometry

BEHAVIORAL OBJECTIVES

Student can . . .

State three reasons geometry is included in the elementary school curriculum.

List the four elements of the structure of geometry taught at the elementary school level.

Describe models that can be extended to describe specific geometric figures.

Describe an involvement activity that can be used to get children to discover closed paths.

Define a simple closed path in terms of crosspoints and endpoints.

Describe a technique for teaching concave and convex.

Describe how various subsets of the set of polygons are classified.

Identify the properties of a circle.

Name specific geometric figures.

Define degrees of an angle.

Describe an involvement technique for teaching symmetry.

Perform specific construction with compass and straightedge.

Identify five specific skills needed in five different vocations.

Describe three methods or techniques of teaching applications.

Describe how to teach coordinates.

List three types of graphs.

Describe a technique for teaching each type of graph.

17.1 INTRODUCTION

Some people might ask, "Why teach geometry in the elementary school?" The answer is simply that geometry is one of the most widely used areas of knowledge that a child will study. The concepts of geometry affect every person from birth to death. Let us examine some common basic applications of geometry.

Why is a circular-shaped manhole cover a better choice of shape than a square-shaped manhole cover?

Answer: Because, unlike a square-shaped cover, a circular-shaped manhole cover can be slid over the hole, and it won't fall in. The nature of a circle's diameter prevents any type of orientation that will allow the cover to fall down the hole.

Why are straight and parallel slats in a baby's crib better than crooked slats?

Answer: It is a safer procedure due to the equidistance of the slats from each other. There is less danger that a baby will get part of his body wedged in the slats.

Why is a rectangular-shaped picture tube in a television set better than an oval-shaped picture tube?

Answer: Because the oval-shaped picture tube would either have distortion around the edges or would omit essential detail.

Why is a triangular-shaped bracing system better than a rectangular-shaped bracing system in a television tower.

Answer: A triangle is a rigid geometric shape, whereas a rectangle is not.

(Hint: Construct models of triangles and rectangles using strips of cardboard, and use straight pins to fasten the ends. Then push the models around on a flat surface and note how the rectangle model deforms, whereas the triangle stays a triangle.)

Why would the choice of a spherical shape for a water tower reservoir be better than a cubical shape?

Answer: A spherical shape would be better able to withstand the water pressure. (The sides of a cubical-shaped water tower would deform unless prohibitively thick sides were used.)

The applications of geometry are almost endless. During the design stage of almost any commercially produced object, consideration is given to geometric principles. However, the applications of geometry go far beyond commercial applications. Numerous vocations require extensive applications of geometric principles. Some people who make major use of geometric principles are architects, engineers, tool and die makers, artists, teachers, pilots, navigators, interior designers, landscape architects, and draftsmen.

Beside a person's need to know geometric principles for their commercial and vocation application, there is a need to know geometric principles because they are used in the learning process of other disciplines.

A sample of the applications of geometry in other disciplines includes:

1. Giving directions in teaching reading and language arts
2. Teaching perspective in art
3. Teaching computation in arithmetic
4. Teaching measurement in mathematics
5. Teaching scale drawings in industrial arts
6. Teaching map reading in social studies
7. Teaching flower arrangement in home economics
8. Teaching drill formations in band

17.2 THE STRUCTURE OF ELEMENTARY SCHOOL GEOMETRY

Each mathematical topic has its own structure. When the teacher is aware of a basic structure of a topic he can integrate this structure into his planning and make his teaching efficient and meaningful.

At the elementary school level the basic structure of geometry involves properties, relationships, classifications, construction, and applications.

The following table gives examples of each element of this structure:

Structural Element	Example	How the Element Fits into the Structure
Properties	——— The path is *straight*.	Properties are used to classify figures
Relationships	⟷ The lines are *parallel*.	Relationships are used to classify figures
Classifications	△ The figure is a *triangle*.	Used in applications
Constructions	Erect a perpendicular.	Used in applications

Incorporating a topic's structure into the learning sequence insures:

1. Unity of the topic
2. An ease in justifying the inclusion of specific concepts in the curriculum, which would be difficult to justify if no thought is given to structure (The teaching of symmetry without regard for its role in the field of applications would be difficult to justify in the curriculum. Similarly, a concept such as congruency of angles would be difficult to justify if one disregarded its role in classification and applications.)

17.3 POINTS, SPACE, AND PLANES

Geometry can be defined as the study of sets of points. This definition contains the undefined word *points*. In our study of geometry, we shall have many undefined words. Although we shall leave these words undefined and develop the concepts intuitively, it still will be possible to talk about properties that these "things" possess.

One of the properties we can attribute to a point is that it has no dimension (size). This property has implications for the teacher. If points

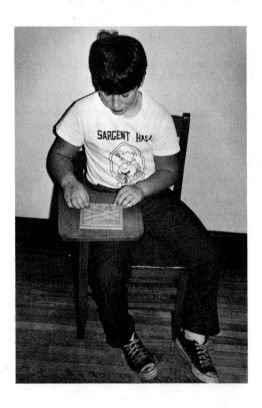

have no size, and we choose to make a dot on a piece of paper to be our model of a point, then the smaller the dot, the better representation. We must be careful that we do not give children misconceptions of geometrical ideas through grossly imperfect models. We shall use small dots to be pictures of points. These dots will give us a rough idea of the location of the point to which we are referring. Sometimes we shall want to make it clearly understood which of the many points we are referring to. In such cases, it will be convenient for us to name the point. We do this by placing a capital letter of the alphabet in close proximity to the dot picturing the point. In Figure 17.1, several points have been named.

B •

    R K •

   •   •Z

       •A

Figure 17.1

The set of all points constitutes *space*. This space goes on and on in all directions forever and ever. It is everywhere dense, which means that there are no locations that are without points. There is nothing especially interesting about space per se; it will be subsets of space that are of prime interest to us.

.The first subset of space we focus our attention on is that set of points identified as a *plane*. Intuitively, we might imagine a plane as being like the surface of a very smooth table (or wall or ceiling) that goes on and on forever. A plane has infinite length and width, without "thickness." One of the properties we can attribute to a plane is that it is everywhere dense. In other words, there are no locations in the plane where there are no points. The teacher has many models available to him for conveying the idea of a plane to his students. Statements such as the following will help in developing the idea of a plane:

"If we were to consider the surface of this desk to be extended right and left and front and back forever and ever, this surface would be a good model of what a plane is like."

Or, "If we were to consider the surface of this wall to be extended up and down and right and left forever and ever, this surface would be a good model of a plane."

Any three points in space determine one plane. This basic idea of planes can be demonstrated to children as follows:

1. Have three children standing fairly close together select three points in space by letting the end of a finger of each mark the approximate location of one of these points.
2. Place a piece of masonite or plastic or other firm material on the tips of the fingers.

3. Have the children shift their fingers to determine another point.
4. Lead the children to see that two points would not fix a plane but, on the contrary, would allow an infinite set of planes to pass through the two points.
5. Lead the children to see that four points may or may not determine one plane.

Some or all of the following concepts can be investigated as the class studies planes:

1. A set of points is *coplanar* if every point of the set lies in the same plane.
2. The intersection of two planes is a *line*.
3. When two planes do not have points in common, the planes are said to be *parallel*.

We shall be especially concerned in this chapter with subsets of this plane. Unless otherwise noted, all figures referred to in the next section will be understood to be subsets of this plane.

17.4 CURVES

The simplest of all geometric figures is the curve. Curves can be classified as those finite in length (in other words, those whose length could be measured if we so wished) and those infinite in length (or nonmeasurable).

Let us see how we might introduce this concept to children. The following dialogue can be used to give children an intuitive "feel" for the variety of figures that comprises the curve that is finite in length:

"Draw two dots on your paper."
"Place the lead of your pencil on top of one of the dots."
"I am going to have you close your eyes and draw around the paper. When I tell you to open your eyes, either draw back to the dot from which you started, or draw to the other dot."
"Close your eyes. Draw around on your paper. Now open your eyes and draw to one of the dots."
(You may wish to have different children display their pictures at this time.)
    "You have each drawn a picture of a curve. How many different curves do you suppose there are?" (Many; so many you can't count them; etc.)
"Which of you drew over to the dot you started with? You have drawn a picture of what we call a *closed curve*. If you draw back to the dot you started from, you will always draw a picture of a closed curve."

At this point, you will wish to classify some pictures on the basis of their using one point or two points. In Figure 17.2, we see several curves classified on the basis of either one- or two-point derivations. Notice that it is

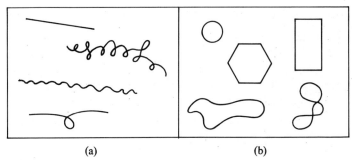

(a)   (b)

Figure 17.2

possible to draw the figures in (a) with two points and the figures in (b) with one point.

After the children have progressed to the stage where they can classify curves on the basis of one- or two-point origins, and thus can classify these paths into closed and nonclosed curves, they are ready to learn further techniques of classification.

Before undertaking this classification, we will introduce the child to two properties that may or may not be properties of a particular curve. The first of these properties is that a path may have *endpoints*. This concept could be developed intuitively as follows:

"Pretend that curve *A* (Figure 17.3) is a narrow road along which you could ride a bicycle. You are not allowed to turn your bicycle around in the road. If you kept on riding in the direction shown, what would happen?" (You would come to the end of the road.)

"We call the point where the curve ends the endpoint. How many endpoints does curve *A* have?" (Two.)

"Pretend that curve *B* is a narrow road. If you kept riding on the curve, would you come to the end?" (No.) "We say that curve *B* has zero endpoints."

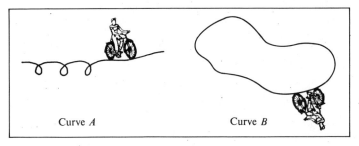

Curve *A*   Curve *B*

Figure 17.3

A second property is that a curve may have *crosspoints*.

"Pretend that you are riding your bicycle along a curve. If you reach a point on the curve where you have a choice of which way you would go, you call this type of point a crosspoint. We could also call these points 'decision points' or 'which way' points. This drawing (Figure 17.4) shows some crosspoints in various curves."

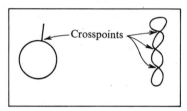

Figure 17.4

So far, we have classified the set of curves as two subsets—those that are infinite in length and those that are finite in length. We have then classified the set of finite curves into two subsets consisting of closed curves and nonclosed curves. We have identified the two properties a curve can have. Now, on the basis of the property of crosspoints, we shall classify the set of closed curves into two subsets.

17.5 SIMPLE CLOSED CURVES

When a closed curve has zero crosspoints, we name it a simple closed curve. Figure 17.5 shows sets of closed curves classified on the basis of having or not having crosspoints.

The simple closed curve partitions every plane into three disjoint sets of points. Let us examine how we might explore this concept with children. Pretend that a farmer has run one strand of wire around a field. In the field is a cow. The cow has learned that she cannot eat the grass directly under the wire, because every time she tries to do so, the wire gives

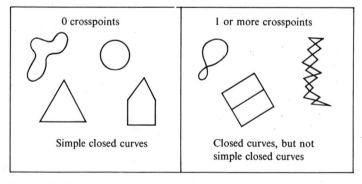

Figure 17.5

her a shock. The cow has also learned that every time she tries to eat the grass on the other side of the wire, she gets a shock. The set of points that corresponds to where the cow can eat grass is called the *interior region*. The set of points corresponding to the grass directly under the fence (or, in other words, the simple closed curve) is called the *boundary*. The set of points that is not the interior region and not the boundary is called the *exterior region*.

We say that the simple closed curve bounds a set of points. This set of points that is bounded is referred to as the interior region. Occasionally, we are interested in classifying the set of interior regions into two disjoint subsets consisting of convex regions and concave regions.

Let us see how we can distinguish a concave region from a convex region. A simple closed curve is pictured in Figure 17.6a. Pretend that we stick pins all around the boundary of this curve, as in Figure 17.6b. If we were to put a rubber band around our pins, as in Figure 17.6c, we would find that it would

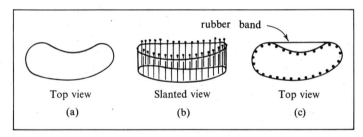

Top view	Slanted view	Top view
(a)	(b)	(c)

Figure 17.6

not follow the boundary of our simple closed curve. When the path is such that the rubber band will not follow the boundary, we describe the figure as *concave*.

Figure 17.7 shows several concave figures paired with the pictures that would result if we did the same thing with the rubber band.

When the rubber band follows the same curve as the simple closed curve, we say the interior region represents a *convex* set of points.

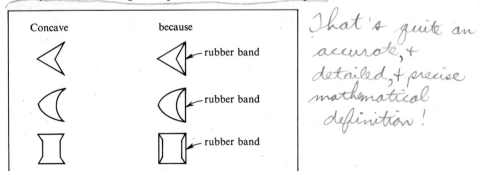

That's quite an accurate, + detailed, + precise mathematical definition!

Figure 17.7

EXERCISES (1)

1. Review the properties of points. Which would be a better picture of a point, a large dot or a small dot?
2. Select a point on your paper. Place a dot to mark the location of your point and give it a name.
3. Name five models that could be used to develop the idea of a plane.
4. Identify whether the following pictures of curves could be constructed via one-point or two-point origins.

    (a)   (b)   (c)   (d)   (e)

5. Identify the properties that each of the following curves have that prevent their being called simple closed curves.

    (a)   (b)   (c)   (d)   (e).

6. Tell whether each of the following figures bounds a convex or a concave region:

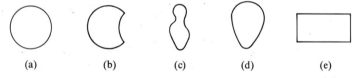

    (a)   (b)   (c)   (d)   (e)

17.6   LINE SEGMENT

Before exploring other concepts relative to the simple closed curve, it will be necessary to develop the concept of a line segment.

If you were to take a very small pebble and let it drop to the floor, the path the pebble took would be like a line segment. Or, if two people were to pull tightly on the ends of a very fine wire, the path that the wire formed would be like a line segment. A line segment has the properties of being finite in length, without thickness, and with two endpoints.

We shall have occasion to refer to a line segment among many line segments. For this reason, it is desirable to be able to give a name to a line segment. In Figure 17.8a we have pictured a line segment. In Figure 17.8b, we have given letter names to the two endpoints. We can now refer to this line segment as $\overline{RK}$ (read line segment RK) or $\overline{KR}$ (read line segment KR).

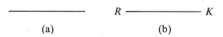

    (a)   (b)

Figure 17.8

17.7 POLYGONS

Line segments serve as the building blocks for a special subset of simple closed curves. When a simple closed curve is composed of line segments only, we call this curve a *polygon*. Figure 17.9 depicts a few members of the class of polygons.

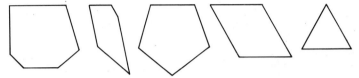

Figure 17.9

When two line segments are joined together in such a way that the joining forms an endpoint common to the two line segments, we refer to this common endpoint as a *vertex*. When more than two line segments are involved and more than one common endpoint is formed, these endpoints are referred to as vertices. In Figure 17.10, the vertices of the polygons have been given names.

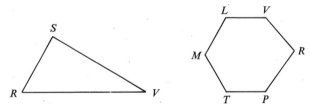

Figure 17.10

The line segments of the polygon are designated *sides* of the polygon. It is on the basis of the number of sides that a polygon has that we are able to classify the polygons further. Three-sided polygons are called *triangles*, four-sided polygons are called *quadrilaterals*, five-sided polygons are called *pentagons*, and so on.

We shall not be able to classify these polygons further until we have explored the relationship called congruency that can exist between two line segments. Two line segments will be said to seem *congruent* if each measures the same length. For this to be a usable definition for children, we need to create a technique whereby they can determine when two pictured line segments measure the same length and hence seem congruent. Figure 17.11 shows how the edge of a piece of paper can be used to demonstrate that two line segments are congruent.

If we compare the sides of a triangle for the relationship of congruency, we can further classify the set of triangles. When we find a triangle in which

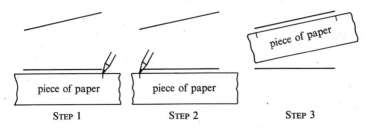

STEP 1   STEP 2   STEP 3

Figure 17.11

no two sides are congruent, we call it a *scalene* triangle. When at least two sides of the triangle are congruent, it is classified as an *isosceles* triangle. When all three sides are congruent, we classify it as an *equilateral* triangle. If we compare the sides of a quadrilateral and discover that opposite sides are congruent, we classify this quadrilateral as a *parallelogram*. When a parallelogram has congruent adjacent sides, we classify this figure as a *rhombus*.

EXERCISES (2)

1. Draw a picture of a line segment. Name the line segment.

2. What properties in each of the following figures prevent its being called a polygon?

(a)   (b)   (c)   (d)   (e)

3. What properties in each of the following figures prevent its being called a triangle?

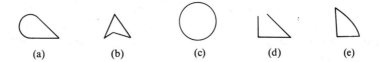

(a)   (b)   (c)   (d)   (e)

4. What properties in each of the following figures prevent its being called a quadrilateral?

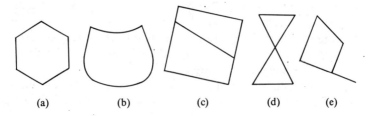

(a)   (b)   (c)   (d)   (e)

5. What properties in each of the following figures prevent its being called a parallelogram?

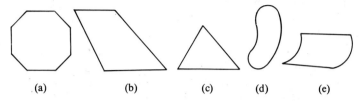

(a) (b) (c) (d) (e)

6. Tell whether each figure is a scalene triangle or an isosceles triangle or an equilateral triangle. (Remember, to be an isosceles triangle, the triangle must have at least two congruent sides.)

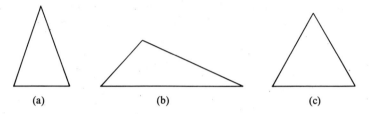

(a) (b) (c)

We need only one further concept to complete our classification of the polygons. We need to develop the concept of a diagonal of a polygon. Any line segment that connects a vertex of a polygon with a vertex not belonging to either of the two line segments forming the first vertex is said to be a *diagonal*. Figure 17.12 illustrates various polygons with and without diagonals.

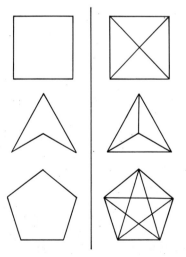

Figure 17.12

The relationship that exists between the number of diagonals of a polygon and the number of sides of the polygon is an interesting one. We find that a polygon with three sides can have only zero diagonals; a polygon with four sides can have only two diagonals; one with five sides can have only five diagonals, and so on. Can you find the pattern? (Start with a quadrilateral. Construct the diagonals. Add a point in the exterior region such that going from this point to two adjacent vertices with line segments forms a pentagon. How many diagonals will this new vertex contribute? Continue this process of adding a dot to form a new vertex.)

We are now in a position to classify the parallelograms further on the basis of their having or not having congruent diagonals. If a parallelogram has congruent diagonals, then we call this parallelogram a *rectangle*. The set of all rectangles for which all sides are congruent is classified as *squares*. Figure 17.13 summarizes how we have classified the closed curve.

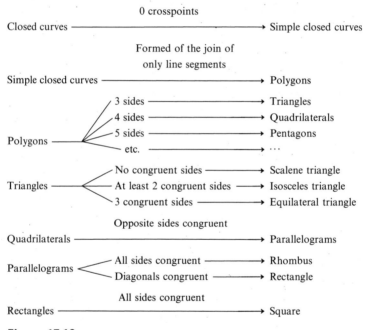

Figure 17.13

17.8   CIRCLE

One other planar figure of general interest that is a simple closed curve but not a polygon is the circle. We can define a circle as a simple closed curve with the property that there exists a point in the interior region of the circle such that all line segments that could be considered with one endpoint as a boundary point and one endpoint as this point would be congruent. In more sophisticated language, the circle is a simple closed curve such that each boundary point is equidistant from some fixed point in the interior. This fixed point, which is equidistant from any point of the boundary, is the *center* of the circle.

A line segment from the center to the boundary is identified as a *radius*. Any line segment that has as endpoints two boundary points and also contains the center point is called a *diameter*. Any line segment with endpoints consisting of boundary points is identified as a *chord*. The diameter satisfies these requirements and can also be called a chord. The set of boundary points between two boundary points is referred to as an *arc*.

17.9 RAYS

We have discussed how some of the curves of finite length are classified. Now we shall study the properties used to classify curves of infinite length.

Let us imagine that a line segment is extended forever in one direction. A geometric figure of this type is called a ray (see Figure 17.14). The

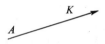

Figure 17.14

arrow denotes that the ray goes on in that direction forever. An endpoint and one point on the ray have been named. We name this ray $\overrightarrow{AK}$ (read ray AK).

17.10 ANGLES

Just as the line segment served as the building block for the polygon, so the ray will serve as the building block for the figures we call angles. When two rays are joined (or the union of the two rays is taken) in such a way that a common endpoint is formed, we define the resultant figure as an angle.

Figure 17.15 depicts an angle. The endpoint common to the two rays is named the *vertex* of the angle. Notice that the vertex and one other

Figure 17.15

point on each of the two rays has been given a name. With three such points named, we can name the angle. This angle is named ∠ *RKZ* (read angle *RKZ*).

Notice that the name of the vertex point is always placed between the names of the points on the ray that are not endpoints. (When there is no chance of ambiguity, it is permissible to refer to the angle by its vertex name only. For example, the previous angle could be designated ∠ *K*.)

It will be convenient to define a measure of an angle. Consider an angle that has a vertex corresponding to the center point of a circle (see Figure 17.16). This circle has been partitioned into 36 arcs of equal length. Each of these arcs is said to be 1 degree in length and is indicated as follows: 10° (read 10 degrees.)

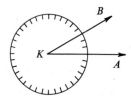

Figure 17.16

The measure of ∠*BKA* is defined as the number of the 360 arcs between points *A* and *B* on the circle, if the number is less than 180. (A figure formed by the joining of two rays, which has a measure of 180, will be defined as a line and not an angle.) In order to facilitate the determination of the measure of an angle, we use an instrument called a protractor, which has the measure of these arcs named. Figure 17.17 depicts how a protractor can be used to determine the measure of ∠*MAT*. (Notice that one ray is placed along the radius defined by *AM*.) The measure of this angle is 30°.

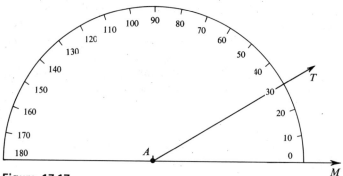

Figure 17.17

If the measure of an angle is 90°, this angle is named a right angle. If the measure is less than 90°, the angle is defined as an acute angle. If the angle's measure is greater than 90° and less than 180°, the angle is defined as an obtuse angle.

17.11 LINE

If we consider a line segment as a subset of a set of points that goes on and on in both directions forever and ever, the line segment is a subset of a figure called a line. Figure 17.18 depicts a line. The arrows indicate that the line goes on and on in both directions without end. Notice that two points on the line have been named. Using these two named points, we give the line a name $\overleftrightarrow{XL}$ (read line XL). The line has the properties of being infinite in length, without thickness, and without endpoints.

Figure 17.18

Two lines are said to be *intersecting* if they have one point in common. Two lines are said to be *parallel* if they have no points in common. (Remember that we have specified that all of the figures we are considering are in a plane.) We now have new properties that will enable us to reclassify some of our polygons.

17.12 TRIANGLES RECLASSIFIED

When children have been acquainted with an angle and its measure, they are in a position to further refine their techniques of classification.

We have classified triangles on the bases of the congruency or non-congruency of pairs of sides. Now, if we consider each pair of sides as determiners of an angle, we are able to reclassify our triangles on the basis of the measure of an angle. We are not saying that these sides are an angle; we are saying only that if each of the sides were extended in a direction away from the common vertex, an angle would result. Notice in Figure 17.19 that when sides AK and KG are extended, they form the angle AKG.

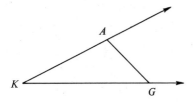

Figure 17.19

If we were to take the measure of this angle, we would find that it is an acute angle. If we find the measure of the angle determined by *AK* and *AG*, we find that this is an obtuse angle. If every angle determined by a triangle is an acute angle (remember that we have defined a measure of an angle as that part of the boundary of the circle that is less than a measure of 180°), the triangle is called an *acute* triangle (see Figure 17.20).

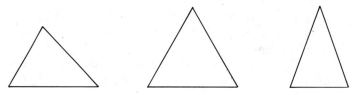

Figure 17.20

If the measure of one angle determined by the sides of the triangle is greater than a right angle, the triangle is classified as an *obtuse* triangle. Figure 17.21 depicts some obtuse triangles.

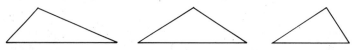

Figure 17.21

If the measure of one of the angles determined by the sides of the triangle is equal to a right angle, then the triangle is classified as a *right* triangle (see Figure 17.22).

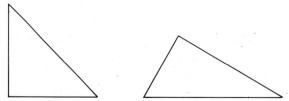

Figure 17.22

If two triangles determine angles with the same measure, the triangles are said to be *similar*. Figure 17.23 depicts similar triangles. We can symbolize this relationship as follows: △*CEF* ~ △*RKZ* (read triangle *CEF* is similar to triangle *RKZ*).

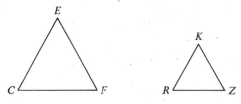

Figure 17.23

If we have two triangles in which one of the sides of one of the triangles is congruent to one of the sides of the other triangle, in which the triangles are similar, and in which the sides that are congruent are oriented the same way with respect to the angles determined by the triangles, then we say the triangles are *congruent*. Figure 17.24 depicts congruent triangles. We can symbolize this relationship as follows: $\triangle ABC \cong \triangle DEF$ (read triangle *ABC* is congruent to triangle *DEF*).

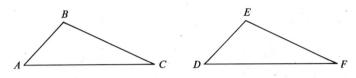

Figure 17.24

17.13 QUADRILATERALS RECLASSIFIED

The concepts of the measure of an angle and parallelism permit us to refine further our techniques for classifying the set of quadrilaterals. Previously, we classified a parallelogram as a quadrilateral with congruent opposite sides. Now, if we consider each of these sides as determining a line, we can say that a parallelogram is a quadrilateral with two pairs of sides, each pair of which determines a set of parallel lines. We can reclassify our rectangle as being a parallelogram with sides that determine four right angles.

EXERCISES (3)

1. What is the name of the longest possible chord a circle can have?
2. Draw a picture of a ray and name it $\overrightarrow{ZM}$.
3. Draw a picture of a triangle and name it $\triangle ACE$.
4. Using a protractor, find the sum of the measure of the three angles determined by various triangles.
5. Can you have an obtuse isosceles triangle?
6. Can you have an obtuse equilateral triangle?
7. Why can't you have a right equilateral triangle?
8. What is the name of the line pictured?

9. Describe a rhombus in terms of its sides determining parallel lines and congruent sides.
10. What would be the best name you could give to a quadrilateral whose opposite sides determine parallel lines and in which one pair of sides determined a right angle?

17.14   THREE-DIMENSIONAL FIGURES

Until now we have been referring to geometric figures in a plane, or, in other words, two-dimensional figures. In this section, we shall explore some of the common three-dimensional figures taught at the elementary level. To do this, we shall introduce the term join. A *join* is defined as the set of points that constitutes line segments connecting a set of points in a plane and a set of points that does not lie in this plane.

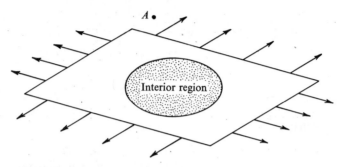

Figure 17.25

Consider the point *A* above the plane in Figure 17.25 and also the set of points in the plane consisting of the circle and its interior region. Figure 17.26 illustrates the resulting three-dimensional figure after we consider the join. The resulting figure is called a *cone* and its interior region.

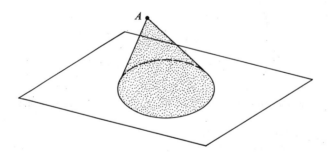

Figure 17.26

By using other simple closed paths in a plane, we can form the join of other three-dimensional figures. For example, in Figure 17.27, we see a perspective view of a square and its interior region in a plane and a point not on this plane. When we consider the join, we call the resulting figure a *square pyramid* and its interior region.

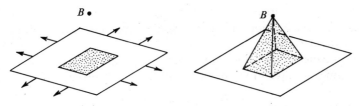

·Figure 17.27

By choosing other polygons, we can construct various types of pyramids and their interior regions. For example, a *triangular pyramid* can be thought of as the join of a triangle and its interior region and a point not on the plane (see Figure 17.28).

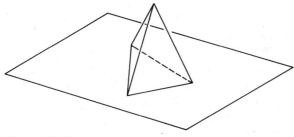

Figure 17.28

By considering the join of two sets of points in two planes, we can investigate some very interesting three-dimensional figures. For example, suppose we consider the join of two circles having radii of equal measure, but on parallel planes. We shall consider the join of these two circles and their interior regions. The resulting figure is called a cylinder. (See Figure 17.29.)

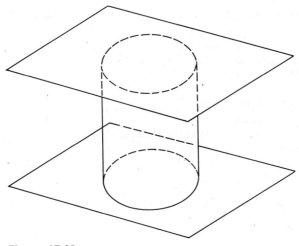

Figure 17.29

If, instead of using circles, we had chosen to form the join of quadrilaterals and their interior regions, we would have called the resulting figure a *quadrilateral prism*.

We have been considering *polyhedrons* (many-faced solids). Figure 17.30 identifies the names we give to various parts of the polyhedrons.

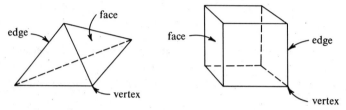

Figure 17.30

17.15   TEACHING SYMMETRY BY INVOLVEMENT

The inclusion of symmetry as a required part of the elementary school mathematics curriculum is a recent development. However, the teaching of symmetry as an incidental part of the curriculum has been done for many decades.

People, in general, when given a choice between symmetrical objects and nonsymmetrical objects will express a preference for symmetrical objects. People generally view symmetrical objects as more satisfying than non-symmetrical objects.

Nature endows numerous of its creatures and things with symmetry. From crystals to plants, from stars to ants, symmetry surrounds us. Two types of symmetry are taught at the elementary level, *bilateral* and *radial* symmetry.

Let's examine how we might use involvement to teach the concept of symmetry.

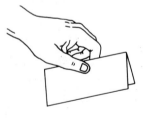

The teacher sees that each child has a piece of plain paper, a pair of scissors, and a pencil.

Teacher: Fold your paper over and press your finger along the crease to make it sharp. (The teacher demonstrates this to the children and the children follow her example.)

Teacher: Starting at the crease and returning to the crease, draw some kind of mark. (The teacher demonstrates this.)

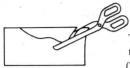

Teacher: Now take your scissors and cut along the mark you made, but don't unfold the paper. (The teacher demonstrates this.)

Teacher: Now unfold your paper. Your shape has bilateral symmetry. This means that the figure has the same shape on either side of this crease line.

As a follow-up the children can (1) create a display of their shapes with bilateral symmetry and (2) find objects in their environment possessing bilateral symmetry.

Radial symmetry (which means having similar parts arranged around a central axis) can be taught by a similar type of involvement.

Fold a piece of paper over several times until it is creased into several congruent "pies."

Draw a path starting at the crease and returning to the crease.

Cut along the mark.

Open up the folded paper and you will have a figure that possesses the property of radial symmetry.

17.16 TEACHING CONSTRUCTIONS

As an elementary teacher, you will find occasions when you will need to know how to make and demonstrate various geometric constructions. Most geometric constructions are generally delayed until the child has reached the intermediate grades. This is due to the fact that geometric constructions with compass and straightedge require good coordination involving the late developing small muscles.

In this section we will discuss some of the basic compass and straightedge constructions. You may wish to use a compass and straightedge to practice the directions in this section.

Making an Arc from a Fixed Point

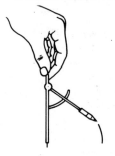

Hold compass like this and twirl or spin with fingers and thumb.

Drawing a Circle

Step 1 Place the needle of the compass at the point you intend to be the center of the circle.

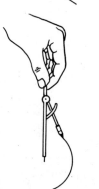

Step 2 Spread the compass so that the distance between the point and the pencil point corresponds to the radius of your circle.

Step 3 Tilt the compass slightly and pull the lead of your compass around.

Constructing a Perpendicular at a Point

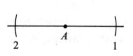

Step 1 Place your compass at point *A*.

Step 2 Spread your compass and arcs 1 and 2.

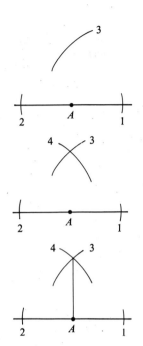

Step 3 Spread your compass some more.

Step 4 Place your compass point in the point where arc 1 crosses the line segment and make arc 3.

Step 5 Place your compass point in the point where arc 2 crosses the line segment and make arc 4.

Step 6 Connect the point where the arcs cross and point *A* with a line segment.

Copying an Angle

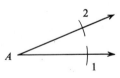

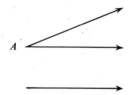

Step 1 Draw a picture of a ray.

Step 2 Place compass needle in point *A*.

Step 3 Spread compass.

Step 4 Swing two arcs crossing the two rays of the angle.

Step 5 Make a large arc on your ray by placing the needle in the endpoint and swinging an arc.

Step 6 Place the needle of your compass in the point where arc 1 crosses the ray.

Step 7 Decrease or increase the spread of your compass so that the pencil lead is on top of the point where arc 2 cuts the other ray.

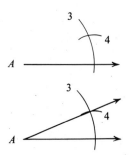

Step 8 Make an arc of this radius, placing your compass needle in the point where the large arc crossed your ray.

Step 9 Connect with a line segment point *A* and the point where arcs 3 and 4 cross. Make this picture of a line segment a picture of a ray.

Bisecting an Angle

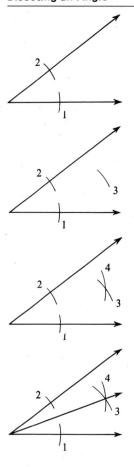

Step 1 Place compass point in point *A* and swing arcs 1 and 2.

Step 2 Place the needle of the compass in the point where arc 1 crosses the ray and make arc 3. (You may need to spread the compass.)

Step 3 Place the needle of the compass in the point where arc 2 crosses the ray and make arc 4.

Step 4 Connect with a line segment point *A* and the point where arcs 3 and 4 intersect. Extend this line segment to form a ray.

Drawing a Line Through a Point Parallel to a Given Line

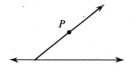

Step 1 Draw a ray from the line through point *P*.

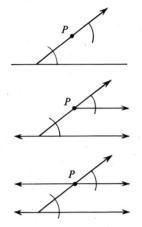

Step 2 Copy angle *PRG* so that the new angle has *P* as a vertex and *PM* as a ray.

Step 3 Extend $\overrightarrow{PK}$ to form line *PK*.

Bisecting a Line Segment, or Constructing a Perpendicular

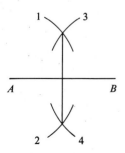

Step 1 Place the needle of the compass in point *A* and swing arcs 1 and 2.

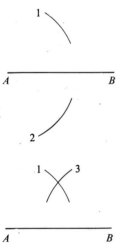

Step 2 Place the needle of the compass in point *B* and swing 3 and 4.

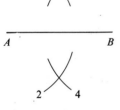

Step 3 Connect with a line segment the point where arcs 2 and 4 cross. Where this line segment crosses the original line segment is the point that partitions the original line segment into two pieces of equal length.

Circumscribing a Circle About a Given Triangle

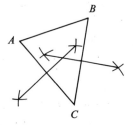

Step 1 Construct the perpendicular bisector of two sides of the triangle.

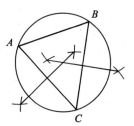

Step 2 Place the needle of your compass in the point where the two constructed line segments cross. Set the spread of your compass to correspond to the distance from the needlepoint to one of the vertices. Circumscribe a circle.

Constructing a Line Segment from a Given Point so that It Is Perpendicular to Another Line Segment

• *A*

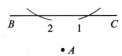

Step 1 Place the needle of your compass in point *A*. Swing arcs 1 and 2.

• *A*

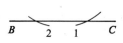

Step 2 Place the needle of your compass in the point where arc 1 crosses $\overline{BC}$. Swing arc 3.

• *A*

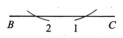

Step 3 Place the needle of your compass in the point where arc 2 crosses $\overline{BC}$. Swing arc 4.

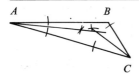

Step 4 Connect with a line segment point A and the point where arcs 3 and 4 cross.

Inscribing a Circle in a Fixed Triangle

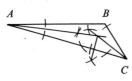

Step 1 Bisect two of the angles determined by the triangle.

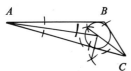

Step 2 Construct a line segment perpendicular to $\overline{AC}$ through point Z where the two angle bisectors cross.

Step 3 Let the distance from point A to $\overline{AC}$ serve as a radius and inscribe the circle.

Copying a Triangle Using One Side and Two Angles

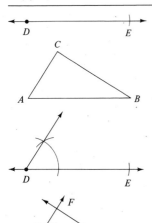

Step 1 Draw a line and mark a point D. Open the compass to the length of $\overline{AB}$. Now make an arc with the point at D.

Step 2 Copy angle A at point D and draw the ray.

Step 3 Copy angle B at point E and draw the ray.

17.17   TEACHING APPLICATIONS

Application of geometry is the keystone to the structure of geometry taught at the elementary school level. Omission of applications leaves a flimsy structure that seldom motivates the child.

The teacher has many approaches she can use in developing applications of geometry. Some of these are:

1. Relating applications of geometry to a vocation
2. Relating applications of geometry to the child's immediate environment
3. Viewing geometrical applications from a historical perspective

In relating applications of geometry to vocations, the teacher can achieve several objectives. He can orient the child to the nature of and requirements of a vocation, which is a basic objective of any elementary school curriculum. He can help the child relate the curriculum to the "real" world. He can help the child relate his interests and capacities to a vocational skill.

Let us examine a sampling of skills needed by various vocations.

	Vocation	Concept
	Navigator	Concept of an angle
	Draftsman	Concept of parallelism
	Carpenter	Scale
	Nurse	Coordinates

Flower arranger   Symmetry

Guest speakers can provide the teacher with an excellent means of developing geometrical applications from a vocational point of view.

Relating geometry to the child's environment can and should be done from a child's first introduction to geometry. The following are sample questions that can be used by a teacher who is interested in developing applications in the environment by discovery:

1. Where do you find rectangular (square, circular, etc.) shapes in the classroom?
2. In this picture of a bridge, what geometric shapes are used?
3. In this slide of a church, where do we find circular shapes used?
4. Where do we find cylinders used in a grocery store?

Interest can also be developed through field trips. Visits to industry, museums, and art exhibits offer a multitude of visual experiences in this area.

There are many techniques that can be used to develop applications of geometry from a historical perspective. The teacher can approach the subject through biographies (Bolyai, Euclid, Hilbert, Lobachevsky, Pythagoras, Riemann, etc.), a cultural point of view (Egyptian, Grecian, Romanic, etc.), a period (Renaissance, Middle Ages, etc.), a field of knowledge (architecture, surveying, astronomy, etc.). Encyclopedias are an excellent research resource for children investigating the development of a particular geometric application.

As has been mentioned earlier in this chapter, there are many direct applications of geometry that can be made in other school subject areas. Let's examine a few applications in the subject area of art.

Type of Art

String figures which employ models of line segments.

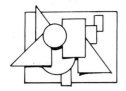

Collages of geometric shapes.

Ornaments and decorations made of poly-hedron paper-fold models.

Geometric compass designs.

Sketches using perspective and scale.

Drawings using basic geometric forms.

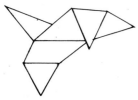

Paper-fold origami using basic geometric shapes.

You will wish to acquaint yourself with the many books in your school library that give examples of applications of geometry.

17.18 COORDINATES

We have discussed how to construct a number line. This number line provided a useful model with which to identify points in the line. By using two of these number lines, we can identify points in a plane.

Let two lines intersect in a plane such that four right angles are determined by the lines. We shall call the point of intersection the *origin*. For convenience, we orient one of the lines in a horizontal manner and the other in a vertical manner. In order, to be able to refer to these lines without having to say "horizontal" and "vertical" each time, we call the horizontal line the □ axis and the vertical line the △ axis.

Starting at the origin, we mark off a number line to the right of the origin along the △ axis. (When negative numbers have been introduced, these will be designated to the left of the origin.) We also mark off a number line starting from the origin and moving in an upward direction along the □ axis. Figure 17.31 illustrates the resulting figure.

It will facilitate our future discussion if we construct a grid using the points named on the two axes. Figure 17.32 illustrates such a grid.

We name points in the portion of the plane that has the grid by naming a pair of numbers. The first number named will refer to a column named on the △ axis; the second number will refer to the row named on the □ axis. The intersection of the column identified by the first number and the row identified by the second number is the point named by the ordered pair. In Figure 17.33, point *A* can also be named by the ordered pair of numbers (5, 4) and point *B* by the ordered pair (1, 3).

We shall treat as exercises some of the relationships that can be explored on our grid.

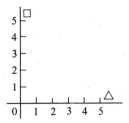

Figure 17.31

Figure 17.32

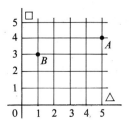

Figure 17.33

EXERCISES (4)

1. Is point (2, 3) the same point as (3, 2)?

2. The ordered pairs (1, 5), (2, 4), and (3, 3) are said to satisfy the equation △ + □ = 6 because:

$$\triangle 1 + \boxed{5} = 6$$
$$\triangle 2 + \boxed{4} = 6$$
$$\triangle 3 + \boxed{3} = 6$$

Copy the following coordinate grid and plot these three points:

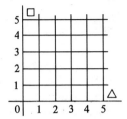

3. If the three points designated in Exercise 2 are connected via line segments, would these line segments determine one line?
4. Find four pairs of numbers that satisfy the equation $\triangle + \square = 5$ such that ordered pairs could be recorded on our grid in Exercise 2. (Fractional numbers are permissible.)
5. If the rule for adding these ordered pairs is as follows: $(a, \ b) + (c, \ d) = (a + c, b + d)$:
   a. Is $(3, 4) + (5, 9)$ equal to $(5, 9) + (3, 4)$?
   b. Is $(3, 4) + (5, 0)$ equal to $(4, 3) + (0, 5)$?
   c. Is $[(3, 4) + (2, 5)] + (3, 1)$ equal to $[(3, 4) + (2, 5)] + (3, 1)$?

17.19 CONSTRUCTION OF GRAPHS

Having established the idea of ordered pairs of numbers, the teacher is now in a position to introduce the concept of *line graphs*. Let us give some applied meaning to our pairs of numbers. For example, let us specify that the numbers along the $\triangle$ axis refer to miles and that the numbers along the $\square$ axis refer to hours. Now we can create a "picture" showing various types of rate situations. Consider the following:

John walks 2 miles per hour.
In 2 hours he will have walked 4 miles.
In 3 hours he will have walked 6 miles.

Figure 17.34 depicts this information as a graph.

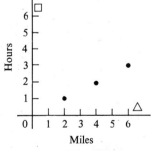

Figure 17.34

If we write a mathematical sentence depicting this relation, we obtain $\triangle = 2 \times \square$, or $\square = \frac{1}{2}\triangle$. We can obtain the ordered pairs $(0, 0)$ and $(2, 1)$ using this equation. Noting that all of the points lie on a straight line, we connect points $(0, 0)$ and $(6, 3)$ with a line segment.

We are now ready to explore with the children how graphs are used. You should demonstrate to them that, given either the hours or the miles traveled, how far John had traveled or how long John had traveled can be determined quickly. For example, suppose we wanted to know how far John had traveled after $2\frac{1}{2}$ hours. Figure 17.35 shows how the answer can be read directly from the graph.

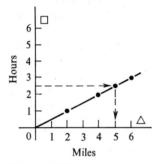

Figure 17.35

We can verify that 5 miles is the correct answer by showing that 5 is equal to $2 \times 2\frac{1}{2}$. Having the children "read off" solutions to problems will help them understand one of the functions of line graphs.

You will also want to introduce the child to the *broken-line graph*. Although its function is not nearly as general as that of the line graph, it is nevertheless quite useful in conveying ordered relationships. This time, instead of comparing numerical relationships, we shall compare the ordered sequences of months with ordered sequences of numbers. In this case, the numerals will reflect the number of words that John spells correctly on each monthly spelling test of 100 words. Figure 17.36 depicts such a relationship.

We can use a broken-line graph to note trends. For example, we note that, except for John's January score, each month his score was better than that of the preceding month. The broken-line graph and the line graph are especially useful when the $\triangle$ variable has many increments. Line and broken-line graphs will be further developed in the exercises.

If the number of increments of $\triangle$ is relatively small, a type of graph called a *bar graph* may be more appropriate than a line graph. The construction of a bar graph is similar to the construction of a line graph. The first step in constructing a bar graph is to make dots on the graph to correspond to the ordered pairs. For example, suppose we were

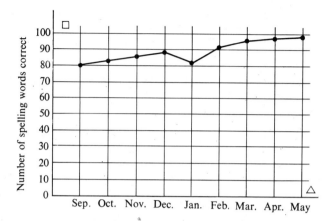

Figure 17.36

given the table in Figure 17.37 depicting John's performance on weekly 20-item mathematics tests. We would first set up a graph with dots corresponding to the ordered pairs (1st, 10), (2nd, 19), (3rd, 11), (4th, 18), and (5th, 10) (Figure 17.38). Then we would construct bars whose lengths

First week	10
Second week	19
Third week	11
Fourth week	18
Fifth week	10

Figure 17.37

correspond to a distance from the △ axis to the dot (Figure 17.39). We can construct the bar graphs in either a vertical manner, as in Figure 17.39, or in a horizontal manner, shown in Figure 17.40.

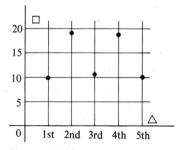

Figure 17.38

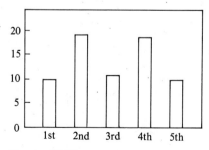

Figure 17.39

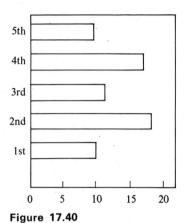

Figure 17.40

Even though bar and line graphs depict ordered relationships, sometimes we are interested in comparing fractional parts to a whole, and these graphs are not appropriate. For example, suppose we spend $\frac{1}{4}$ of our budget for food, $\frac{1}{4}$ for rent, $\frac{1}{8}$ for transportation, $\frac{1}{8}$ for medical fees, $\frac{1}{8}$ for entertainment, and $\frac{1}{8}$ for insurance. A circle graph would be appropriate for depicting these relationships. In Figure 17.41, we can easily see that we spend twice as much for food as we do for transportation. Comparative expenditures for various things are easily noted when using a circle graph.

Sometimes we are not especially interested in very precise relationships but only in more general relationships. In this case, the most appropriate graph to use might be the pictograph. In constructing a pictograph, we

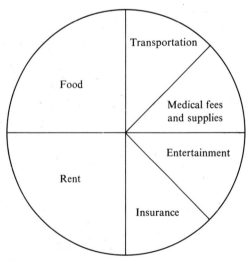

Figure 17.41

select some picture that will show a certain number of a given unit. For example, suppose we are interested in showing aluminum production from 1920 through 1960. We might let a picture of an aluminum ingot stand for 100,000 tons of aluminum. Figure 17.42 shows how our pictograph of aluminum production might look.

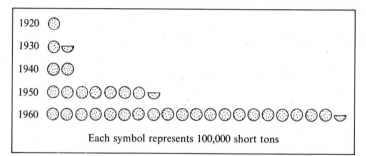

Figure 17.42

Notice that this type of graph gives only a gross comparison of the ratios involved. We can increase the usefulness of a graph of this type by accompanying the pictures with the numerical data.

EXERCISES (5)

1. Name three relationships for which a line graph can be constructed.
2. Using one of the following sources, construct a table that can be used to construct a broken-line graph:

   a. *World Almanac*   c. Newspaper
   b. Business magazine   d. Farm magazine

3. Using the same sources, construct a table that can be used to construct a bar graph.
4. Using the same sources, construct a table to show data for a pictograph that would be an appropriate graph.
5. List four sets of relationships that lend themselves to description by circle graphs.

BIBLIOGRAPHY

Alspaugh, C. A. "Kaleidoscopic Geometry," *The Arithmetic Teacher* (February 1970), pp. 116–117.

Black, J. M. "Geometry Alive in Primary Classrooms," *The Arithmetic Teacher* (February 1967), pp. 90–93.

Brune, I. H. "Some k-6 Geometry," *The Arithmetic Teacher* (October 1967), pp. 441–447.

Buck, C. "Geometry for the Elementary School," *The Arithmetic Teacher* (October 1967), pp. 460–467.

Coltharp, F. "Simple Constructions Introduce Geometry," *The Instructor* (October 1965), p. 42.

Carrol, E. C. "Creatamath, or—Geometric Ideas Inspire Young Writers," *The Arithmetic Teacher* (May 1967), pp. 391–393.

D'Augustine, C. H. "Developing Generalizations with Topological Net. Problems," *The Arithmetic Teacher* (February 1965), pp. 109–112.

Girard, R. A. "Development of Critical Interpretation of Statistics and Graphs," *The Arithmetic Teacher* (April 1967), pp. 272–278.

Hartung, M. L., and R. Walch. *Geometry for Elementary Teachers* (Chicago: Scott, Foresman and Company), 1970.

Ibe, M. D. "Better Perception of Geometric Figures Through Folding and Cutting," *The Arithmetic Teacher* (November 1970), pp. 583–586.

Inskeep, J. E. "Primary-Grade Instruction in Geometry," *The Arithmetic Teacher* (May 1968), pp. 422–426.

May, L. J. "String and Paper Teach Simple Geometry," *Grade Teacher* (February 1967), pp. 110–112.

Paschal, B. J. "Geometry for the Disadvantaged," *The Arithmetic Teacher* (January 1967), pp. 4–6.

Richards, P. L. "Tinkertoy Geometry," *The Arithmetic Teacher* (October 1967), pp. 468–469.

Sganga, F. "A Bee on a Point, a Line, and a Plane," *The Arithmetic Teacher* (November 1966), pp. 549–552.

Sullivan, J. J. "Some Problems in Geometry," *The Arithmetic Teacher* (February 1967), pp. 107–109.

Walter, M. "Some Mathematical Ideas Involved in the Mirror Cards," *The Arithmetic Teacher* (February 1967), pp. 115–125.

Walter, M. "A Second Example of Informal Geometry: Milk Cartons," *The Arithmetic Teacher* (May 1969), pp. 368–370.

18

Teaching measurements

BEHAVIORAL OBJECTIVES

Student can . . .

List seven basic elements of the structure of teaching measurement.

Given a type of measure, describe a comparison that can be demonstrated to teach when two observations of this type of measure are equal in measure.

Describe nonstandard units that can be used for a specific type of measure.

Identify a scale for a specific type of measure.

List six standard units for a specific measure.

Describe a direct and an indirect method of determining a specific measure.

Discuss the nature of precision and the approximate nature of measure.

Use a ratio approach to make a conversion.

Use a nonratio approach to make a conversion where zero in one scale is not equal to zero in another scale.

Describe how different types of measures can be combined to form new measures.

18.1 INTRODUCTION

The methods of teaching measure are distinct from those employed in teaching number and numeration systems. Whereas we have been concerned with such things as patterns, place value, properties, and computation, in teaching measure we shall be concerned with things such as standards, precision, approximations, scientific notation, accuracy, and special measurement systems.

The study of measurement offers the elementary teacher a much greater opportunity to be creative than does the teaching of numeration and number systems. For example, any time we touch an object that is mass-produced in our society, we can be sure that one or more standard measures are associated with it. A shirt (sleeve length, neck size), light bulb (wattage, voltage), cardboard box (volume, breaking strength), ink (color, amount), air conditioner (Btu, horsepower, amperage, voltage), pump (water pressure, gallons per minute), gasoline (octane, cost), and so on, all involve measure.

There are few things we come in contact with for which standards of measure have not been created. The teacher is in a position to act as a connoisseur, selecting and developing basic principles of measure from those types of measure promising the greatest chance to reflect creative effort at problem solving.

18.2 TEACHING MEASUREMENT USING ITS BASIC STRUCTURE

If a teacher were to disregard the basic structure of measurement, he could still probably teach the elementary school child concepts about measures of length, area, volume, weight, value, and time. But by disregarding the structure of measurement in his teaching, the teacher would do little to help the child generalize his learning for the literally thousands of types of measures the child will encounter during his lifetime.

By using the study of measures of length, area, volume, weight, value, and time as vehicles for studying the basic structure of measurement, the teacher accomplishes two objectives:

1. The child learns six commonly used types of measurement.
2. The child is taught the basic structure that will give him a systematic way to study each new type of measurement he encounters.

There are several major elements to the structure of measurement, which we shall discuss in the following subsections.

1. Comparison Each type of measurement is based on some type of comparison.

Type of Measure	Sample Comparison	Equal in Measure
Linear A B	Which is longer?	Two objects are lined up end to end. When both sets of ends match, the two objects are said to be equal in length.
Area 	Does the piece of paper sitting on top of B have more or less area than B?	Two regions are said to have the same area if each can be used to cover up the region of the other.
Volume A B	Does object A or B have the greater volume?	Two objects are said to have the same volume when they occupy the same amount of space (displace the same amount of water).
Weight 	Who weighs the most?	Two objects are said to be equal in weight when they both are pulled toward the Earth with the same force (the balance balances).
Money value 	Which object was worth more?	Two objects are said to have the same money value when two people are willing to trade.
Time 	Who took the least amount of time to finish the race?	If two events start together and finish together, we say they took the same amount of time.

It is not always possible to make comparisons directly. Sometimes it is desirable to bring in a model of one of the objects, things, or events being compared. For example, if we wanted to cut a Christmas tree in the woods so that it would be the same height as a room in a window display, then we might cut a string to correspond to the height of the room and use the string to determine the length the tree should be cut.

Sometimes we want to go beyond the point of determining the equality or inequality of two measurements. Very often we want to assign a quantitative value to the measurement. As soon as a quantitative value was sought, a basic unit had to be created in that type of measurement.

2. Unit (Nonstandard) Quantitative values assigned to measurements require the use of units. In the past, the use of units varied from day to day and from place to place. For example, during the colonial period, a farmer might have purchased six rifle balls with two pouches of tobacco one day, and another day he might purchase six rifle balls for eighteen eggs.

To help children understand the arbitrariness of units and the nature of how units are selected you may wish to have your class create their own units at the introductory stage when studying a new type of measure. The following table suggests some arbitrary units that can be used.

Type	Nonstandard Unit
Linear	Toothpick, nails, straws
Area	Sheets of paper, ceramic tiles, trading stamps
Volume	Marbles, ceramic tiles, sugar cubes
Weight	Bricks, books, bottle caps
Money value	Baseball cards, pencils, gum
Time	Burning candles, sand pouring out of cones, swings of rock on string

As society changed from agrarian to technological, there arose the need to communicate measurements via mail, over a phone, and so on. The more measurements we communicated, the greater the need for standard measurements. (Imagine having a tire blow out on the road without having a spare. You call up a garage and ask the garage man to send out a tire with a diameter of six thumbs' widths. You would not be able to communicate the needed width with this nonstandard unit of length.)

3. Standard Units Every type of measure has standard measures associated with it. The following table lists some of the common standard units associated with each type of measure.

Type	Standard Unit		
Linear	Inch	Mile	Light year
	Foot	Centimeter	Kilometer
	Yard	Meter	Rod
Area	Square inch	Square centimeter	
	Square foot	Square kilometer	
	Square yard	Acre	
Volume	Pint	Liter	Cup
	Quart	Milliliter	Tablespoon
	Ounce	Gallon	Teaspoon
Weight	Ounce	Centigram	
	Pound	Kilogram	
	Gram	Ton	
Money value	Penny	Dollar	Mill
	Pound	Mark	Lire
Time	Minute	Decade	
	Hour	Eon	
	Year	Nanosecond	

Imagine the inefficiency of having to use nothing but units. Pretend you select an item in a store that cost 35 cents. You have nothing but units to pay for the item so you have to count out 35 pennies. Imagine the enormous amount of time that business transactions would take if we were forced to use only units.

In order to increase the efficiency of working with standard units, scales are developed.

4. Scales A scale is a technique or device for combining units so that the number of multiple units may be determined quickly. The following table identifies some of the common scales associated with measures.

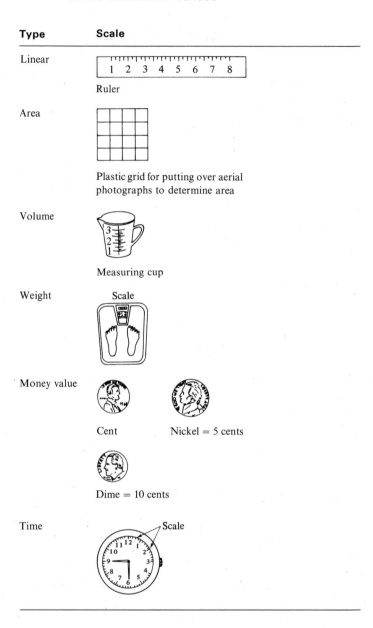

Type	Scale
Linear	Ruler
Area	Plastic grid for putting over aerial photographs to determine area
Volume	Measuring cup
Weight	Scale
Money value	Cent Nickel = 5 cents Dime = 10 cents
Time	Scale

Sometimes it is possible to determine a measure directly, but often an indirect measuring technique must be used to determine a measure.

5. Direct Versus Indirect Measurements Many ingenious indirect methods of measuring have been developed. The following table describes some of the common methods of measuring.

Type	Indirect Method
Linear
Radar used to determine distance
Area
Grid used on aerial photograph
Volume
Displacement of water
Weight
Weight of water displaced by a floating body
Money value
Credit card
Money value determined by cash price plus interest charges
Time
Age of rock determined by measuring the amount of radioactive carbon 14. |

As children begin to measure directly and indirectly they will realize there are many different size units for a given type of measure. They will learn that the smaller the unit, the greater the precision. They will also learn that measurements are not exact but only approximate.

As children begin working with different units the need will arise to convert from one unit to another.

6. Conversion There are two types of conversion the child must be taught at the elementary school level. The most common type of conversion is when zero in one type of unit is zero in the other type of unit. For example, zero feet is equal in measure to zero inches. When both units of measure have a common zero, and when there is a linear relation associated with the scales of both units, then conversion from one unit to

another can be accomplished by a ratio approach. Thus we can convert 8 yards to feet as follows:

$\dfrac{3 \text{ feet}}{1 \text{ yard}}$ Basic conversion ratio

$\dfrac{3}{1} = \dfrac{x}{8}$ $3 \cdot 8 = x$

$x = 24$

8 yards = 24 feet

When two units possess different zeros (e.g., 0°F is not equal to 0°C) it is not possible to use a ratio approach to effect the conversion. Let us examine a step-by-step procedure that can be used to make a conversion when units do not have the same zero point. (It is necessary to know two equivalent conversions before one can make use of this technique. For example, 32°F is equal in measure to 0°C and 212°F is equal in measure to 100°C.)

Let us assume we want to find out how many zings is equal in measure to 4 gabs. We know 2 zings equal 1 gab and 12 zings equals 7 gabs.

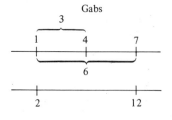

Step 1 We find what fractional part of the way 4 is from 1 to 7. Since $7 - 1 = 6$, it is 6 units from 1 to 7. Since $4 - 1 = 3$, 4 is 3 units from 1. Therefore 4 is $\frac{3}{6}$ of the way between 1 and 7 or $\frac{1}{2}$ of the distance.

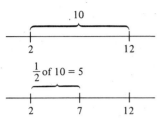

Step 2 Find the number which is $\frac{1}{2}$ of the distance from 2 to 12. Since $12 - 2 = 10$, there are 10 units from 2 to 12.

$\frac{1}{2}$ of 10 is 5.

Therefore the number we are looking for is 5 units from 2 or $5 + 2 = 7$.

4 gabs = 7 zings.

Most conversions that the child encounters at the elementary level involve ratio-type conversions. The nonratio conversion is limited at the elementary school level to converting units of temperature.

As a child masters units and conversions he is slowly taught to integrate and combine measures into new types of measures. This process of deriving new measures and relationships between measurements results in almost unlimited possibilities of new types of measures and new applications of measures.

7. Applications and Mixed Formulas Notice in the following table how by combining the six types of measures we can create new measures:

	Linear	Area	Volume	Weight	Money Value	Time
Velocity	X					X
Pressures		X	X			
Cost			X	X		
Flow rate			X			X

Although the applications of mixed formulas are developed extensively in the students postelementary school experience, there are numerous explorations with mixed formulas at the elementary school level. The most common of these are:

		Example
Costs	Money value per linear	If rope costs 5 cents per foot. ...
Costs	Money values per volume	If gasoline costs 39 cents per gallon. ...
Costs	Money values per area	If a rug costs 6 dollars per square yard. ...
Rate	Linear per time	If a car travels 30 miles per hour. ...

Not every part of the basic structure is developed with children at every level, but some structural aspect is developed at every level. It is the teacher's responsibility to view the total curriculum and see that his teaching plays a part in the development of the basic structure of measurement.

18.3 TEACHING TIME

A child entering school for the first time comes with a great many misconceptions about time. He has heard his mother say, "In a minute we will do such and such," or "Wait a second," followed by varying degrees of passing time before an event. A minute and a second do not represent fixed units of time to the child; they represent ideas synonymous with "a little while."

The teacher will need to develop a child's perception of a minute, an hour, and a day, along with the establishment of a unit. A child's first experiences with measures of time should be through gross comparison. Comparing the length of time it takes to empty two containers and comparing the length of time it takes two people to run the same distance are activities that lend themselves to comparison of a gross nature. Similar activities can be used to establish the same length of time.

The teacher can exercise her creativity in the manner in which she promotes the selection of a unit of time. An excellent motivational device is to display some historical attempts to arrive at a unit of time, such as the water clock, candle clock, rope clock, hourglass, and sun dial. Let the class suggest other means of arriving at a unit and try as many of these as is feasible. Although some of them may not be the right type of unit to measure time, it is probably best to allow the children to come to this conclusion through experimentation rather than serve as the rule-maker with your adult perceptions.

With the derivation of a unit of time, the need to associate a number with this unit becomes obvious. For example, we did something 4 fleegens* ago, or John can run to the tree in 5 goops. A question such as the following will motivate the need for a standard unit of measure: "Mary can hold her breath 8 tingles; John can hold his breath 3 wintles; who can hold her or his breath longer?"

Early experiences with standard measure should not only teach the child to "read" measures (such as looking at a clock and being able to announce the time) but should also help him gain a "feel" for the standard being taught. For example, to help the child relate to the 1-hour idea, you might say, "The clock now says 10 o'clock; in 1 hour we shall go out to the playground." Or to help create the feel of 1 minute, you might say, "The bell will ring in 1 minute."

Generally, the child is first taught to read a clock by hours. This learning experience should be cyclic. That is, not only is it desirable that the child be able to read a clock, but it is also necessary that he be able to construct or draw or set a clock showing a designated time. Half hours, quarter hours, five-minute intervals, minutes, minutes to, minutes after—all these sequentially follow the introduction of the concept of an hour. Certain generalizations such as "any 15 consecutive minutes constitute a quarter of an hour," or "any 30 consecutive minutes constitute a half hour," should be taught.

---

* Along with the creation of a unit, we also create a name for the unit.

Let's examine how oral involvement might be used to teach a child to read time involving multiples of 5 minutes.

Teacher: Hold your nose with your left hand. This will be the small hour hand of the clock. Hold your right hand over your head. We are going to count by fives and move our right hand as the minute hand moves around the clock.

Teacher and class (counting orally and moving their arms):
5 ... 10 ... 15 .... This is continued around until 60 is reached.

(Next a clock face is used which contains only the minute hand.)
Teacher: I want you to count silently by fives as I move the minute hand around the clock face.

(Making pronounced stops on the 1, 2, 3, and 4 and making a sound on each of these stops to aid the child in his silent counting.)

Teacher: Count silently by fives as I move the hand around the clock. When I say "go" tell me what you have counted to.

Teacher: Go!
Children: 20.

(Next a clock face with only the hour hand is used.)

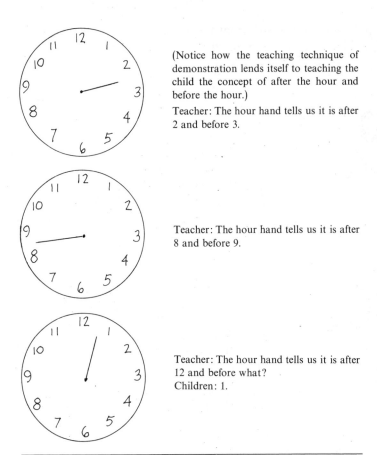

(Notice how the teaching technique of demonstration lends itself to teaching the child the concept of after the hour and before the hour.)

Teacher: The hour hand tells us it is after 2 and before 3.

Teacher: The hour hand tells us it is after 8 and before 9.

Teacher: The hour hand tells us it is after 12 and before what?
Children: 1.

After several experiences with each of these activities the child is taught by using a real clock with both hands on it.

The child's concepts of time are gradually extended to the idea of days, weeks, months, years, and so on. Gradually, his concepts of measure are extended to include the incorporation of measures of time. For example, he will learn that a light year (the distance light travels in a year) is a standard for measuring distances, or that miles per hour is a standard for measuring velocity, or that foot-pounds per second is a measure of rates of work, or that particle bombardments per second is a measure of radiation intensity.

You, as the teacher, will find some of the following motivational devices useful in the exploration of the concept of the measure of time.

1. A collection of various types of timepieces
2. Demonstrations of how timepieces are used

3. A play where there is an attempt to identify the role of measure during some period of history
4. Exhibits the students have prepared that represent novel ways they have created to tell time
5. Student-created games involving time as a measure
6. Bulletin board displays that depict, with cutouts from newspapers and magazines, the role that measurement of time plays in our society
7. Creative writing experiences, such as a science-fiction story about measures of time on a nonrotating planet with two suns
8. Students' research into the history of the measurement of time

18.4 TEACHING LINEAR MEASURE

The child comes to school with certain conceptions about length. The preschool child has many experiences with gross discriminations that involve discrimination in terms of length or one of its related concepts. He already has command of such concepts as taller than, shorter than, bigger than (in height), smaller than (in height), nearer than, and farther than.

Even though he has had certain experiences in gross discrimination of length, he will need help in refining these concepts. For example, you will need to demonstrate refined techniques of comparing lengths, such as a side-by-side comparison or the construction of a moveable model of one of the lengths. For example, in order to compare lengths you might use a picture of a line segment that corresponds in length to one of the objects being compared.

Comparison of lengths of objects such as pencils, children, shoes, fingers, strips of paper, plants, leaves, and ropes provides a natural environment for building readiness for the concept of "less than" in measure, "greater than" in measure, "the same" in measure.

Following experiences with gross comparisons, it is the teacher's responsibility to define what will be meant when we say two objects are the same in length. This is not a trivial concept; it requires careful development. Children start comparing heights and lengths on a visual basis, and such factors as color and nearness of objects play a role in distorting their perception of length. Such concepts as "the shortest distance between two points is the measure of a line segment whose endpoints are the two points" and the "necessity of a strictly vertical comparison for comparing heights" must be developed by the teacher.

These techniques are best taught through demonstrations using proper measurement techniques. Such concepts as the shortest distance between two points can easily be demonstrated with string, where the nonextended piece of string is compared with itself extended. Figure 18.2 depicts how the edge of a piece of paper can be used to compare the lengths of two line

Figure 18.1

segments. Our conclusions about two line segments having the same length are limited by our ability to perceive and our ability to master the skills of measurement.

Following gross comparisons and the establishment of what will be meant by saying that two objects have the same length, it is necessary to develop the concept of unit and scale. Children again should be encouraged to see the arbitrariness of the unit we select. At this point, they should be given measuring experiences to point out that precision is increased as we decrease the size of our unit. For example, suppose we measure $\overline{AB}$ in Figure 18.3 with units M, J, and K. We find that the measure is between 2 and 3 measures of M, and between 4 and 5 measures of J, and between 9 and 10 measures of K. It is quite easy to see that if we are to be "off," at most, by $\frac{1}{2}$ unit of measure, the smaller unit of measure gives us the greatest precision.

In teaching children how to measure things of a "nonstraight" nature (such as the circumference of a circle), the teacher has a wonderful opportunity to develop their ability to attack real problems creatively. The teacher should encourage the children to suggest techniques of finding

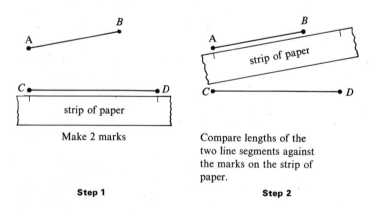

Figure 18.2

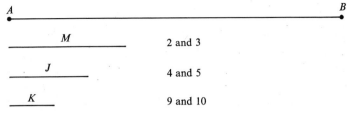

Figure 18.3

the measure. Several "promising suggestions" should be tried. The following represent a few of the creative solutions to linear measurement problems suggested by children:

Problem: To find the length of a tangled fishline. Cut off a unit length and weigh this piece. Weigh the rest of the fishline. Divide the weight of the tangled fishline by the weight of a unit in order to derive the number of units.

Problem: To measure the distance around a lake that is very marshy around the edge. This solution was suggested by a sixth-grade class. Take a picture of the lake from the air. Mark off a unit on the picture. See how long this unit is at the lake. Find out how many of these units it takes to go around the picture of the lake. Multiply this number times the number of the length 1 unit corresponds to in terms of the lake.

Problem: To measure the depth of water in a well. Let out a string with a rock attached until the rock touches the bottom. Measure the length of wet string.

The creation of a wheeled measuring device is appropriate at this stage of developing a measure. Even though devices of this nature are generally circular, noncircular ones are also suitable. Let the children create various devices to speed up the measuring process. Figure 18.4 depicts some devices created for this purpose.

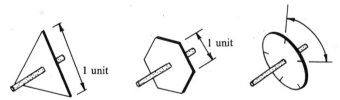

Figure 18.4

Devices such as an odometer, a pedometer, and a cyclometer will stimulate discussion. These devices will also underscore the advantage of creating a scale.

Measurement of distance and length in everyday situations is rarely of the "put the ruler down and measure it off" variety. Such things as radiation, radio waves, and sound waves are some of the more exotic units that are used to measure distance and height. The student should be made aware that in mastering the use of a tape measure or a ruler he has only reached the threshold of determining linear measure, and that we strive always for more and better ways to measure things linearly. The teacher should promote creative effort in the search for such devices and standards.

Until now we have not identified the standards of linear measure that will be taught. Certainly the child needs to be familiar with inches, feet, yards, and so on. This need involves not only knowing that 12 inches is equal in measure to 1 foot, but also involves the child's gaining a "feel" of what an inch is and what a foot is. The development of this feel involves measuring things in inches, feet, and so forth.

Development of a feel for larger units can be accomplished by relating these measures to the experiences a child has had. For example, a mile might be described as being about as far as walking around the school grounds five times. A similar feel can be developed for smaller measures. For example, you might compare $\frac{1}{128}$ of an inch to the width of a hair.

Although we have an obligation to introduce the child to our common linear measures, we also need to familiarize him with the metric system of linear measure, which the United States will be using in the future. The metric system is used universally in science and by a large proportion of the civilized world, and it has many advantages as a measuring system.

The *meter* is the basic unit of measurement of length in the metric system. The following list designates the decimal multiples of the meter:

1 myriameter $\overset{m}{=}$ 10,000 meters

1 kilometer $\overset{m}{=}$ 1000 meters

1 hectometer $\overset{m}{=}$ 100 meters

1 decameter $\overset{m}{=}$ 10 meters

1 meter

1 decimeter $\overset{m}{=}$ $\frac{1}{10}$ meter or .1 meter

1 centimeter $\overset{m}{=}$ $\frac{1}{100}$ meter or .01 meter

1 millimeter $\overset{m}{=}$ $\frac{1}{1000}$ meter or .001 meter

In the development of concepts relative to the metric system, it is important to establish a feel for a meter, centimeter, or kilometer in terms of lengths of common objects in the child's environment.

Some experience in converting from our system of measure to the metric system and back will establish a feel for the various types of units. A ratio approach offers a convenient means to translate between systems of measure that have the same zero and that both employ a multiple-unit approach to measure. (This is in contrast to such measures as temperatures, which have different zeros and scales of measure, or such measures as atomic half-life measures, which use an exponentially derived scale.)

In Figure 18.5, we see several ratios that will prove useful in converting either from our system to the metric system or from the metric system to our system.

2.54 centimeters: 1 inch ∷ □ centimeters: △ inches, or $\frac{2.54}{1} = \frac{\square}{\triangle}$

.3048 meter: 1 foot ∷ □ meters: △ feet

.9144 meter: 1 yard ∷ □ meters: △ yards

5.029 meters: 1 rod ∷ □ meters: △ rods

1.6093 kilometers: 1 mile ∷ □ meters: △ miles

Figure 18.5

It is important that the teacher stress the ease of converting within the system. For example, 3.5 meters easily translates to $3.5 \times 100 \overset{m}{=} 350$ centimeters.

As the children are developing a feel for linear measure, you will want to be developing the generalizations that relate to linear measure. A useful technique to employ is to record measures in tabular forms and have children look for a number pattern that might be useful in determining a linear measure. For example, suppose we have measured the sides of several rectangles in order to determine the perimeter (see Figure 18.6). A question such as "What would be the fewest number of sides of a rectangle that we could measure and still determine the perimeter of a rectangle?" will lead the children to the generalization that $P \overset{m}{=} 2 \times (l + w)$.

By similar activities, it could be discovered that the perimeter of a square is equal in measure to four times the measure of one side.

Rectangle	w_1	l_1	w_2	l_2	Perimeter
A	3	5	3	5	16
B	1	8	1	8	18
C	14	26	14	26	80

Figure 18.6

18.5 TEACHING AREA MEASURE

Techniques of determining a number to assign to a surface have been with us since antiquity. The Egyptians of the pre-Christian era used area measure to reassign land to the farmers after the flooding Nile had obliterated the previous year's boundary markers.

Unlike linear measure, area measure is a concept about which the preschool child has had few opportunities to develop misconceptions. His first experiences with area measure, then, should involve activities requiring him to make gross discriminations involving surface. Such questions as the following will help him focus on the nature of area measure:

"If we painted this wall and that wall, which wall would take the most paint?"
"Can I cover all the glass on the window with this sheet of paper?"
"Could I write more on this piece of paper (very small piece), or on this piece (very large piece)?"

Comparison of areas such as lawns, sidewalks, floors, ceilings, and walls will help develop an intuitive awareness of "less than," "greater than," and "the same as," in measure.

In early work with selecting a unit of measure for area, it is suggested that the children be allowed to try a variety of units, including circular regions for units, polygonal regions for units, and nonsymmetric regions for units. The teacher should lead them to see that the circular region would not be a wise choice, because it leaves some surface uncovered, even when the circles are touching. Figure 18.7 illustrates the derivation of the surface area using units areas of various shapes.

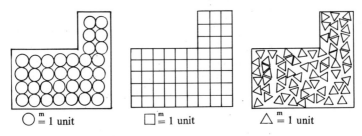

Figure 18.7

When we were concerned with linear measure, we could assert that our measurement was correct to the nearest $\frac{1}{2}$ unit. However, when finding the area of a certain surface, we can assert only that the measure of area is between the number of units that is completely within the figure being measured and the number of units required to completely cover the region. This idea is illustrated by Figure 18.8, where we find that there are 12 units completely within the region, but that it took 28 units to completely cover the region. If we were to decrease the size of our units, we would find the precision of our measure would increase accordingly.

A useful teaching aid to incorporate when studying area is a grid printed on a sheet of clear acetate. This grid can be quickly superimposed over the regions whose areas you want to determine.

It is suggested that you encourage the children to determine novel ways of finding the areas of such things as:

1. A flat island of which you have only an aerial photograph

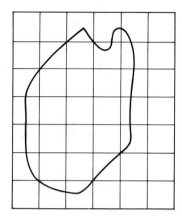

Figure 18.8

2. One face of an object such as a coin
3. One surface of a roll of aluminum foil in which you are not allowed to unroll the foil more than 1 inch
4. The surface of a mountain

After the children have explored such concepts as units, types of units, and the creation of a scale, you will want to undertake activities involving standard units. Again you should stress the fact that a standard unit is selected to facilitate communication involving area measure.

The children should be introduced to the square inch, square foot, square yard, acre, square mile, and so on. They can gain a feel for these standard measures either by measuring off various surfaces with the unit under consideration or by relating the surface to their environment. This can be done by saying that Billy's house is located on 1 acre of land, or that a football field is a little more than 1 acre of land.

Just as it was important to introduce linear metric measure, it is important that the children be exposed to area measure based on metric units. The following designate the decimal multiples of the square meter:

1 square meter $\overset{m}{=}$ 1 centare

100 square meters $\overset{m}{=}$ 1 are

10,000 square meters $\overset{m}{=}$ 1 hectare

Some experience in converting from our system of measure to the metric system and back serves to establish a feel for the various types of units. A ratio approach will prove helpful, because both systems have the same zero and both utilize a multiple-unit approach. Figure 18.9 presents several ratios that are useful either in converting from our system to the metric system or in converting from that system to ours.

6.45 square centimeters: 1 square inch ⁙□ square centimeters: △ square inches

.093 square meter: 1 square foot ⁙□ square meters: △ square feet

.405 hectare: 1 acre ⁙□ hectares: △ acres

Figure 18.9

When teaching the metric system, stress the ease with which conversions can be made within the system. For example, 2.5 centares easily translates to $2.5 \times .01 \overset{m}{=} .025$ are.

You will want to have your students exploring such relationships as the area of a rectangle $= l \times w$ and the area of a triangle $= \frac{1}{2} \times bh$. Even though tabular recordings can be used to focus the children's attention on these relationships, we shall explore an alternate approach to discovering these relationships.

If you mark off the unit squares on a rectangle, it is a simple matter to relate the array formed to the multiplication operation and hence to area of rectangle $= l \times w$ (or number of rows times the number in each row).

Figure 18.10 shows how a parallelogram can be partitioned and reconstructed to become a rectangle. In this way, the children can be led to see that the area of a parallelogram $= b \times h$.

Similarly, Figure 18.11 shows the relationship of the area of a triangle to the area of a parallelogram formed by using two triangles congruent to the original triangle.

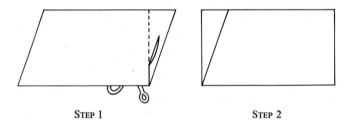

STEP 1   STEP 2

Figure 18.10

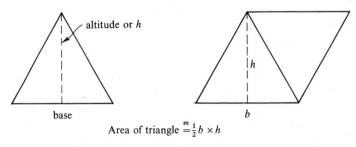

altitude or h

base

Area of triangle $\overset{m}{=} \frac{1}{2}b \times h$

Figure 18.11

Although we have concentrated on direct measures of area, the indirect measures of area offer a chance for the child to exercise creative solutions to area problems and to relate more closely to the means whereby he will derive area in social situations.

18.6 TEACHING MEASURE OF VOLUME

It is generally not possible to measure the volume of an object directly. It is seldom feasible to examine the number of cubic units of a given object by the process of counting these units, because volumetric measure is concerned with a three-dimensional measure, whereas area measure was concerned with a two-dimensional figure.

One of the child's first experiences with measure of volume should be in making gross comparisons where he determines that one object is larger than another. Such activities as comparing a tennis ball to a softball, a book to a radio, or a tree trunk to a can are useful in establishing an intuitive awareness of volume.

It is important to relate the volume of an object to the space it occupies. One way to focus on this aspect is to say, "Suppose you were packing a football and a marble; which object would take up more space in the box?"

A useful technique with which to develop this idea of a unit of volume is to do it through the vehicle of water displacement. For example, fill a jar about half full of water. Mark the level of the water on the side of the jar with a grease pencil. Add a marble to the water and mark the new level

of water. Keep adding marbles and marking the new water levels. Remove the marbles from the water and add a few drops to return the level of the water to its starting point. Now you have a series of marks on the side of the jar that correspond to the volume of water displaced by various numbers of marbles.

By defining a unit of volume as the amount of water displaced by one marble, you can proceed to compare the volume of various objects with respect to marble units. This technique allows you to determine the volume of irregularly shaped objects such as jewelry, figurines, or rocks. By working with modeling clay, you can use other types of units such as cubes and rectangular boxes to establish units of displacement.

Another technique for establishing volume is to construct a model of a given object using unit cubes. In Figure 18.12, we can see that a model of

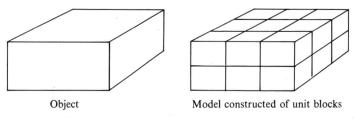

Object   Model constructed of unit blocks

Figure 18.12

the rectangular box has been constructed using unit cubes. After a model is constructed, the number of units used is determined in order to find the volume.

The technique of constructing models using unit cubes will prove useful in getting children to discover generalizations such as "the volume of a rectangular box is equal in measure to $l \times w \times h$."

Rectangular box	l	w	h	Volume
A	1	1	1	1
B	2	2	2	8
C	2	3	2	12
D	4	5	2	40

Figure 18.13

The table in Figure 18.13 was derived using unit cubes to make up models for rectangular boxes. Ask the children to see if they can find the relationship between the length, width, and height and the volume.

This type of activity will lead them to the technique of determining indirectly the volume of a rectangular solid, simply through determining the measure of length, width, and height, and then utilizing the generalization that the volume = $l \times w \times h$.

By exposing children to a great many techniques for determining volume, you will give them an opportunity to appreciate fully the complexity involved in the everyday application of volume determination. You may want to have them explore one or more of the following problems:

1. How can a lumberman estimate how much lumber he can get from a given tree?
2. How can a miner estimate the amount of gold a given mine will produce?
3. How can an astronomer estimate the size of a given star?
4. How can a car manufacturer determine how much steel will be used in a new car?
5. How can a mason estimate how many units of bricks will be needed for a building?
6. How can a road engineer estimate how many trucks of dirt he will need to fill a roadway?

While the children are exploring the nature of volume, the role of the standard units will need to be developed. One of the first experiences that a child will have with standard units is discovering that there is a wide variety of standards for volume, and that our selection of an appropriate standard depends on the nature of the object we are measuring. For example, we have measures such as ounce, pint, quart, gallon, liter, teaspoon, tablespoon, cup, and dram. All these are associated with liquid measure. Others, such as cord, board-foot, bushel, peck, cubic inch, cubic foot, and cubic yard are associated with solid measure.

It is important to develop general conversion techniques for the more common measures that will be encountered in everyday life. However, it is equally important that children view the measure of volume in its broader perspective so that in the future they will be able to interpret and translate from one standard to another, working with measures that have not yet been created.

Allow children to create their own units of measure. Let them describe the ratio of this new measure to one of the standard measures. Require that they determine various translations to and from their system to the standard system. It has been stressed all along that it is essential for children to get a feel for the various standard units. This is no less important for volumetric measure. It will be useful to display various containers holding standard units such as quarts, pints, and cups. Allow the children to fill these containers and to transfer the material from container to container so that they become sensitive to relative capacities. It is also desirable to have a large number of cubic-inch blocks on hand so that relationships such as the following can be shown:

1728 cubic inches = 1 cubic foot.

Halving two of the dimensions of a rectangular solid decreases the volume to one-fourth the original volume.

Doubling three of the dimensions of a rectangular solid makes the new volume eight times as large as the original volume.

EXERCISES

1. Describe how you would teach the comparison of each of the following:

a. Time
b. Weight

c. Viscosity*
d. Hardness*

2. Make up a nonstandard unit for:

a. Money value
b. Length

c. Viscosity*
d. Tensile strength*

3. Make up a scale for using your nonstandard units for:

a. Money value
b. Length

c. Viscosity*
d. Tensile strength*

4. Identify two metric standards units for each of the following:

a. Area
b. Volume

c. Weight
d. Length

5. Identify an indirect method of measuring

a. Length   b. Time   c. Temperature

6. Use a ratio approach to make the following conversions:

a. 19 ft = □ yd
b. 85 oz = □ pt

c. 388 sq in. = □ sq yd
d. 2.5 tons = □ lb

*7. Make the following conversions using a nonratio method:
If 3 bings equals 7 zags and 8 bings equals 20 zags, what does 5 bings equal?

8. Identify each new type of measure which involves the combination of:
a. Distance and time   b. Area and weight

BIBLIOGRAPHY

Archbold, J. C. "Measuring with Maps," *The Arithmetic Teacher* (May 1967), pp. 393–395.

Banks, J. H. "Concepts of Measurement," in National Council of Teachers of Mathematics, *27th Yearbook* (Washington, D.C.), 1963, pp. 108–125.

Bourne, H. N. "The Concept of Area," *The Arithmetic Teacher* (March 1968), pp. 233–243.

Helgren, F. J. "The Metric System in the Elementary Grades," *The Arithmetic Teacher* (May 1967), pp. 349–352.

Jackson, S. B. "Congruence and Measurement," *The Arithmetic Teacher* (February 1967), pp. 94–102.

National Council of Teachers of Mathematics. *30th Yearbook* (Washington, D.C.), 1969, pp. 389–434.

* The asterisk indicate a high level of difficulty.

19

Management and evaluation

BEHAVIORAL OBJECTIVES

Student can . . .

Given a set of behavioral objectives, construct an inventory test.

Given a set of behavioral objectives, construct achievement test items.

Given a set of behavioral objectives, construct a learning sequence chart.

Describe the nature and purpose of anecdotal records.

19.1 INTRODUCTION TO TESTING

At the beginning of each school year, each child enters the classroom differing in every respect from each other child. No two children have had exactly the same set of experiences. Ideally, the teacher should meet the needs of each child during each moment of each school day. Even though the impossibility of such a task is self-evident, the goal of constantly trying to meet each child's needs is a desirable one.

A basic theme of this chapter is the idea of meeting the different needs of children within group-learning situations involving elementary school mathematics. To learn to meet individual needs, we shall need to discuss methods of identifying differences in terms of skill levels, abilities to abstract, abilities to pursue independent activities, abilities to organize and synthesize, abilities in related skills—reading, science, language arts, and so forth.

After each child's abilities and deficiencies are identified, we shall examine techniques of meeting the needs of children who differ radically from the norms, such as the nonreader, the child transferring into the school system with gross deficiencies, the gifted child, the handicapped child, and the "slow" learner.

19.2 INVENTORYING SKILLS AND CONCEPTS

The teacher virtually lives with his students several hours a day, five days a week. If he is sensitive to his students, he will be able to develop a better insight into each child's overall mathematical ability than any test ever devised.

But although the teacher can develop the ability to classify his students in terms of their general overall competence, there are times when specially

devised tests can identify "specifics" better than any amount of direct observation. One of these times is at the beginning of the school year when each child is usually "new" to the teacher. Another time is when the teacher is going to teach a particular unit and wants to identify each child's skill level relating to the unit. The teacher will also be interested in testing the attainment of particular skills and concepts at the completion of a unit.

Let us first examine the inventory test that is given at the beginning of the year. The first task in the construction of an inventory is a listing of those skills and concepts we want to inventory. A very good source for items for this list will come from your school system's curriculum guide. You will want to inventory not only those skills listed as major concepts and skills for the previous grade but also those you plan to teach that year (in order to identify those children who may need special activities and assignments while certain concepts are being developed).

A second source of items for your inventory is an index of a textbook. Also, the teacher of the preceding grade often can be helpful in suggesting items for inclusion.

To gain insight into how to go about developing such a test, let us pretend that you are a second-grade teacher. Assume that you have decided on inventorying the following major areas:

1. Sets
2. Place value

3. Order and relations
4. Addition of whole numbers
5. Subtraction of whole numbers
6. Numbers and numerals
7. Fractional numbers and fractions
8. Geometry
9. Measurement
10. Multiplication

In each of these areas, there will be some items that are best inventoried with paper and pencil and others that will require oral responses. For example, let us examine some of the skills in the area of "numbers and numerals" and decide which of the two techniques—written or oral—might be the most appropriate for inventorying each skill:

1. Number concept of zero—oral
2. Cardinal number of a set—written
3. Number-numeral distinction—oral
4. Recognition of numerals—written and oral
5. Writing numerals—written
6. Reading numerals—oral
7. Counting—oral

After compiling a list of items you want inventoried, and after deciding on the mode of inventory, you will want to construct test items. Some skill levels can be ascertained by sampling techniques. For example, having a child count by fives, starting at 65 and counting to 95, is a good test of whether he can start at 5 and count to 95. (If the child fails this test item, you can have him start at 5 and see how far he can count by fives.)

Other skills must be examined comprehensively. For example, you will want to inventory all of the basic addition facts involving 6 as an addend. It would not be possible to test two of the 6 facts and then render valid judgments about knowledge of the other 6 facts.

A useful technique in administering an inventory test is to stagger its administration. Figure 19.1 shows how a staggered administration might be used in order to inventory various addition skills.

Notice that when some of the students are occupied by the test, the teacher can be working with students found deficient in certain skills as measured by an earlier inventory test. As information is obtained from the test, the teacher may want to construct a checklist for each child. Figure 19.2 depicts a section of such a checklist for the area of measurement.

Notice that this checklist is being used to maintain a continuous inventory of the child's skills. This type of record is a very valuable addition to the permanent records that accompany the pupil from one grade to the next.

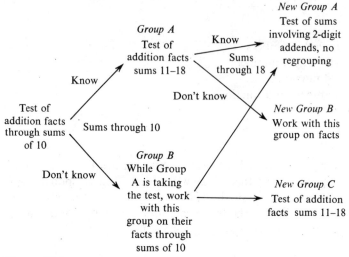

Figure 19.1

	September	November	January
Money			
Cent	✓	✓	✓*
Nickel	✓	✓	✓
Dime			✓
Time			
Hour	✓	✓	✓
Half-hour	✓	✓	✓
Quarter-hour		✓	✓
Minute			✓
Day			✓
Month			
Season	✓	✓	✓
Linear measure			
Inch	✓	✓	✓
Foot	✓	✓	✓
Yard			
Liquid measure			
Pint		✓	✓
Quart	✓	✓	✓
Gallon			✓

* The child knew about a cent measure at each checking period.

Figure 19.2

We do not inventory the skills of a class in order to try to get everyone to the same skill level. On the contrary, to attempt to get everyone to the same skill level is most undesirable. However, inventory tests will prove useful in grouping your class for effective instruction in a particular unit.

These groups of students determined on the basis of inventory tests can be classified conveniently as one group of individuals whose skill level is below that necessary to profit by grade-level instruction, one group whose skill level matches the skills required for mastery of grade-level instruction, and one group that already possesses these grade-level skills.

To meet the needs of these three groups, it is necessary to develop very flexible teaching units. For example, assume that you are interested in developing the generalization that the area of a rectangular region is equal in measure to the product of the measure of the length and the measure of the width. Some of your students will need to work with the basic concept of area as being measured by the number of units of surface required to cover a given surface, others are ready for the generalization, and some students already possess this generalization and are ready for other concepts.

The teacher has several approaches he might use in meeting the needs of these three groups. Figure 19.3 shows two approaches he might use in meeting the needs of his students.

	Group A	Group B	Group C
Longitudinal approach	Students are involved in determining areas of various regions by covering with units.	Students are involved in constructing rectangular arrays working with unit square regions where they record the rows and columns and area after constructing the rectangular array.	Students are involved in converting parallelogram regions to rectangular regions and deriving a formula for determining the area of a parallelogram.
Horizontal approach	Students are involved in determining the area of various rectangular regions by covering with various types of units.	Same as above.	Students are investigating ways that areas of rectangular regions were determined in the past.

Figure 19.3

19.3 ASSESSING MENTAL POTENTIAL

Not only will you want to ascertain what skill levels various children have reached, but you will also want to determine each child's mental potential. Although day-to-day observations of the children may lead you to make speculations about this or that child's potential, there will be times when obscure factors will lead you to faulty speculations. If the child has vision defects, malnutrition, hearing defects, anemia, or lack of adequate sleep, you may identify him as having little potential, when he really may have much potential once these defects or conditions are corrected. On the other hand, high motivation leading to intense concentration on a given area, possibly coupled with parental tutelage, may lead you to identify an individual as a gifted child when he is of only "average" potential but working inordinately more than the other children. (To avoid this problem, we define gifted in mathematics as being capable of a high level of abstraction, coupled with creative and imaginative problem-solving ability.)

Because of the possibility of misclassifying a child on the basis of his potential, there exists the need to administer or to have administered to the children individual intelligence tests. These tests should be of such a nature as to yield profiles for each child. Profiles should include special aptitudes such as numerical comprehension, spatial apperception, numerical reasoning, and so on.

When the results of these tests deviate from your expectations, you should proceed to investigate what factors might account for such deviations. You will want to utilize the results of these tests in developing a flexible program to meet the different needs. Some characteristics of such a program for meeting the needs of children differing widely in mental potential are as follows:

Instructional materials
1. Less abstract materials for the less mentally able.
2. Differentiation in use of concrete materials, with the less able utilizing for a longer time the concrete materials.

Instructional techniques
1. Differentiation in the amount of independent study and self-direction.
2. Differentiation in review and reteaching, with the less able receiving more frequent and intensive reviews and reteaching.
3. Programed materials and supplemented units for the more able student.
4. Encouragement given to the more able student to deviate from prescribed routines in searching for new algorithms, properties, and patterns.

EXERCISES (1)
1. Make up an inventory test for each of the following: division facts; addition of fractional numbers; common divisor; measure of volume (liquid); two-step story problems.

2. Look up the difference between a group intelligence test and an individual intelligence test.
3. Look up the difference between diagnostic tests and group achievement tests.
4. Look up the uses that can be made of group achievement test scores.

19.4 TESTING ACHIEVEMENT

As a unit is being administered, you will want to assess its value in raising skill levels and teaching concepts. This assessment may take many forms. For example, you might give a test, have the children summarize what they have learned, present a play depicting the concepts learned, have the children write a report giving a self-evaluation of what they have learned, or measure the children's attainments on the basis of how they attack related problems. The most common type of assessment is probably a test. The types of concepts that might be tested and suggested test items are shown in Figure 19.4.

	Sample Items
Vocabulary	1. In $3 + 4 = 7$, which numeral names the sum? 2. A figure formed by the join of two rays having a common endpoint is called either a line or an _____.
Meanings	1. In 342 the 4 names a number that is how many times as large as the number named by the 2? 2. In the division problem below, what does the 4 name? $$\begin{array}{r} 359 \\ 7)\overline{2513} \\ 21 \\ \hline 41 \\ 35 \\ \hline 63 \\ 63 \\ \hline \end{array}$$
Computational skills	1. Find the product of 35 and 78. 2. Find the measure of the angle pictured below: How many degrees less than 45° does this angle measure?
Problem-solving skills	1. What operations are needed to solve each of the following problems: (a) John buys 3 gallons of gasoline at 32 cents per gallon. How much did the 3 gallons of gas cost? (b) Mary bought 35 yards of ribbon. She cut the ribbon into 5-yard strips. How many strips could she get?
Generalizations	1. $3 + \square = \square + 3$ 2. $9\,\square = 9$

Figure 19.4

Every test need not be comprehensive; some may represent only a sampling of the concepts taught. You will use the results of the test to help identify those individuals who would profit by more work in the area being tested. At the same time, the tests will point out weaknesses or misconceptions being developed that may require your immediate attention to correct.

19.5 ASSESSING NONMATHEMATICAL SKILLS AND ABILITY

You will need to know which of your children have reading or language problems so that you can make provisions for these deficiencies. Standardized reading and language tests provide some useful information. You can supplement the information from these tests with mathematics-vocabulary tests and with oral reading tests of material of a mathematical nature. When children with special reading handicaps are identified, special provisions must be made for them. One or more of the following can be used to help the child who is handicapped in reading to develop problem-solving skills:

1. A variety of story problems placed on tape or inexpensive records the student can listen to with earphones.
2. Filmstrips pictorially depicting stories the student can view.
3. Another student acting as reader for the story problems. (Since the basic goal is to develop a child's ability to solve problems of a numerical nature and not to solve "word problems" per se, the teacher must be concerned with maintaining and developing the child's problem-solving skills until such time as he improves his reading skill level to the point of independence. If this is not done, the child will one day develop his reading skills only to find that the gap between his problem-solving ability and that of the others is so great as to be insurmountable. There is no reason to create a double handicap simply because the child is deficient in reading skills, providing his skills are not otherwise deficient.)

Sometimes a child's low skill level in mathematics is due to a physical disability. The diagnosis and treatment of these disabilities should be left to professionals. If no special provisions, such as special instruction, can be made for those who have visual or hearing defects, you should make every provision possible in your classroom to meet their needs.

19.6 INTRODUCTION TO PLANNING THE LESSON

How a learning experience in mathematics is organized depends to a large extent on the type of experience and the objectives of the experience.

Learning-Sequence Chart
Type of Instruction

Introduction of algorithm	Review skills and properties that will be needed for algorithm. Motivation: recognition of need for an efficient algorithm.	→ Basic presentation including: (1) format of algorithm; (2) meaning behind algorithm; (3) discussion of alternate algorithms.	→ (1) Practice. (2) Application.
Basic facts	Introduce basic meaning of the operation.	→ Exploration and discovery of facts.	→ (1) Practice. (2) Motivate a need for memorization; memorize. (3) Study properties that relate to this operation.
Geometric construction	Demonstration of construction technique.	→ Practice.	→ Application or utilization of construction in more complex construction.
Information	Presentation: ── → Application. a. Report b. Demonstration c. Display d. Exhibit e. Film or filmstrip f. Audio tape g. Television h. Books or magazines		
Vocabulary	Pronunciation. ── → Application. Meaning. Spelling.		
Story problems	See units at end of Chapters 4, 5, 6, and 7.		
Properties	See specific units in chapters on operations.		
Geometry	Exploration and → Application. classification. Constructions. Model building.		
Generalizations	Discovery. ── → Application. Summarization. Presentation. Development via direct teaching.		

Figure 19.5

For example, disseminating information requires quite a different organization for learning than does the technique of having children discover structural properties. On the other hand, reteaching a concept requires that the teacher deviate from his original teaching plan to promote interest and meet the needs of those children who failed to attain the concept the first time. Reviewing a skill requires a different approach than does teaching for enrichment. Creative explorations require a freer learning environment than does the introduction of an algorithm.

Figure 19.5 suggests a framework for planning various types of learning experiences. It would not be possible to construct a chart to show every possible modification and deviation. This chart is designed solely for the purpose of exposing you to a framework—not *the* framework—for planning an activity. As your competence in teaching grows, you will develop many different learning sequences.

19.7 ORGANIZING THE CLASSROOM

Ideally, when each new learning experience is begun, the classroom should be organized into as many groups as there are skill levels. Practically, however, a teacher can never attain this ideal. How many groups a teacher manages effectively will depend on his managerial ability. Some teachers can maintain an extremely effective learning environment with several groups simultaneously engaged in different learning experiences. Other teachers, lacking managerial skill, would have a better learning experience if they did not group, because confusion reigns within groups that are not receiving the teacher's attention.

Let us examine some of the basic principles for grouping in mathematics. The first principle is that the more groups you maintain, the greater variety of instructional materials you must have available to meet the needs of different groups. The more groups you have, the greater the amount of time you must spend in planning how these children will spend their time in the groups. The greater the number of groups, the more flexible these groups will be in terms of children moving from one group to another as new needs occur. The more groups you have, the better "chance" you will have of meeting the needs of your children.

Since our primary goal is to meet the educational needs of our students, this factor must take precedence when we decide to group. Groups organized for effective mathematics instruction are different from groups organized for other learning experiences in the elementary school. For example, groups organized for reading are semistable groups that do not have many children moving from one group to another throughout the year. In contrast, mathematics grouping is highly flexible, varying not only in who is in any given group on any given day, but also in the number of groups on any given day.

Let us examine two different types of grouping situations that can arise in teaching. The first of these involves introducing a multiplication algorithm. After an inventory test, we find that three children who transferred in from another system indicate that they have mastered this algorithm, seven children indicate that they are extremely weak in regard to the basic multiplication facts, and 19 give evidence of being ready to learn this algorithm. Thus we have three groups. (Notice that these three groups are quite disproportionate in number.) Figure 19.6 depicts the types of activities

Group A	Group B	Group C
Need to learn the basic facts.	Need to learn algorithm.	Need for extension.
1. Work with arrays, sets, recording of facts.	1. Presentation of the algorithm.	1. Allow these children to investigate how ancient peoples multiplied numbers
2. Work with flash cards or similar devices to aid in memorizing the facts.	2. Practice with the algorithm.	or
3. Practice tests.		2. Introduce them to a different algorithm.
4. Study on facts missed.		

Type of Teacher Involvement for Each Group

Have planning session with group. Check with group to see that they are proceeding in an orderly way.	Check each child as he is practicing the algorithm in order to aid those having trouble.	Let the children report to you on their progress or let them construct an exhibit with your help in their search for materials to place in the exhibit.

Figure 19.6

we might plan for each of these groups. Notice that it is possible to have a group where you do not do any formal introduction but where the nature of the learning experience is self-instructional

Let us examine a second type of grouping situation where fewer groups are involved. Assume that you are going to develop the skill of partitioning a segment into five congruent pieces. Yesterday you demonstrated how to copy an angle, since being able to copy an angle is prerequisite to learning today's skill. However, three children were absent yesterday and thus missed the instruction. In this case, you could present the technique to the whole group and, when you had finished, while the majority of students practiced partitioning a segment, you could work with the group of three children, demonstrating this skill to them. Or you might allow a child proficient in this skill to come over to the group of three and help them. After the three begin their practice, you could return to the larger group and aid those having trouble with partitioning a segment.

In planning your grouping, do not feel that you need to meet with each group each day, although you may need to meet with some groups several times in one day. Utilize your better students to aid those who have been absent or have recently transferred in. Let children participate in presenting instructional units.

Your skill in grouping will grow with your skill as a teacher. In your early experiences with grouping, limit the number of groups you attempt to coordinate. Remember that it is not the number of groups that you can maintain but the effectivenesss of the learning taking place within the groups that is most important.

19.8 INTRODUCTION TO SPECIAL MANAGEMENT PROBLEMS

In this section, we shall suggest some general guidelines to serve as a nucleus of ideas around which you can add other techniques as you mature as a teacher.

Question: What do you do when a child transfers in?

When a child transfers in, you will want to determine his various skill levels as soon as possible. You should study his permanent records in order to determine if previous teachers have cited any unusual traits, skills, or deficiencies in the area of mathematics. You should talk with the child and inquire what concepts he has been learning and what self-image he has in regard to mathematics. If you are in the middle of a mathematics unit, administer the inventory test you used at the beginning of this unit. If several gaps are noted that are probably due to his transfer from a class studying topics at a different pace or in a different sequence from your class, you may want to utilize one or more of the following:

1. Assign the child a helper who can update his skills.
2. Request that the parents secure a tutor or provide the child with some assistance.
3. Assign the child programed units on the topics that have been identified as deficiencies.
4. Give the child assistance after school or during your free periods.*

Question: What do you do with the child who always finishes early?

When a child finishes before the rest of his group, do not punish him by assigning him more of the same type of problem. Post in a con-

---

* Give preference to this technique.

spicuous place activities of a mathematical nature that the children are free to engage in when they have completed their assignment. These activities may entail working with mathematical puzzles, reading biographies of mathematicians, writing a play on mathematics, constructing geometric models, constructing exhibits, reading the history of mathematics, working on a deficiency such as mastery of the basic facts.

You will probably want to question some who finish early. Their speed in completion may be contributing to excessive errors or sloppiness. When this is the case, encourage these children to take a little more time in order to reduce their error rates or improve the neatness of their papers. (Remember, however, that neatness is not a mathematical skill but a general study skill that relates to every area of learning. Excessive insistence on neatness when the child does not have adequate muscular control to write neatly can aid in developing negative attitudes toward mathematics.)

Question: What do you do with the child who is continually revealing to the class the discovery of a generalization before the class has had a chance to make the discovery?

You will want to prevent children from revealing a discovery before others have had a chance to make the discovery. Possibly the best positive technique to use is to ask each child to test his discovery with other examples. Request that the children try to find a way to prove their discoveries. When you feel that further work will not significantly increase the number of children making discoveries, you can call on those children to announce their discoveries. (Notice that we have specified *discoveries*, rather than discovery. It is a good technique to structure more than one potential discovery in each learning situation. When the children come to expect more than one discovery, they will be less likely to reveal what they have discovered before they think that they have exhausted the number of possible discoveries.)

19.9 ASSESSING A YEAR'S WORK

Although you probably will want to maintain a constant evaluation of how your class is progressing from day to day, you will also want to know if your class is deficient in any major concepts normally taught at your grade level. For assessing your class's attainments and deficiencies, you have at your disposal any number of good standardized group achievement tests.

If you administer an achievement test at the beginning of the year, it will not only provide you with a "starting" point from which to measure the class achievement under your tutelage, but it will also show you in which areas the class has overall weaknesses. You may want to postpone this first administration until you have had an opportunity for an overall review.

You will probably administer an achievement test during the later months of the school year. If you administer it when you think that the basic "core" of material has been presented, you will be able to reteach those areas showing weakness. You should record the scores from the mathematics achievement test in the child's permanent record, because this information will help his next teacher.

19.10 ANECDOTAL RECORDS

In addition to the inventory checklist, achievement-test scores, and mental-ability scores, you should include anecdotal records within the child's permanent records. These anecdotal records consist of comments about any unusual behavior from a child with respect to mathematics. The following represent typical comments that might be included:

> Johnny is quite motivated by measurement concepts. Following a unit on measurement, he constructed an exhibit on his own initiative that showed how the Egyptians found the area of land following a flood. He repeatedly brings in objects relating to measure and explains their uses to the class. He is an excellent resource person when the class is studying measurement.
>
> Mary uses her fingers to determine sums and differences. I have found that since introducing her to a simple slide rule she has made less use of her fingers. (Later.) She now appears to be developing some independence of both her fingers and the slide rule.
>
> Philip has very poor coordination. This must be considered in terms of the neatness one expects from him. He is extremely bright and is quick to anticipate generalizations. He has developed several unusual algorithms for multiplying and dividing. He is quite proficient with these algorithms, even though they require a high level of skill in mental calculation.

At the end of the year, screen your anecdotal records and remove any comments that did not prove to represent a consistent description of the child. For example, you may have recorded earlier that a child was weak in a particular area in which he has since become proficient.

EXERCISES (2)

1. Find out what each of the following words means when applied to an achievement test: reliability, validity, norms.
2. Go to an elementary school and study some children's permanent records. Record the types of information you find that might at some time be a factor in your teaching the child mathematics.
3. Observe a class being taught mathematics. Concentrate your observation on one or two children. Record specific comments about these children with respect to their performance, temperament, attitudes, skills, deficiencies, study habits, and apparent motivation.
4. Prepare a lesson plan for teaching a unit in geometry. Outline the objectives of your lesson and tell how you will evaluate whether the lesson has met each objective.

BIBLIOGRAPHY

Evaluation

Burns, P. C. "Analytical Testing and Follow-up Exercises in Elementary School Mathematics," *School Science and Mathematics* (January 1965), pp. 34–38.

Epstein, M. G. "Testing in Mathematics: Why? What? How?" *The Arithmetic Teacher* (April 1968), pp. 311–319.

National Council of Teachers of Mathematics. *26th Yearbook* (Washington, D.C.), 1961.

Riedesel, C. A. *Guiding Discovery in Elementary School Mathematics* (New York: Appleton-Century-Crofts), 1967, pp. 402–430.

Westcott, A. M., and J. A. Smith. *Creative Teaching of Mathematics in the Elementary School* (Boston: Allyn and Bacon), 1967, pp. 181–192.

Management

Hess, A. L. "Discovering Discovery," *The Arithmetic Teacher* (April 1968), pp. 324–327.

Jackson, Humphrey C. "Motivation," *The Arithmetic Teacher* (October 1964), pp. 402–406.

Kersh, B. Y. "Learning by Discovery: Instructional Strategies," *The Arithmetic Teacher* (October 1965), pp. 414–417.

Leblanc, J. F. "Pedagogy in Elementary Mathematics Education—Time for a Change," *The Arithmetic Teacher* (November 1970), pp. 605–611.

Price, E. B., A. L. Prescott, and K. D. Hopkins. "Comparative Achievement with Departmentalized and Self-Contained Classroom Organization," *The Arithmetic Teacher* (March 1967), pp. 212–215.

Sandel, D. H. "Teach so Your Goals Are Showing!" *The Arithmetic Teacher* (April 1968), pp. 320–323.

Weaver, J. F. "Some Ways to Individualize Instruction," *The Instructor* (February 1967), p. 75.

Answers
to
Exercises

CHAPTERS 1–3

Independent study chapters with self-scoring tests.

CHAPTER 4

1. Reading assignment.
2. $3 - \square = 1$
3. Answers will vary.

CHAPTER 5 (1)

1. SAMPLE ANSWER: An apple, a cherry, a grape, and a bald-headed man.
2. SAMPLE ANSWER:

 Leafiness, greenness, shininess

3. SAMPLE ANSWER: $\{\triangle, \square\}$; triangle, square; $\triangle, \square$; $\triangle \ \square$
4. SAMPLE ANSWER: All sets will be said to have the number property of 4 if they can be matched one-to-one with $\{1, 2, 3, 4\}$.
5. All sets will be said to have the property of zero if they can be matched one-to-one with $\{\ \}$.
6. It should read: The teacher wrote the numeral 3 on the board.

CHAPTER 5 (2)

1. SAMPLE ANSWER:
   a. Giving the child a set of 4 objects and having him find other sets of 4 by matching one-to-one.
   b. Having the child learn dot patterns of 4 and development of readiness for $0 + 4$, $1 + 3$, $2 + 2$, $3 + 1$, and $4 - 0$, $4 - 1$, $4 - 2$, $4 - 3$, $4 - 4$.
   c. Counting 4 objects and counting 4 objects out of a set of objects.

2. SAMPLE ANSWER:

a. Pairing off members of one set with members of another set and observing which set has fewer or more members.

b. Ordering numerals.

c. Working with expressions where the correct inequality symbol must be furnished to complete a true sentence.

3. Because you use the skill of counting by tens to develop the concept of counting by ones to 100.

4. Have the child count: 10, 20, 30, 40, 42. Then have him identify that there are 42 dots. Have the child identify how many tens are present. Have the child identify how many ones are present. Review the idea that 4 tens and 2 ones is 42.

5. Have the numeral 240 read.

Then have the children read each 240 with you supplying the periods name.

6. Reading assignment.

CHAPTER 6 (1)

1. Counting by elevens. Ones place pattern: 0, 1, 2, 3, ... Tens place pattern: 1, 2, 3, ...

2. Provide readiness for mental addition of elevens.

3. 3, 7.

4. SAMPLE ANSWER:

Tens	Ones
	‖‖‖‖‖‖‖‖
	‖‖‖‖‖

$\longrightarrow$

Tens	Ones
	‖‖‖‖‖‖‖‖‖
	‖‖‖‖‖

$\longrightarrow$

Tens	Ones
‖	
	‖‖‖‖‖

5. SAMPLE ANSWERS: $35 = 30 + \square$ $28 = \square + 8$ $\square = 60 + 6$

$\square = 60 + 4$ $95 = 90 + \square$

6. Step 1: renaming or expanded notation. Step 2: associative property. Step 3: addition facts. Step 4: renaming or expanded notation.

7. SAMPLE ANSWER:

$$n\{A, B, C, D\} = 4$$
$$n\{3, 5, 6, 9, 11\} = 5$$
$$\{A, B, C, D\} \cup \{3, 5, 6, 9, 11\} = \{A, B, C, D, 3, 5, 6, 9, 11\}$$
$$n\{A, B, C, D, 3, 5, 6, 9, 11\} = 9$$

8. 6 plus 7 is 13; 6 plus 7 equals 13; the sum of 6 and 7 is 13; the sum of 6 and 7 equals 13; 7 added to 6 is 13.

9. Addends: 3, 9, 7, 4. Sums: 12, 11.

10. $6 + 0 = 6$, zero is called the identity element.

11. SAMPLE ANSWERS:

Paired problems: $3 + 5 = \square$ $5 + 3 = \square$

Single solution: $8 + 6 = 6 + \square$

Multiple solution: $\square + 9 = 9 + \square$

12. SAMPLE ANSWERS:

Paired problems: $6 + (7 + 8) = \square$ $(6 + 7) + 8 = \square$

Single solution: $(9 + 3) + 2 = 9 + (\square + 2)$

Multiple solution: $(8 + 4) + \square = 8 + (4 + \square)$

CHAPTER 6 (2)

1. SAMPLE ANSWERS:

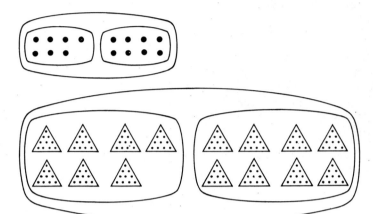

2.

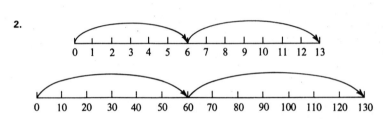

3. Answers will vary.
4. Step 1: renaming or expanded notation. Step 2: associative property. Step 3: addition facts. Step 4: renaming or expanded notation. Step 5: associative property. Step 6: addition of tens. Step 7: renaming or expanded notation.
5. Answers will vary.
6.

$38 + 47$	
$(30 + 8) + (40 + 7)$	expanded notation or regrouping
$30 + (8 + 40) + 7$	associative property
$30 + (40 + 8) + 7$	commutative property
$(30 + 40) + (8 + 7)$	associative property
$70 + 15$	addition of tens and basic facts
$70 + (10 + 5)$	renaming or expanded notation
$(70 + 10) + 5$	associative property
$80 + 5$	addition of tens
85	renaming or expanded notation

7. Order: first to last read from left to right.

$$
\begin{array}{ccccc}
8 & 23 & 40 & 16 & 33 \\
+7 & +3 & +30 & +9 & +29 \\
\hline
\end{array}
$$

8. Order: first to last read from left to right (if adding down).

$$
\begin{array}{ccc}
2 & 3 & 1 \\
2 & 5 & 9 \\
+5 & +6 & +4 \\
\hline
\end{array}
$$

9. Order: first to last read from left to right (if adding down).

21	31	48
32	52	16
+45	+63	+29

CHAPTER 6 (3)

1–4. Answers will vary.

5. SAMPLE ANSWERS: a. John got 3 points in the first half of the game and 10 points in the second half. How many points did he get in all?   b. Bill learned 15 new spelling words each week. How many words did he learn in 3 weeks?   c. Bob spent 30 cents for balloons, 40 cents for cookies, and 10 cents for candles. How much money did he spend in all?   d. A town has 4567 parking meters. It orders 3487 more meters. How many will it have in all?

CHAPTER 7 (1)

1.   SAMPLE ANSWER:

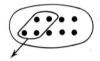

2.   SAMPLE ANSWER:

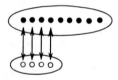

3. 6 minus 5 equals 1; 6 minus 5 is 1; the difference of 6 and 5 is one; the difference of 6 and 5 equals 1; 5 from 6 is 1.

4. Minuends: 7, 8. Subtrahends: 3, 2. Differences: 4, 6. Sum: 7, 8. Known addends: 3, 2. Unknown addends: 4, 6.

5. 53, 44, 35, 26, 17, 8; ones pattern: 3, 4, 5, 6, 7, 8; tens pattern: 5, 4, 3, 2, 1, 0.

6. Sample answer: Pair each block with one cylinder. How many are not paired?

7.

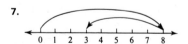

8. SAMPLE ANSWER:

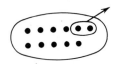

9. $7 + 6 = 13$; $6 + 7 = 13$; $13 - 6 = 7$.
10. Answers will vary.

11.

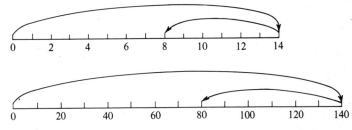

12–14. Answers will vary.
15. a. Yes. b. Yes. c. Compliment him. d. It would depend on the class' mastery of addition and subtraction of integers. This skill is not normally mastered at a third-grade level.
16. SAMPLE ANSWER: $(5 - 4) - 2 \neq 5 - (4 - 2)$.
17. SAMPLE ANSWERS:
  Paired problems: $6 - 4 = \square$ $(6 + 3) - (4 + 3) = \square$
  Single solution: $8 - 5 = 9 - \square$
  Multiple solution: $13 - \square = 20 - \triangle$
18. SAMPLE ANSWERS:
  Paired problems: $8 - (4 + 2) = \square$ $(8 - 4) - 2 = \square$
  Single solution: $13 - (6 + 4) = (13 - 6) - \square$
  Multiple solution: $18 - (5 + \square) = (18 - 5) - \square$
19. SAMPLE ANSWERS:
  Paired problems: $(9 + 8) - (5 + 2) = \square$ $(9 - 5) + (8 + 2) = \square$
  Single solution: $(8 + 4) - (3 + 2) = (8 - \square) + (4 - 2)$
  Multiple solution: $(13 + 5) - (4 + \square) = (13 - 4) + (5 - \square)$
20. SAMPLE ANSWERS:
  Paired problems: $(8 + 4) - 2 = \square$ $8 + (4 - 2) = \square$
  Single solution: $(9 + 3) - 1 = 9 + (3 - \square)$
  Multiple solution: $(9 + 5) - \square = 9 + (5 - \square)$
21.   35 $(20 + 15) - 7 = 20 + (15 - 7)$
      $-\ 7$ $(\square + \triangle) - \bigcirc = \square + (\triangle - \bigcirc)$

      30      $(20 + 10) - 2 = 20 + (10 - 2)$
      $-\ 2$ $(\square + \triangle) - \bigcirc = \square + (\triangle - \bigcirc)$

      $30 + 4$ $(30 + 4) - 2 = 30 + (4 - 2)$
      $-\ \ 2$ $(\square + \triangle) - \bigcirc = \square + (\triangle - \bigcirc)$

      $20 + 8$ $(20 + 8) - (10 + 6) = (20 - 10) + (8 - 6)$
      $-(10 + 6)$ $(\square + \triangle) - (\bigcirc + \bigcirc) = (\square - \bigcirc) + (\triangle - \bigcirc)$

CHAPTER 7 (2)

1–4. Answers will vary.

5. SAMPLE ANSWERS: a. Beth has 27 ribbons; 9 of the ribbons are red. How many are not red? b. Sam has 32 baseball cards. Henry has 25 baseball cards. How many more cards has Sam than Henry? c. Ken has 35 cents. He spends some money at the store. He then has 28 cents. How much money did he spend at the store? d. Sue has 88 pictures. She has 34 more than Ann. How many pictures does Ann have? e. Jim has some pepper plants. Jill gave him 45 more plants. He now has 68 plants. How many plants did he have before Jill gave him some? f. John traveled 91 miles the first 2 hours of his trip. At the end of 4 hours he had gone a total of 165 miles. How far did he travel the second 2 hours?

CHAPTER 8 (1)

1. Counting by nines.

2. SAMPLE ANSWER:

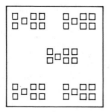

How many sets of 7 are on the board? How many pieces are on the board? What is the product of 5 and 7?

3.

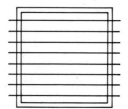

How many rows of pegs do we have? How many pegs in each row? How many pegs in all? 8 times 6 equals what?

4. SAMPLE ANSWER:

Put 8 sticks on your frame in the same way I have done.

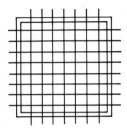

Now put 7 sticks on your frame so that each new stick crosses the 8 sticks. How many places do the sticks cross? What is 8 times 7 equal to?

5.

How long is each jump? How many jumps did we take? 3 times 5 equals what?

6.

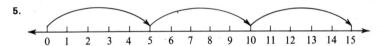

How long is each jump? How many jumps did we take? The product of 9 and 20 is equal to what?

7. $8 \times 90 = 8 \times (9 \times 10)$
    $= (8 \times 9) \times 10$
    $= 72 \times 10$
    $= 720$

8. $8 \times 28 = 8 \times (20 + 8)$
    $= (8 \times 20) + (8 \times 8)$
    $= 160 + 64$
    $= 224$

Dialogues will vary.

9. Answers will vary.

10.

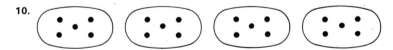

11. ● ● ● ● ● ● ●
    ● ● ● ● ● ● ●
    ● ● ● ● ● ● ●

12. SAMPLE ANSWER:

13. The product of 5 and 9 is 45; the product of 5 and 9 equals 45; 5 times 9 is 45; 5 times 9 equals 45; 9 multiplied by 5 is 45.

14. Factors: 8, 9, 6, 3. Products: 72, 18.

15. $88 \times 1 = 88$. Identity property for multiplication.

16. SAMPLE ANSWERS:
Paired problems: $7 \times 4 = \square$ $\qquad$ $4 \times 7 = \square$
Single solution: $8 \times 5 = \square \times 8$
Multiple solution: $\square \times 3 = 3 \times \square$

17. SAMPLE ANSWERS:
Paired problems: $(3 \times 2) \times 5 = \square$ $\qquad$ $3 \times (2 \times 5) = \square$
Single solution: $(4 \times 9) \times \square = 4 \times (9 \times 6)$
Multiple solution: $8 \times (5 \times \square) = (8 \times 5) \times \square$

18. SAMPLE ANSWERS:
Paired problems: $4 \times (5 + 6) = \square$ $\qquad$ $(4 \times 5) + (4 \times 6) = \square$
Single solution: $8 \times (3 + 5) = (\square \times 3) + (\square \times 5)$
Multiple solution: $3 \times (7 + \square) = (3 \times 7) + (3 \times \square)$

19. SAMPLE ANSWERS:
Paired problems: $8 \times (9 - 3) = \square$ $\qquad$ $(8 \times 9) - (8 \times 3) = \square$
Single solution: $4 \times (3 - 2) = (4 \times 3) - (4 \times \square)$
Multiple solution: $\square \times (8 - 1) = (\square \times 8) - (\square \times 1)$

CHAPTER 8 (2)

1–2. Answers will vary.

3. $300 \times 4000 = (3 \times 100) \times (4 \times 1000)$
$$= 3 \times (100 \times 4) \times 1000$$
$$= 3 \times (4 \times 100) \times 1000$$
$$= (3 \times 4) \times (100 \times 1000)$$
$$= 12 \times 100,000$$
$$= 1,200,000$$

4. $35 \times 182 = 35 \times (100 + 80 + 2)$
$$= (35 \times 100) + (35 \times 80) + (35 \times 2)$$
$$= [(30 + 5) \times 100] + [(30 + 5) \times 80] + [(30 + 5) \times 2]$$
$$= (30 \times 100) + (5 \times 100) + (30 \times 80) + (5 \times 80) + (30 \times 2) + (5 \times 2)$$
$$= 3000 + 500 + 2400 + 400 + 60 + 10$$
$$= 6370$$

5.
```
      237
  ×    46
  ───────
       42
      180
     1200
      280
     1200
     8000
  ───────
   10,902
```

6. Answers will vary.

CHAPTER 8 (3)

1–4. Answers will vary.

5. SAMPLE ANSWERS: a. A triangular piece of metal is .17 of an inch on a side. What is its perimeter? b. Betty bought 3 cans of beets for 17 cents a can. What was the total cost of the beets? c. Bill had 2 pages of stamps with 5 stamps on each page and 3 pages of

stamps with 6 stamps on each page. How many stamps were on the 5 pages in all?
d. The farmer planted 34 rows of pine trees. There were 67 trees in each row. What was the total number of pine trees planted?

CHAPTER 9 (1)

1.
$$
\begin{array}{r}
24 \\
\times\ 6 \\
\hline
144
\end{array}
$$

2. Because there is a whole number 8 that when multiplied by 9 gives the product of 72.

3.
$$
\begin{array}{r}
3 \\
\times\ 5 \\
\hline
15 \\
+\ 1 \\
\hline
16
\end{array}
$$

4. 5 $\overline{)15}$ $15 \div 3 = 5$ $\frac{15}{3} = 5$ $15/3 = 5$

5. The quotient of 6 and 2 is 3; the quotient of 6 and 2 equals 3; 6 divided by 2 is 3; 6 divided by 2 equals 3.

6. Products: 20, 16, 15. Divisors: 2, 3. Dividends: 15, 16, 20. Quotients: 8, 2.

7. SAMPLE ANSWERS:
Paired problems: $(18 - 6) \div 3 = \square$ $(18 \div 3) - (6 \div 3) = \square$
Single solution: $(24 - 12) \div 6 = (24 \div \square) - (12 \div 6)$
Multiple solution: $(36 - 12) \div \square = (36 \div \square) - (12 \div \square)$

8. SAMPLE ANSWERS:
Paired problems: $32 \div 8 = \square$ $16 \div 4 = \square$
Single solution: $10 \div 5 = (10 \times 2) \div (5 \times \square)$
Multiple solution: $72 \div 12 = (72 \div \square) \div (12 \div \square)$

CHAPTER 9 (2)

1. $12 \div 2 = 6$; $12 \div 6 = 2$; $12 \div 3 = 4$; $12 \div 4 = 3$; $(12 \div 1 = 12$ and $12 \div 12 = 1$ are not basic facts, but could be discovered).

2. SAMPLE ANSWER:

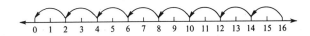

3. Answers will vary.

4.
2)6		2)6		2)6		2)6	
2	1	2	1	4	2	6	3
4		4		2		0	3
2	1	4	2	2	1		
2		0	3	0	3		
2	1						
0	3						

5. $36 \div 4 = \square$ You would introduce the algorithm working with a division problem for which he already knew the answer. In this way he could focus on the mechanics of the algorithm.

6. SAMPLE ANSWERS: $600 - (2 \times 100) = \square$ $1524 - (2 \times 500) = \square$
7. SAMPLE ANSWERS: $356 - (4 \times 70) = \square$ $890 - (7 \times 30) = \square$
8. Answers will vary.
9. 39 tens; 39 hundreds; 39 tens.

CHAPTER 9 (3)

1-4. Answers will vary.
5. SAMPLE ANSWERS: a. A farmer had 394 peaches. He placed 6 peaches in each package. How many packages did he pack?   b. Six boys earned a total of 4 dollars and 94 cents. If they each earned the same amount of money, how much did each boy earn? c. Tom took a bag of 36 quarters and a bag of 40 quarters to the bank. How many dollar bills could he get in exchange for these quarters?   d. Judy had 16 shells and found 4 more at the beach. If she packed these shells 5 to a box, how many boxes would she use?   e. Robert put up a fence for 3 days. He put up the same amount of fence each day. If he put up 900 feet of fence in all, how many feet did he put up each day? f. Mary made 80 pieces of chocolate candy and 60 lemon drops. She bagged the chocolate 5 pieces to the bag and she boxed the lemon drops 10 pieces to the box. If she sold a bag for a nickel and a box for a nickel, how many nickels could she get by selling all the bags and boxes?

CHAPTER 10 (1)

1. SAMPLE ANSWER: Pentagon: fifths, tenths. Octagon: halves, fourths, eights, sixteenths.
2. Check to see that each disjoint subset has the same number of elements and that there are six of these subsets equal in number.
3. SAMPLE ANSWER:

4. SAMPLE ANSWER:

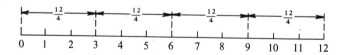

5. SAMPLE ANSWER:

6. SAMPLE ANSWER:

7. SAMPLE ANSWER:

CHAPTER 10 (2)

1. SAMPLE ANSWER:

2. SAMPLE ANSWER:

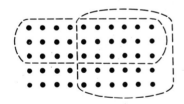

3.

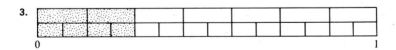

4.

5.

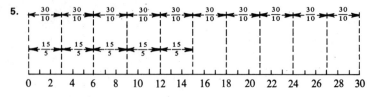

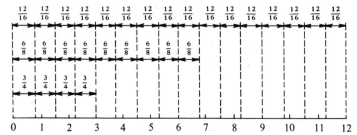

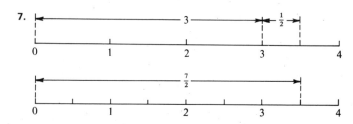

6.

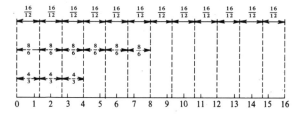

7.

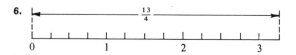

8. a. Yes.   b. There are many names for zero.

9. SAMPLE ANSWERS:

a. $\frac{9}{7} \times \frac{8}{8} = \frac{72}{56}$

$\frac{9}{8} \times \frac{7}{7} = \frac{63}{56}$

$\frac{9}{8} = \frac{63}{56} = \frac{63 \times 1,000,000}{56 \times 1,000,000} = \frac{63,000,000}{56,000,000}$

$\frac{9}{7} = \frac{72}{56} = \frac{72 \times 1,000,000}{56 \times 1,000,000} = \frac{72,000,000}{56,000,000}$

9 million fractional numbers with denominators of 56,000,000 from $\frac{9}{8}$ to $\frac{9}{7}$. By a similar argument you could extend number to 9 billion, 9 trillion, and so forth.

b. $\frac{9}{8} < (\frac{9}{8} + \frac{9}{7}) \div 2 < \frac{9}{7}$

$\frac{9}{8} < \{[(\frac{9}{8} + \frac{9}{7}) \div 2] + \frac{9}{7}\} \div 2 < \frac{9}{7}$

Could be extended on and on.

CHAPTER 11 (1)

1.

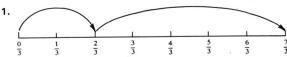

$$\frac{0}{3} \quad \frac{1}{3} \quad \frac{2}{3} \quad \frac{3}{3} \quad \frac{4}{3} \quad \frac{5}{3} \quad \frac{6}{3} \quad \frac{7}{3}$$

2.

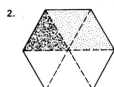

3. $\frac{4}{3} + \frac{\triangle}{\square} = \frac{7}{3}$

4. SAMPLE ANSWERS: a. $\frac{2}{5}$ plus $\frac{5}{5}$ equals $\frac{7}{5}$; $\frac{2}{5}$ plus $\frac{5}{5}$ is $\frac{7}{5}$; the sum of $\frac{2}{5}$ and $\frac{5}{5}$ equals $\frac{7}{5}$; $\frac{5}{5}$ added to $\frac{2}{5}$ is $\frac{7}{5}$. b. $\frac{7}{8}$ minus $\frac{3}{8}$ is $\frac{4}{8}$; the difference of $\frac{7}{8}$ and $\frac{3}{8}$ equals $\frac{4}{8}$; $\frac{3}{8}$ subtracted from $\frac{7}{8}$ is $\frac{4}{8}$; $\frac{7}{8}$ less $\frac{3}{8}$ is $\frac{4}{8}$.

5. Sum: $\frac{8}{4}$. Addends: $\frac{3}{4}, \frac{5}{4}$.

6. Differences: $\frac{1}{4}$ in a, $\frac{3}{4}$ in b. Minuend: $\frac{4}{4}$. Subtrahend: $\frac{1}{4}$. Known addend: $\frac{3}{4}$. Unknown addend: $\frac{1}{4}$. Sum: $\frac{4}{4}$.

7. SAMPLE ANSWERS:

Paired problems: $\frac{3}{4} + \frac{5}{7} = \frac{\triangle}{\square}$ $\frac{5}{7} + \frac{3}{4} = \frac{\triangle}{\square}$

Single solution: $\frac{6}{7} + \frac{3}{4} = \frac{\triangle}{\square} + \frac{6}{7}$

Multiple solution: $\frac{\triangle}{\square} + \frac{2}{3} = \frac{2}{3} + \frac{\triangle}{\square}$

8. SAMPLE ANSWERS:

Paired problems: $(\frac{1}{5} + \frac{4}{6}) + \frac{2}{3} = \frac{\triangle}{\square}$ $\frac{1}{5} + (\frac{4}{6} + \frac{2}{3}) = \frac{\triangle}{\square}$

Single solution: $(\frac{4}{9} + \frac{1}{7}) + \frac{2}{5} = \frac{4}{9} + (\frac{\triangle}{\square} + \frac{2}{5})$

Multiple solution: $(\frac{\triangle}{\square} + \frac{3}{4}) + \frac{7}{8} = \frac{\triangle}{\square} + (\frac{3}{4} + \frac{7}{8})$

CHAPTER 11 (2)

1. SAMPLE ANSWERS:

Paired problems: $\frac{6}{7} - \frac{1}{5} = \frac{\triangle}{\square}$ $(\frac{6}{7} + \frac{2}{5}) - (\frac{1}{5} + \frac{2}{5}) = \frac{\triangle}{\square}$

Single solution: $\frac{13}{11} - \frac{4}{11} = (\frac{13}{11} + \frac{4}{5}) - (\frac{4}{11} + \frac{\triangle}{\square})$

Multiple solution: $\frac{11}{5} - \frac{7}{5} = (\frac{11}{5} - \frac{\triangle}{\square}) - (\frac{7}{5} - \frac{\triangle}{\square})$

2. a.

0   1   2

b.

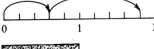

c.

0   1

3. a. $\frac{6}{2} + \frac{8}{2} = \frac{6+8}{2}$ b. $\frac{12}{5} + \frac{4}{5} = \frac{12+4}{5}$

c. $\frac{4}{7} - \frac{2}{7} = \frac{4-2}{7}$ d. $\frac{30}{6} - \frac{12}{6} = \frac{30-12}{6}$

4–5. Answers will vary.

6. $3 + \frac{4}{7} \rightarrow 3 + \frac{44}{77}$

$\dfrac{2 + \frac{9}{11} \rightarrow 2 + \frac{63}{77}}{5 + \frac{107}{77} = 5 + \frac{77}{77} + \frac{30}{77} = 6\frac{30}{77}}$

7. Answers will vary.

8. $3 + \frac{4}{7} \quad\rightarrow\quad 3 + \frac{44}{77} \rightarrow 2 + \frac{77}{77} + \frac{44}{77} \rightarrow \quad 2 + \frac{121}{77}$

$\dfrac{-(2 + \frac{9}{11}) \rightarrow -(2 + \frac{63}{77}) \rightarrow\ -(2 + \frac{63}{77}) \rightarrow\quad -(2 + \frac{63}{77})}{\frac{58}{77}}$

9. SAMPLE ANSWERS: a. If you are interested in comparing the $\frac{6}{10}$ to a decimal expression. b. If you are interested in comparing $\frac{77}{100}$ with a percent expression.   c. If you are being paid by the half-hour.   d. If you are making change in quarters of a dollar.   e. If you are buying yards of cloth.

CHAPTER 12 (1)

1.

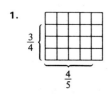

2. SAMPLE ANSWERS: a. $\frac{3}{8} = \frac{7}{8} \times \frac{\triangle}{\square}$ b. $\frac{9}{2} = \frac{8}{3} \times \frac{\triangle}{\square}$ c. $\frac{2}{4} = \frac{3}{4} \times \frac{\triangle}{\square}$ d. $\frac{3}{4} = \frac{4}{3} \times \frac{\triangle}{\square}$

3. SAMPLE ANSWERS: a. Three-sevenths times nine-eighths equals twenty-seven fifty-sixths; three-sevenths times nine-eighths is twenty-seven fifty-sixths; the product of three-sevenths and nine-eighths is twenty-seven fifty-sixths; the product of three-sevenths and nine-eighths equals twenty-seven fifty-sixths. b. Three-sevenths divided by nine-eighths is twenty-four sixty-thirds; the quotient of three-sevenths and nine-eighths is twenty-four sixty-thirds; the quotient of three-sevenths and nine-eighths equals twenty-four sixty-thirds.

4. Factors: $\frac{3}{8}, \frac{8}{7}, 3\frac{1}{4}$. Product: $\frac{24}{33}, 12\frac{1}{4}$. Partial products: $\frac{1}{4}, \frac{3}{2}, 9\frac{3}{4}$.

5. Products: $\frac{6}{35}, \frac{16}{3}$. Dividend: $\frac{16}{3}$. Divisor: $\frac{3}{2}$.

6. SAMPLE ANSWERS:

a. Paired problems: $\frac{4}{7} \times \frac{9}{3} = \frac{\triangle}{\square}$ $\frac{9}{3} \times \frac{4}{7} = \frac{\triangle}{\square}$

Single solution: $\frac{6}{3} \times \frac{3}{4} = \frac{\triangle}{\square} \times \frac{6}{3}$

Multiple solution: $\frac{1}{2} \times \frac{\triangle}{\square} = \frac{\triangle}{\square} \times \frac{1}{2}$

b. SAMPLE ANSWERS:

Paired problems: $(\frac{3}{4} \times \frac{9}{7}) \times \frac{1}{5} = \frac{\square}{\triangle}$ $\frac{3}{4} \times (\frac{6}{7} \times \frac{1}{5}) = \frac{\square}{\triangle}$

Single solution: $(\frac{7}{6} \times \frac{6}{9}) \times \frac{2}{3} = \frac{\triangle}{\square} \times (\frac{6}{9} \times \frac{2}{3})$

Multiple solution: $(\frac{11}{3} \times \frac{4}{2}) \times \frac{\triangle}{\square} = \frac{11}{3} \times (\frac{4}{2} \times \frac{\triangle}{\square})$

c. SAMPLE ANSWERS:

Paired problems: $\frac{7}{9} \times (\frac{16}{3} + \frac{4}{3}) = \frac{\triangle}{\square}$ $(\frac{7}{9} \times \frac{16}{3}) + (\frac{7}{9} \times \frac{4}{3}) = \frac{\triangle}{\square}$

Single solution: $\frac{2}{13} \times (\frac{4}{7} + \frac{2}{3}) = (\frac{2}{13} \times \frac{\triangle}{\square}) + (\frac{2}{13} \times \frac{2}{3})$

Multiple solution: $\frac{5}{4} \times (\frac{3}{2} + \frac{\triangle}{\square}) = (\frac{5}{4} \times \frac{3}{2}) + (\frac{5}{4} \times \frac{\triangle}{\square})$

d. SAMPLE ANSWERS:

Paired problems: $\frac{3}{4} \times (\frac{11}{2} - \frac{1}{2}) = \frac{\square}{\triangle}$ $(\frac{3}{4} \times \frac{11}{2}) - (\frac{3}{4} \times \frac{1}{2}) = \frac{\square}{\triangle}$

Single solution: $\frac{8}{3} \times (\frac{6}{7} - \frac{4}{5}) = (\frac{\square}{\triangle} \times \frac{6}{7}) - (\frac{\square}{\triangle} \times \frac{4}{5})$

Multiple solution: $\frac{\triangle}{\square} \times (\frac{35}{3} - \frac{17}{2}) = (\frac{\triangle}{\square} \times \frac{35}{3}) - (\frac{\triangle}{\square} \times \frac{17}{2})$

e. SAMPLE ANSWERS:

$\frac{6}{4} \times \frac{4}{6} = \frac{\triangle}{\square}$ $\frac{3}{5} \times \frac{\triangle}{\square} = \frac{15}{15} = 1$ $\frac{\triangle}{\square} \times \frac{9}{8} = \frac{72}{72} = 1$

$\frac{8}{3} \times \frac{3}{8} = \frac{\triangle}{\square}$ $\frac{4}{7} \times \frac{\triangle}{\square} = 1$

CHAPTER 12 (2)

1. SAMPLE ANSWERS:

Single solution: $\frac{3}{4} \div \frac{5}{8} = (\frac{3}{4} \times \frac{5}{6}) \div (\frac{5}{8} \times \frac{\triangle}{\square})$

Multiple solution: $\frac{4}{9} \div \frac{2}{7} = (\frac{4}{9} \times \frac{\square}{\triangle}) \div (\frac{2}{7} \times \frac{\square}{\triangle})$

2. SAMPLE ANSWERS:

Paired problems: $(\frac{6}{5} + \frac{3}{5}) \div \frac{7}{3} = \frac{\triangle}{\square}$ $(\frac{6}{5} \div \frac{7}{3}) + (\frac{3}{5} \div \frac{7}{3}) = \frac{\triangle}{\square}$

Single solution: $(\frac{21}{13} + \frac{4}{11}) \div \frac{7}{10} = (\frac{21}{13} \div \frac{7}{10}) + (\frac{4}{11} \div \frac{\triangle}{\square})$

Multiple solution: $(\frac{8}{5} + \frac{3}{7}) \div \frac{\triangle}{\square} = (\frac{8}{5} \div \frac{\triangle}{\square}) + (\frac{3}{7} \div \frac{\triangle}{\square})$

3. SAMPLE ANSWERS:

Paired problems: $(\frac{7}{2} - \frac{4}{2}) \div \frac{6}{17} = \frac{\triangle}{\square}$ $(\frac{7}{2} \div \frac{6}{17}) - (\frac{4}{2} \div \frac{6}{17}) = \frac{\triangle}{\square}$

Single solution: $(\frac{4}{6} - \frac{1}{6}) \div \frac{3}{7} = (\frac{4}{6} \div \frac{3}{7}) - (\frac{1}{6} \div \frac{\triangle}{\square})$

Multiple solution: $(\frac{14}{2} - \frac{\triangle}{\square}) \div \frac{3}{4} = (\frac{14}{2} \div \frac{3}{4}) - (\frac{\triangle}{\square} \div \frac{3}{4})$

4. Answers will vary.

5. a. Compensation property   b. Multiplication algorithm   c. Reciprocal property
d. Multiplication facts   e. Division by one

6. a. Compensation property   b. Multiplication algorithm   c. Multiplication facts   d. Concept of $\frac{3}{6}$ and $\frac{4}{6}$ e. Compensation property   f. Fraction notation

7–8.

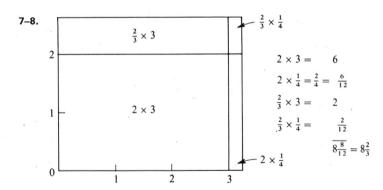

CHAPTER 13 (1)

1. Repetitive, no place value, no zero, additive, base 4.
2. Not repetitive, place value, no zero, additive, base 3 (note *aa* means 1 three 1 one).
3. Not repetitive, place value, zero, additive, base 4.
4. Repetitive (in *kak* both *k*s mean 5), no place value, no zero, additive and subtractive, base 5.
5. Repetitive, no place value, no zero, multiplicative, additive, no base.
6. Repetitive, no place value, no zero, additive, base 5. .

CHAPTER 13 (2)

1. a. Pile (a): 75 cups; pile (b): 10 cups; pile (c): 2 cups. Total cups: 87.

b. Pile (a): 4 cups; pile (b): 2 cups; pile (c): 0 cups. Total cups: 6.

c. Pile (a): 18 cups; pile (b): 0 cups; pile (c): 2 cups. Total cups: 20.

2. SAMPLE ANSWERS:

$$4567_{\text{eight}} \rightarrow (\underline{} \times 8^3) + (\underline{} \times 8^2) + (\underline{} \times 8^1) + (\underline{} \times 8^0)$$

$$3 \times 8^3 + 7 \times 8^0 \rightarrow \underline{}_{\text{eight}}$$

3. SAMPLE ANSWER:

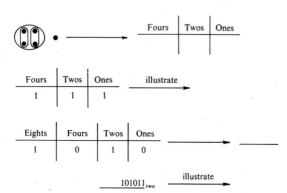

Fours	Twos	Ones

illustrate →

Fours	Twos	Ones
1	1	1

illustrate →

Eights	Fours	Twos	Ones
1	0	1	0

$$\underline{} 101011_{\text{two}}$$ illustrate → $\underline{}$

4. SAMPLE ANSWERS:

$300 \rightarrow \square \times 10^2$

$7000 \rightarrow 7 \times 10^{\square}$

$460 \rightarrow 4.6 \times 10^{\square}$

$3854 \rightarrow \underline{} \times 10^3$

Express in scientific notation: a. 40,000 b. 3,700,000. Express in standard notation: a. 3.6×10^6 b. 4.798×10^8

CHAPTER 14 (1)

1. a. $\frac{375}{2} \times \frac{5}{5} = \frac{1875}{10} = 187.5$ b. $\frac{41}{5 \times 5} = \frac{41}{5 \times 5} \times \frac{2 \times 2}{2 \times 2} = \frac{164}{100} = 1.64$

c. $\frac{3714}{2 \times 5 \times 5} = \frac{3714}{2 \times 5 \times 5} \times \frac{2}{2} = \frac{7428}{100} = 74.28$

2. a. $\frac{3}{10} + \frac{6}{10} = \frac{9}{10}$ $.3 + .6 = .9$

b. $\frac{4}{10} + \frac{7}{100} = \frac{40}{100} + \frac{7}{100} = \frac{47}{100}$ $.40 + .07 = .47$

c. $\frac{3}{10} - \frac{1}{10} = \frac{2}{10}$ $.3 - .1 = .2$

d. $\frac{8}{10} - \frac{9}{100} = \frac{80}{100} - \frac{9}{100} = \frac{71}{100}$ $.80 - .09 = .71$

3. SAMPLE ANSWERS: a. $\frac{3}{10} + \frac{5}{100} = \frac{\triangle}{\square}$ $\frac{5}{100} + \frac{3}{10} = \frac{\triangle}{\square}$

b. $\left(\frac{4}{1000} + \frac{3}{10}\right) + \frac{25}{100} = \frac{\triangle}{\square}$ $\frac{4}{1000} + \left(\frac{3}{10} + \frac{25}{100}\right) = \frac{\triangle}{\square}$

c. $\frac{8}{10} - \frac{3}{10} = \frac{\triangle}{\square}$ $\left(\frac{8}{10} - \frac{4}{100}\right) - \left(\frac{3}{10} - \frac{4}{100}\right) = \frac{\triangle}{\square}$

d. $\frac{17}{100} - \frac{3}{100} = \frac{\triangle}{\square}$ $\left(\frac{17}{100} + \frac{4}{10}\right) - \left(\frac{3}{100} + \frac{4}{10}\right) = \frac{\triangle}{\square}$

e. $\frac{35}{100} + \frac{1}{10} = \frac{\triangle}{\square}$ $\left(\frac{35}{100} - \frac{2}{10}\right) + \left(\frac{1}{10} + \frac{2}{10}\right) = \frac{\triangle}{\square}$

f. $\frac{6}{10} + \frac{0}{10} = \frac{\triangle}{\square}$ $\frac{0}{10} + \frac{6}{10} = \frac{\triangle}{\square}$

4. a. {0, 1, 2, 3, ... 15, 16}   b. {0, 1, 2, 3, ... 257, 258}

c. {0, 1, 2, 3, ... 369, 370}

d. {0, 1, 2, 3, ... 179,387,239, 179,387,240}

5. a. .11$\overline{1}$ b. .22$\overline{2}$ c. .33$\overline{3}$ d. .44$\overline{4}$ e. .55$\overline{5}$ f. .66$\overline{6}$

   g. .0909$\overline{09}$ h. .1818$\overline{18}$ i. .2727$\overline{27}$ j. 9.0909$\overline{09}$

   k. .9090$\overline{90}$ l. 11

CHAPTER 14 (2)

1. a. $\frac{3}{10} \times \frac{17}{100} = \frac{51}{1000}$ $.3 \times .17 = .051$

   b. $\frac{4}{100} \times \frac{5}{100} = \frac{20}{10,000}$ or $\frac{2}{1000}$ $.04 \times .05 = .0020$ or $.002$

   c. $\frac{42}{10} \times \frac{35}{100} = \frac{1470}{1000}$ $4.2 \times .35 = 1.470$

2. SAMPLE ANSWER:

a.
```
  64)471.00
     384.00 | 6
    ─────────
      87.00
      64.00 | 1
    ─────────
      23.00
      19.20 | .3
    ─────────
       3.80
       3.20 | .05
    ─────────
        .60 | 7.35 or 7.4 to the nearest tenth
```

b.
```
  64)47.10
     44.80 | .7
    ────────
      2.30
      1.92 | .03
    ────────
       .38 | .73 or .7 to the nearest tenth
```

   c. $47.1 \div 6.4 = (47.1 \times 10) \div (6.4 \times 10)$ or $471 \div 64$ by the same methods as a and b; answer: 7.36

   d. $471 \div .064 = (471 \times 1000) \div (.064 \times 1000)$; use the same method as a and b; answer 7359.4

   e. $47.1 \div .64 = (47.1 \times 100) \times (.64 \times 100) = 4710 \div 64$; use the same method as a and b; answer: 73.6

3. a. 120 miles   b. 12 feet   c. 27

4. SAMPLE ANSWERS: $\frac{6}{14}, \frac{9}{21}, \frac{12}{28}, \frac{15}{35}, \frac{18}{42}.$

5. SAMPLE ANSWER: $\frac{4 \times 16}{7 \times 16} = \frac{64}{112}$ and $\frac{9}{16} \times \frac{7}{7} = \frac{63}{112}.$

6. $\frac{3}{100}$ and $1\frac{30}{100}$ or $1\frac{3}{10}$ or $\frac{130}{100}.$

7. .22, .04, .001.

CHAPTER 15 (1)

1. SAMPLE ANSWER: Give each child a set of blocks. Have him determine which number of blocks can be arranged into only two arrays.

2. Answers will vary.

3. Answers will vary.

CHAPTER 15 (2)

1–3. Answers will vary.

4. 1

   1 + 4

   1 + 4 + 7

   1 + 4 + 7 + 10

   1 + 4 + 7 + 10 + 13

   $1 + 4 + 7 + 10 + 13, \ldots + [1 + 3(n - 1)]$

CHAPTER 16 (1)

1. Commutative property for subtraction of integers. The operation of subtraction on the set of integers is not commutative.
2. Associative property for subtraction of integers. (It does not hold.)
3. n plus m is equal to n minus the opposite of m.
4. Compensation property.

CHAPTER 16 (2)

1. a. Since $^-3 \times {}^-2 = {}^+6$; $^+6 \div {}^-3 = {}^-2$
   b. Since $^-3 \times {}^+2 = {}^-6$; $^-6 \div {}^-3 = {}^+2$
   c. Since $^+3 \times {}^+2 = {}^+6$; $^+6 \div {}^+3 = {}^+2$

2. SAMPLE ANSWERS:

   $^+16 \div {}^-2 = \square$

   $(^+16 \times {}^-3) \div (^-2 \times {}^-3) = \square$

   $^-48 \div {}^+6 = \square$

   $(^-48 \div {}^+3) \div (^+6 \div {}^+3) = \square$

   $^-15 \div {}^-3 = \square$

   $(^-15 \times {}^-2) \div (^-3 \times {}^-2) = \square$

   $^-12 \div {}^-4 = \square$

   $(^-12 \div {}^-2) \div (^-4 \div {}^-2) = \square$

3. SAMPLE ANSWERS:

   $(^-27 + {}^+9) \div {}^+3 = \square$

   $(^-27 \div {}^+3) + (^+9 \div {}^+3) = \square$

   $(^-72 + {}^-60) \div {}^-12 = \square$

   $(^-72 \div {}^-12) + (^-60 \div {}^-12) = \square$

   $(^+18 + {}^-36) \div {}^-6 = \square$

   $(^+18 \div {}^-6) + (^-36 \div {}^-6) = \square$

   $(^-8 + {}^-6) \div {}^+2 = \square$

   $(^-8 \div {}^+2) + (^-6 \div {}^+2) = \square$

4. SAMPLE ANSWERS:

   $(^-14 - {}^+16) \div {}^+2 = \square$

   $(^-14 \div {}^+2) - (^+16 \div {}^+2) = \square$

   $(^-21 - {}^-6) \div {}^-3 = \square$

   $(^-21 \div {}^-3) - (^-6 \div {}^-3) = \square$

CHAPTER 16 (3)

1. SAMPLE ANSWERS: Which sentences are false?

   a. $^-6 < {}^-7$
   b. $^-6 \times {}^+4 < {}^-7 \times {}^+4$
   c. $^-4 < {}^+8$
   d. $^-4 \times {}^+5 < {}^+8 \times {}^+5$
   e. $^+8 < {}^+11$
   f. $^+8 \times {}^+2 < {}^+11 \times {}^+2$

   g. $^-6 < {}^-7$
   h. $^-6 \times {}^-4 < {}^-7 \times {}^-4$
   i. $^-4 < {}^+8$
   j. $^-4 \times {}^-5 < {}^+8 \times {}^-5$
   k. $^+8 < {}^+11$
   l. $^+8 \times {}^-2 < {}^+11 \times {}^-2$

2. SAMPLE ANSWERS: Which sentences are false?

   $^-2 < {}^+6$
   $^-2 \div {}^+2 < {}^+6 \div {}^+2$
   $^-2 \div {}^-2 < {}^+6 \div {}^-2$

   $^+24 < {}^+32$
   $^+24 \div {}^+8 < {}^+32 \div {}^+8$
   $^+24 \div {}^-8 < {}^+32 \div {}^-8$

   $^-12 < {}^-6$
   $^-12 \div {}^+3 < {}^-6 \div {}^+3$
   $^-12 \div {}^-3 < {}^-6 \div {}^-3$

CHAPTER 17 (1)

1. A small dot.
2. SAMPLE ANSWER: R
3. SAMPLE ANSWERS: Surface of a tabletop extended; surface of a wall extended; surface of a ceiling extended; surface of a floor extended; surface of a smooth lake extended.
4. (a), (b), and (e) must be drawn with two-point origins; (c) and (d) were most probably drawn with a one-point origin.
5. (a) Crosspoints   (b) Endpoints   (c) Crosspoints and endpoints   (d) Endpoints (e) Crosspoints
6. Convex: (a), (d), (e); concave: (b) and (c)

CHAPTER 17 (2)

1. SAMPLE ANSWER:

R   S

2. (a) Not the join of just line segments   (b) Crosspoints   (c) Endpoints   (d) Endpoints (e) Crosspoints
3. (a), (b), (c), and (e)   Not the join of three line segments
(d) Endpoints
4. (a) Not the join of 4 line segments   (b) Not the join of only line segments (c) and (d) Crosspoints   (e) An endpoint
5. (a) and (c) Not the join of only 4 line segments
(b) Diagonals are not congruent
(d) and (e) Not the join of only line segments
6. (b) Scalene   (a) and (c) Isosceles   (c) Equilateral

CHAPTER 17 (3)

1. Diameter

2.
Z   M

3.

4. 180°.
5. Yes.
6. No.
7. Each angle determined by each pair of sides is 60°.
8. $\overleftrightarrow{RK}$.
9. A rhombus is a quadrilateral with four congruent sides which has parallel opposite sides.
10. A rectangle.

CHAPTER 17 (4)

1. No.

2.

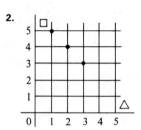

3. Yes.

4. SAMPLE ANSWERS: $(2, 3)$, $(4, 1)$, $(0, 5)$, $(\frac{1}{2}, 4\frac{1}{2})$.

5. a. Yes   b. No   c. Yes

CHAPTER 17 (5)

1. SAMPLE ANSWERS: sales of ice cream per month; growth of bean plant per day; automobile accidents per year.

2–5. Answers will vary.

CHAPTER 18

1. SAMPLE ANSWERS:
   a. Comparing two events such as sand pouring from two cans.
   b. Comparing what happens when children are placed on ends of a teetertotter.

2. SAMPLE ANSWERS:
   a. Matchbox cars
   b. Toothpicks

3. SAMPLE ANSWERS:
   a. 1 matchbox car equals 10 baseball cards
   b. 5 toothpicks equal in length to 1 straw

4. SAMPLE ANSWERS:
   a. Square centimeter
   b. Liter
   c. Kilogram
   d. Kilometer

5. SAMPLE ANSWERS:
   a. Odometer
   b. Half-life of radioactive elements
   c. By the color of molten steel

6. a. $\dfrac{3}{1} = \dfrac{19}{n}$; $n = \dfrac{19}{3}$ or $6\frac{1}{3}$ yd

   b. $\dfrac{16}{1} = \dfrac{85}{n}$; $n = \dfrac{85}{16}$ or $5\frac{5}{16}$ pt

   c. $\dfrac{1296}{1} = \dfrac{388}{n}$; $n = \dfrac{388}{1296}$ or $\dfrac{97}{324}$ sq yd

7. $12\frac{1}{5}$ zags

8. a. Rate
   b. Pressure

CHAPTER 19 (1)

1. Answers will vary.
2–4. Reading assignments.

CHAPTER 19 (2)

1. Reading assignment.
2–3. Observation experiences.
4. Preparation of a lesson plan (see Section 19.6).

Index

77 9 8 7 6 5 4